The Commonplace Book of WILLIAM BYRD II of Westover

The Commonplace Book of
WILLIAM BYRD II
of Westover

Edited by

Kevin Berland,

Jan Kirsten Gilliam,

and

Kenneth A. Lockridge

*Published for the
Omohundro Institute of
Early American History and
Culture, Williamsburg, Virginia,
by the University of North
Carolina Press, Chapel Hill
and London*

The Omohundro Institute of

Early American History and Culture

is sponsored jointly by the College

of William and Mary and the

Colonial Williamsburg Foundation.

On November 16, 1996, the Institute

adopted the present name in

honor of a bequest from

Malvern H. Omohundro, Jr.

© 2001
The University of North Carolina Press
Manufactured in the United States of America

Library of Congress
Cataloging-in-Publication Data
Byrd, William, 1674–1744.
The commonplace book of William Byrd II of
Westover / edited by Kevin Berland, Jan Kirsten
Gilliam, and Kenneth A. Lockridge.
    p. cm.
Includes bibliographical references (p.   )
and index.
ISBN 0-8078-2612-x (cloth: alk. paper)
1. Virginia—Social life and customs—To 1775.
2. Byrd, William 1674–1744. 3. Commonplace-
books. 4. Plantation owners—Virginia—
Biography. 5. Gentry—Virginia—Biography.
6. Gentry—Virginia—Attitudes—History—18th
century. I. Berland, Kevin, II. Gilliam, Jan
Kirsten. III. Lockridge, Kenneth A. IV. Title.
F229 .B94 2001
975.5′02′092—dc21   00-056363

05   04   03   02   01   5   4   3   2   1

ACKNOWLEDGMENTS

KB would like to acknowledge assistance from the College of Liberal Arts at the Pennsylvania State University for research development grants to support participation in this project. Guidance, support, and suggestions have been supplied by Professors Nancy Mace, Charles Mann, James May, and Linda Merians and by other colleagues and friends on the Internet forum C18-L. Sincere thanks to all the librarians I have been lucky enough to work with, especially the indefatigable Fran Freed, Sandy Stelts, and the staff at the Rare Book Room of Penn State's Pattee Library; Susan Anderson of the Historic Library of the Pennsylvania Hospital; and the kind people at the Library Company of Philadelphia, the Philadelphia College of Physicians, the Folger Shakespeare Library, the Houghton Library at Harvard University, the Huntington Library, the William Andrews Clark Memorial Library at the University of California, Los Angeles, the Virginia Historical Society, and other collections. My part in this project would not have been possible without the generosity of Kevin J. Hayes, who made available to us advance copies of *The Library of William Byrd of Westover*. Thanks also to Professors David Shields and Fred Leeds, to Donna Brodish, to Peggy McCann, and to Madonna Brown, and to Jan and Ken for bringing me into the project.

*   *   *

JKG would like to thank first and foremost Margaret Beck Pritchard for introducing me to William Byrd II and encouraging me to take on this project. She has been a constant source of help and support throughout. My thanks also go to Betty Leviner, who allowed me the time to work on the project and lent her support in many ways. Other colleagues in the Department of Collections at Colonial Williamsburg offered their interest and support during this long process, particularly Graham Hood and John Sands. John Ingram and Mark R. Wenger generously gave their time to read early drafts and to offer expert advice. I would also like to give my thanks to those at the Institute, particularly Fredrika J. Teute and Ron Hoffman, who have been supportive and patient with us. The Virginia Historical Society has also been generous in allowing us to work with the original manuscript and granting permission to publish it. I wish to offer my thanks to Kevin for coming aboard and adding to the scholarship of the project. Finally, I wish to thank Ken for boosting my morale throughout and convincing me this book would one day be published. It has taken several years, and would have been impossible (and dull) without his input and insights.

* * *

KAL would like to thank Graham Hood, Margaret Beck Pritchard, and Virginia Lascara for the encouragement and support that enabled us to begin this project, and to thank as well the entire Collections staff at Colonial Williamsburg, where the project has found a good home in Jan Gilliam's hands. Susan Juster offered special wisdom at a crucal moment, as did John Stagg. Ronald Hoffman gave us a second home at the Institute, where Fredrika J. Teute and her reader, David Shields, offered still more help, not the least of which was sending Jan and myself to Kevin Berland. The Virginia Historical Society was kind enough to approve publication of the manuscript, and Nelson Lankford has given us particular support. Without Jan and Kevin, however, all might have been in vain, and I thank them for skill, wisdom, friendship, and perseverance.

CONTENTS

EDITORIAL METHOD

In 1964 the Virginia Historical Society acquired a manuscript notebook identified as the commonplace book of William Byrd II of Westover (Mss2b9964a3). To date, the only section that has been published is a sequence of letters to "Charmante" (*Correspondence*, 332–341). The full text of William Byrd's commonplace book is presented here as it appears in the manuscript, a notebook of 108 unlined pages, measuring 6⅛″ x 3¾″, in a modern binding. Each page contains writing in the unmistakable hand of William Byrd II. The notebook has no title page, nor are there topical indexes or headings. The 573 entries range over a variety of topics without acknowledging any sources. A few entries include a Latin phrase, and two conclude with a line of the same shorthand in which Byrd composed his diaries.

In transcribing the manuscript we have tried to remain faithful to the original text as much as possible to preserve Byrd's intent, his style, and the feel of the work. No changes in capitalization, punctuation, or spelling have been introduced; we have not retained the eighteenth-century long *s*. It is sometimes difficult to determine Byrd's intention in using upper- or lowercase letters, especially in regard to the the letter *s*. This letter appears in our transcription as lowercase unless Byrd clearly intended the uppercase; we have attempted to use our best judgment to bring this into line with Byrd's other capitalization practices. No attempt has been made to add periods or to delete unnecessary marks from the text. Byrd's interlineations have been preserved here as superscripts (or subscripts) in the text. Underlined words reflect Byrd's own underscoring. A few words or lines are printed in bold to denote Byrd's own practice of emphasizing a word by larger, bolder writing. Repeated words have been retained, but the catchwords used in several entries have been omitted. The few words in the manuscript erased but still legible are reproduced here, struck through with a line to indicate cancellation. In one entry in the manuscript Byrd introduces a line interrupting the middle of a sentence, printed in the transcription as it appears in the original. Occasionally Byrd left a gap between words; these gaps have been silently closed up. Hyphens and dashes have been regularized, as have been Byrd's own ellipsis points. Hyphenated words at the ends of lines have been silently incorporated into the text unhyphenated.

For easier reference and clarity we have assigned numbers to each entry (complete or fragmentary); these numbers appear within brackets at the beginning of the transcription and run consecutively with no attempt to account for the possibility of missing entries or missing pages. Byrd did not number his entries. In most cases he separated each entry with a line (not retained in this transcription) beginning at the left and running about a quarter of the page width, indenting the first line of each entry. Byrd assigned page numbers to most of the first forty-four pages (in the upper left corner of the manuscript). These numbers will appear within brackets in the body of the text. Because he did not continue numbering the pages, we have also included within these brackets, following a slash, another page number, that assigned by the Virginia Historical Society (written in pencil on the bottom, outer corner of each page of the manuscript). Thus: [3/3], [44/39], [/47].

The manuscript is in fairly good condition, and most of the writing quite clear, but there are areas that are torn, stained, or illegible. Missing or illegible words are indicated in brackets by ellipses [. . .]. The extent of the missing text is not noted, but it is generally limited to a few letters or only a couple of words. The only exceptions are found in the first pages, which have sustained the most damage over time. With some caution we have supplied a few missing letters or words, where the intent is easily discernible, in brackets.

We have tried to offer the text with as few interruptions as possible. For this reason the Commentary follows the commonplace book, keyed by entry number. The few footnotes that appear in the body of the text refer to physical characteristics of the manuscript as they affect the text.

Establishing the date of the notebook has been a challenging task. Byrd's handwriting changed very little over time; judging by Byrd letters and other manuscripts in the Alderman Library of the University of Virginia and in the Virginia Historical Society, we can date the hand only roughly to 1715–1735. Other internal evidence helps to narrow this range somewhat. In §388 Byrd mentions the year 1723, using a formulation suggesting either the recent past or the virtual present. In another entry (§91) he discusses old age in terms repeated in an extant letter dated July 1723. In §393 he refers to an event of May 1723 as if it had occurred recently, and he mentions figures for the French national debt for 1725 (§555). He transcribes excerpts from books published in the early 1720s, such as William Wollaston's *Religion of Nature Delineated* (§526). Three-quarters of the way through the notebook he mentions a phenomenon found also "among the Females of this island" (§489). This indicates that he was writing in England before his return to Virginia in 1726. It is our view that the commonplace book period is approximately 1721–1726 (though the activity might conceivably have started a little before Byrd's return to London in 1721 or 1722, or continued for a time after he left for Virginia in 1726).

Following the transcription of the manuscript we have provided a Commentary on many of the entries. The range of Byrd's reading is indicated by the multiplicity of topics that he recorded in his commonplace book. When we have been able to identify his immediate sources, we have done so, sometimes by consulting extant copies of books formerly in his library. Otherwise, we have attempted to identify the ultimate source of a story or saying. Plutarch, for instance, is the wellspring from which many of the entries originally came. However, because Plutarch was so thoroughly absorbed and recycled by early modern writers, it is extremely difficult to determine whether Byrd read Plutarch in Greek, in French or English translation, or was consulting any one of the countless intermediary authorities.

The purpose of the Commentary is to provide cultural and historical contexts for the entries, together with observations on the significance of material as it relates to Byrd's life and writings. It has been our intention to make Byrd's commonplace book available to readers and scholars as a text for continuing research, and we look forward to future developments in Byrd scholarship that may result.

ABBREVIATIONS & SHORT TITLES

ASD
> William Byrd, *Another Secret Diary of William Byrd of Westover, 1739–1741, with Letters and Literary Exercises, 1696–1726,* ed. Maude W. Woodfin, trans. Marion Tinling (Richmond, Va., 1942).

Bacon, *Apophthegmes*
> [Francis Bacon], *Apophthegmes New and Old* (London, 1625), in Bacon, *Philosophical Works.*

Bacon, *Philosophical Works*
> *The Philosophical Works of Francis Bacon,* ed. John M. Robertson (from edition of Spedding, Ellis, and Heath) (1905; Freeport, N.Y., 1970).

Burnet, *History*
> Gilbert Burnet, *History of His Own Time,* ed. Thomas Stackhouse (London, 1979).

Churchill, *Voyages*
> Awnsham Churchill, comp., *A Collection of Voyages and Travels . . . ,* 4 vols. (London, 1704).

Correspondence
> *The Correspondence of the Three William Byrds of Westover, Virginia, 1684–1776,* ed. Marion Tinling, 2 vols. (Charlottesville, Va., 1977).

CWF
> Colonial Williamsburg Foundation, Williamsburg, Va.

Diodorus Siculus
> *Diodorus of Sicily: The Library of History,* trans. C. H. Oldfather et al., 12 vols., LCL (1940–1967).

Diogenes Laertius *Lives*
> Diogenes Laertius, *Lives of Eminent Philosophers,* trans. R. D. Hicks, 2 vols., LCL (1925).

Erasmus, *Adages*
> Erasmus, *Adages,* ed. R. A. B. Mynors (Toronto, 1982–1992), vols. XXXI–XXXIV of *Collected Works of Erasmus.*

Erasmus, *Apophthegmes*
  Apophthegmes, That Is to Saie, Prompte, Quicke, Wittie, and Sentencious
  Saiyings . . . First Gathered . . . by . . . Erasmus of Roterdame, trans. Nicholas
  Udall (London, 1542).

Guardian
  John Calhoun Stephens, ed., *The Guardian* (Lexington, Ky., 1982).

Hayes
  Kevin J. Hayes, *The Library of William Byrd of Westover* (Madison, Wis.,
  1997).

LCL
  Loeb Classical Library (New York, London, Cambridge, Mass.).

LD
  William Byrd, *The London Diary (1717–1721) and Other Writings*,
  ed. Louis B. Wright and Marion Tinling (New York, 1958).

Lockridge, *Diary, and Life*
  Kenneth A. Lockridge, *The Diary, and Life, of William Byrd II of Virginia,*
  1674–1744 (Chapel Hill, N.C., 1987).

Lockridge, *Patriarchal Rage*
  Kenneth A. Lockridge, *On the Sources of Patriarchal Rage: The Commonplace*
  Books of William Byrd and Thomas Jefferson and the Gendering of Power in
  the Eighteenth Century (New York, 1992).

Lucian *Works*
  [The Works of] Lucian, trans. A. M. Harmon, K. Kilborn, and
  M. D. Macleod, 8 vols., LCL (1913–1967).

Montaigne, *Essays*
  The Essays of Michel de Montaigne, trans. George B. Ives
  (1925; New York, 1946).

OED
  The Oxford English Dictionary, compact ed. (Oxford, 1971).

Plutarch *Lives*
  Plutarch's Lives, trans. Bernadotte Perrin, 11 vols., LCL (1914–1926).

Plutarch *Moralia*
  Plutarch, *Moralia*, trans. Frank Cole Babbitt et al., LCL (1928–).

Quintus Curtius
  Quintus Curtius [History of Alexander], trans. John C. Rolfe, 2 vols., LCL
  (1946).

SD
  The Secret Diary of William Byrd of Westover, 1709–1712, ed. Louis B. Wright
  and Marion Tinling (Richmond, Va., 1941).

Spectator

    The Spectator, ed. Donald F. Bond, 5 vols. (Oxford, 1965).

Stanley, *History*

    Thomas Stanley, *The History of Philosophy: Containing the Lives, Opinions, Actions, and Discourses of the Philosophers of Every Sect,* 2d ed., 3 vols. (London, 1687).

Stobaeus

    Iohannes Stobaeus, *Ioannis Stobaei Sententiae, ex Thesauris Graecorum Delectae,* and *Loci Communes Sententiarum, ex S. Scriptura, Veteribus Theologis, et Secularibus scriptoribus, collecti per Antonium et Maximum Monachos, atque ad. I. Stobaei locos relati* (Aureliae Allobrogum, Pro Francisco Fabro, Bibliopola Lugdunensis, 1609).

Tatler

    The Tatler, ed. Donald F. Bond, 2 vols. (Oxford, 1987).

Valerius Maximus, *Acts and Sayings of the Romans*

    Quintus Valerius Maximus, *Romae Antiquae Descriptio: A View of the Religion, Laws, Customs, Manners, and Dispositions of the Ancient Romans . . .* (London, 1678).

Venette, *Tableau*

    Nicolas Venette, *De la génération de l'homme, ou tableau de l'amour conjugal,* 8th ed. (Cologne, 1702).

VMHB

    Virginia Magazine of History and Biography.

WMQ

    William and Mary Quarterly.

Works

    The Prose Works of William Byrd of Westover: Narratives of a Colonial Virginian, ed. Louis B. Wright (Cambridge, Mass., 1966).

Prologue

William Byrd II (1674–1744) was an important figure in the history of colonial Virginia. Inheriting extensive lands from his father, Byrd expanded his
holdings and founded new settlements, including Richmond. He was active in
the political life of Virginia, serving as a member of the House of Burgesses and
the Council of Virginia and as the Virginia representative to the commission
charged with establishing the border between Virginia and the Carolinas.

But Byrd is best known today for his diaries, records that have offered modern readers an unparalleled glimpse into the private life of a Virginia gentleman.
Half a century ago Louis B. Wright and Marion Tinling decoded and published
three manuscript diaries. These diaries reveal a powerful tension between Byrd's
private sense of self and his sense of the appearance of the self in the public
sphere. Private diaries may appear to be a more promising source for revelations
of character than commonplace books, which record notions gleaned from
reading and conversation. However, we are convinced that this manuscript does
indeed contain material that contributes significantly to a deeper understanding
of Byrd's public and private life, and therefore we have transcribed it and furnished both annotation (identifying and discussing topics and sources) and
interpretation (linking ideas found in the manuscript to what is already known
about Byrd).

* * *

Unless a reader were to search the secret diaries of William Byrd II for just such a
thing, it might be easy to overlook what is written there about the way he used
his commonplace book:

> I rose about 7 o'clock and wrote a little in my commonplace. I said my prayers
> and ate milk and potato for breakfast.

> I rose about 7 o'clock and read a little in my commonplace. I ate some boiled
> milk for breakfast and said a short prayer.

His statements are characteristically terse, and, while they do not specify his
purpose in writing and reading, they do indicate that the activity was usual for
him. These entries appear in the diaries Byrd kept during a period nearly a

decade before he started to make entries in the commonplace book here published, the only one known to survive. Since Byrd regularly maintained a number of similar private activities all through his life—daily readings in Greek, Latin, and Hebrew, diary writing, nightly prayer—it is reasonable to conclude that recording interesting thoughts in a commonplace book was a literary activity he exercised habitually.[1]

What is a commonplace book? Dr. Johnson described it simply as "A book in which things to be remembered are ranged under general heads."[2] In its simplest form it serves as an aid to memory, a book of blank pages on which an individual could record passages from readings and snippets of conversation, to which he could refer when he felt a need to refresh his memory or to kindle his imagination about specific topics. In effect, this commonplace book appears to be a collection of moral wit and wisdom, ancient and modern, transcribed and rephrased by its owner, together with a miscellaneous jumble of anecdotes, jokes, and recipes.

The small, pocket-sized volume was important enough to Byrd that he wrote in it and referred to it often and even carried it with him when he traveled. On a dozen occasions in the early diary Byrd mentions using his commonplace book; in May 1710, Byrd recorded reading in his commonplace book between his turns in a game of billiards with friends at Westover, and he occasionally records reading parts of it aloud.[3] Byrd selected the material in this commonplace book for several discernible reasons. Some of the entries pertain to serious matters that concerned him throughout his entire life, some reflect issues that were of paramount importance to him at a specific time in his life, and still others provide insight into what kinds of things he found entertaining.

Byrd's commonplace book contains evidence of an intellectual process at work, a process that reveals a stage in the development of his mind. The nearly six hundred entries document Byrd's course of reading over a period of several years in which he had to make some momentous decisions about his future. By looking at the books he chose to read at this time and the material he considered important enough to reproduce in his commonplace book, therefore, it may be possible to learn more about his ideas on several important issues at a crucial time in his life, as we will endeavor to demonstrate in the following sections of the Prologue.

1. *SD*, 514, 515, from the diary entries for Apr. 14, 15, 1712. See Chapter 8, below, for a discussion of the dates of the commonplace book manuscript.

2. Samuel Johnson, *A Dictionary of the English Language* (1755; rpt. New York, 1979).

3. *SD*, 102, 122, 137, 148, 177, 181, 229, 403, 514, 515, 517. "I read several things to them out of my book" (*LD*, 137).

The extrapolation of Byrd's ideas from the record of his reading is not a simple task. To begin with, firm details are hard to come by. The commonplace book itself provides no sources for its entries, and, while his diaries frequently mention reading, they say little about exactly what he was reading, with a few exceptions. He hardly ever records in the diaries anything concerning what he thought or felt about what he had read. Still, the diaries establish that reading was important enough to him that he made it a point to read something—and sometimes a great deal—nearly every day.[4]

This dedication to reading is borne out by the importance of books in his life. Byrd's remarkable library at Westover eventually held at least three thousand titles, a good number of which he had in London with him in the 1720s. Of course, there are inherent difficulties in any attempt to draw conclusions about the exact nature of the way book owners used their libraries. Collectors do not always read the books they assemble; in fact, there is not enough physical evidence in those of Byrd's books that have been found to reveal much about the way he read them (that is, most of them are free of marks such as underscoring, marginalia, and interlineations). Indeed, there is usually no physical evidence to confirm whether he read them at all. Then, too, library catalogs are not always accurate; some of a private collector's books may be dispersed (loaned, given away, or misplaced) during their owner's lifetime and hence may not appear in the library catalog.[5] Moreover, not all the books important to readers are to be

4. In the *Secret Diaries* he records reading John Tillotson's sermons fairly often (*SD*, 4, 16, 175, 210, inter alia); he read Henry Sacheverell not long after his impeachment, as well as Bishop Gilbert Burnet on the case (*SD*, 226, 238–239); he read Mary Delarivière Manley's *New Atalantis* and worked out a key (*SD*, 277–279), and papers such as the *Tatler*. He also mentions reading classical authors in Greek and Latin (including Anacreon, Dio Cassius, Herodian, Homer, Horace, Josephus, Lucian, Petronius, Pindar, Plutarch, Sallust, Terence, and Thucydides) and reading the Scriptures in Hebrew and Greek.

His recorded reponses to Tillotson's sermons are exceptional. A sermon he read on May 7, 1709, affected him "very much," producing "some tears of repentance" (*SD*, 175). This spiritual catharsis is, perhaps, a function of sermon reading easier to explain than the time his wife read to him "a sermon in Dr. Tillotson" immediately after a "flourish . . . performed on the billiard table" (*SD*, 211).

5. Some years ago Edwin Wolf 2nd found a number of books formerly in the library at Westover; his essays "The Dispersal of the Library of William Byrd of Westover" and "More Books from the Library of the Byrds of Westover" appeared in American Antiquarian Society, *Proceedings*, LXVIII (1958), 19–106, LXXXVIII (1978), 51–82. Wolf's work has been greatly expanded by the recent reconstruction of the library at Westover by Kevin J. Hayes, which includes references to notes in Byrd's hand. The most copious annotation is reserved

found in their personal libraries; for Byrd, access to college libraries and the private collections of several gentlemen was an important part of the cultural life of London. This means that the range of Byrd's reading certainly extends beyond his own books—already a large field of inquiry.

Nevertheless, it is clear that selectivity in reading is important, and thus it is safe to say that the commonplace book—edited and sourced—discloses what Byrd *chose* to read in the early 1720s. The entries themselves, the transcriptions, distillations, and comments he recorded in his notebook, also involve a selectivity that invites speculative analysis.

---

for legal texts. An account of influences on Byrd by Sir William Temple and Jonathan Swift, authors known to have been in his library, appears in Donald T. Siebert, Jr., "William Byrd's *Histories of the Line:* The Fashioning of a Hero," *American Literature,* XLVII (1976), 543–547.

Hayes has found several books once part of Byrd's collection (with signatures or bookplates) but not included in the catalog of the Philadelphia sale of Byrd's library. For example, Byrd's copy of Locke's *Essay on Human Understanding* (Hayes B4), now in the collection at Gunston Hall, Virginia, must have left the Westover library before the library was cataloged and broken.

1. WILLIAM BYRD II OF WESTOVER

At the time of William Byrd II's birth in 1674, Virginia was an emerging British colony inhabited by settlers still putting down roots.[1] The great dynastic Virginia families were just beginning to take shape. When he was eighteen, William Byrd I had been invited to join his uncle Thomas Stegge in Virginia. Stegge, a fur trader, planter, and Virginia's auditor-general, died in 1670, leaving his young nephew his entire estate (more than thirty thousand acres in Virginia as well as property in England). The first Virginia Byrd quickly adapted to Virginia life, expanding his fur trade, prospering as a planter, and entering the political world, eventually assuming the offices of receiver-general, auditor, and king's councillor. In 1673 he married Mary Horsmanden Filmer. Their son, William Byrd II, was born in the following year.

Notwithstanding the commitment to the colony felt by William Byrd I, the younger Byrd did not grow up in Virginia. His father sent him to be educated in England when he was seven years old. Byrd attended the Felsted Grammar school in Essex during the era in which Christopher Glasscock was headmaster. Felsted, with more than one hundred "gentlemen's sons" as students, had gained a reputation for piety and learning under Glasscock's predecessor Martin Holbeach, attracting students from many areas of England. It is not always easy to discover what kinds of things students learned in any but the most prominent schools in such distant times, though historians of education agree that in general the traditional humanist curriculum of the sixteenth-century schools persisted well into the eighteenth century. Some sense of the school's program can be found in the autobiography of Dr. John Wallis, a student at Felsted in the 1630s. Wallis looked back on his years of learning Latin and Greek, "having read divers Authors therein (such as at Schools are wont to be read)." He had become accomplished in the grammar of both tongues "and in such other Learning as is

1. For a full account of Byrd's life, see Lockridge, *Diary, and Life;* Pierre Marambaud, *William Byrd of Westover, 1674–1744* (Charlottesville, Va., 1971); the introductory essays by Percy G. Adams and William K. Boyd in *William Byrd's Histories of the Dividing Line betwixt Virginia and North Carolina* (New York, 1967); and in Hayes. On the social origins and establishment of dynastic families in Virginia, see James Horn, *Adapting to a New World: English Society in the Seventeenth-Century Chesapeake* (Chapel Hill, N.C., 1994), 24–38, 328.

commonly taught in such Schools." This learning included sufficient fluency in Latin that he spoke it at school, and he also learned Hebrew, French, logic, and music. Glasscock himself had attended Felsted around the same time as Wallis and appears to have continued the tradition when he became headmaster. We can reasonably conclude that Byrd received a high-quality classical education, fit for a gentleman. He learned Greek, Latin, and Hebrew as well as mathematics, history, and other subjects. His mastery of these ancient languages is evident in his lifelong habit of reading Scripture and the classics in the original languages nearly every day.[2]

However, the next phase of his education was somewhat out of the ordinary. Byrd did not make the usual transition from grammar school to university. Instead, around 1690 his father sent him to learn about business matters in the Netherlands under the care of Rotterdam merchants connected with his business agents Perry and Lane. It may be that the father believed the son who would one day inherit all the lands, plantations, and business ventures he had accumulated in Virginia would find an education in commerce beneficial.[3] Byrd put up with this training for a year, but he was apparently dissatisfied, for he asked to be allowed to return to England. In London he decided to substitute the study of law for continued practical training in commerce. In April 1692 he entered the

2. See M. L. Clarke, *Greek Studies in England, 1700–1830* (1945; rpt. Amsterdam, 1986): "The system had taken shape in the sixteenth century and was not seriously modified until well into the nineteenth" (10). On the prevalence of spoken Latin in seventeenth-century schools, see Clarke, *Classical Education in Britain, 1500–1900* (Cambridge, 1959), 34–35. On Felsted, see Michael Craze, *A History of Felsted School, 1564–1947* (Ipswich, 1955), 41, 51, 62, 66, 69, 70–75. Dr. Wallis considered his education there to be comparable with that provided by the other great grammar schools. It is possible to underestimate Byrd's mastery of Greek, Latin, and Hebrew if we consider only the paucity of translations by his hand. In fact, Byrd usually read *in* these languages, without "Englishing." This mastery of language was a primary objective of early modern schools; at Eton and other schools, Clarke notes, "written translations into English were unknown" (*Greek Studies in England*, 18).

3. Louis B. Wright suggests that Byrd's father thought university unnecessary for a man of business (*Works*, 4–5). Richard Grassby, in *The English Gentleman in Trade: The Life and Works of Sir Dudley North, 1641–1691* (Oxford, 1994), points out: "In fact no law in England prohibited gentlemen from entering business; gentility was by long established convention distinguished from rank and defined in terms of personal virtue rather than by source of income. What was considered a suitable occupation depended as much on the subjective perception of parents, who made the final choice, as on roles allocated by the formal value system" (19). Nonetheless, Byrd might have felt the lack of university education keenly, which could explain his dedication to improving his knowledge and his public displays of erudition.

Middle Temple and by 1695 was admitted to the bar. Byrd's direct move into the study of law without attending university was unusual but by no means un-precedented. The following year he became a fellow of the Royal Society, which from its inception opened its membership to members of the gentry who ex-pressed scientific interest.[4] Byrd's membership at the Inns of Court and in the prestigious scientific society gave Byrd the opportunity to meet and mingle with some of the prominent men of London society. He became lifelong friends with men like Sir Robert Southwell (president of the Royal Society), Charles Boyle, and Charles Wager, all of whom had marked influence on Byrd.[5]

After a brief visit home in 1696—long enough for him to garner an appoint-ment to the House of Burgesses—Byrd returned to London. He made the Atlan-tic crossing again in 1705 to take up the vast estates in Virginia left to him upon the death of his father. While in Virginia he became increasingly involved in the politics and government of the colony; he served on the council and was named commander in chief of the Henrico and Charles City County Militia. The Vir-ginia council's struggle to retain its authority soon pitted the ambitious young lawyer Byrd against the new governor, Alexander Spotswood, who had passed a law allowing him to convene a special court of oyer and terminer to hear cases in

4. On patterns leading to the study of law, see Michael Van Cleave Alexander, *The Growth of English Education* (University Park, Pa., 1990), 220. Bishop Thomas Sprat, charter mem-ber of the Royal Society and its first historian, reveals the genteel cachet of membership in his account of the levels of society from which the Royal Society drew its members: "Though the *Society* entertains very many men of *particular Professions;* yet the farr greater Number are *Gentlemen,* free, and unconfin'd" (*The History of the Royal-Society of Lon-don . . .* [London, 1687], 67). Byrd's copy of Sprat's *History* [Hayes 943, 944] is now in the Logan collection of the Library Company of Philadelphia.

5. See *Correspondence* for Byrd's epistolary friendship with Southwell and Charles Boyle, earl of Orrery. On Byrd's relationship with Southwell, see Lockridge, *Diary, and Life,* 31–34. The importance of these men to Byrd may be seen in the fact that he kept a portrait of Southwell in his library, and many years later he mentioned these men in the text of the epitaph he designed for his own interment:

He was early sent to England for his education,
Where under the care and direction of Sir Robert Southwell,
And ever favored with his particular instructions,
He made a happy proficiency in polite and varied learning.
By the means of this same noble friend,
He was introduced to the acquaintance of many of the first persons of his age
For knowledge, wit, virtue, birth, of high station,
And particularly contracted a most intimate and bosom friendship
With the learned and illustrious Charles Boyle, Earl of Orrery. (*LD,* 11)

which council members might be concerned, superseding the Virginia General Court. The battle was long and drawn out, and in the end neither party could claim victory. Spotswood criticized the way Byrd carried out his office of receiver-general and sent a bill to the council to reform the collection of quit-rents, which passed over Byrd's objections. Also during this time Byrd married Lucy Parke, and soon his first son was born, only to die shortly thereafter. The Byrds subsequently had two daughters, Evelyn and Maria, who survived into adulthood.

In 1715, at the age of forty, Byrd was again back in London tending to the colony's business and his own. It was his mission to persuade the Board of Trade to reverse Spotswood's policies (in 1718 the Virginia House of Burgesses would again name him agent for Virginia, ignoring Spotswood's veto). Byrd's campaign on behalf of the Virginia planters essentially involved an attempt to limit the crown's prerogative in the colony in the interest of the liberties of Virginians. Not surprisingly, Lord Orkney and the other court officials in charge of the plantations looked coldly upon Byrd's endeavors. George I ruled in favor of the governor, and the council accepted Spotswood's power to appoint judges. Spotswood then attempted to have Byrd and two others removed from the council, arguing that Byrd had been away from Virginia too long. The Board of Trade agreed to support Byrd if he would make his peace with the governor, and the king granted his petition to be allowed to remain in England an additional year without losing his seat. The support of the king and the Board of Trade reassured him that he could return to Virginia in safety, despite Spotswood's enmity. This effectively ended his campaign to supplant Spotswood as governor of Virginia.

His wife, Lucy, had joined him in London in 1716, but she died of smallpox soon after her arrival. After the mourning period, Byrd began to consider remarrying. He paid court to Miss Mary Smith, known in Byrd's letters as "Sabina." Despite—or perhaps because of—his holdings in Virginia, Byrd did not receive the approval of her father, and soon the courtship ended in humiliation. Curiously, Byrd did not set up a household in England. Even when his daughters came to live in England, he quartered them with friends and kept his rooms in the Middle Temple.

Despite assurances, Byrd did not find the political climate in Virginia welcoming or safe on his return in 1720. Still fearing Spotswood's retribution, Byrd remained in Virginia only until 1721. Once again in London he continued his search for a well-to-do wife, this time pursuing Lady Elizabeth Lee, the "Charmante" of his letters (some of which appear in this commonplace book).

She too rejected his suit. Finally, in 1724 he married Maria Taylor, an educated Englishwoman of respectable family but no fortune.[6]

It is evident from his diaries that Byrd considered himself a Londoner throughout his sojourns in England, but the prestige of his status as a colonial landlord was not always recognized by those he wished to impress. Of his first thirty-one years, all but eight were spent in England. He had grown up and had been educated in the society of early-eighteenth-century London and was an eager participant in the cultural life of the eighteenth-century English gentleman. His education, his connections with wellborn friends, his membership in the Royal Society, his membership in the legal society of the Middle Temple, and his status as the representative of the Virginia colony, all gave him an entrée into good society. He frequented the theater, where he saw played out on stage the great comedies and heroic tragedies of the age and met and rubbed elbows with English society as well. He sat for a portrait by Sir Godfrey Kneller and acquired a number of other portraits. His collection of portraits, eventually the largest such collection in the American colonies, included family members, notable English acquaintances, and public figures from circles in which it is unlikely that Byrd traveled but that would suggest a level of sophistication Byrd would certainly have wished to project.[7]

At the coffeehouses—he frequently visited Will's, the favorite haunt of John Dryden a generation earlier—and at salons he participated in discussions of current ideas and heard the latest gossip. He had access to the latest works of poets, historians, theologians, scholars, and the new scientists, either by purchasing books for his own library or reading them in libraries at the Royal Society, Lincoln's Inn, various colleges, or the homes of his friends.[8]

6. See *Correspondence,* 348; Maria's ability to read Greek he considered an unexpected bonus.

7. Among the portraits at Westover were a portrait of William Byrd II (attributed to Hans Hysing) and portraits of his father-in-law Daniel Parke II, his mentor Sir Robert Southwell (a copy of Sir Godfrey Kneller's portrait), the marquess of Halifax, the duke of Argyll, Sir Robert Walpole, and Alexander Pope's friend Teresa Blount—all probably acquired during Byrd's years in London. Though there is no evidence that Byrd met Walpole or Pope and Blount, he would have been acquainted with Halifax and Argyll, who were both active in the Royal Society when Southwell sponsored Byrd's induction. The Westover portraits are now in the collection of the Virginia Historical Society; they are reproduced in Paula A. Treckel, " 'The Empire of My Heart': The Marriage of William Byrd II and Lucy Parke Byrd," *VMHB,* CV (1997), 127, 129, 132.

8. In the *London Diary* Byrd records meeting many learned gentlemen at the top of London society, including Charles Boyle, fourth earl of Orrery; the Spanish and Muscovite

By 1726, he felt he could no longer afford to live in England without attending to business in Virginia. He hoped to make this stay in Virginia as brief as his previous ones, but, as it turned out, he never returned to London. Once back in Virginia, Byrd busied himself for the next eighteen years with family, estate, and government. He and Maria had four children, including his only son, William Byrd III (1728–1777). Westover, the plantation left to him by his father, was now his home, and he was continually involved in the business of running the plantation and improving the house. As a member of the council of Virginia, he made frequent trips to Williamsburg. He also explored and surveyed the land of the colony, including the dividing line between North Carolina and Virginia, an experience about which he wrote two well-known accounts. As a final cap to his government career he was appointed president of the council, but in the following year, 1744, he died at the age of seventy.[9]

———

ambassadors; William Congreve; John Perceval, earl of Egmont; Sir Charles Wager; Sir John Randolph (a Virginian like himself); Sir Robert Southwell; the duke of Buckingham; and Horace Walpole. Byrd also mentions visiting libraries at Magdalen College, Oxford, and the homes of Southwell and Lord Islay.

[Abel Boyer], *Letters of Wit, Politicks, and Morality . . .* (London, 1701), discusses the company at Will's, which then included people Byrd later met and admired, including Samuel Garth and the earl of Orrery (215–223, 290–291). Byrd owned a copy of this book (Hayes 1101).

9. Byrd's *History of the Dividing Line* and the *Secret History of the Line*, two accounts of the survey of the Virginia–North Carolina boundary, were based on diary notes and fleshed out at a later time. Both accounts circulated in manuscript during Byrd's lifetime but were not published until much later; for the publication history of these works, see *Works*.

2. MAKING A GENTLEMAN:
WILLIAM BYRD AND EARLY MODERN EDUCATION

The common purpose of early modern educators was to make gentlemen. That is, they were concerned with instilling in young men of good families both the moral values vital to the well-being of society and the personal skills, talents, and strengths indispensable for a life of public responsibility and power. Locke explains the charge of all educators:

> The great Work of a *Governour* is to fashion the Carriage, and form the Mind; to settle in his Pupil good Habits, and the Principles of Virtue and Wisdom; to give him by little and little a view of Mankind; and work him into a love and imitation of what is Excellent and Praise-worthy; and in the Prosecution of it to give him Vigour, Activity, and Industry.

At the time Byrd received his training as a gentleman, English society was still rigidly structured and hierarchical, though expansion and redefinition of certain social categories were starting to be discernible. Birth, family, land, wealth, and leisure time made a gentleman; education prepared him for public life, especially for his primary task of governing and exercising authority over the public weal. The crucial element in Locke's view is that attaining mastery over others is impossible without first attaining the virtue possible only with self-mastery.[1]

The gentry moved back and forth between country estates and the city, but the wealth of some city merchants rivaled that of the established gentry (and even that of the nobility). The commingling of gentlemen with other urbanites blurred social boundaries, so that it became increasingly difficult to know how to recognize a gentleman. By the beginning of the eighteenth century one writer was able to conclude, "Any one that, without a Coat of Arms, has either a liberal or genteel education, that looks gentleman-like (whether he be so or not) and has the wherewithal to live freely and handsomely, is by the courtesy of England usually called a gentleman." Although the manner, deportment, and learning of a gentleman could be acquired with time, practice, and money, it was by no

1. John Locke, *Some Thoughts concerning Education,* ed. John W. Yolton and Jean S. Yolton (Oxford, 1989), 156, and introduction, 8–9; Mary Thomas Crane, *Framing Authority: Sayings, Self, and Society in Sixteenth-Century England* (Princeton, N.J., 1993), 30–31, 101.

means an open field. The gentry were confident that interlopers would give themselves away. Indeed, gentlemen were convinced that they differed from commoners in their fundamental nature, thoughts, and makeup. They knew they were important to society. They were the ones who made events happen, who gave orders to others, who were supposed to bring their community of dependents economic and social stability.[2]

According to commonly accepted eighteenth-century belief, social rank and conduct were closely linked. Gentility, or "Good Breeding," was not simply a matter of birth; rather, it was a social quality marked by appropriate conduct in all situations. Locke sums up this belief in his account of what gentlemen expect educators to instill in their sons—"*Virtue, Wisdom, Breeding,* and *Learning*":

> I place *Vertue* as the first and most necessary of those Endowments, that belong to a Man or a Gentleman; as absolutely requisite to make him valued and beloved by others, acceptable or tolerable to himself.

Locke recommends prudence or practical wisdom, "a Man's managing his Business ably, and with fore-sight in this World," and good breeding is that aspect of manners dealing with the estimation of one's own worth in relation to others, governed by the precept *"Not to think meanly of our selves, and not to think meanly of others."* The manifold parts of learning, which Locke outlines in detail, are all subsumed to the cause of virtue:

> The great Business of all is *Vertue* and *Wisdom. Nullum numen abest si sit prudentia.* ["No heavenly power is wanting if there be wisdom."] Teach him to get a Mastery over his Inclinations, and *submit his Appetite to Reason.* This being obtained, and by constant practice settled into Habit, the hardest part of the Task is over.[3]

The character of a gentleman involves two aspects, the private and the public. The private must serve the public self. To a degree Byrd's contemporaries recognized the importance of personal growth and psychological equilibrium—this is, of course, really a more modern preoccupation—but they did not ordinarily see it as an end in itself. Rather, they believed that the strength and greatness of private character is realized only in the public sphere, where the gentleman is

---

2. Guy Miège, *The New State of England under Our Sovereign Queen Anne* (London, 1703), as quoted by Peter Earle, *The Making of the English Middle Class: Business, Society, and Family Life in London, 1660–1730* (Berkeley, Calif., 1989), 6. On the changing definitions of gentility, see 5–10.

3. Locke, *Some Thoughts concerning Education,* ed. Yolton and Yolton, 194–199, 255.

called to fulfill a complex set of social requirements. John Clarke, in his *Essay upon Study,* epitomizes these demands:

> The proper Business of *Gentlemen* as such, is, I presume, to serve their Country, in the Making or Execution of the Laws; as likewise in preventing the Breach and Violation of them, by preserving the Peace and good order of the World about them, as much as possible; by the Encouragement of Virtue, especially Industry and Frugality; and the Discouragement of Vice; by finding out Ways and Means of employing the Poor; and thereby keeping them from Idleness and Starving. . . . And how much is he obliged to his Maker, that has so noble a Situation in Life assigned him, wherein he may have the most delicious Enjoyment of it, and constantly feel the greatest and most exalted of all pleasures to a generous mind, by being the Instrument of so much good in his Fellow-Mortals.[4]

Clarke's definition characteristically emphasizes responsibility rather than privilege, reflecting the Anglican doctrine of stewardship, which maintains that birth, social position, material wealth, and every sort of ability are all given in trust, so the individual can make use of them for the greater good. The doctrine of stewardship thus places the most fortunate members of society under a serious obligation.

How did the educators of Byrd's day teach their charges to approach this obligation? They taught them about the nature of virtue—true greatness and magnanimity—and attempted to demonstrate how it could be achieved. At the heart of English education was the conviction that the classics contained the best articulation of public values available anywhere. M. L. Clarke explains, "In particular, classical literature was thought of as inspiring manliness, patriotism and a love of liberty." Byrd's education was English, and these were precisely the qualities of character to which young English gentlemen were encouraged to aspire.[5]

4. John Clarke, *An Essay upon Study* . . . (London, 1731), 224–225. Byrd owned Clarke's *Essay upon the Education of Youth in Grammar-Schools* (Hayes 889) and his *Introduction to the Making of Latin* (Hayes 1586, 1587) as well as his editions of Justin, Suetonius, and Cornelius Nepos (Hayes 1568–1571).

5. M. L. Clarke, *Greek Studies in England, 1700–1830* (1945; rpt. Amsterdam, 1986), 13. These ideals were equally part of the education of colonial gentlemen. Meyer Reinhold states, "The value of the Classics as an instrument for inculcating moral truths was advocated by Puritans and Virginians alike" ("The Classics and the Quest for Virtue in Eighteenth-Century America," in Susan Ford Wiltshire, ed., *The Usefulness of Classical Learning in the Eighteenth Century,* American Philological Association [1976], 9). The con-

Such lofty aspirations may be inculcated easily enough, especially with the great examples of magnanimity provided by classical narratives, but something further is required to equip young men to achieve them. More immediate gratifications of various sorts may seem attractive enough to distract them from their higher goals. The desire for pleasure and aversion from pain are natural innate tendencies; they must be moderated by reason, or they will lead us astray, as Locke makes clear:

> Its seems plain to me, that the Principle of all Vertue and Excellency lies in a power of denying our selves the satisfaction of our own Desires, where Reason does not authorize them.

Locke's sense of the urgency of attaining rational control over desires and emotions—something shared by classical moralists and Anglican divines alike—is central to Locke's view of education. The essential lesson all people must learn is how to control their actions in order to achieve the ends most appropriate and rewarding in the long run. "Present desires may close future options, the desire for immediate pleasure may stand in the way of future (and especially of eternal) happiness."[6] A number of entries in Byrd's commonplace book participate in this cautionary tradition; consider, for instance, §297:

> Tis a more noble conquest to get the better of what we love than of what we hate: For what we hate, if it do its Worst, can but destroy our Bodys, but what we love, may destroy both Body and Soule.

At the time Byrd was entering such messages to himself in the commonplace book, he was no longer a young man struggling with the task of forming himself into a gentleman recognized by other gentlemen. Nonetheless, as the commonplace book makes clear, the same heedfulness is evidently necessary throughout life.

It was particularly important for a gentleman to be in full control of his passions, because there were so many external threats. The public life was fraught with dangers: the protean, unreliable nature of many personalities, dissimulation and intrigue, fraud and flattery, and the widespread pursuit of selfish ends under

------

tention put forward by some historians that the emphasis of colonial educators on civic virtue anticipated the later revolutionary opposition to hereditary privilege does not take into account the earlier traditional role of civic virtue in English education (as outlined here); see Reinhold, 6–9.

6. Locke, *Some Thoughts concerning Education,* ed. Yolton and Yolton, 107, and introduction, 15.

the guise of disinterested attitudes. Considering that their task included preparing their pupils to meet such opposition, educators recognized that codified rules of conduct, though valuable, needed to be supplemented with a more direct appeal to intuitive recognition. Bringing about perceptions of moral qualities in practice can be a powerful aid in moral education. Example served to underscore precept; indeed, many educational theorists held that example is a stronger method. Locke explains the superior force of example on formative minds:

> Vertues and Vices can by no Words be so plainly set before their Understandings, as the Actions of other Men will shew them, when you direct their Observation, and bid them view this or that good or bad Quality in their Practice. And the Beauty or Uncomeliness of many Things, in good and ill Breeding, will be better learnt, and make deeper Impressions on them, in the *Examples* of others, than from any Rules or Instructions can be given about them.[7]

Greek and Roman poets, historians, and orators provided early modern educators with a body of work plentifully supplied with narratives of the actions of representative men. Anthony Blackwall expounds on how a wide experience of such narratives will help young men accommodate themselves to the inconstancy of fortune and the humorous variability of human character.

> The Reflections that are made by these *noble* Writers upon the Conduct and Humours of Mankind, the Interests of Courts, and the Intrigues of Parties, are so curious and instructive, so true in their Substance, and so taking and lively in the manner of their Expression, that they satisfy the soundest Judgment, and please the most sprightly Imagination. From these glorious *Authors,* we have Instruction without the common Formality and Dryness of Precept; and receive the most edifying Advice in the pleasing Way of Insinuation and Surprize.[8]

Both greatness and meanness are thus figured in ancient letters. Henry Felton advised the noble pupil to whom he addressed his *Dissertation on Reading the Classics* that his studies would provide both cautionary tales and models for emulation:

---

7. Ibid., 143.

8. Anthony Blackwall, *An Introduction to the Classics* . . . , 2d ed. (London, 1719), 27–28. In the commonplace book, Byrd indicates his awareness of this principle: "For tis a settled truth, that naked Example without precept is more instructive, than the most edifying Precept can be without Example" (§355).

Your Lordship will meet with great and wonderful Examples of an irregular and mistaken Virtue in the *Greeks* and *Romans,* with many Instances of Greatness of Mind, of unshaken Fidelity, Contempt of humane Grandeur, a most passionate Love of their Country, Prodigality of Life, Disdain of Servitude, inviolable Truth, and the most publick disinterested Souls, that ever threw off all Regards in Comparison with their Country's Good; Your Lordship will discern the Flaws and Blemishes of their fairest Actions, see the wrong Apprehensions they had of Virtue, and be able to point them right, and keep them within their proper Bounds. Under this Correction Your Lordship may extract a generous and noble Spirit from the Writings and Histories of the Ancients.[9]

Here too we may see evidence in the commonplace book that Byrd was culling from the exemplary tradition to which his education had exposed him. There are anecdotes or sayings that recount the public spirit and civic virtue of figures such as Cato, Epaminondas, and Phocion and maxims enjoining self-discipline from Socrates and other philosophers. And there are negative figures as well, including Alexander and Caesar, whose great military achievements are held to be inferior to the conquest over one's own unruly passions (§325).

Other important benefits could be drawn from classical education. An attention to detail, for instance, was a valuable attribute in a gentleman of affairs. Classical education provided young men with training in mental acuity; the "habit of accuracy" instilled by rigorous study of grammar was understood to be transferable to other serious endeavors throughout life.[10]

Furthermore, an intimate knowledge of the classics was deemed necessary in the development of a true taste, one of the essential marks of gentility. Taste is "the internal sense of a harmonic order perceived in certain objects and belonging to them and to the perceiving mind as well." The ability to distinguish between real and fallacious aesthetic values was an important asset in polite eighteenth-century society. Taste is *"that Faculty of the Soul,"* Addison explains, *"which discerns the Beauties of an Author with Pleasure, and the Imperfections with Dislike."* As an innate faculty, it appears in differing degrees among men; it may diminish with neglect, but it also improves with training (reading and conversation). Moreover, according to some eighteenth-century aesthetic theorists, taste, as a refined, discriminating perception of value, is implicitly connected to moral discrimination. It must also be acknowledged that taste is often

9. Henry Felton, *A Dissertation on Reading the Classics, and Forming a Just Style . . . ,* 2d ed. (London, 1715), 15–16.

10. Clarke, *Greek Studies in England,* 13.

used as an instrument of displaying social status, in that only young men of a limited social stratum had access to the requisite education and training. Developing and displaying taste became for many gentlemen a considered attempt to shine in one another's eyes, to thrive in a public, genteel society whose purpose to a large extent was to furnish these gentlemen with self-confirmation.[11]

Be this as it may, taste also has a practical application, as a key component of eloquence, a vital part of the public life. Here especially the study of the classics was invaluable, since so many of the surviving Greek and Roman texts dealt with civic and political history. Clarke explains: "In England as in Athens and Rome public speaking was an essential part of public life, and Demosthenes and Cicero were the undisputed models of oratory."[12] These classical models for emulation were particularly important to those whose place in society required them to speak publicly on important matters:

> Besides the other Advantages of studying the *Classical Historians,* there is one which *Gentlemen* of Birth and Fortune, qualify'd to manage *Public Business,* and sit as Members of the most *August Assemblies,* have a more considerable Share in than People of meaner Condition. The Speeches of the great Men among the *Greeks* and *Romans* deserve their peculiar Study and Imitation, as being Master-pieces of clear *Reasoning* and genuine Eloquence.[13]

At all stages of Byrd's public career, as a representative of the colonial planters, as a legislator, and as a leading man of Virginia politics, he was able to call upon this training in reasoning and eloquence. In fact, Byrd's life embodies the ideal of education as proposed by Francis Bacon:

11. Giorgio Tonelli, "Taste in Aesthetics," in *Dictionary of the History of Ideas* (New York, 1968–1974), IV, 355; Joseph Addison, *Spectator,* no. 409 (June 19, 1712). Byrd had an extensive collection of Addison's writings, including *Notes upon the Twelve Books of Paradise Lost* (Hayes 901), *Remarks on Several Parts of Italy* (Hayes 224), the collected *Spectator* papers (Hayes 870), and the six-volume edition of the *Works* (Hayes 1848).

As an instance of the acceptance of class limitations for classical education, see Richard Steele's comments about classical studies inappropriate to lower-class youth, *Tatler,* no. 173 (May 18, 1710): "Whatever Children are designed for, and whatever Prospects the Fortune or Interest of their Parents may give them in their future Lives, they are all promiscuously instructed the same way; and *Horace* and *Virgil* must be thrummed by a Boy as well before he goes to an Apprenticeship as to the University. This ridiculous Way of treating the Underaged of this Island has very often raised both by Spleen and Mirth." Steele follows this with a lampoon of such an unfortunate youth and his pseudolearned malapropisms. Byrd owned two sets of the *Tatler* (Hayes 996–997).

12. Clarke, *Greek Studies in England,* 13.

13. Blackwall, *An Introduction to the Classics,* 59.

Studies serve for delight, for ornament, and for ability. Their chief use for delight, is in privateness and retiring; for ornament, is in discourse; and for ability, is in the judgment and disposition of business.[14]

In Byrd's case, we have evidence of his delight in his private studies—his daily course of reading in Greek, his episodes of intense concentration on the works of particular authors, and in his occasional literary productions. Studies ornamented his discourse in conversation and in letters. The third of Bacon's ends, the judgment and disposition of business, was Byrd's lifelong occupation as a major figure in the public life of his community.

So, in the end, what significance can we draw from Byrd's classical education and from the continuities discernible in his diaries and especially in this commonplace book? Not enough attention has been paid to this essential part of Byrd's life; indeed, many Byrd scholars have dismissed it outright.[15] The primary function of the classical education gentlemen of Byrd's station received was *preparation of the gentleman for public life:* at the university, had he gone there, Byrd would have continued the course of studies that he began in public school. Essentially, by choosing to study law (and in his continuing private studies) Byrd did just that. In Byrd's day mastery of languages was viewed as a means to an end, which was access to the wisdom of the ancients. The devotion to the minutiae of philological matters of high scholarship was for the most part a stock target for farce rather than an option Byrd was not allowed to pursue.

Byrd's education, then, was successful, since it produced the qualities it set out to instill and prepared him for the public life of a responsible Christian gentleman, a preparation that served him well in his endeavors in Virginia politics and his career as a planter and a leading citizen in his community.

14. Francis Bacon, "Of Studies" (*Essays; or, Counsels Civil and Moral* [1625]), in Bacon, *Philosophical Works,* 797.

15. See, for instance, Louis B. Wright: "Byrd's father, a realistic businessman as well as a member of the aristocratic landed class in Virginia, had no notion of making a *mere scholar* of his son and heir" ("Introduction: William Byrd as a Man of Letters," *Works,* 4, emphasis added); and Pierre Marambaud, *William Byrd of Westover, 1674–1744* (Charlottesville, Va., 1971), who similarly states it was not William Byrd I's "intention to make a bookworm" of his son (17). In regard to Wright's dismissive term, "a mere scholar," we must ask, How many among the countless young men who received a classical education such as that offered at Felsted Grammar School, and later at the universities, actually devoted their lives to scholarship? This was not the function of universities; in fact, there is no contradiction between the education offered by Felsted and the universities and the complicated business tasks Wright outlines. It seems that Wright has mistakenly equated the term "scholar" with the term "pedant."

His education planted in him a strong sense of the desirability of social order (though his place in this order was not always clear to him).[16] The running commentary on public life scattered through the commonplace book gives evidence that Byrd continued to build upon this preparation. Bacon explains that studies support a gentleman in judgment and disposition of business; Byrd needed judgment to find his way among the conflicts and confusions of trade and politics, to remain firm and centered while others around him were sometimes inconsistent and humorous, and to draw on inner strength when his plans were checked by the actions of those with more power. The ancients continually warned their readers to be on guard against the vicissitudes and disappointments of life. Byrd studied these warnings, knowing he had to learn to keep himself ready to act purposefully, to speak winningly, and to accept defeat and victory gracefully.

16. Marambaud sums up this position: "Byrd, like most members of his group, despised barbarity, disorder, idleness, intemperance, and selfishness. He valued industry, frugality, moderation, responsibility, justice, and respect for authority" (*William Byrd,* 200). On order in Byrd's public writing, see Ross Pudaloff, "'A Certain Amount of Excellent English': The Secret Diaries of William Byrd," *Southern Literary Journal,* XV, no. 1 (Fall 1982), 108–109; Susan Manning, "Industry and Idleness in Colonial Virginia: A New Approach to William Byrd II," *Journal of American Studies,* XXVIII (1994), 170–171.

3. THE COMMONPLACE BOOK IN EDUCATION

In the project of making gentlemen, schools extended the program of classical reading by extensive emphasis on developing skill in argument, training the memory, and gaining a broad acquaintance with the world. Commonplace books emerged as a means of supporting these pedagogical ends. In the late seventeenth century, when Byrd was educated at Felsted, schools regularly assigned their students the task of condensing and registering the essential lessons they were learning in personal commonplace books. By thus reconstructing elements of lectures, readings, conversation, and personal discoveries in their own words, students were encouraged to participate in their own education through a time-tested exercise of controlled discovery.

The origin of this process lies in ancient forms of education. According to the classical logicians and orators, students learning the ways of reasoning needed to learn the best ways to test a statement for truth. Writers such as Aristotle, Cicero, and Quintilian recommended that students commit to memory certain useful forms of argument, which were known as "places"—τόποι (*topoi*) in Greek, *loci communes* in Latin. The knowledge of these forms would help in the invention (discovery and construction) of arguments. Arguments could be used to discover the truth, or to test the truth of a proposition or another disputant, and thus the places were an essential tool in moral as well as practical education. They were valuable as aids in developing the proper use of reason. Locke explains "the use and end of right Reasoning" is "to have right Notions, and a right Judgment of things; to distinguish betwixt Truth and Falshood, Right and Wrong; and to act accordingly."[1] On a moral level, the development of reason in young gentlemen supported their endeavors to find the best way to live their lives; furthermore, on a practical level, the ability to plumb the character or truthfulness of others was essential for making one's way in the world.

The places were the common property of all educated people; they could be

1. John Locke, *Some Thoughts concerning Education,* ed. John W. Yolton and Jean S. Yolton (Oxford, 1989), 240–241. Locke also distinguishes between practical learning (leading to virtue) and the far less desirable disputatious learning, warning against raising sons "in the Art and Formality of Disputing," for fear of producing wrangling and opinionated men.

considered virtually as locations in the public mind, or perhaps as existing in some sphere of higher knowledge. The original topics were rhetorical forms of argument (from cause, from effect, by definition), which Greek and Roman educators expected their students to commit to memory. Gradually, however, over the centuries the term "place" and "commonplace" expanded to include every sort of element useful in argumentation: strategies of argumentation, turns of logic, rhetorical figures, illustrations, and amplifications. Students were encouraged to keep a record of anything that could prove useful in argumentation. Some collections of commonplaces were little more than a vocabulary of rhetorical tricks, but the early modern humanist educators revived the original idea of collecting commonplaces to support moral philosophy as well as rhetoric. Roger Ascham, in his *Scholemaster* (1570), urged students to keep three separate notebooks: one for translation, one for retranslation, and the third for a collection of phrases and grammatical notes taken in the course of their reading. Juan Luis Vives, in his *De tradendis disciplinis* (1523), required each boy to keep a large book in which to record maxims from his master, from his readings of the great writers, and from conversation.[2]

Erasmus provided schoolmasters with the best-known advice on such matters. His book *De copia*, first published in London in 1569 and running to many editions during the next two centuries, was the leading schoolbook in the sixteenth century. Erasmus takes for granted the moral dimension of the *topoi* (*copia, exempla*), emphasizing the use of rhetoric in service to the commonwealth. His understanding of *copia* includes "variation, abundance or richness, *eloquence,* and the *ability* to vary or enrich language and thought." A book of copia provided material for students to use when practicing translation from one language to another and turning prose to verse and back again, an activity that was supposed to improve fluency and style. Erasmus's collected topics would find their way into the memory, where they would be readily accessible to enhance speech or writing even if his book were not at hand. Drawing on one's copia could help one to illustrate a subject and persuade an audience to a particular point. Because legitimate persuasion properly depended on the truth

2. For the history of commonplace books, see Joan Marie Lechner, *Renaissance Concepts of the Commonplaces* (New York, 1962); William G. Crane, *Wit and Rhetoric in the Renaissance: The Formal Basis of Elizabethan Prose Style* (New York, 1937); Wilbur Samuel Howell, *Eighteenth-Century British Logic and Rhetoric* (Princeton, N.J., 1971); John Guillory, "The English Common Place, Lineages of The Topographical Genre," *Critical Quarterly,* XXXIII, no. 4 (Winter 1991), 3–27. On Ascham and Vives, see Foster Watson, *The English Grammar Schools to 1660: Their Curriculum and Practice* (Cambridge, 1908), 7–8, 123–126, 263.

of the assertion, Erasmus insisted on the importance of selecting commonplaces from authors known for their wisdom, such as Plato and Cicero.[3]

Erasmus held that a reader can understand a text fully only if he can make it his own. One of the best ways is to recapitulate the text using the methods of amplification—paraphrase, analogy, parallel, versification, illustration—and commonplacing is named as one of the most effective methods. Eloquence springs naturally from familiarity with the important parts of meaningful texts:

> Whoever trains himself for eloquence ought to examine individual places and go over them in detail to see what he can elicit from them. Practice will result in their suggesting themselves automatically in a never ending series. . . .
>
> . . . Therefore, if anyone is willing to collect a great number of ornaments of speech from his reading he can produce an oration as copious as he wishes; and yet it will not be a lifeless mass of words, and through its variety will avoid tedious monotony.

Thus the proper procedure for creating a comprehensive collection:

> Therefore, whoever has resolved to read through every type of writer (for he who wishes to be considered learned must do that thoroughly once in his life) will first collect as many topics as possible.[4]

Such collections include a mélange of topics: historical deeds and sayings, common customs of peoples, and exempla from historians, poets, and philosophical and theological writers. The diversity of nations provides a rich store, as do different historical eras and social conditions—some deal with princes, some with magistrates, parents, slaves, paupers, rich men, women, maidens, boys. All this Erasmus breaks down into detailed classes and categories. The topics chosen are to be arranged either alphabetically or in pairs of opposites, such as piety and impiety:

3. Watson, *English Grammar Schools,* 438; Desiderius Erasmus, *On Copia of Words and Ideas (De utraque verborem ac rerum copia),* trans. Donald B. King and H. David Rix (Milwaukee, Wis., 1963), 9, 16–17. Byrd would have encountered Erasmus at Felsted; later, Byrd's library contained numerous books by Erasmus, including his edition of the New Testament (Hayes 1288), *Adagia* (Hayes 1608, 1609), *Adagiorum epitome* (Hayes 1534), *De utraq verborum ac rerum copia* (Hayes 1549), *Erasmi vita* (Hayes 1559), *Colloquies* (Hayes 828, 1560, 1799), *Apophthegmata* (Hayes 1767). Erasmus might have served as a source for Byrd's commonplace book entries §29, 96, 108–110, 124, 218, 277. On the late-seventeenth-century revival of Erasmus, see Irwin Primer, "Erasmus and Bernard Mandeville: A Reconsideration," *Philological Quarterly,* LXXII (1993), 314–315.

4. Erasmus, *On Copia,* trans. King and Rix, 67, 87.

Then after you have collected as many headings as will be sufficient and arranged them in the order you wish, and have placed the appropriate divisions under each, and to the divisions have added the commonplaces or *sententiae*, then whatever you come across anywhere in any author, especially if it is very noteworthy, you will immediately mark down in its proper place. . . . This method will also have the effect of imprinting what you read more deeply on your mind, as well as accustoming you to utilizing the riches of your reading.[5]

By the seventeenth century the convention of having students keep commonplace books was well established. In England, students concentrated on learning the classical languages; writing, arithmetic, reading, and so forth were supplementary tasks. The commonplace book was an educational device that served both to advance the learning of languages and to instill virtue. Passages were sought out and assigned because of their grammatical and syntactic function, but, whenever possible, such passages were also selected on the basis of their ability to serve as a vehicle for another, deeper lesson. The student was directed to texts that could "teach all things, framing him to eloquence in talke, and virtue in deeds." This practice of gathering and framing was central to humanist education, directing students to texts "where the cultural codes of antiquity and modern Europe coincided," invoking (or repatterning) the values and morals of the ancients, insofar as they had relevance to the present age. In this way students were able to write and speak on modern subjects supported by the weight and authority of the ancients. In committing these topics to memory, the student assimilated proper values.[6]

Francis Bacon recognized the value of collecting commonplaces, though he also expressed some concern that artificiality and preciosity might cancel the productiveness of the activity:

There can hardly be anything more useful even for the old and popular sciences, than a sound help for the memory; that is a good and learned Digest of Common-Places. I am aware indeed that the transferring of the things we read and learn into common-place books is thought by some to be detrimen-

5. Ibid., 68, 89. It is interesting to note that Byrd's commonplace book touches on nearly every one of Erasmus's topics. The concept of pairing opposing concepts or examples may be linked to the influence of the biographical method of Plutarch, whose biographies were written in pairs to provide contrasts.

6. Mary Thomas Crane, *Framing Authority: Sayings, Self, and Society in Sixteenth-Century England* (Princeton, N.J., 1993), 58–59, 60, 62–63.

tal to learning, as retarding the course of the reader and inviting the memory to take a holiday. Nevertheless, as it is but a counterfeit thing in knowledge to be forward and pregnant, except a man be also deep and full, I hold diligence and labour in the entry of common-places to be a matter of great use and support in studying; as that which supplies matter to invention, and contracts the sight of the judgment to a point. But yet it is true that of the methods and frameworks of common-places which I have hitherto seen, there is none of any worth; all of them carrying in their titles merely the face of a school and not of a world; and using vulgar and pedantical divisions, not such as pierce to the pith and heart of things.

Disposing or collocating what is read can focus the digesting of what is being read. In Bacon's approach we can see how the use of commonplace books expands beyond its educational function as a collection of classical "places" to a useful compendium of ideas appropriate for appropriately learned gentlemen.[7]

It must be acknowledged that other educational writers took a dim view of the commonplace book. Henry Felton, in his *Dissertation on Reading the Classics,* offers several cautions:

> The first is, that Your Lordship would never be persuaded into what they call *Common-Places,* which is a Way of taking an Author to Pieces, and ranging him under proper Heads, that You may readily find what he hath said upon any Point, by consulting an *Alphabet.* This Practice is of no Use but in Circumstantials of Time and Place, Custom, and Antiquity, and in such Instances where Facts are to be remembred, not where the Brain is to be exercised. In these Cases it is of great Use: It helpeth the Memory, and serveth to keep those Things in a Sort of Order and Succession. But, my Lord, *Common Placing* the *Sense* of an Author is such a stupid Undertaking, that, if I may be indulged in saying it, they *want Common Sense* that practise it. What Heaps of this Rubbish have I seen! O the Pains and Labour to record what other People have said, that is taken by those, who have Nothing to say themselves! Your Lordship may depend upon it, the Writings of these Men are never worth the Reading; the Fancy is cramp'd, the Invention spoiled,

---

7. Bacon, *De augmentis scientiarum,* in Bacon, *Philosophical Works,* 519. Bacon assembled late in his life a collection of apothegms, intermixing classical and modern references, reputedly dictated from memory; see *Apophthegmes New and Old* (London, 1625), in Bacon, *Philosophical Works,* 859–899. Byrd owned an extensive collection of works by Bacon, including the *Advancement of Learning* (Hayes 925), the *Essays* (Hayes 856), and the *Opera omnia* (Hayes 623). Bacon might have been one of the authors Byrd consulted and transcribed into his commonplace book; see §72, 124, 218, 220, 246, 288, 358.

their Thoughts on every Thing are prevented, if they think at all; but 'tis the peculiar Happiness of these *Collectors* of Sense, that they can write without *Thinking*.[8]

Yet Felton appears to be criticizing the *abuses* of commonplacing—especially the reliance on rubbishy miscellanies as an attempt to disguise empty-headedness—rather than the practice itself, which he allows to have some merit for the particular purposes he names.

One hundred years later, almost as if to answer Bacon's call for the articulation of a better approach to the collection of commonplaces, John Locke's posthumous *New Method of Making Common-Place-Books* offered a useful statement of purpose and detailed instructions. Locke extends the Erasmian approach by providing clear, detailed instructions for the student. The *New Method* furnishes a step-by-step guide on how to create a useful notebook of commonplaces, beginning with the choice of a blank book, and going on to describe how to divide the pages, create an index, and label the entries with headings, which should consist of a key word. Once the form was established, an entry could be recorded on the appropriate page and if necessary carried over to other pages, skipping pages set aside for other topical categories. Locke stresses the importance of recording the source in full (even going so far as to record the page on which the entry was found against the total number of pages in the edition used, creating a reference resembling fractional notation, to help find the source even in a different edition). Locke's method was so influential that printers made up blank paper books prefaced with Locke's instructions.[9]

Throughout the early modern period readers also had access to books that supplemented the moral instruction instilled by the schools, in the form of collections of wise sayings, apothegms, and moral essays as well as advice or courtesy books. An early example of this is William Baldwin's sixteenth-century compendium, *A Treatise of Morall Philosophie,* which adds to a brief survey of great philosophers several collections of "worthy Sentences, notable Precepts,

8. Henry Felton, *A Dissertation on Reading the Classics, and Forming a Just Style . . .* , 2d ed. (London, 1715), 35–37. Crane, in *Framing Authority,* has contended that commonplacing reduces the authority of established texts to a manageable (and hence reductive) size.

9. John Locke, *A New Method of Making Common-Place-Books* (London, 1706). Originally part of a letter from Locke to Nicolas Toinard, the remarks were published (in French) at Toinard's urging; the English translation was published in 1706, after Locke's death. The pamphlet itself was not in Byrd's library, but it does appear in Locke's *Posthumous Works* (London, 1706), which Byrd owned (Hayes 2127). Joseph Spence, *Observations, Anecdotes, and Characters of Books and Men, Collected from Conversation,* ed. James M. Osborn (Oxford, 1966), I, 302.

Counsels, and Parables" arranged under headings such as "Of the Soule," "Of Kings and Rulers," "Of Iustice and Iniustice," "Of Temperance," "Of Envie and Malice," and so forth. In their approach to the assembly of discrete bits of wisdom, such collections parallel the commonplace book. Educational writers recommended using them as models for students in developing their own commonplace books; published collections of copia helped students achieve eloquence as well as exemplify how such collections could be compiled independently. John Brinsley explains, in his *Ludus Literarius* (1612), that such collections can also serve as an aid to versifying. Students provide themselves with a storehouse of appropriate topics and ideas to use in the composition of verse for all occasions. Like Erasmus, Brinsley believed the importance of such a collection was to serve as a stepping-stone to eloquent speech and writing.[10]

Charles Hoole's *New Discovery of the Old Art of Teaching School* (1660) extended the exercise still further by enumerating the sources from which students should compile their own commonplace book. Hoole recommended selecting the headings and then collecting under these a variety of material, including histories, fables, adages, emblems, ancient laws and customs, witty sentences, and descriptions of things natural and artificial. Under each of these choices he

10. [John Brinsley], *Ludus Literarius; or, The Grammar Schoole; Shewing How to Proceede from the First Entrance into Learning, to the Highest Perfection* . . . (London, 1612); William Baldwin, *A Treatise of Morall Philosophy* . . . (London, 1557); Pollard and Redgrave's *Short-Title Catalogue* lists two dozen editions of *A Treatise*. Other similarly arranged collections of ancient wisdom, stories, maxims, and sententious similes include Baldwin, *A Myrroure for Magistrates* (1559); Haly Heron, *A Newe Discourse of Morall Philosophie* (1579); Thomas Crewe, *The Nosegay of Morall Philosophie* (1580); Anthony Fletcher, *Certaine Very Proper, and Most Profitable Similies* (1595); Nicholas Ling, *Politeuphuia* (1595); John Bodenham, *Belvedére* (1600); Robert Cawdrey, *A Treasurie; or, Store-house of Similies* (1600); Francis Meres, *Palladis Tamia* (1598); John Spencer, *Things New and Old; or, A Store-house of Similies, Sentences, Allegories, Apophthegms, Adagies, Apologues, Divine, Morall, Political, etc. with Their Severall Applications* (1658). Other similar sources of such topics are the learned early modern collections of Latin proverbs, such as Polydore Vergil, *Proverbiorum Libellus* (1498), Domenico Nani Mirabelli, *Polyanthea* (1503), and Joannes Stobaeus, *Sententiae* (1555). Some of this material found its way into English in Thomas Stanley's *History of Philosophy* (1655), based on Diogenes Laertius with material culled from ancient histories and later anthologists such as Stobaeus.

On the importance of advice books to the formation of gentlemen, see John E. Mason, *Gentlefolk in the Making: Studies in the History of English Courtesy Literature and Related Topics, from 1531 to 1774* (Philadelphia, 1935); and Richard L. Bushman, *The Refinement of America: Persons, Houses, Cities* (New York, 1992), especially the section "The Courtesy-Book World," 30–60. The editors would like to thank Kevin R. Hardwick for helpful information in this area.

provided a list of the most appropriate sources, naming authors and titles, from which to choose. Byrd might have been familiar with Hoole's text from his school days and might have learned to compile a commonplace book according to Hoole's method. Hoole also sets forth a system for students to use commonplace books as an educational tool: the student consults the recommended authors and writes the commonplaces under the appropriate headings (making sure the schoolmaster approves the selections), and then each student reads his excerpts aloud while the other students write them down in their books. In this way each student accumulates a wider range of commonplaces than he might have gathered on his own. Like Brinsley, Hoole also recommends that the school keep some published collections for additional reference.[11]

Thus, many gentlemen of the seventeenth and eighteenth centuries gained an early familiarity with the practice. They learned how to read for understanding by extracting commonplaces and became well read in a variety of topics that would be useful to them in later life. Through this education they also took possession of a pool of common knowledge and values that would benefit them as they made their way in society. Upon leaving school, many young men found it convenient to continue the collecting, adapting it to their station in life as gentlemen.

11. Watson, *English Grammar Schools,* 457. Commonplacing was almost certainly part of Byrd's early education; however, as we shall demonstrate, in eschewing topical arrangement and identification of sources, Byrd employs neither Hoole's nor Erasmus's nor Locke's recommendations.

4. THE COMMONPLACE BOOK AND THE COMMON CULTURE

English literary and social culture of the seventeenth and eighteenth centuries was highly referential and allusive. Within the community of educated writers and readers, the free play of intertextual reference included purposeful direction to those sources of practical wisdom that all gentlemen were expected to have absorbed. These sources were, of course, the stuff of commonplace collections: maxims, anecdotes, proverbs, classical allusions, and epigrams. Writers assembled such elements in their own collections of commonplaces stored in memory, in notebooks, and even in published collections. The kind of material assembled in eighteenth-century commonplace books tends to fall within fairly predictable boundaries. That this is so should not be surprising; after all, the purpose in collecting copia was to facilitate participation in the common culture, to help gain acceptance in a public sphere where one was expected to understand the core body of knowledge.

The commonplace book served as a device for ordering and framing the culture's most important ideas, a function evident in the way the practice of collecting copia found its way into the literature of the period. In Steele's *Tatler* papers, the "grave and facetious" fictional author, Isaac Bickerstaff, appointed himself spokesman for the values of the educated gentry, summing up ancient and modern wisdom and tempering it with wit. Henry Felton's praise of Bickerstaff establishes the nature of his appeal:

> 'Squire *Bickerstaff*... hath drawn Mankind in every Dress, and every Disguise of Nature, in a Style ever varying with the Humours, Fancies, and Follies he describes. He hath showed himself a Master in every Turn of his Pen, whether his Subject be light, or serious, and hath laid down the Rules of common Life with so much Judgment, in such agreeable, such lively and elegant Language.[1]

Occasionally Bickerstaff referred to his own commonplace book as a source for inspiration. In 1709 Bickerstaff entertained a sorrowful gentleman who sought his advice.

---

1. Henry Felton, *A Dissertation on Reading the Classics, and Forming a Just Style . . .* , 2d ed. (London, 1715), 252.

Much Experience has made me particularly sagacious in the Discovery of Distempers, and I soon saw that his was Love. I then turned to my Commonplace Book, and found his Case under the word *Coquette;* and reading over the Catalogue which I have collected out of this great City of all under that Character, I saw at the name of *Cynthia* his fit came upon him.[2]

As successor to the *Tatler,* Addison and Steele's *Spectator* continued to produce topical essays rich with anecdotes, classical references, and other items of copia. In a discussion on the disposition and abilities of young people, Steele writes of looking for historical precedents:

> My common-place Book directs me on this Occasion to mention the Dawning of Greatness in *Alexander,* who being asked in his Youth to contend for a Prize in the Olympick Games, answered he would if he had Kings to run against him.[3]

Following this, Steele adduces the examples of Cassius, Scipio, and Marius, all of whom gave proleptic evidence as children of the kind of men they would become. In this way authors in the public eye continued to demonstrate the use of commonplaces, whether ancient or modern, to amplify their arguments.

Of course, the use of commonplaces could get out of hand. Bickerstaff is, to some degree, a figure of parody. Swift, too, was particularly exercised by the abuses of commonplacing, and he returned repeatedly to the ludicrous prospect of a man who collected fragments of information but knew virtually nothing. In *A Tale of a Tub,* for instance, he ironically recommends that the moderns adopt the method to avoid running out of things to say:

> Our *Modern* Wits are not to reckon upon the Infinity of Matter, for a constant Supply. What remains therefore, but that our last Recourse must be had to large *Indexes,* and little *Compendiums.* . . . But above all, those judicious Collectors of *bright Parts,* and *Flowers,* and *Observanda's,* are to be nicely dwelt on; by some called the *Sieves* and *Boulters* of Learning, tho' it is left undetermined, whether they dealt in *Pearls* or *Meal;* and consequently, whether we are more to value that which *passed thro',* or what *staid behind.*
>
> By these Methods, in a few Weeks, there starts up many a Writer, capable of managing the profoundest, and most universal Subjects. For, what tho' his

---

2. *Tatler,* no. 107 (Dec. 15, 1709). Byrd owned the *Tatler* as well as bound copies of other popular magazines of the period: *Guardian* (Hayes 867), *Free-holder* (Hayes 868), *Englishman* (Hayes 869), *Spectator* (Hayes 870), *Examiner* (Hayes 989), and *Medleys* (Hayes 995).

3. *Spectator,* no. 157 (Aug. 20, 1711). This anecdote appears in Byrd's commonplace book as §218.

> *Head* be empty, provided his *Common-place-Book* be full; And if you will bate him but the Circumstances of *Method,* and *Style,* and *Grammar,* and *Invention;* allow him but the common Priviledges of transcribing from others, and digressing from himself, as often as he shall see Occasion; He will desire no more Ingredients towards fitting up a Treatise, that shall make a very comely Figure on a Bookseller's Shelf.[4]

Swift here outlines the mechanical production of literature, which provides a marketable product without requiring of an author any of those qualities ordinarily required of literary creation. A similar parody occurs in Swift's *Complete Collection of Genteel and Ingenious Conversation,* in which an editorial persona, Simon Wagstaff, expresses an absurd confidence in the value of his collection of the "choisest expressions," all guaranteed to be "at least one hundred Years" old and therefore all "genuine, sterling, and authentick." His readers are to learn these expressions by rote, so they will never be "at a Loss in applying the right Answers, Questions, Repartees, and the like immediately, and without Study or Hesitation." Wagstaff anticipates the accolades of society because he is sure that his compilations will provide them with an invaluable aid to conversation. True wit, he believes, is nothing more than the ability to say the appropriate thing at all times, so he proceeds to list approved sayings in an astonishingly wooden dialogue and proposes that his readers should learn them by rote. The number of traditional sayings is limited—though the accumulated clichés, dull jests, and utterly predictable repartees of the *Complete Collection* seem to go on forever—and Wagstaff complains of the difficulty of collecting sayings in polite company, since conversation keeps "degenerating into smart Sayings of their own Invention, and not of the true old Standard."[5]

In spite of the laughable excesses of Wagstaff's approach, we can see that a large part of the common culture found expression in polite conversation. In the

4. Jonathan Swift, *A Tale of a Tub,* in Herbert Davis, ed., The Prose Works of Jonathan Swift, I (Oxford, 1957), 93.

5. Jonathan Swift, *A Complete Collection of Genteel and Ingenious Conversation, according to the Most Polite Mode and Method, Now Used at Court, and in the Best Companies of England* (1737), in Davis, ed., Prose Works of Jonathan Swift, IV (Oxford, 1957), 102–103, 106–107.

Swift satirically indicates Wagstaff's appalling ignorance through his identification of Newton, whom he ludicrously identifies as one of his rivals for fame, as a mere "Instrument-Maker, formerly living near *Leicester* Fields, and afterwards a Workman in the Mint," knighted for improvements in making sundials, and "thought to be a Conjurer, because he knew how to draw Lines and Circles upon a Slate, which no Body could understand" (122–123).

public setting of coffeehouses a new kind of socializing began during the Restoration and early eighteenth century. This public discourse was not completely random; gentlemen were guided by traditions of politeness, especially acted out in words and deeds. But it was in conversation that a gentleman proved himself. Politeness governed the social interaction between gentlemen for the betterment of the individual and society. Papers like the *Spectator* aided in the dissemination of politeness to a wider public. The periodicals were filled with polite essays that discussed morals and refinement in an informal, conversational style. In these literary forms the coffeehouses are portrayed as sites for this "conversable sociability conducive to the improvement of society." Gentlemen participating in the coffeehouse discourse needed to be practiced in the recognized forms of eloquence and thus required access to the original body of reference, which we see represented in commonplace books.[6]

Such practitioners of polite conversation (and such polite authors) as the duke of Buckingham, the earl of Egmont (Byrd's friend), the marquess of Halifax (whom Byrd met at the Royal Society and whose portrait he later owned), and the earl of Shaftesbury all compiled commonplace books. At the same time, another tradition ridiculed those who depended on the tired, trite observations that often emerged from commonplace books. Buckingham satirized Dryden's denying that he used a commonplace book and pretending that his brilliance was all spontaneous.[7]

Byrd's contemporaries in Virginia also compiled such collections of copia. Few of these books survive, but their existence is recorded in contemporary inventories, letters, and diaries. For instance, George Carter in his will of 1742 left to a colleague in England "my Ms. notes taken in the Courts of Westminster, and my Common place Book, 8 fol. vols." This probably refers to a legal commonplace book (a compilation of cases annotated by the author). Byrd himself

6. As Lawrence E. Klein states, "Conversation was the paradigmatic arena for politeness" (*Shaftesbury and the Culture of Politeness: Moral Discourse and Cultural Politics in Early Eighteenth-Century England* [Cambridge, 1994], 4). See also David H. Solkin, *Painting for Money: The Visual Arts and the Public Sphere in Eighteenth-Century England* (New Haven, Conn., 1993), 30–31. Early modern gentility appropriated and transformed Cicero's notion that appropriate conversation was one of the preeminent components of social life (*De officiis* 1.37).

7. Christine Phipps, ed., *Buckingham: Public and Private Man: The Prose, Poems, and Commonplace Book of George Villiers, Second Duke of Buckingham, 1628–1657* (New York, 1985); Mark N. Brown, ed., *The Works of George Savile, Marquis of Halifax* (New York, 1989), particularly the "Appendix: Common Place Book," III, 310–314. The British Library has the commonplace books of Sir John Perceval, second and third baronets, and the books of the first and second Lords Egmont (BM 47111–47113, 47137–47139, 47126–47130B).

kept such a grouping of cases with notes; in the early diary he mentions several times when he read law and "wrote the most remarkable part of it in a book" or "abridged it in my book."[8]

Thomas Jefferson kept both a literary and a legal commonplace book. His literary collection follows the format recommended by Erasmus and Locke. Jefferson originally compiled it early in his career (in the 1760s and 1770s), and he referred to and amended entries in later years. There are no topical headings, but the sources for all the entries are recorded. The book includes Greek, Latin, and English entries and concerns matters of moral philosophy and literature; there are none of the anecdotal, witty, satirical, and gossipy entries of Byrd's collection.[9]

Another Virginian, Robert Beverley, kept a commonplace book, found in the library of his Spotsylvania County estate and listed in a 1734 inventory as "2 commonplace books begun by Mr. Beverley. Quarto." John Custis's commonplace book, one of the few to survive the passage of two hundred years, contains seventy-five pages of medical remedies complete with an index, and the remaining seventy-four pages contain verses and sayings in English and Latin. Joseph Ball considered his commonplace book important enough that he specifically directed it should be shipped to London with his other books. At midcentury Robert Bolling kept a book that acquired the title of *A Collection of Diverting Anecdotes, Bon-Mots, and Other Trifling Pieces.* The collection combined items transcribed from other sources along with some of his own composition.[10]

Another famous Virginian educated in the classical tradition was Landon Carter. Though he did not record his collection of commonplaces in a separate notebook, he did scatter topical extracts from the Bible, Blackstone's *Commentaries,* and other books dealing with law, religion, and agriculture throughout his diary and daybooks, creating a kind of dispersed commonplace book.[11]

8. "Virginia Gleanings in England," *VMHB,* XV (1907–1908), 426–427; *SD,* 563, 565. Byrd's legal commonplace book of cases and notes, written in his special code, is bound (upside down) together with the 1709–1712 diary at the Huntington Library (BR61).

9. Thomas Jefferson, *Jefferson's Literary Commonplace Book,* ed. Douglas L. Wilson (Princeton, N.J., 1989).

10. W. G. Stanard, "Major Robert Beverley and His Descendants," *VMHB,* III (1895–1896), 389. The John Custis commonplace book is in the collection of the Chicago Historical Society (CWF microfilm M-97). Bolling's *Collection* book survives in a nineteenth-century copy made by Robert Alonzo Brock in 1869 from the 1764 original (now missing), Virginia Historical Society (Mss5:5 B6385:1).

11. Jack P. Greene, ed., *The Diary of Colonel Landon Carter of Sabine Hall* (Charlottesville, Va., 1965), II, 785–790, 909–917, 953–963, 1067–1070, 1086, 1135.

This is just a sampling of Byrd's contemporaries known to have kept commonplace books. Other surviving books may remain to be discovered, cataloged under a bewildering range of headings, or even ignored, perhaps because the practice of making commonplace books, and the common culture it fed, scarcely exist any longer.

5. WILLIAM BYRD AS A WRITER:
BETWEEN THE PRIVATE AND PUBLIC SPHERES

Byrd is best known today for his private writings, especially the frank, laconic, encrypted diaries, of which three large volumes have been discovered, decoded, and published only in this century. These writings have provided historians with valuable insight into eighteenth-century private life; Byrd scholars have been involved in explicating and interpreting these private texts since they first came to light some half a century ago.[1]

There were times in Byrd's life when he sought recognition for his more public literary productions, as a number of extant works he wrote for a particular audience will attest. Byrd did not aspire to the highest literary ranks, serious poetry and drama. Rather, he saw himself as a gentleman of letters (or aspired to that distinction). Such a self-definition (or aspiration) was often part of the package of the well-educated English gentleman—thus his indulgence in trans-

---

1. *SD, ASD, LD.* On the terse, "formulaic," and "affectless" tone of the diaries, see Ross Pudaloff, " 'A Certain Amount of Excellent English': The Secret Diaries of William Byrd," *Southern Literary Journal,* XV, no. 1 (Fall 1982), 102–103. In *The Family, Sex, and Marriage in England, 1500–1800* (New York, 1977), Lawrence Stone calls the diaries "a cold and bloodless account of the bare facts of his daily routine. . . . entirely lacking in colour, warmth, imagination, or self-revelation" (563). Though secret, the diaries do not in fact contain very much information of the private sort one might expect Byrd to want to keep hidden—in this regard they fall far short of those maintained by Pepys. In the biographical introduction to *Works,* Louis B. Wright declares that the reasons Byrd compulsively recorded his "most trivial or intimate actions" remain a mystery (35). The psychological significance of the diaries as an attempt to overcome fears and self-doubt by imparting a shape, order, and regularity was suggested by Donald T. Siebert, Jr., in "William Byrd's *Histories of the Line:* The Fashioning of a Hero," *American Literature,* XLVII (1976), 535–551. Norman S. Grabo, in "Going Steddy: William Byrd's Literary Masquerade," *Yearbook of English Studies,* XIII (1983), also considers the diaries "an instrument for creating as well as recording the kind of figure that Byrd wished to be" (85). This approach culminates in Lockridge, *Diary, and Life,* where the diaries are fully explicated as a key document in Byrd's self-fashioning.

Evidence suggests Byrd might have tried his hand at another ambitious project; see Margaret Beck Pritchard and Virginia Lascara Sites, *William Byrd II and His Lost History: Engravings of the Americas* (Williamsburg, Va., 1993).

lating classical poems.[2] Byrd composed witty letters, character sketches, occasional verse, scientific notes, and, later, memoirs of historic events. Significantly, all these works feature a motley of elements considered necessary to a gentleman's writing—classical allusions, anecdotes, epigrams, historical parallels, moral-philosophical ruminations, and pieces of scientific information—all elements, as we shall see, to be found here among the entries in his commonplace book.[3]

Another related activity at which Byrd excelled is letter writing. Many of his letters (not including those devoted to business) adhere to the epistolary style of the eighteenth century, which extended Horace's warrant for poetry—its purpose is to delight and instruct—to yet another literary form. The writer, in selecting and arranging the subject matter of a letter, could take the opportunity

2. Byrd's translation "The Ephesian Matron" appears in *ASD*, 224–227. Wright speculates that Byrd might also have collaborated with William Burnaby in translating *The Satyr of Titus Petronius Arbiter . . .* published in 1694 (*Works*, 7). Wright cites Byrd's interest in Petronius (the surviving translation, references in the diaries) and Burnaby's membership in the Middle Temple. Byrd also collected Petronius (Hayes 841, 1131, 1406, 1688, 2515, A42), though the Burnaby translation was apparently *not* in his library.

3. On Byrd's efforts as a poet, see Carl Dolmetsch, "William Byrd of Westover as an Augustan Poet," *Studies in the Literary Imagination*, IX (1976), 69–77. On the role of Byrd's belles lettres in his aspirations to genteel status at Tunbridge Wells, see David S. Shields, *Civil Tongues and Polite Letters in British America* (Chapel Hill, N.C., 1997), 41–42. Byrd's extant light verse may be found in the selections attributed to Byrd ("by Mr. Burrard") in *Tunbrigiala; or, Tunbridge Miscellanies, for the Year 1719* (*ASD*, 401–409), and "A Poem upon Some Ladys at Tunbridge 1700" (*ASD*, 248–249). The Byrd canon is not fixed; see Cameron C. Nickels and John H. O'Neill, "Upon the Attribution of 'Upon a Fart' to William Byrd of Westover," *Early American Literature*, XIV (1979), 143–148; but see Carl Dolmetsch's reply, *Early American Literature*, XV (1980), 276–277. Robert Bolling reports that Byrd once claimed to have contributed to Colley Cibber's comedy *The Careless Husband* (recorded in "Anecdotes relating to *The Careless Husband*," in transcript of "Letter Book of Joseph Ball, 1750–1759," July 17, 1745, Nov. 14, 1746 [CWF microfilm]). Byrd's supposed collaboration with Cibber is considered by Carl R. Dolmetsch in "William Byrd II: Comic Dramatist?" *Early American Literature*, V (1971), 18–30. Dolmetsch identifies Byrd's contribution as the song "Sabina with an Angel's Face," which appears in the notebook (published in *ASD*) of Byrd's original compositions of 1703–1706, the same time Cibber's comedy was first acted and published. Dolmetsch acknowledges the difficulty of verifying whether Cibber used Byrd's song, or Byrd copied a song by Cibber (or from an earlier source) into one of his own notebooks (27; Pierre Marambaud, *William Byrd of Westover, 1674–1744* [Charlottesville, Va., 1971], 93). Dolmetsch insists, however, that Byrd's version predates Cibber's. Byrd owned Cibber's collected plays (Hayes 982) and *Apology for the Life of Mr. Colley Cibber* (Hayes 1097).

to construct an epistolary voice. Byrd's letters, then, are often more than accounts of local news and family gossip. Their tone and content reveal something of Byrd's intentions, not through candid descriptions of his feelings (as we might expect from modern letter writers); rather, we must approach them indirectly, examining the "William Byrd" the letters are meant to project. Sometimes the letters are practically essays designed to entertain and to instruct—and to give the recipient the impression that the writer was the sort of man eminently capable of wit and wisdom.[4] For instance, in a letter written from London to his friend John Custis in 1723, Byrd declares that love no longer holds sway over him, reason having triumphed over inclination. This, he explains, is due less to his advancing age than to growth in understanding. What follows is a kind of essay recommending that age should be measured by experience, not years (this observation closely parallels the commonplace book).[5]

Again, in a letter to Mrs. Anne Taylor Otway (ca. 1729) he includes a small essay about marriage and those who remain unmarried; two anecdotes featured in this set piece are also found in the commonplace book. The rest of the letter follows the pattern typical of essays of the time (such as the *Spectator*): a variety of examples elaborate the chosen theme. At the end of the letter Byrd writes: "Thus for want of news I am forced like the spider, to spin something out of my own bowels for my dear sisters entertainment." With this image, Byrd is not literally apologizing for having nothing to say. Rather, he is alluding to the distinction between literature produced through imitation (*mimesis*) and literature produced by inspiration, figured respectively in the bee who visits all the flowers of the field and gleans their essence, and the spider who spins a web out of its own bowels. Byrd thus allusively offers his "dear sister" entertainment ostensibly provided by his own inspired wit. It is somewhat ironic to note that Byrd's very claim to original wit is based on allusion gleaned from the commonplaces of literary culture.[6]

Another literary form in which Byrd engaged with considerable success was the *character* (or character sketch). The originator of this genre was the Greek writer Theophrastus (ca. 370–285), who sketched "the typical manifestations in

---

4. On the Addisonian model for the "conversible prose" of Byrd's letters, see Susan Manning, "Industry and Idleness in Colonial Virginia: A New Approach to William Byrd II," *Journal of American Studies*, XXVIII (1994), 175–180.

5. Byrd to John Custis, July 29, 1723, *Correspondence*, I, 346; see §91.

6. Byrd to John Perceval, June 10, 1729, *Correspondence*, I, 402. The first anecdote is only partially recorded in the surviving portion of the letter; see §473, 485. On the bee and the spider, see Jonathan Swift, *The Battle of the Books*, in Herbert Davis, ed., The Prose Works of Jonathan Swift, I (Oxford, 1957), 147–151.

human nature of some one quality of character" in the form of a generalized character type marked by some kind of folly or vice. The Theophrastan character offers the reader "an account of the characteristic behavior of a plausible man who suggests an entire, special, familiar moral branch of the human family."[7]

The character was revived in the seventeenth century in France by Jean de La Bruyère, and in England by many English writers, including Joseph Hall, Thomas Overbury, John Earle, John Suckling, Nicholas Breton, Richard Brathwaite, Donald Lupton, and John Dryden, and it continued into the eighteenth century with the marquess of Halifax, Joseph Addison and Richard Steele, and many others. Seventeenth-century authors (including La Bruyère) featured references to actual people and events, sometimes explicated with a key. Byrd's characters followed the traditional English form, either in the negative mode, casting telling characteristics of people he knew in a satirical light, or in the positive mode, praising one distinctive virtuous quality to form a eulogistic sketch. The moral and social standards by which the objects of these sketches are measured are perfectly consistent with the normative principles of Byrd's era. His satirical characters belong to the comic enterprise of laughing folly and vice out of existence; his positive characters bestow applause upon the praiseworthy. In either case, the author of characters aligns himself with the normative values of society and establishes himself as both a witty and a judicious observer of human nature. It is interesting to note that a number of the moral themes running through Byrd's character writing are also discernible in the commonplace book. That Byrd should have been interested in fashioning such a public voice for himself as an author is significant, for by articulating his wise observations the character writer places himself well above folly. Indeed, by bestowing praise he implicitly places himself among the worthy.[8]

Byrd's diaries reveal an abiding practical interest in "physick," or medicine. He records countless occasions on which he provided servants, family, friends,

---

7. Benjamin Boyce, *The Theophrastan Character in England* (Cambridge, Mass., 1947), 5, 177.

8. Byrd owned copies of works by character writers La Bruyère (Hayes 825, 2392), Joseph Hall (Hayes 1141), John Suckling (Hayes 961), John Dryden (Hayes 807), and the marquess of Halifax (Hayes 834, 991). Historians such as Bishop Gilbert Burnet wrote characters, as did many Restoration and early-eighteenth-century writers. For Byrd's own characters, see *ASD*, 193–194, 203–212, 228–229, 274–298. The English translation of La Bruyère (*The Characters; or, The Manners of the Age* [London, 1699]) included a "key to the characters." Byrd's copy is now in the Logan Collection at the Library Company of Philadelphia (Hayes 825). La Bruyère wrote brief, one-paragraph characters embedded in longer essays on moral topics. Byrd's characters do not suggest French influence; rather, they tend to resemble those of the English school.

and neighbors with advice and treatments of various sorts. The only one of Byrd's works published separately in his lifetime, *A Discourse concerning the Plague, with Some Preservatives against It* (London, 1721), appeared in the same period during which he was writing in the commonplace book, which also features several entries concerning the preservation of health.[9] (Byrd's activities in this area will be discussed in some detail in Chapter 7.) For now, it must suffice to point out that, in his medical writings, and in his frequent advice to others concerning sickness and health, Byrd was successfully projecting an image of himself as a knowledgeable, expert, and generous dispenser of knowledge.

Byrd's major extant literary enterprise, the one on which he worked longest, was the *History of the Dividing Line betwixt Virginia and North Carolina,* written in the 1730s and circulated in manuscript, though not published in his lifetime. This narrative of the official excursion to survey the wilderness and establish the border between Virginia and North Carolina is much more than a factual account of the expedition. In its final form, Byrd winds into his story a number of narrative strands. The basic structure is a chronicle of the preparations for and progress of the expedition. Byrd's commitment to the scientific project of empirical observation may be seen in the record of plant life, animal habits, cultural customs, and medical recipes—all amplified with classical allusions, parallels, and other commonplaces. These amplifications may strike some readers as affectedly erudite digressions, ranging as they do so far afield: China, Egypt, and Asia, the Hottentots, the ancient Scythians. However, they are not little modules of learning randomly inserted into the text: the amplifications function rhetorically to focus the reader's attention on certain themes, working from the commonly held principles of his time that human nature is essentially the same in all ages and places and that analogies and historical parallels aid understanding. Along the way Byrd also describes the local people (contrasting their rustic behavior with the more cosmopolitan conduct of the Virginian party) and the crudity of the Carolinians.[10]

The *History's* treatment of individual personality (extended in character form in Byrd's *Secret History*) makes up one of the most interesting strands.

9. Reprinted in *ASD,* 411–443.

10. On the literary qualities of *The Dividing Line,* see Wright (*Works,* 27); David Smith, "William Byrd Surveys America," *Early American Literature,* XI (1976), 296–310; Manning, "Industry and Idleness in Colonial Virginia," *Journal of American Studies,* XXVIII (1994), 183–187. Jeffrey F. Folks, in "Crowd Types in William Byrd's Histories," *Southern Literary Journal,* XXVI, no. 2 (Spring 1994), proposes a connection between the sexual elements in Byrd's writings and his account of colonial abundance, both of which spring from his "fascination with the principles of increase" (3).

Byrd's account of the manners of a wide range of individuals and types adopts the Theophrastan approach, skewering some of the same vices and follies he ridiculed in his earlier character sketches. Indeed, the very same vices and follies, and the virtues from which his companions on the expedition have departed, also appear in numerous entries in Byrd's commonplace book. Some of these thematic parallels are in fact so close that it seems likely that Byrd consulted this commonplace book as he worked on the *History*. Other textual parallels support this contention. For instance, the descriptions of certain animals in the *History* closely parallel entries in the commonplace book: the Indians' taming of wolves for domestic use (§513), the elk's defense of the herd (§510), and the peculiar habits of the Egyptian ibis (§522). And in the *History* he might have drawn on his commonplace book note (§173) about miscegenation for a proverbial figure— washing an Ethiopian white—to support his discussion of intermarriage with Indians.

Keeping a commonplace book could be a valuable practice for a man of letters. In looking briefly at Byrd's life as a writer, we have suggested that the commonplace book recorded thoughts and phrases for later use in conversation and writing. Many of Byrd's writings concern the projection of a public character, in turn adventurous, learned, bold, witty, risqué, and judicious. The commonplace book might have served as a repository for the basic elements of this self-creation. To this discussion we shall return after we have examined Byrd's method of commonplacing and considered several major areas of his interest and concern, as reflected in the topics he compiled in the pages of his commonplace book.

6. GATHERING AND COMPILING
THE COMMONPLACE BOOK

The method of gathering and recording commonplaces recommended by educators such as Erasmus and Locke redistributes material under topical headings. Such arrangement may be seen in many manuscript commonplace books and in published collections of sayings. It was not, however, the method Byrd used.

The 573 entries simply run from one topic to another without any apparent scheme of organization or topical coherence. A careful examination of the subject matter of the entries does reveal the existence of what might be called strands or clusters of related entries. For instance, the nature of sleep and dreams is taken up by entries §189–194; family pride is the subject of §148, 151, and 152; a series of entries concerning friendship runs from §212 to 215; the dangers and comforts of hope appear in §316–320; a set of detailed physiological expositions runs from §515 to 520; in several places there are clusters of jests or anecdotes dealing with figures from Byrd's time or the immediately preceding era; and there is a remarkable series of entries concerning human sexuality and reproduction, running (with a few interruptions) from §439 to 498. Furthermore, there are so many instances of recurring themes that the entries would lend themselves to topical reorganization under such headings as Hope and Despair, Trust and Dissimulation, the Perils of Love, and so forth. A look at the index we have provided will confirm that Byrd's topical interests, though inclusive, still show a remarkable degree of consistency. This consistency suggests that Byrd sought out certain kinds of books to read and that he found certain themes particularly apt during a specific period of his life (the years 1719–1726).

By identifying some of the books that served as sources for the entries, we have been able to distinguish patterns in Byrd's commonplacing. He sometimes transcribes material exactly, but he also condenses and rearranges the order of sentences. He sometimes interjects his own observations or comments. When entering a series of extracts from a single book, he does not always follow the order in which the material appears in the source; that is, he may skip back and forth among the pages of the source text. This may indicate that he returned to the source text after first reading, using a guide such as slips of paper (bookmarks) or notes indicating page numbers. However, our examination of books formerly in Byrd's library has not uncovered any such markers or notes, nor is there any useful evidence of marginal notation or commentary in his hand, so our hypothesis about his reading and commonplacing habits remains speculative.

In several instances, we are able to be more certain about the specifics of transcription. The entry concerning numismatics (§26) comes from Addison's "Dialogue III: A Parallel between the Ancient and Modern Medals." The detailed, parallel comparison of the texts undertaken in the Commentary demonstrates the probability that Byrd compiled this entry from notes taken while reading the "Dialogue": the arrangement he follows disrupts the order of Addison's text, but the wording remains very close to the original. Byrd rearranges the elements he has extracted, perhaps because he was interested in justifying the study of medals. Indeed, this explanation for the presence of this entry in the commonplace book is supported by further evidence of Byrd's interest in the lore of medals and numismatic history. The catalog of his library documents this interest, for he owned many books on emblems, medals, and related curiosities.[1]

A similar treatment occurs in Byrd's redaction of the argument of William Wollaston's *Religion of Nature Delineated* (§526). The analysis of Byrd's response to Wollaston (provided in the Commentary) indicates that Byrd studied this text very carefully. His précis is highly selective, omitting the entire apparatus of logic and the detailed metaphysics in which Wollaston specialized and zeroing in on passages that could have practical value for him. What remains is a series of notes on the nature of virtue and vice, of the soul, and of understanding and the basic tenets of Anglican eschatology. Byrd's notes follow the original text fairly

1. *The Works of the Right Honourable Joseph Addison, Esq* (London, 1721), I. Among the books in Byrd's library were these important studies of medals: Giovanni Pietro Bellori, *Veterum illustrium philosophorum, poetarum, rhetorum, et oratorum imagines, ex vetustis nummis . . .* (Rome, 1685?) (Hayes 99); Pierre Bizot, *Medalische Historie der Republyk van Holland* (Amsterdam, 1690) (Hayes 1991); Louis Joubert, *La science des medailles* (Paris, 1692?) (Hayes 1320); Claude François Menestrier, *Histoire du regne de Louis le Grand par les medailles . . .* (Paris, 1700) (Hayes 2035).

Byrd also owned an extensive collection of emblem books (a form closely related to the symbolic part of numismatics), including Andrea Alciati, *Emblemata* (1548?) (Hayes 2441); Philip Ayres, *Emblems of Love* (London, 1683?) (Hayes 1945); Jean Baudoin, *Recueil d'emblemes divers* (1638?) (Hayes 2440); *Symbola Politica* (Hayes 2229, probably Jakob Bornitz, *Moralia bornitiana, hoc est: symbola et emblemata politica-sacra et historia-politica*); Everard van Bronckhorst, *Aphorismi politici* (Leiden, 1623) (Hayes 2228); Victorinus Bythner, *Lyra prophetica Davidis regia* (1650?) (Hayes 2022); Jacob Cats, *Alle de Werken* (Amsterdam, 1650?) (Hayes 1988); Christian Matthias, *Systema politicum* (Hayes 208); Louis Du Moulin, *Morum exemplar seu characteres* (Leiden, 1654?) (Hayes 233); Cesare Ripa, *Iconologie* (Paris, 1637) (Hayes 92); Diego de Saavedra Fajardo, *The Royal Politician Represented in One Hundred Emblems . . .* (London, 1700) (Hayes 2390).

closely, but he also introduces comments relating the text to his own circumstances. Most notable is his application of Wollaston's reasoning to the problem of carnal temptation. Wollaston defines vice as a contradiction of known truth; Byrd likewise defines libertine sexuality as a contradiction of the truth about the real nature of the relationship with women: "If I am incontinent, and lye with every Woman I meet, I use those women as if they belongd to me when they really do not." These are Byrd's own words, superimposed upon the structure of Wollaston's moral reasoning. In this we can see how complex the process of commonplacing really was for Byrd, involving at least three levels of activity: accurate transcriptions of important ideas, loose paraphrase or summary, and personal commentary based upon but moving beyond the original text.[2]

Byrd transcribed material from several accounts of foreign countries published in Awnsham and John Churchill, *A Collection of Voyages and Travels*.[3] The first volume provides the source for two entries. In §216 Byrd takes the account of a remarkable Chinese architectural feat from the Jesuit Dominick Fernandez Navarette's account of his travels in China. Byrd follows the original phrasing closely, but he makes two rather interesting changes: he deletes all of Navarette's references to the missionary purpose of the Jesuits in China (he was never friendly to Roman Catholicism), and he translates Navarette's measurements in fathoms into the more familiar feet.

Byrd combines accurate transcription from the same source with expansion and commentary in §238. To Navarette's statement that the Chinese consider the trunk of the elephant and the paw of the bear great dainties, he adds two additional elements: the tail of the beaver is another great dainty, and these three items are fit for the richest of all monarchs, the Sophi of Persia, the Grand Mogul, and the emperor of China. The first of these additions springs, no doubt, from his own Virginia experiences or his knowledge of Native American foods. The latter may come from his recollection of one or more of several accounts in the Churchill *Voyages* of the vast wealth of these particular oriental potentates.

More entries come from the fourth volume of the Churchill *Voyages*. Thus, §419 and 426, describing the Hottentots of southern Africa, come from William ten Rhijne's *Account of the Cape of Good Hope and the Hottentotes, the Natives of That Country*. Here Byrd transcribes very accurately, without additional comment; but, as the parallel readings in our annotations establish, Byrd's transcriptions skip passages and scramble the sequence of the original.

2. William Wollaston, *The Religion of Nature Delineated* . . . (London, 1724).

3. Awnsham Churchill and John Churchill, comps., *A Collection of Voyages and Travels* . . . , 6 vols. (London, 1704–1732) (Hayes 79).

Three more miscellaneous entries come from *A Voyage round the World, by Dr. John Francis Gemelli Careri,* also featured in the fourth volume of the Churchill *Voyages.* In §422 he extracts most of Careri's description of elephants from the account of the way of life of the Indostanis; there are some excisions, but the rest adheres to Careri's wording fairly accurately. In §423 he follows Careri's exemplary Chinese tale of patriotic duty still more faithfully. The story of the eastern wives' hoodwinking distant husbands (§426) also comes from Careri. Byrd retains the humorous approach and the censorious tone at the close found in the original, though he omits another story Careri provides illustrating the "foolish Opinion" that women can conceive simply by thinking about their husbands.

From these sample comparisons of Byrd's entries and the sources from which he drew them it is now possible to get a clearer picture of how the commonplace book came to be. Byrd, recording ideas he encountered in reading or conversation, makes them his own. This is the "digestion" that early modern educational writers insisted should accompany reading. Condensation and paraphrase are the simplest procedures in this digestion; extension and commentary are the advanced forms.

At several points in the Introduction and Commentary we have occasion to refer to the commonplace book period. Neither the manuscript notebook itself nor the individual entries bear any record of the date. Nonetheless, Byrd mentions several dates in passing, and these afford some points of reference. The "Charmante" letters included in the notebook are dated 1722, Byrd mentions visiting Hammersmith in 1723 (§388), and he mentions the figures for the French national debt for 1725 (§555). A further set of dates provides confirmation: several of the sources Byrd used were newly available to him in the early 1720s—the Jacob Tonson edition of Addison's *Works* (1721), the first four volumes of the Churchill *Collection of Voyages and Travels,* and the first edition of William Wollaston's *Religion of Nature Delineated* (1722).

The presence of Charmante letters in the manuscript notebook calls for further explanation. In the midst of the brief commonplaces there appears a sudden interpolation of eight pages (four leaves) of love letters sent in 1722 to a woman he called Charmante, together with Byrd's commentary on the relationship.[4] This interpolation presents a puzzle. To begin with, a portion of the series of letters seems to be missing; the first interpolated leaf begins suddenly in the middle of one of the letters (§502). The letters appear to be written in the same hand as the rest of the manuscript, but on these four pages the writing is slightly

---

4. Pp. 85–92 in the VHS manuscript; §502–508.

clearer, and the rising and descending lines are more slanted than in the commonplace pages preceding and following. Further, these four leaves appear to interrupt a strand of commonplace entries concerning the threat presented by women; commonplaces on the same subject resume on the next leaf as if there were no interpolation. How, then, did these pages get there?

One possibility is that Byrd did not himself place these letters to Charmante among the leaves of the commonplace book. The binding in place when the notebook was acquired by the Virginia Historical Society fixed these peculiar leaves at the point where they now appear, but there is no conclusive evidence that it was the original binding. The letters are dated 1722, and in the pages immediately preceding the letters a reference to "this Island" indicates that they were written in England, between his return after the visit to Virginia in 1719–1721 and his final return in 1726.

Byrd's commentary on the Charmante letters (§508) has given rise to some controversy about dating. If, as Maude Woodfin suggested in the Introduction to *Another Secret Diary,* the eligible widow Charmante was Lady Elizabeth Lee (1693–1741), and the witty, successful rival for her hand was the poet Edward Young, then §508 would have to be dated after their marriage in 1731. Marion Tinling, however, has cast doubt on Woodfin's identification, demonstrating that Lady Elizabeth could not have been a widow in 1722.[5]

Even if the identification of events in 1731 were supportable, it would not be easy to reconcile the corollary that Byrd must have stopped writing in his commonplace book shortly before 1726 and resumed in 1731, after adding these letters. Such a scenario is rendered even less likely by the fact that after the letter the entries resume with the same theme (fear and women) as those preceding—and in the same hand. Again, it might be possible, if the 1731 date were to be accepted, that Byrd at a date later than 1722 copied these old love letters and his commentary onto some blank pages remaining at the end of the completed commonplace notebook. Then, perhaps much later, part of the binding disintegrated, the letters came loose and were rebound at a different point in the manuscript, and somehow all but these leaves were lost. The existing binding neither confirms nor refutes this hypothesis.

A more persuasive explanation is that these copied letters belong at this point in the sequence of the commonplace book because they were intentionally

---

5. Woodfin, introduction, *ASD,* xxxiii; Tinling, *Correspondence,* 333n. The death of Charmante's child that she had by his rival, mentioned in §508, does not correspond to the facts of Lady Elizabeth's life in 1731, rendering insupportable both Woodfin's identification of Charmante and the dating of the addition of the letters to the notebook in 1731.

inserted there by Byrd, probably before his return to Virginia in 1726; the fact that some of the letters are now missing neither confirms nor denies this view. Alternatively, Byrd might have copied out the entire commonplace book at a later date (perhaps even later than 1731), adding at this specific point in the original sequence the Charmante letters and his commentary. The homogeneity of handwriting throughout the notebook might allow this possibility, though there is no conclusive evidence one way or the other. Another theory about the placement of the Charmante letters appears below in "The Commonplace Book of a Colonial Gentleman in Crisis."

7. SCIENCE AND MEDICINE IN
THE COMMONPLACE BOOK

In 1696, through the sponsorship of Sir Robert Southwell, Byrd entered the ranks of the Royal Society. It was certainly a signal honor for a twenty-two-year-old, but Byrd evidently considered it more than simply an entrée into another level of polite society. He took the society's charge seriously; indeed, he continued to consider himself a man of science all through his life. The first historian of the Royal Society, Bishop Thomas Sprat, explains the society's project in terms that help us understand Byrd's involvement: "The true Philosophy must be first of all begun, on a scrupulous, and severe examination of particulars." The society was particularly interested in accumulating empirical observations that might lead to the discovery of things *of use* to people. Byrd's contribution to the examination of particulars was modest but consistent—he collected data in the field, the minute particulars of natural history.[1]

The ultimate mark of his success in this field was the publication of a brief report, "An Account of a Negro-Boy That Is Dappel'd in Several Places of His Body with White Spots, by Will. Byrd, Esq, F.R.S.," in the Royal Society's *Philosophical Transactions*:

> There is now in *England,* in the Possesion of Captain *Charles Wager,* a Negro-Boy, of about Eleven Years Old, who was born in the upper Parts of *Rappahanock* River, in *Virginia:* His Father and Mother were both perfect Negroes, and Servants to a Gentleman of that Country, one Major *Taylor.* This Boy, till he came to be Three Years Old, was in all Respects, like other Black Children, and then without having any Distemper, began to have several little White Specks in his Neck and upon his Breast, which, with his Age, have since been observed to increase very much, both in Number and Bigness; so that now from the upper part of his Neck (where some of his Wool is already turn'd White) down to his Knees he is every where dappel'd with White Spots, some of which are broader than the Palm of a Man's Hand, and others of a smaller Proportion. The Spots are wonderfully White, at least equal to the Skin of the

1. On Byrd's scientific interests, see Pierre Marambaud, *William Byrd of Westover, 1674–1744* (Charlottesville, Va., 1971), chap. 6, "Virtuoso"; Tho[mas] Sprat, *The History of the Royal-Society of London . . .* (London, 1687), 31.

fairest Lady, and have the Advantage in this, that they are not liable to be Tann'd. But they are, I think, of a Paler White, and do not show Flesh and Blood so lively through them as the Skin of White People, but possibly the Reason of that may be, because the Skin of a Negro is much thicker. This Boy never had any Sickness, but has all along been very Sprightly and Active, and has more Ingenuity too, than is common to that Generation. His Spots grow continually larger and larger, and 'tis probable, if he lives, he may in time become all over White; but his Face, Arms and Legs are perfectly Black.[2]

This account, describing a condition perhaps caused by a skin disease such as leucoderma, is exactly the kind of factual report the Royal Society collected in its concerted attempt to gather enough data to build a solid body of empirical science.

Another attempt to participate in the scientific project is recorded in Byrd's botanical correspondence with Hans Sloane, the eminent English physician, naturalist, and president of the Royal Society. Soon after he arrived in Virginia in 1706, Byrd wrote to Sloane, apologizing for his hasty departure from London without receiving the society's charge and offering his services as a correspondent from the New World:

The country where fortune hast cast my lot, is a large feild for natural inquirys, and tis much to be lamented, that we have not some people of skil and curiosity amongst us. I know no body here capable of makeing very great discoverys, so that nature has thrown away a vast deal of her bounty upon us to no purpose.

He explains that the complexities of settling his father's estate have prevented him from collecting many observations on the country, but he is able to send two specimens of medicinal plants, rattlesnake root and "the true hypoquecuana [ipecac]."[3]

2. William Byrd, "An Account of a Negro-Boy That Is Dappel'd in Several Places of His Body with White Spots," Royal Society, *Philosophical Transactions*, XIX (1695–1697), 781–782.

3. Byrd to Hans Sloane, Apr. 20, 1706, *Correspondence*, I, 259–261. It is interesting to note that, many years earlier, William Byrd I had also furnished Sloane with samples of botanical materials, such as sassafras berries, acorns, and seeds, and notes on cypress, euonymus, yucca, and other plants (Byrd to Sloane, [ca. March 1687?], Mar. 6, 1694, *Correspondence*, I, 71, 171).

After Hans Sloane (1660–1753) completed his medical studies in France, he made a botanical voyage to the West Indies, returning with more than eight hundred species of plants. In addition to his London medical practice, Sloane was a tireless natural historian

Nearly two years later the discussion continued; this time Byrd sent Sloane more ipecac, some pokeberry root, poisonous seeds of "Jamestown weed," the vermifuge Jerusalem oak seeds, the styptic root of "stickweed," and an unknown root that by its taste Byrd judged "to have a great deal of virtue." Byrd is interested in Sloane's opinion whether there might be a market in England for Virginia ipecac, pokeberry dye, and wormseed and asks for ore samples for the purpose of geological comparison. He modestly offers his services again as a collector of scientific data:

> I have strong inclinations to promote naturall history, and to do service to the society: I wish I were qualify'd to do it with effect, but my best endeavours you may always depend on.

In his reply Sloane corrects the identification of several plants, refers Byrd to botanical authorities, and discusses the use of medicinal plants.[4]

Byrd wrote once more, and then a hiatus of twenty-seven years followed. The epistolary silence was broken by a new discussion of medicinal plants, including rattlesnake root and ginseng. Byrd's letters to various other correspondents show he had become a self-appointed champion of the North American ginseng, though he was aggrieved that Sloane was unwilling to admit it was the "true sort."[5]

In a number of letters Byrd describes the Virginia landscape in considerable detail. Some details furnish picturesque effects; others carefully describe plants (including botanical medicines), animals, geographical details, and other particulars that might interest the London scientific circles. Thus, Byrd's correspondence provides a rich store of evidence of his lifelong interest in the scientific project. His letters often take the form of episodic travel writing, often achieving the same attention to detail that characterizes the two *Dividing Line* histories. In this way he puts into practice the "scrupulous, and severe examination of par-

---

and collector. He was knighted in 1716. Sloane donated his books, manuscripts, and miscellaneous collections to the nation in 1749, a gift that became the core of the British Museum collections.

4. Byrd to Sloane, Sept. 10, 1708, Sloane to Byrd, Dec. 7, 1709, *Correspondence,* I, 266–267, 272–273. Byrd's library contained many of the botanical reference books to which Sloane refers.

5. Byrd to Sloane, June 10, 1710, May 31, 1737, *Correspondence,* I, 274, II, 511. During part of these intervening years Byrd was in London, where he would have had opportunities for more direct contact with Sloane and the Royal Society. Byrd mentions ginseng in numerous letters: Byrd to Charles Boyle, earl of Orrery, June 18, 1730, to Sloane, May 31, 1737, Aug. 20, 1738, Apr. 10, 1741, to Mark Catesby, June 27, 1737, to Peter Collinson, July 10, 1739, *Correspondence,* I, 431, II, 512, 518, 528, 533, 585–586.

ticulars" that Bishop Sprat assigned as the primary task of the fellows of the Royal Society. Travel narratives, with their manifold particular details concerning the natural history and social customs of distant lands, had proved to be a useful mode of communicating scientific information. Indeed, Sprat included several in his *History of the Royal-Society,* shorter accounts of voyages appeared regularly in the *Philosophical Transactions,* and the Royal Society's library had an extensive collection of published travel narratives. One such book was John Ray's *Collection of Curious Travels and Voyages,* which included—in addition to the accounts of the travels of Rauwolff, Belon, Vernon, Spon, Smith, Huntingdon, Greaves, Alpinus, Veslingius, and Thevenot—catalogs of Levantine trees, shrubs, and herbs. The full spectrum of descriptive activity is furnished in the full titles of other voyages, such as John Fryer's *New Account of East-India and Persia, in Eight Letters: Being Nine Years Travels, Begun 1672, and Finished 1681, Containing Observations Made of the Moral, Natural, and Artificial Estate of Those Countries: Namely, of Their Government, Religion, Laws, Customs; of the Soil, Climates, Seasons, Health, Diseases; of the Animals, Vegetables, Minerals, Jewels; of Their Housing, Cloathing, Manufactures, Trades, Commodities; and of the Coins, Weights, and Measures, Used in the Principal Places of Trade in Those Parts.*[6]

In a letter to Lord Perceval dating from the *Dividing Line* period, Byrd relates the amazing conditions he found in the Dismal Swamp and the beauties of the country along the Roanoke:

> The worst of all was a dreadfull bogg of vast extent, call'd the Dismal, being 30 miles in length and 15 in breadth where we past it. . . . The exhalations that rise out of it infect all the adjacent country, insomuch that like the Lake Avernus the birds dont venture to fly over it. The ground of this bog is all a quagmire trembling under the feet of those that walk upon it, and every impression is instantly filled with water. Whenever our people made a fire, so soon as the crust of leaves and trash was burnt through, the coals sunk down into a hole, and were instantly extinguished. . . . In our way we forded several rivers, one of which being the south branch of Roanoke, was the most beautifull stream I ever saw. The banks of it were fringed with tall canes which are

6. Byrd owned many travel narratives, including John Ray's *Collection of Curious Travels* . . . (London, 1693?) (Hayes 75) and John Fryer's *New Account of East-India and Persia* . . . (London, 1698) (Hayes 173). Travel collections provide material for many entries in Byrd's commonplace book.

For the Royal Society's collection, see Alan J. Clark, *Book Catalogue of the Library of the Royal Society* (Frederick, Md., 1982).

perpetually green. The water was as clear as liquid crystal, the bottom gravelly, and spangled very thick with flakes of mother of pearl, that dazzled our eyes, and the sand on either shoar sparkled with the same shineing substance. . . . A finer country I never saw, nor do I believe the world can afford than that lying near the mountains. The land is rich, the clymate is mild, the water clear, all the woods full of timber, and the hills full of marble and alabaster. Did the poor people in the Old World, that groan under tyranny and priesthood, know how happy a retreat they might find here, it would not long lye uninhabited. But men are so wedded to the place of their nativity that they rather chuse want and oppression at home than liberty and affluence abroad.[7]

We can see several interwoven elements: evocative, picturesque description, literary allusion, a record of natural historical phenomena, and a suggestion of the benefits the discovery of this region could offer mankind—the same benevolent motive for all Byrd's projects for developing the unsettled regions of Virginia. In this way, the duty of the gentleman (to improve the lot of those under his care) and of the scientist (to turn discoveries to the benefit of humanity) are combined. A similar attention to detail and a similar set of underlying values may be discerned all through Byrd's *History of the Dividing Line*, rendering it important to scholars interested in the early history of the scientific project in the colonies.

The commonplace book also includes plenty of evidence of Byrd's involvement in scientific matters, at least at one remove, in the sense that he continued to collect particulars as he read. He clearly read extensively (and miscellaneously) during the commonplace book period, recording brief notes on many sorts of information, indicating his continued fascination with a wide variety of things. Thus, it is reasonable to conclude that he considered himself a *virtuoso*, one who "has a general interest in arts and sciences, or one who pursues special investigations in one or more of these; a learned person; a scientist, savant, or scholar" (*OED*). This was the term applied in the seventeenth century to practitioners of the New Science as well as antiquarian collectors.[8]

7. Byrd to [John Perceval], June 10, 1729, *Correspondence*, I, 402–405.

8. For uncritical use of the term, see [Robert Boyle], *The Christian Virtuoso: Shewing, That by Being Addicted to Experimental Philosophy, a Man Is Rather Assisted, than Indisposed, to Be a Good Christian* (London, 1690); and Eusebius Renaudot, *A General Collection of Discourses of the Virtuosi of France, upon Questions of All Sorts of Philosophy, and Other Natural Knowledge . . .* , trans. George Havers (London, 1664). Both books were in Byrd's library (Hayes 927, 1038, 2260).

Another, less positive sense of the word developed when it came to be applied to collectors "of all antiquities, natural curiosities or rarities," which in turn devolved into "a connoisseur, freq[uently] one who carries on such pursuits in a dilettante or trifling manner." In this last sense the term became part of the arsenal employed in the comic assault on the Royal Society and its imitators, attacks such as Thomas Shadwell's farce, *The Virtuoso,* or Addison's *Tatler,* no. 216, and *Guardian,* no. 112.[9] Byrd also participates in this satiric tradition, using the term facetiously in §36, naming those who study the animal kingdom "fellow creatures" of the mule:

> The Virtuosi who Study the nature of their Fellow creatures affirm, that a mule cannot only carry a great deal upon his back, but also a great deal in his head, for not Quantity of strong drink will make him drunk.

Nonetheless, in other writings, Byrd takes the scientific project much more seriously and uses the term *virtuoso* in a positive sense, as when he comments on the "nice" (that is, precise) distinctions made by numismatists in §28. As well, in the *History of the Dividing Line* he describes the attraction of the Virginia river-beds for scientific collectors:

> A virtuoso might divert himself here very well in picking up shells of various hue and figure and amongst the rest that species of conch shell which the Indian peak is made of. The extremities of these shells are blue and the rest white, so that peak of both these colors are drilled out of one and the same shell, serving the natives both for ornament and money, and are esteemed by them far beyond gold and silver.[10]

Byrd's library contained an impressive collection of important scientific works by Francis Bacon, Robert Boyle, Anders Celsius, Galileo, Edmund Halley, Robert Hooke, Antoine Le Grande, Nicolas Lémery, Isaac Newton, Pliny, John Ray, John Wilkins, and many others as well as a complete set of the *Philosophical Transactions* of the Royal Society. In fact, in his commonplace book Byrd drew more frequently upon voyages than upon these serious scientific works, mining them to create the verbal equivalent of a cabinet of curiosities. Thus, in the commonplace book he transcribes many details about the customs of people in exotic countries, such as the Hottentots of Africa, the Islamic people of Barbary, Morocco, and Turkey, the Chinese, and the Muscovites.

There are also several botanical entries drawn from various books. Pliny is

9. Thomas Shadwell, *The Virtuoso* (London, 1676); Addison, *Tatler,* no. 216 (Aug. 26, 1710); *Guardian,* no. 112 (July 20, 1713).

10. *Works,* 178.

the ultimate source for the information about the way the balsam tree is cut to extract its sap (§542). Other botanical entries have a more immediately practical value, that is, notes on treating cankers on fruit trees (§19), on preventing the regrowth of wooden fenceposts (§20), on the treatment of walnuts for table use (§32), and the use of a "Layhouse" or greenhouse structure for growing "Southern Plants" such as pineapples, coffee, and spice trees in less clement regions (§383, 384).

Zoological entries are still more profuse and reflect a marked diversity of sources and functions. Some tend toward the marvelous, as in the case of §77:

> In the Island of Zeylon in the East Indies they have Elephants Milk White, and some of them 18, & some 22 feet high. In Spain they have Asses that are 15 or 16 hands high.

In §521, however, he expresses some skepticism about reports of this sort:

> Travellors, who are Seldome Slaves to the Truth, tell us very gravely, that in the East Indies there's a sort of serpent call'd a Boa, which measures 120 feet in length & is big in proportion, So that he often swallows a Buck horns and all for his Dinner, & it don't sit heavy upon his stomach.

Many of these entries spring from much older traditions, particularly ancient treatises on the animal kingdom and later works building upon them. One of the main features of such works, in addition to the appeal to wonderment, is fabulistic interpretation or moralizing, as in Matthew Barker's collection of commonplaces, *Flores Intellectuales:*

> In a certain Island in *India,* called *Titon,* they say the Trees never shed their Leaves. A good Emblem of perseverance in Grace.

> I have read of certain poysonous Herbs in *Africa* that bees draw a luscious Honey from, but it will cause a frenzy in them that eat it. So sinful Pleasures may delight the Sense, but intoxicate the Mind.[11]

Each "fact" related similarly produces positive or cautionary advice. In the same spirit Byrd records the legendary aversions of mighty animals for lesser creatures—the Leviathan fears the swordfish, the elephant the mouse, and the lion the cock—turned to a jest on woman, who fears neither her husband nor the devil himself, but is irrationally frightened "out of her sences at the sight of an harmless Spider, or a nimble Frogg, which have much more reason to be affraid

---

11. Matthew Barker, *Flores Intellectuales; or, Select Notions, Sentences, and Observations . . .* (London, 1691), 116, 130. Byrd owned a copy of this book (Hayes 2271).

of Her" (§509). The succeeding entries are a little more serious; he describes the elk (§510), the reindeer of Lapland (§511), and the red deer (§512). In each case the behavior of the animal is moralized in the ancient tradition: we learn from loyalty of the elk the value of friendship, from the docility of the reindeer the value of humility, and from the red deer's tears the danger of paying too much regard to weeping.

Byrd evidently saw no inconsistency in combining such traditional wisdom with actual observation in the field, as he did on several occasions in both the commonplace book and the *History of the Dividing Line.* In §513 Byrd relates that the Indians domesticate wolves:

> The Wolf is tamed by the Indians, and used like a dog but a Fox like a Shrew, can never be made tame either by kind or by Cross usage.

The same observation recurs in the *Dividing Line:*

> This beast is not so untamable as the panther, but the Indians know how to gentle their whelps and use them about their cabins instead of dogs.

This statement might well have resulted from Byrd's own observations, yet he also records fabulous material in the midst of such observation. For instance, in the *Dividing Line* he describes seeing an ibis, adding a piece of traditional lore: "And this long-necked fowl will give itself a clyster with its beak whenever it finds itself too costive or feverish." The information also appears in §522, where it is attributed to those same travelers, "Seldome Slaves to the Truth," who tell of towering white elephants and asses. The legend that people learned the value of purgation by clyster from the ibis originates with Pliny and Aelian; curiously, it also recurs occasionally in the writings of those who questioned the claim to innovation made by the moderns concerning some of their discoveries or inventions. Byrd owned one such book, Thomas Baker's *Reflections upon Learning,* possibly the source for this entry, but the skepticism apparent in Byrd's introductory words in §522 is nowhere to be seen in the reiteration of the story in the *Dividing Line.*[12]

The apparent contradiction in Byrd's approach is really not so surprising, although it explicitly goes against the Baconian principle of supplanting the schoolmen's traditions with empirical observations and induction. In fact, it was still not uncommon for empirical observers of Byrd's day to combine observation of wildlife in their natural habitat with references to ancient authorities.

12. *Works,* 240, 305; [Thomas Baker], *Reflections upon Learning, Wherein Is Shewn the Insufficiency Thereof . . . ,* 2d ed. (London, 1700), 72.

Throughout the commonplace book scientific and medical entries exist side by side with the fabulous.

As we have already seen, Byrd's scientific curiosity was largely directed toward what he called "Physick," what today we would call medicine. Indeed, it could be argued that his scientific activities were all focused on medicinal applications. Though Byrd never studied medicine formally, he managed to educate himself sufficiently that he felt competent to prescribe treatment, diet, and medication for his family, servants and slaves, neighbors and friends—and throughout his life, if we can accept Byrd's word for it in a myriad of diary entries, they apparently complied with his treatment. In his earliest letter to Hans Sloane, Byrd laments the primitive state of medicine in Virginia:

> Here be some men indeed that are call'd doctors: but they are generally discarded surgeons of ships, that know nothing above very common remedys. They are not acquainted enough with plants or the other parts of natural history, to do any service to the world, which makes me wish that we had some missionary philosopher, that might instruct us in the many usefull things which we now possess to no purpose.[13]

Byrd might have been wishing for further instruction or, in his role as planter (and head of a large family and establishment), for assistance in maintaining the health of his "family." His concern for their health may be seen in ubiquitous diary entries recording his offers of advice on diet and in his continual activity prescribing bleeding, purges, and other "physick."[14]

It may be that Byrd was as well prepared for medicine as many London practitioners. He studied medical texts, he acquired extensive knowledge of medicinal plants, he accumulated considerable practical knowledge of physick, and he wrote and published anonymously a learned treatise on the plague. He owned a very strong medical, herbal, and pharmaceutical library, featuring works by George Bate, François Bayle, Jan van Beverwijck, Patrick Blair, Herman Boerhaave, Robert Boyle, George Cheyne, John Colbatch, Nicholas Culpeper, Pierre Dionis, James Drake, Bartolomeo Eustachius, Hieronymous Fabricius, John Freind, Thomas Fuller, Galen, John Gerard, Johann Rudolf Glauber, Gideon Harvey, Jean Baptiste van Helmont, Hippocrates, James Keill, Théodore Turquet de Mayerne, Richard Mead, Archibald Pitcairne, Pierre Pomet, John

13. Byrd to Sloane, Apr. 20, 1706, *Correspondence,* I, 259–261.

14. Byrd returned in his letters to the notion of instituting a series of medical lectures in Virginia, "improving the scheme" proposed by Dr. Radcliffe; see Byrd to Sloane, May 31, 1737, to Perceval, July 2, 1737, to Collinson, July 5, 1737, *Correspondence,* II, 512, 521, 524.

Radcliffe, Henricus Regius, Thomas Sydenham, Daniel Tauvry, John Tennent, Andreas Vesalius, and many others.[15]

The commonplace book, too, reflects Byrd's absorption in matters of physick. A series of six detailed entries lays out the basic facts of the human physiology of the bones, muscles, heart, brain, digestion, and circulation (§515–520). Several medical recipes are also recorded (§6, 52, 79, 476–479, 501, 515, 535, 566).

Thus the commonplace book provides important evidence of Byrd's involvement in scientific inquiry, learning, and practical medicine. Signifcantly, these activities served two essential functions: they contributed to his sense of status as an English gentleman, and they provided practical support for his career as a gentleman planter and leader in colonial Virginia.

15. On Byrd's collection of medical books, see Hayes, pp. 83–84.

8. WILLIAM BYRD'S RELIGIOUS VIEWS

William Byrd II appears to have been a conventionally devout Anglican gentle-man, concerned with attaining balance through moderation and pious acts. He was a frequent communicant, he was habitually pious in his daily course of prayer, he often read sermons and other religious writings, still more often he read Scripture in the original Greek and Hebrew, and he was manifestly aware of the responsibility for the well-being of others entailed by his position as a gentleman in society. This is not to say, of course, that he was a model of sanctity in his daily conduct or that he led a life untroubled by religious doubt and moral conflict. Indeed, as his diaries show, he often strayed from the path, so there were many occasions when in his evening prayers he felt compelled to ask forgiveness for some reprehensible action or another. These sins were usually sins of excess, failures to control his temper, or matters of sexual misconduct.[1]

The commonplace book shows evidence of several distinct phases of his religious life: discussion of important parts of Christian doctrine, interest in exercises of piety, and searches for explanations of (and help with) his insurgent passions. One of the most pervasive and recurring topics in the commonplace book is the danger of an uncontrolled temper. Concern for the sin of anger runs through the diaries in disclosures of angry outbursts at his wife and his servants.

> When you find anger begin to disorder your mind Suffer it not to break out into any bitter words, or boistrous actions, til you have said over this pacify-ing Prayer, Forgive us O God our Trespasses, as we forgive them that trespass against us. (§554)[2]

1. For Byrd's religious beliefs, see his manuscript creed from the Huntington Library notebook, published in *SD*, xxviii. Louis B. Wright and Marion Tinling wrongly ascribe to this creed "a tinge of deistic rationalism" (xxi). In fact, Byrd's declaration of belief is well within the bounds of mainstream Anglicanism. The "rationalism" to which they refer is nothing more than the reliance upon the use of reason in religious matters: Anglican doctrine states that reason is providentially supplied for the purpose of apprehending the existence of the Supreme Being and to distinguish between good and evil; reason supple-ments revelation and is in fact necessary in comprehending Scripture. This falls far short of the deist's claim for a form of natural religion discernible by reason alone *without* revelation.

2. Like Byrd's "creed" and the manuscript devotions examined below, this "pacifying

Bitter words and boisterous actions were worse than undignified; they betrayed a failure of self-mastery and hence a fundamental weakness of character. The commonplace book is filled with historical examples of great men whose will was strong enough to withstand both terrible deprivations and alluring distractions—great men, all worthy of emulation. One such man is Alexander the Great, who was the outstanding classical exemplar of magnanimity, ambition, and thirst for greatness. But he also was a mixed character, given to drunkenness and bursts of uncontrollable, violent anger and susceptible to the most ridiculous forms of flattery. In this light Alexander became a warning against relaxing the reins on one's temperament:

> A conquest the most difficult, as well as the most glorious any Hero can obtain, is over his own unruly Passions; & this is the only conquest of which a good naturd man woud be ambitious, because tis beneficial to others, as well as to himself. And thus it is a man may be a Conquerour without being a Robber and Destroyer of mankind, like Caesar & Alexander. (§325)

The benefit of such self-conquest goes beyond the health of the private individual's soul, extending into the well-being of the community of which he is an integral part. This kind of heroic effort is different from, and greater than, the conventional notions of warlike heroism. Most of all, because it allows the individual to contribute unselfishly to the community, self-control is the essential characteristic of the Christian gentleman. This accounts for the presence in the commonplace book of so many prescriptive and exemplary accounts of moderation, temperance, and control of the passions.[3]

Byrd willingly assumed the gentleman's obligation to exercise responsibility for those entrusted to his care, as several entries suggest. The Anglican doctrine of stewardship taught that all God's gifts of birth, social position, material wealth, and abilities are given in trust, so the individual can make use of them for the greater good:

> Tis a most excellent frame of Mind in any Person, the more highly he is exalted in his Fortune, to be the more lowly in his behavior, and to esteem the good things of this world to be only lent, and not given him by Providence,

---

Prayer" is not an original composition as such, but consists of a scriptural or liturgical text (the Lord's Prayer) recast into a practical application.

3. On the relation of self-control to the exercise of social power over others, see Kathleen M. Brown, *Good Wives, Nasty Wenches, and Anxious Patriarchs: Gender, Race, and Power in Colonial Virginia* (Chapel Hill, N.C., 1996), 324–328.

because he must be accountable for the right employment & disposition of them. (§267)

Based on the parable of the talents (Matt. 25:14–30), this doctrine places the most fortunate members of society under a serious obligation; a similar teaching is elsewhere attributed to the Greek philosopher Bion:

T'was observd by Bion, that God dos not give, but only lends the good things of this world, & by no means has conveyd the property of 'em to us, but only the use. (§301)

It is therefore important to avoid the pride and arrogance too often attendant upon privilege and power; the commonplace book contains many entries recommending a modest disposition:

The way to be highly esteemd by God and man, is to think lowly of our Selves for tho' humble People may not be good in other Respects, yet they are very capable of being so: but the proud and high-minded are incorrigable. This was the difference between the Publican and the Pharisee. (§363)

It could be argued that the doctrine of stewardship provides the religious underpinning of Byrd's paternalistic colonial enterprise. As one of Virginia's leading gentlemen, Byrd made sure that he improved the gifts left in trust to him, in his business affairs, his management of his extended family, his participation in governance, and his New Eden project of expanding the agricultural use of lands into the western regions.

Yet in spite of the satisfactions provided by his personal and political successes, or by his slow-learned ability to endure setbacks and failures, Byrd's religious experience does not appear to be very self-assured. Christians must always be concerned about their preparation for the future state of rewards and punishments, and Byrd is no exception. In the commonplace book Byrd is clearly concerned with the question of divine justice and divine mercy. He knows God is just; in several entries Byrd records very strong statements outlining divine judgment and vengeance, chronicling the parallels between ancient Greek and Christian views of God's anger at impiety and sin:

Plato usd to teach his Disciples, that Vengeance continually waits on Gods right hand, ready to execute his Pleasure on all that presume to violate his sacred Laws. And if offenders are not immediately chastiz'd, yet their punishment, like a debt at Interest, will increase by forbearance.

The same said frequently, that the vengeance of the Almighty, like his

Providence, never nods, but grasping the glowing Bolt, is always ready to hurl it at the workers of Impiety. (§143–144)[4]

St. John Chrysostom is introduced to warn that escaping chastisement for sin in this life will only increase the inevitable punishment in the next (§177), and other similar observations recur throughout the commonplace book. This vision of an angry God, however, is tempered by other entries that establish that God is also merciful. Providence furnishes beneficial messages; in such dire events as plague we can see a providential warning: "Even the Terrors of Gods Justice are Instruments of his Love, to affright us from our Sins & make us capable of his Mercy" (§398). Christians must school themselves to rely on divine mercy and submit to whatever events and developments Providence provides: "How easy and resignd ought mankind to be in every change of Fortune, since tis not doubted but all Events are directed by infinite Wisdom prompted by infinite goodness?" (§271).

For ordinary men, as Byrd was aware, such reliance on God's mercy is not as easy as this entry suggests. Their daily life is a battle between inclination and judgment, between the strong draw of the passions and the restraining power of reason. Byrd was sufficiently aware of the weakness of his own nature that he often sought guidance and aid in this battle. The first step in repentance is always the recognition of the sin or infraction of law. Although Byrd was not strong enough to resist some temptations, he was still troubled by what he perceived as his sinful nature. The nightly prayers registered in his diaries suggest a degree of repentance, although these records are so laconic that it is virtually impossible to tell what form these prayers might have taken. Still, several entries in the commonplace book may provide an intimation of Byrd's approach to prayer. It is easy enough to put up a front to deceive men, but deception (and self-deception) is transparent to God:

> Never do a shamefull thing with the hopes of keeping it a Secret, because tho' it may escape the knowledge of Men, yet you can never conceal it from God, & your own Conscience; and if it shoud remain a Secret in this world, yet it will be exposd, & made very publick in the next both to men & angels. (§335)

> **Time** will unmask our Secrets, and unveil all those dark Disquises that hide Truth at present from our knowledge; and then all our Hypocrisy towards

4. Although the sources of these two sayings have not been identified, the attribution of such teachings to Plato is fairly common in early modern divinity, a tradition of the Christianized Plato stretching from Marsilio Ficino and Erasmus well into the eighteenth century.

God, our Falsood to men, & our Treachery against our Selves will be thoroughly laid open & exposd, to our utter confusion. (§348)

According to seventeenth- and eighteenth-century Anglican teaching, the prayers of sinful Christians should combine acknowledgment of sin with a petition for assistance in growing stronger in grace:

Approach not the tremendous Throne of God wth any petition for Prosperity, but pray for such a portion of grace & wisdome, as may enable you in all conditions to behave in a manner suitable to the Dignity of your nature, & the firmness of your dependence. (§277)

Such entries indicate Byrd's interest in the efficacy of private devotions. Like many of his contemporaries, he composed a more or less formal set of "devotions," or private meditations, to be used in the task of self-examination enjoined by Christian tradition and ancient wisdom alike. In *The Christian's Pattern*, a popular English version of Thomas à Kempis's *Imitation of Christ*, the translator George Stanhope recommends the preparation of such devotions and provides a number of samples, mostly comprising scriptural extracts.[5]

Byrd's own devotions exist, written in his hand in his copy of another text by an influential Anglican divine, Jeremy Taylor's *Worthy Communicant*, now in the collection of the Virginia Historical Society:

1 Have mercy upon me o Lord after thy great Goodness according to the. multitude of thy mercyes do away mine offenses

2 Wash me thoroughly from my wickedness and cleanse me from all my sin

3 ffor I acknowledge my faults, and my sins is ever before thee

4 Against thee onely have I sinned, and done evil in thy sight tht. thou mayest be justified in thy saying, and clear when thou art Judged

5 Behold I was shapen in wickedness and in sin did my mother conseave me

6 O purge me with [t]hy sope and I shall be clean, wash me and I shall be whiter than snow

7 and make me to hear of Joy and Gladness tht. the. bones wch. thou hast broken may rejoyce

8 ffor my soul is full of trouble and my life draweth nigh unto hell

9 O draw nigh unto my soul and save it, and deliver me for thy mercyes sake

5. Thomas à Kempis, *The Christian's Pattern; or, A Treatise of the Imitation of Jesus Christ,* trans. George Stanhope (London, 1698), sig. Z3r–v. Byrd's copy of this book (Hayes 1181), inscribed with an ornate signature and the motto "Virtus instar omnium [virtue is worth everything]," is now in the collection of the Library Company of Philadelphia.

10 and sat me upon the. rock that is higher than I for thou art my hope and [*sic*] a strong tower for me against the enemy.

11 therefore do I streatch furth my hands unto thee my soul gaspeth after thee as a thirsty land

12 ffor thou o God art full of compassion and mercy, and plentious in goodness and truth

13 Turne thy face from my sins and blot out all my misdeeds

14 If thou, o lord shouldest be extream to mark what is done amiss, who can abide it

15 Make me a clean heart o God and renew a right spirit within me

16 cast me not away from thy presence, and take not thy holy spirit from me

17 then shall I teach sinner's in the way and the wicked shall be converted unto thee

18 then also will I sing praises unto the lord as long as I live and I will praise my God whilest I have a beeing.

19 blessed by the name of his majestie for ever for all the. earth is filled with his majestie, and great Glory

Gloria patri:[6]

This devotion consists of verses from Psalm 51, sometimes slightly altered, ending with the Latin version of the first words of the responsive words of praise used to conclude prayers ("Glory to the Father, to the Son, and to the Holy Spirit"). Its presence on the flyleaf of a book about the spiritual preparation for the Eucharist is significant, though not surprising. This psalm is incorporated into the calendar of the Church of England, as part of the proper liturgy for Ash Wednesday, the beginning of the penitential season of Lent. A devout communicant is expected to devote time during Lent to stern self-examination and contrition. Indeed, such preparation is always appropriate; Psalm 51 appears in the section of *The Whole Duty of Man* offering texts for private devotions preparatory to receiving the Sacrament. Byrd's prayer, then, follows the traditional form, moving through a sense of sin and penitence into grateful confidence in God's mercy and forgiveness.[7]

6. MS autograph notation, back paste-down flyleaf, Byrd's copy of Jeremy Taylor, *The Worthy Communicant; or, A Discourse of the Nature, Effects, and Blessings Consequent to the Worthy Receiving of the Lords Supper; and of All the Duties Required in Order to a Worthy Preparation* . . . (London, 1683). The autograph MS is quoted here with the permission of the Virginia Historical Society.

7. [Richard Allestree], *The Whole Duty of Man* . . . (London, 1673), 458–459; here the devotion ends with the same tag Byrd uses: "Glory be to the Father, and to the Son, and to

The longest and most detailed of Byrd's commonplace book entries is his précis of William Wollaston's *Religion of Nature Delineated* (§526). Byrd ignores Wollaston's complex epistemological logic and metaphysics, focusing instead on the personal, experiential part of religion. Thus it is clear that he is searching for answers to questions that concern him. In various forms the same questions recur throughout the commonplace book as well—What is the real nature of virtue? In what does the soul consist? What changes will occur after death? How does God's knowledge of our secret motives affect our choice of behavior? Byrd recapitulates Wollaston's definition of morality as congruence with truth and works through several instances of immorality as a violation of God's will. Significantly, while the theological argument defining the construction of immorality is Wollaston's, the practical instances are supplied by Byrd himself: fraud, violence, hard-heartedness, gluttony, and especially sexual incontinence. The combination of the selectivity of reading and the personal application of the normative definitions clearly indicates Byrd's seriousness of intent in his approach to Wollaston.

The commonplace book provides a rich source of material for the study of the religious aspect of Byrd's life. The entries shift back and forth from serious to lighthearted material, from ancient wisdom to Christian teaching, from sources of strength for use in public life to spiritual helps for translating private convictions to public life. The only consistent element among all these passages is an emphasis on practicality. Byrd's religion is nowhere theoretical or metaphysical; it deals with the practical, day-to-day challenges of existence. These challenges are best faced with faith that God will supply the grace that allows reason to moderate the passions and resist the downward pull of vice.

———

the Holy Ghost. As it was in the beginning, is now and ever shall be, world without end, *Amen.*" Fragments of Psalm 51 also appear in the section "Pious Ejaculations Taken out of the Book of Psalms," under the headings "For Pardon of Sin" and "For Grace" (439–440).

9. "INVECTIVES AGAINST WOMEN, AND . . . LAMPOONS UPON MATRIMONY"

The most remarkable array of entries in Byrd's commonplace book concerns the nature of women and the disadvantages of marriage. The cumulative effect of these entries suggests that the compiler was at best radically ambivalent about women; indeed, his selection of material for contemplation indicates an unresolved misogyny, which, in its extreme phases, projects a contempt for women so profound as to suggest fury. It is not our intention here to offer a detailed reading of this material; rather, we will endeavor to provide some contexts for interpretation.[1]

Specifically, the commonplace book period coincides with a particular era of Byrd's life, an eight-year hiatus between marriages. William Byrd's first marriage, to Lucy Parke, had been both turbulent and passionate. The diaries record many instances of her intransigence and volatile temper as well as Byrd's own stubbornness, frustration, and anger, but they also reveal his strong attachment to her, his joy in her company. His real grief at her death may be seen in his moving letter to his closest friend, John Custis.[2]

After a short period of mourning, Byrd began to consider remarrying. He paid court to several women, serially, without success. These courtships were much more than campaigns to improve his fortune, or to find a mother for his orphaned children, or to acquire a newer, better wife. His diaries record the powerful hold "Sabina" exerted on his imagination—he dreamed about her, he wrote

---

1. On Byrd's misogyny, see Lockridge, *Diary, and Life*, 95; this argument is enlarged in Lockridge, *Patriarchal Rage*. On Byrd and the pattern of domestic patriarchalism in marriage provided by conduct books, see Paula A. Treckel, " 'The Empire of My Heart': The Marriage of William Byrd II and Lucy Parke Custis," *VMHB*, CV (1997), 137–145.

2. Byrd to John Custis, Dec. 13, 1716, *Correspondence*, I, 296. He might have been experimenting with the power of irony to mask the intensity of his emotions when he wrote this entry: "A man must be very hard-hearted that feels not some concern for the death of a Wife notwithstanding she may have had some failings, for an Ox will weep when his yoke fellow comes to dye, tho' he may sometimes have pull'd against him, and perhaps have galld his neck by his restiveness" (§309). On the turbulent nature of the relationship, see Lockridge, *Diary, and Life*; Michael Zuckerman, "William Byrd's Family," *Perspectives in American History*, XII (1979), 255–311; Treckel, " 'The Empire of My Heart,' " *VMHB*, CV (1997), 125–156.

love letters, he risked boring his friends with incessant talk of her, he loitered in the streets or at the theater hoping for a chance glimpse of her, he exulted in a few signs of her favor, and he took the ultimate failure of his courtship very hard. Eventually, after several other attempted courtships—somewhat less fervent, perhaps, but equally unsuccessful—he met Maria Taylor, whom he married in 1724.

The extant diaries for this unmarried period (between 1716 and 1724) are particularly fascinating in their revelation of a man who is both a rake and a romantic. He was ordinarily quite active sexually, keeping a mistress and seeking additional encounters with streetwalkers. He seems to have been unable to resist temptation—indeed, he seems to have been unable to avoid rushing out to meet temptation more than halfway. Still, he recognized that his taste for illicit sexual encounters redoubled his danger. First, it tended to render him foolish, as hindsight repeatedly demonstrated. In the calm following the emotional storm, he reflected on the way he had allowed himself to be swept away. Numerous entries in the commonplace book stress that folly attends every defeat of reason by emotion and desire. Being ruled by unmoderated passion exposes a man to the worst of tyrannies: "To be Subject to an arbitrary Prince is a more honorable Slavery, than to be Subject to his own more arbitrary Passions" (§162).[3]

Moreover, the pursuit of pleasure steals time and energy that might be devoted to more important things. Byrd records several instances of wise men who took steps to counteract that "hankering after Pleasure, which clouds the understanding, and cloggs all those Talents, which might otherwise distinguish us from the rest of of our Neighbours." Demosthenes, for instance, aware of his "great Byas to pleasure," shaved one side of his head so he would be too embarrassed to be seen in public and thus prevented himself from visiting the courtesan Phryne (§172). Though the matter was serious enough, Byrd was able to jest on the subject in a letter to John Custis, assuring him that in the matter of women his reason was beginning "to get the better part" of his inclination, moving him out of danger.[4]

---

3. On the details of Byrd's sexual life with his mistresses, streetwalkers, and servants, see Lawrence Stone, *The Family, Sex, and Marriage in England, 1500–1800* (New York, 1977), 565–568. Stone describes Byrd's rush to temptation: "Byrd's diary reveals the irresistible tidal force of sexual passion which was driving him during these years, despite his scrupulous piety" (568). Other historians conjecture that Byrd was driven by a sense of threatened identity. Byrd's sexual exertions in the London years strike Norman S. Grabo "as essentially gestures of frustrated power" ("Going Steddy: William Byrd's Literary Masquerade," *Yearbook of English Studies,* XIII [1983], 90). See Lockridge, *Diary, and Life,* for a detailed reading of these issues. For commonplace book entries concerning self-control, see also §188, 330–332, 336–337.

4. Byrd to [Custis], July 29, 1723, *Correspondence,* I, 346.

More seriously still, Byrd knew that such pursuits were certain to place his soul in danger. He might have felt a real sense of sin each night when he looked back on his day in prayer. Several of the texts he transcribed into his commonplace book entries go much further toward emphasizing the consequences of failing to act on the knowledge of sin:

> St Basil tells us, that pleasure as beautifull as it appears to be in the Eyes of young People, has nevertheless a very monstrous Posterity, for t'is the own-mother of Sin and the Grandmother of Death and Damnation. (§296)[5]

Byrd's attitude toward sexuality, then, was fully compartmentalized, divided into clearly demarcated categories, providing modern readers with a unique insight into the sexual code of the era. He acted the part of a rake, keeping a mistress, taking prostitutes to the bagnio, prevailing upon his servant Annie to fondle him, and prowling the streets for the cheapest thrills. At the same time, he was romantically involved with a woman he considered to be of a different sort entirely—he was deeply smitten with Miss Smith (Sabina). Still another fervid romantic attachment is recorded in the letters to "Charmante," some of which are included in this commonplace book. These episodes of love produced a tumult of emotions, a sense of precarious balancing between idyllic happiness and tragedy. But there is no indication anywhere that Byrd experienced any sense of personal inconsistency at living in two separate realms of experience, erotic indulgence and high romance.[6]

Yet there may be discerned in the commonplace book a pattern connecting these realms. In the records of his experiences of romantic love, Byrd expressed the same apprehensions: romantic love, as much as erotic desire, can be so strong that it can overmaster reason and will. His romantic letters, though conventional enough in most respects, portray a love-struck correspondent painfully aware of his vulnerability (or endeavoring to project such vulnerability).[7]

---

5. It must be acknowledged that Byrd's laconic diary entries usually fall short of clearly indicating a sense of sin, as for instance his account of Apr. 30, 1719: "Then we went to Kensington Garden where we walked till 8 o'clock and then returned and I went to see my French whore where I supped and ate some fricassee of chicken. I gave the whore two guineas and committed uncleanness and then I went home in the chair and said my prayers" (*LD*, 263). On his most active nights (as when on May 13, 1719, he proudly chronicles meeting a young woman whom he "rogered . . . three times") he concluded his account by noting, "I neglected my prayers" (*LD*, 268, 269).

6. The Charmante letters, *Correspondence*, I, 332–341; §502–507. In §508, Byrd looks back on the failed courtship with some bitterness.

7. Although Byrd's use of the rhetorical conventions of eighteenth-century love letters

He repeatedly manages to fall hopelessly in love, and, as soon as his beloved lets him down, he reproaches himself for his weakness, his failure to exert rational control over his passions. He reproaches himself with his inability to maintain emotional equilibrium and seeks assistance from received wisdom. However, in a letter to "Zenobia," Byrd playfully describes the ineffectiveness of such treatments in "curing" the distemper of love:

> My Wits were in no small danger by the resolution I had taken to smother the Passion I had for Zenobia. I fancy'd the good old Remedys of Time and absence would cure me, tho Reason & Philosophy had fail'd. I had already taken advice of Seneca Plutarch and Epictetus, I had read over all the Invectives against women, and all the Lampoons upon matrimony. But alas they all toucht my distemper no more than Hellebore dos Folly, and such rules are of no more consequence against Love than Remedys would be against Old Age. T'is a sage thing to preach up patience to a man in a fit of the stone, and discretion to a Lunatique, and very discreet to prescribe good sence to a violent Inclination. But this is really throwing away Wisdom, of which theres so little in this world that I'd have it reserv'd for better purposes. Pray Dont expect that medicines wch never had any effect upon a man in my circumstances shou'd work upon me.[8]

Seneca, Plutarch, and Epictetus are the classical sources of wisdom concerning temperance, the abatement of the passions, and self-control. Byrd, raised in a humanist-Anglican tradition that stressed the importance of such wisdom, confesses to Zenobia his inability to translate his understanding of these teachings into practice. The letter is certainly flirtatious, featuring as it does the gallant avowal that his love for her is too tenacious to be suppressed by the wisdom of the ancients or any other strong medicine. Nonetheless, readers familiar with Byrd's accounts of his unsuccessful wooing may recognize an element of seriousness only partly hidden in the jest. In the commonplace book, Byrd records a proverbial observation about the excesses of love: "Rage differs from madness in nothing but the length of the Fit, & so dos Love from Folly" (§46). When love grows out of proportion and becomes disconnected with any basis in reality, and when (as in Byrd's experience) the emotional attachment of one party develops unanchored by a connection to the real feelings of the object of his affections,

---

has led some scholars to condemn them as insincere (see Stone, *The Family, Sex, and Marriage*, 564), the fact of Byrd's real attraction and emotional involvement is corroborated in the diaries.

8. *ASD*, 261. This letter comes from the longhand manuscript notebook published in *ASD* as "Letters and Literary Exercises, 1696–1726." Zenobia has not been identified.

then love is merely extended folly. This evaluation of fantastic, irrational, fool-hardy love is clearly presented in §202:

> Love is a longing desire to injoy any Person, whome we imagine to have more perfections than she Really has. It is a kind of Natural Idolatry, by which our Fancy sets up an Imaginary Deity, and then we falls down and worships it. Fancy will needs have a Woman to be an Angel, when perhaps, if Reason might have leave to speak, twoud tell us she was a Devil, and many a mis-guided marryd man knows this to be wofully true. If men woud therefore please to make a little use of their understandings when they judge of Fe-males, or even of their Sences, they might discover in them so many imper-fections of mind, so many impuritys of body, & so much perversness of Temper, that they woud never agree to sacrifice their Innocence, their charac-ter, their health, their Quiet, and Estates to injoy them.[9]

In this account Byrd explicitly applies the lessons of the importance of rational control of emotions and desires to his relations with women. And, in his letter to Zenobia, Byrd is clearly making a bold jest about what concerns him seriously—he *does* appear to have felt that his wits were in danger.

If Byrd's playfulness about attempting to regulate passion with philosophy is grounded in reality, it seems likely that other such attempts are similarly grounded in experience. It seems highly probable, in fact, that this portion of the commonplace book consists of a record (in a substantial collection of entries) of Byrd's reading "all the Invectives against women, and all the Lampoons upon matrimony."

One entry in particular makes it clear that he considered entering into mar-riage a calculated risk at best:

> We shoud enter upon Matrimony as we enter upon a Voyage, not look upon the dangers but the Profits of it, else no man woud either go to Sea, or marry. (§375)

His commonplace book testifies that he considered the dangers of marriage quite thoroughly, reading widely in the readily available antifeminist tracts of his day. Scraps of these invectives against women, scurrilous jokes, scornful ac-counts of marriage, and misogynist citations from ancient authorities pepper the commonplace book. There existed in Byrd's day a boundless store of such readings, part of the long-standing paper war over the status of women. Though

---

9. See also §424, which ironically declares that a mistress never wishes her gallant had good sense, for then he might recognize that her supposed charms are only the product of his imagination.

we have not identified all the sources for this material, it may be useful to outline a few of the notions about women that Byrd sought out and noted.[10]

Several of these topics are entirely conventional, simply repeating the standard complaints. All women need to learn to govern their tongues (§34, 107, 251, 514). They are overly fond of scandal and detraction (§223, 253, 365). They become increasingly ill natured, declining into scolds, shrews, and termagants, deafening their husbands with their complaints and attempting to rule the household (§74, 115, 330, 446). One husband tells his friend that his wife's long hours of sleep are not a fault; indeed, he enjoys the respite while she sleeps, "the most innocent & peaceable part of her life" (§193).

Women are undeveloped intellectually, either through lack of capacity, lack of education, or an inherent reluctance to engage themselves in anything but trivial activities. Byrd characterizes them as flighty (§84), gullible (§169, 405), and subject to foolish fears and antipathies (§509). This is also the attitude of Byrd's satire, "The Female Creed," which (with bitter humor) attributes to women every sort of superstition and folly.[11]

Women are vain creatures, overly fascinated by their "own dear charms," and proud of fancy dress.[12] One of the sharpest censures of women (here attributed to Aristotle) calls such a woman "one Insect bloated with the gaudy Spoils of another" (§221). They foolishly elevate appearance to a level of self-adoration: "A Fine Woman that spends most of her time in adorning & admireing of her self, is at the same time both the Idol and the Idolater" (§83). They even go so far in their attempts to preserve a pale complexion as to imperil their health with invasive medical self-treatment (§338). Their characteristic vanity makes them

10. A passage in *A Progress to the Mines in the Year 1732* suggests that proverbial sayings directed against marriage were usual in his circle: "In the meantime, I observed my old friend to be very uxorious and exceedingly fond of his children. This was so opposite to the maxims he used to preach up before he was married that I could not forbear rubbing up the memory of them. But he gave a very good-natured turn to his change of sentiments by alleging that whoever brings a poor gentlewoman into so solitary a place, from all her friends and acquaintance, would be ungrateful not to use her and all that belongs to her with all possible tenderness" (*Works*, 356).

11. "The Female Creed," *ASD*, 447–475. On Byrd's targets (credulity, superstitious religion, the follies of the gentry, and superstitious women) and the creed's misogynist satire, see Peter Wagner, "'The Female Creed': A New Reading of William Byrd's Ribald Parody," *Early American Literature*, XIX (1984), 122–137. On the "Female Creed" and Byrd's misogyny, see Lockridge, *Patriarchal Rage*, 29–45.

12. There is, however, a counterexample in the story of Phocion's wife, a woman free from vanity (§120).

particularly susceptible to predatory men, who know that the best way to hunt females is with flattery (§169).

The commonplace book records a number of rather crude anecdotes or jests, based on formulaic sexual comedy. The very first entry in the commonplace book mocks women's eagerness to take a lover. In this anecdote a woman eagerly hurries to let a man in at the door, her hope for a lover encouraged by his words (the double entendre doubtlessly important to the jest has been obliterated in the wear and tear on the first pages of the manuscript), but then disappointed to find him only a "dirty Dyer." The libertine Rochester caps Charles II's boast of male sexual prowess with a remark that his sister could perform her "Exercizes" at least as often as the king claimed to do. An indulgent husband allows his pregnant wife her request, "One Inch only of a young Fellows Virility," only to learn that she measures differently than he had expected (§122). An Irishman recently married to a lusty widow is outsmarted in his attempt to avoid her inconveniently frequent schedule for "**Procreations**" (§123). When a foppish gentleman asks a farmer why his children are so healthy and fine, the farmer tells him it is because *he* takes the trouble of getting them himself (§416, 430). A servant woman wittily signals her would-be lover that her favors may be purchased for twice the offered price (§454). Two anecdotes involve a woman drenching a man with urine poured from an upper window; in one story the accident discourages a would-be gallant (§351), and in the other the victim marries the offending woman, "his way of being revengd for the injury she had done him" (§389).

The most serious charge leveled at women is their appetite for intrigue and sexual infidelities, as we have already seen in the first entry. Women have a very infirm grip on their virtue:

> T'is very hard upon the poor Women, that every man liveing has a kea to the greatest Treasure they have in the world, and therefore no wonder if the poor Creatures cant preserve it long very safe without looseing it. (§405)

The same message underlies the tale of the "Ephesian Matron" from the *Satyricon* of Petronius, which Byrd translated.[13] A number of other entries deal with the way women's ungoverned sexual appetite can lead them to violate moral and social codes (§175, 405, 488, 498). The threat of cuckoldry appears (§109, 279, 494, 512), and all relations between husbands and wives are subjected to an unrelentingly cynical scrutiny:

13. *ASD*, 224–227.

> When a Wife dresses to stay at home, tis to engage the affection of her Husband: but when she only dresses to go abroad, it may be suspected, that she dos it with a traiterous intent to tempt other people. (§343)

This discouraging perspective is exemplified in the words of the Greek poet Philoxenus, who answered the question why all the women in his plays were bad, and all those in Sophocles' plays were good: "Because Sophocles shewd women as they shoud be: but I follow nature, & shew them just what they are" (§383).

At their worst, women can be extremely dangerous, as Socrates warns: "Avoid the kisses of a beautiful Woman as you woud the bite of a deadly Serpent, this may putrify your Body, but that will poison your Soul" (§205). The commonplace book contains several stories of terrible women who delighted in the destruction of men, including legendary courtesans, queens, and an "antique Lady" knowledgeable in occult lore and married to a younger man so very unsatisfactory that he was made to suffer the consequences of the "female Passion of Revenge" (§561).

Men would be well advised to be as careful in the search for a wife as they should be in the most dangerous activities they might otherwise encounter. If they make the wrong choice, they risk humiliation, betrayal, constant irritation, and worse. Once the choice has been made, there can be no remedy but endurance:

> There are 2 things for which t'is impossible to find any Remedy on this side the Grave, Old Age, & a bad Wife. (§341)

Clearly, then, the commonplace book features a collection of unequivocal warnings about the hazards of allowing unconsidered desire or love to overrule rational considerations. Love, Byrd noted, is no more than "a longing desire to injoy any Person, whome we imagine to have more perfections than she Really has" (§202). The entries we have reviewed here, together with many others bearing similar messages, counteract the treachery of the unrealistically hopeful imagination:

> Fancy will needs have a Woman to be an Angel, when perhaps, if Reason might have leave to speak, twoud tell us she was a Devil, and many a misguided marryd man knows this to be wofully true. (§202)

There was enough turmoil in Byrd's first marriage to make him wary of taking on another such adversary. The evidence of Byrd's diaries and letters suggests that, in his search for a second wife, he interpreted the disappointing conduct of the ladies he courted as indicating they were less than angels, so ultimately each romantic setback could be reevaluated and shown to be a lucky break.

Byrd perceived his powerful amatory and sexual urges to be a serious problem. He sought to understand the nature of human sexuality so that he could better understand his own behavior and attempt to regain control. The commonplace book offers some new information concerning Byrd's libertine way of life during his London years. From time to time, Byrd resorted to the words of various authorities who might offer guidance in handling problems that he was encountering. His primary source was the immensely popular handbook by Dr. Nicolas Venette, *De la génération de l'homme, ou tableau de l'amour conjugal.* This was a remarkably heterogenous book, containing detailed accounts of human anatomy, techniques of sexual intercourse, the physiology of conception, fetal development, childbirth, sexual excesses, sexual defects, sexual therapeutics, fertility and barrenness, sexual curiosities, and reports of sexual customs of other ages and cultures, together with expositions of church doctrine on marriage, discussion of the ethical dimensions of social practices in marriage (parental authority, arranged marriage), and rhapsodies on good women and good marriages. Venette cannot be called consistent, for he often contradicts himself, as when he sets forth without comment received wisdom and folk traditions about human sexuality in one chapter, only to undercut or contradict these reports elsewhere.[14]

14. Byrd owned two copies of Venette's work, both with French titles, neither of which has been found (Hayes 1405, 1469). Establishing which edition of Venette's work Byrd consulted is complicated; Roy Porter points out that Venette was a "best-seller" in France, with at least thirty-one editions in the eighteenth century. The book was translated into English, German, Dutch, and Spanish (" 'The Secrets of Generation Display'd': *Aristotle's Master-piece* in Eighteenth-Century England," in Robert Purks Maccubbin, ed., *'Tis Nature's Fault: Unauthorized Sexuality during the Enlightenment* [New York, 1987], 1–2). We have ruled English translations out as Byrd's source, because they are severely truncated, omitting material by Venette that is present in the commonplace book extracts. The first of many editions was *Tableau de l'amour consideré dans l'estat du mariage* (Parma, 1686); during Venette's lifetime the book was revised and considerably expanded. We concluded that Byrd used a later edition, again because there is material in the commonplace book extracts that is not in the earliest French editions. We have referred here and in the Commentary to the latest edition (accessible to us) in the commonplace book period, *De la génération de l'homme, ou tableau de l'amour conjugal,* 8th ed. (Cologne, 1702).

Our identification of Venette as the source for most of Byrd's commonplace book entries concerning sexuality indicates that his ideas about sexual anatomy were *not* "derived from the leading scientific thinkers of his day" or from his membership in the Royal Society, as Kathleen M. Brown has suggested (*Good Wives, Nasty Wenches, and Anxious Patriarchs: Gender, Race, and Power in Colonial Virginia* [Chapel Hill, N.C., 1996], 333), but from a much older tradition. Still, Byrd's interest in Venette does support Brown's contention that Byrd's diaries and commonplace book are an important part of "mainstream male gentry

Byrd read Venette selectively. In fact, he appears to have jumped around a little, for the entries taken directly from Venette come from different places in the *Tableau,* and the sequence of entries does not always follow the sequence of the original. He also appears to interrupt his transcriptions or translations from Venette to interject material from other sources, not always relevant to the subject matter of the Venette entries. The first entry taken from Venette (§439) follows two entries discussing the sexual appetite and performance of males and females. After writing three extracts from Venette, Byrd shifts into a different mode, recording a series of jests and miscellaneous trivia for two dozen entries. He then returns to an extended series of extracts from Venette (§467–501), which are interrupted by only six extraneous but related entries. This is the same sort of interrupted reading (or transcribing) we have already seen in instances of material drawn from other sources.

The sequence of entries Byrd selected from Venette does not, however, reveal a clear pattern of topic selection. Essentially, it seems that Byrd was reading and transcribing out of a powerful sense of curiosity. Some of the entries are sensational, such as the one describing the horrible course Faustina took to remedy an unsuitable infatuation (§441), and others are practical, such as those describing the best sexual position for promoting conception (§442). Still others record remarkable facts about sexual organs and sexual customs. Although modern historians of sexuality have suggested that sex guides such as Venette's *Tableau,* *Aristotle's Master-Piece,* and John Marten's *Gonosologium novum* were often read for their salacious content, there is no indication in the commonplace book that Byrd sought out or transcribed titillating passages.[15]

Nonetheless, two thematic patterns emerge from a careful examination of Byrd's highly selective reading of Venette. First, he is very interested in the nature of sexual desire, an interest that focuses on the differences between male and female sexual appetite. In several parts of the commonplace book Byrd records comments about the powerful, inherent lasciviousness of women: it may be

---

culture in the colony." For studies of Venette, see Roy Porter, "Spreading Carnal Knowledge or Selling Dirt Cheap? Nicholas Venette's *Tableau de l'Amour* in Eighteenth-Century England," *Journal of European Studies,* XIV (1984), 233–255; Porter, "Love, Sex, and Medicine: Nicolas Venette and His *Tableau de l'amour conjugale,*" in Peter Wagner, ed., *Erotica and the Enlightenment* (Frankfort, 1990), 90–122; Porter and Lesley Hall, *The Facts of Life: The Creation of Sexual Knowledge in Britain, 1650–1950* (New Haven, Conn., 1995), esp. chap. 3, "Doctors and the Medicalization of Sex in the Enlightenment."

15. See Peter Wagner, "The Discourse on Sex—or Sex as Discourse: Eighteenth-Century Medical and Paramedical Erotica," in G. S. Rousseau and Roy Porter, eds., *Sexual Underworlds of the Enlightenment* (Chapel Hill, N.C., 1988), 46–49.

expected to increase among menstruating or barren women (§438, 492), and, although the accepted purpose of coitus is to allow conception, pregnant women do not experience an abatement of desire (§122, 439, 442, 493). Taken together, the commonplace book entries discussing women's appetite for sex clearly demonstrate that it was at least as strong as that felt by men. From Venette, Byrd drew a number of passages emphasizing female sexual appetite; in §498 he records the anger of women directed against those overmoderate philosophers who recommended the abatement of sexual activities, thus denying them their rightful due. Elsewhere, Byrd records humorous versions of this controversy (§121–123). To a certain extent, Byrd no doubt concluded, women's sexual appetite provided opportunities for men like him to exploit: §175 explains the strategy of using a bawdy story to gauge the sexual readiness of a woman.[16]

But the power of women's sexual nature could also be threatening. Byrd's commonplace book records several instances of female sexual appetite so excessive that it becomes dangerous. The legendary Egyptian courtesan, Rhodope, had so many lovers that they built her a pyramid (§377). Another Egyptian queen, Cleopatra, had sex with more than a hundred men in one night, and the Roman empress Messalina prostituted herself to twenty-five men in twenty hours, without having enough (§498). Worse yet, the Assyrian warrior queen Semiramis rewarded her numberless lovers with immediate death, to preserve her public appearance of modesty (§495). The Roman noblewoman Faustina considered her infatuation for a gladiator so "low" that she was willing to undertake his murder in search of a cure (§441). Thus, women "very strongly inclind to the passion of Love" can prove fatal to men, particularly those whose uncontrolled sexual appetite renders them vulnerable to their wiles. It is interesting to note that in each of these cases female lasciviousness is associated with women of considerable status and political power, and at its worst it produces tyranny and murder.

On the other hand, Byrd does not consider excessive sexual appetite among males to be especially dangerous; indeed, he does not appear to take the legends of male sexual prowess as seriously as he does the legends of voracious women. He records Venette's account of Hercules and Pomponius Proculus, but he shares Venette's forthright skepticism about the vanity of male claims to the frequency of sexual intercourse:

> Man, considering how frail, how dependent, & depravd a creature he is, never
> makes so ill a figure, as when he is vain of his Perfections, & gives himself airs

16. Porter and Hall agree that "Venette saw men and women as equally lascivious" (*The Facts of Life*, 70).

of sufficiency. . . . Amongst the rest of our Vanitys, there is none more ridiculous than when we make ostentation of our Exploits with the women. Whereas supposeing every word we said of our might in that particul[ar] were true, theres hardly a Brute in the Creation but is able to perform oftener with his Female than we can do. (§497)

Byrd recorded a jest about such boasters, when Charles II gave "himself ayrs what Feats he was able to perform in the Feild of Love, and how oft he coud gratify a Lady in one night" (§121). He also noted the ram's superior potency (§437), and in other entries he records comments that undercut male vanity concerning the size and efficacy of the penis (surely the pun is deliberate):

> Tis a *standing observation,* that men on whome nature has bestowd the largest Privitys, have the least understanding. (§472; emphasis added)

According to Venette, the notion of heroic sexual performance is nothing more than a myth, so that men need not attempt to compare themselves with such an impossible standard. Furthermore, no sensible woman expects it; only those women afflicted with excessive, insatiable desire will demand heroic measures. Thus women are portrayed in the commonplace book as potentially dangerous, if their desire is not held in check, but a man whose desire is also moderated by reason will avoid the danger of being consumed and destroyed.

The commonplace book also contains recipes, therapeutic formulas for various sexual inconveniences or afflictions. Byrd notes some of his contemporaries' methods of counteracting exposure to venereal disease (§79) and transcribes from Venette a recipe for making a sexually active woman's vagina as tight as that of a virgin (§478), and another for making a "strait maid" more easily penetrable (§479). Byrd approves Venette's recommendation of rubbing the penis with lavender oil to procure an erection and adds his own recommendation of an aphrodisiac drink (§476).

Perhaps the most interesting of these treatments, however, are those recommended for men of "too amorous a complexion," which Byrd records in §501. Here he draws on Venette's discussion of the problem of controlling male sexual desire, including Venette's recommendations of measures to limit the production of semen. Certain medicines such as chicory and lettuce and a cooling diet may have this effect, and others have advised wearing leaden belts and other procedures. A more effective measure, short of considerations of virtue and religion, Venette maintains, is to avoid the company of women who stimulate this passion and to avoid additional stimuli such as nude paintings and statues or erotic books—in short, to overcome the problem by flight. Byrd took remarkable liberties in transcribing this material. His version completely omits Venette's doubt about the remedies as well as his suggested alternative, avoiding the occasion of sinful desire or exerting moral self-discipline. Byrd appears to be most interested in the possibility of an immediate, medical cure for the desire that leads him to dangerous women, even if it means half poisoning with hemlock.

There is one more recommendation implicit in the passage in Venette from which §501 is drawn. The "too amorous" man may be considered to suffer from an excessive supply of semen; constitutional temperament and the production of various bodily fluids vary from individual to individual. The prevailing view of sexuality from ancient times through the eighteenth century, Lawrence Stone reminds us, was the "hydraulic" view—that is, it advocated maintaining a balance of bodily fluids. Semen ought to be conserved for the purposes of procreation, but complete abstinence might cause an oversupply and hence a mental or physiological affliction. The release of semen in sexual intercourse was extremely beneficial; Roy Porter and Lesley Hall comment, "Venette regarded an eager libido as a barometer of bodily and psychic health, and sexual performance as medicinal." Physicians advised men of an amorous complexion to make sure they released semen regularly, and thus justified visits to bagnios and streetwalkers. Venette alludes to masturbation as a practical remedy that nature herself presents, but he passes over it quickly and obscurely, since the church considered masturbation to be self-pollution. Byrd does not refer to this part of Venette's discussion, but he must have considered this explanation of his own driving desire, often gratified by visits to prostitutes and episodes in which he paid streetwalkers and servants to caress him until he discharged his seed—"committed uncleanness" or "polluted" himself.[17]

We have already seen that at least part of Byrd's remorse after such episodes was probably genuine. What Byrd's exploration of Venette suggests is that he might have found in the *Tableau* an articulation of sexuality that could provide an explanation of, if not a justification for, his urgent nocturnal ramblings in search of sexual release.

Byrd's commonplace book reveals a nearly obsessive concern with the dangers posed by the failure to moderate male desire and the concomitant dangers

17. Lawrence Stone, "What Foucault Got Wrong," review of Porter and Hall, *The Facts of Life*, *TLS*, Mar. 10, 1995, 4–5; Porter and Hall, *The Facts of Life*, 77. Venette reports that Saint Martin's total abstinence resulted in the shrinkage or atrophy of his penis (§470). Similar instances of Byrd's seminal "uncleanness" recur throughout the *London Diary:* "I kissed the maid until my seed ran from me" (68); "I . . . went home in the chair and said my prayers, and kissed the maid till I polluted myself, for which God forgive me" (72).

of female sexuality. Curiously, at the same time, the commonplace book reveals a concern with the *decline* of sexual appetite and power that accompanies old age. To understand the significance of the juncture of these two topics, the issue must be considered in the context of Byrd's personality as embodied in the common-place book, and especially his concerns at the specific stage of his life during which he recorded his thoughts in this particular manuscript from the 1720s.

10. THE COMMONPLACE BOOK
AND SELF-FASHIONING

From their earliest beginnings, commonplace books existed on the borderline between the private and the public and in the gray area triangulated by print, writing, and oral performance. Gathered in private readings of publicly available printed sources or in conversation based on or paralleling these sources and written down in private for personal development, commonplace books also had from the beginning clear overtones of rehearsal for public oral performances. Initially little more than schoolboy exercises, they became instruments of genteel self-creation for adults as well. In its complexity and variability—amid a gentleman's arsenal of books-of-the-self, amid his diaries and his letterbooks, and amid his public oral performances—the commonplace book takes on an almost protean character.

In Byrd's commonplace book we can distinguish several related functions. It is a medium for expression; some entries, such as the "Charmante" letters, are Byrd's own compositions, and many other entries are filtered through his paraphrase and commentary. It provides a supply of good counsel, particularly in the maxims and examples of the great and wise men of the past. It serves as a tacit confessional, where, as Byrd contemplates the dangers men face in public and private life, he registers obliquely the nature of the catastrophes he hopes to avoid. When the entries keep returning to subjects the compiler feels most grave and threatening, it suggests an attempt at understanding and mastering the major challenges of the compiler's life. The commonplace book offered compilers like Byrd a place where the self could be expressed, consoled, and reconstructed.

William Byrd was fixed by his birth both to his native soil of Virginia and to the culture of early-eighteenth-century Britain. He was educated as a gentleman in England and for many years considered himself a Londoner, yet repeatedly he encountered scornful treatment from those who considered his origins and status as a propertied gentleman to be peripheral or suspect. These conditions appear to have created in him a degree of conflict that undercut his sense of himself as a gentleman.[1] Establishing a claim to metropolitan gentility would

---

1. For an account of Byrd's sense that his status was peripheral, see Lockridge, *Diary, and Life.*

place him firmly among the socially exalted rather than among the excluded. Practically, it would give him access to the noble patrons and state patronage that would confirm his claim with honors and wealth. The quest to establish his claim to gentility appears in many of the commonplaces he collected during his London years. The urgency of this quest may be seen in the fact that many of these commonplaces are essentially reiterations of material he must have absorbed many years earlier, beginning with his readings in school. These commonplaces include advice about developing strength of character and self-reliance, warnings about the dangers of intrigue and dishonesty in public life, and consolations for those who cannot attain their goals or who fall from high positions (referring to the traditional inconstancy of fortune). They also included some of the raw material for projecting the necessary image of eloquence and wit.

Modern studies in the concept of the self have suggested that the personal character individuals project in company with other people is to a large extent fashioned through deliberate selection:

> The self is an image we construct from the materials at hand. In a sense, a self resembles a wardrobe: we pick up bits and pieces of identity along the way, and as long as these elements fit and are suitably stylish, we will wear them for the time being.[2]

This concept is valuable in its emphasis on the *performance* of character. To apply the theory of self-construction to early-eighteenth-century figures, it is necessary to factor in an additional consideration: an individual may perceive a need for specific elements in his identity, may seek them out, and may endeavor to incorporate them into the "performance" of his daily life. In Byrd's day, such an effort would be supported, arguably required, by the duty of self-examination and improvement enjoined by secular and religious wisdom alike. The educational principle of emulation assumes that individuals can perceive the moral strength of exemplary figures and apply it to their lives, a form of refashioning the self that involves voluntary ethical patterning of one's own values and actions.[3]

2. James J. Dowd, "Aporias of the Self," in Linda Marie Brooks, ed., *Alternative Identities: The Self in Literature, History, Theory* (New York, 1995), 246. Dowd states that postmodern theory goes beyond the earlier (Romantic and Freudian) theories of the supremacy of the self (the self antagonistic to society), and the traditional sociological view of an entity created by early socialization processes. The levity of Dowd's imagery here may misrepresent the seriousness of the process of *choosing* the materials at hand.

3. See especially Stephen Greenblatt, *Renaissance Self-Fashioning from More to Shake-*

Byrd's continual study of the conduct of public life, as represented in the commonplace book, merges with his campaign to establish his claim to gentility in the art of conversation. Knowledge must be put into practice, tempered, expanded, given perspective by conversation. Saint-Évremond explained, "Knowledge begins the Gentleman, and the Correspondence of the World compleats him." Thus, the complete gentleman must engage in both an active life in the public sphere and the witty and well-informed discourse of public conversation. Byrd entered a fashionable circle of London men, including lawyers, poets, physicians, scientists, and members of the nobility. Often in their company, he frequented the theaters and coffeehouses of London, the most public venues for the emerging public sphere of genteel discourse. In both ventures he had need of fine conversation with which to craft an appropriate public self. The commonplace book includes a hoard of anecdotes and bons mots for use in coffeehouse conversations and in letters. Byrd seems to have felt that the new public sphere chiefly expected epigrammatic wit and that it was most often bound to long-past events and historical traditions as a source of wisdom and guidance.[4]

Reading the right books and digesting style and the substance by commonplacing could help an aspiring gentleman to prepare for participation in this polite society by granting access to a common culture. Periodicals like the *Spectator* and public venues like the coffeehouses provided the forum for the display and popularization of the genteel common culture. The letters and literary sketches are clearly performances in this forum, literary activities designed to project a coherent image of the man he wished others to see.

The use of commonplace books was predicated on the idea that gathering and manipulating extracts of writings by or about wise men could help produce an eloquent, wise, and moral human being. Ordinarily, this wisdom encompassed religious and ethical values and tended toward personal and political

----

speare (Chicago, 1980). See also Lawrence E. Klein, *Shaftesbury and the Culture of Politeness: Moral Discourse and Cultural Politics in Early Eighteenth-Century England* (Cambridge, 1994); Robert Folkenflik, ed., *The Culture of Autobiography: Constructions of Self-Representation* (Stanford, Calif., 1993); Brooks, ed., *Alternative Identities*.

4. Klein, *Shaftesbury and the Culture of Politeness*, 6. John Locke recommends that a young man be "made acquainted with Men, to secure his Vertue" by introducing him to pitfalls of adult life, especially the temptations of various pleasures and the perils of trusting others overmuch—the "Dangers of Conversation" (*Some Thoughts concerning Education*, ed. John W. Yolton and Jean S. Yolton [Oxford, 1989], 129). On the concept of the public sphere, see Jürgen Habermas, *The Structural Transformation of the Public Sphere: An Inquiry into a Category of Bourgeois Society*, trans. Thomas Burger (Cambridge, Mass., 1989); on the coffeehouse in the public sphere, see Peter Stallybrass and Allon White, *The Politics and Poetics of Transgression* (London, 1986), 94–100.

stability. The individual learned from historical examples and precepts the value of living one's life in tranquillity and productivity, of pleasing the monarch and serving the state. Commonplace books, as part of the educational method often extended into adult life, became part of the construction of gentility.

According to Norbert Elias, this "civilizing process" involves gathering and framing, collecting and controlling oneself, one's thoughts, body, dress, emotions, and behavior. In this sense, the genteel collection of commonplaces was subtly a part of the larger project of defining the self through its ability to assemble, control, and retain.[5] The emphasis may tend to be placed on the framed appearance of value rather than on achieving value itself. Indeed, though the discourse of public conversation was important and could contain substantive issues, it could also be manipulated by glib practitioners, as Byrd himself recognized:

> Reason and good sence are not so powerfull in the art of Perswasion as a sweet Pipe, and an Engageing action. (§119)[6]

Perhaps the best way to perceive the way the commonplace book served Byrd as an instrument of self-construction is to place it beside the autobiographical character he wrote a few years earlier, humorously entitled "Inamorato L'Oiseaux." This self-portrait reflects many of the characteristics of personality discernible in the work of the compiler of places.[7] Byrd describes himself thus:

5. Norbert Elias, *The Civilizing Process* (New York, 1978); see also Richard L. Bushman, *The Refinement of America: Persons, Houses, Cities* (New York, 1992).

6. On the dangers of empty rhetoric, see also §171, 308.

7. The character "Inamorato L'Oiseaux," dated 1723 (but certainly written much earlier), is found in *ASD*, 276–282. Byrd scholars usually refer to this as a single, integral title; however, as in the case of several of Byrd's characters published in *ASD*, the given title conflates both the fictitious name of the anonymous target and the key: "Duke Dulchetti. Argyle," "Cavaliero Sapiente. Southwell." Thus the nickname "Inamorato" (that is, "the enamored one") is identified by the key (L'Oiseaux, that is, Byrd).

Donald T. Siebert, Jr., in "William Byrd's *Histories of the Line:* The Fashioning of a Hero," *American Literature*, XLVII (1976), explains the prose character as an exercise in self-analysis by comparison with standards implicit in the common culture as set forth by Sir William Temple (548–549). Ross Pudaloff ("A Certain Amount of Excellent English: The Secret Diaries of William Byrd," *Southern Literary Journal*, XV, no. 1 [Fall 1982]) points out the rhetorical situation entailed by the occasion for writing—it was intended for a woman he was courting—which explains why he "simultaneously stresses his sexual drive, his social graces, and his ability to speak in an ambiguous manner about personal and intimate details" (107n). Susan Manning extends the rhetorical view ("Industry and Idleness in Colonial Virginia: A New Approach to William Byrd II," *Journal of American Studies*, XXVIII [1994]), discussing the frankness of the presentation that "exudes gentlemanly tact

He has learning without ostentation. By Reading he's acquainted with ages past, and with the present by voyageing & conversation.

The extent and quality of his learning and his acquaintance with the past are readily seen in the allusive quality of his public writings and the daily program of classical reading registered in the diaries. Likewise, we know he had traveled to the Netherlands, France, and throughout England, not to mention Virginia, and, like his Royal Society colleagues, he had made it a point to learn of foreign lands by reading travel narratives. His education was extended and finished by his social circle in London, where he participated in both the serious and the less staid sorts of conversation. The self-portrait thus opens with a positive evaluation of Byrd's sense of his own strengths—or at least of what Byrd would like to think were his strengths. But the Theophrastan character is not a genre that lends itself to self-delusion, and Byrd was fully aware of the tradition warning against becoming complacent about oneself:

> Of all the Flatterers in the world, said Thales, be sure to avoid Him that is the most dangerous & most difficult to guard against, Your Self. (§235)

Accordingly, Byrd frankly introduces a conflict within the constitution of Inamorato: he must struggle ceaselessly to maintain rational control of his passions, to live according to his convictions, and to avoid the drift into inconstancy:

> *The struggle between the Senate and the Plebeans in the Roman Common-wealth, or betweext the King and the Parliament in England, was never half do violent as the Civil war between this Hero's Principles and his Inclinations.*[8]

The commonplace book, too, reflects Byrd's sense of the importance of the struggle to achieve a mature, stable personality; many entries establish the need to control one's passions for one's own good as well as for others.

> Pythagoras was wont to to inculcate, that no thing is so tyranical as our Passions, when they have dethroned Reason, and usurped the government of our actions; very like the tyrany of Slaves, who exercize the most insolent dominion over their natural Lords, and never fail to add cruelty and injustice to their usurpation. (§332)[9]

---

in keeping the personal in a public framework" (181). Taking a different tack, Lockridge, *Diary, and Life*, considers the character to be a stilted exercise in painful self-exposure.

8. *ASD*, 276, 280 (italics in *ASD*).

9. See also §188, 325, 329–331, 337.

Both the sketch and the commonplace book recommend controlling and focusing one's passions by fixing on a goal and conserving all one's energy to expend in attaining that goal.

> The great **Secret** of thriveing, and being happy in this world, is to keep some worthy & profitable End in view, and after that to find out the properest means of attaining that End. (§356)

Nonetheless, while he recognized the pivotal importance of this secret, he also recognized a countervailing diffidence in himself:

> Nature gave him all the Talents in the World for business except Industry, which of all others is the most necessary. This is the spring and life and spirit of all preferment, and makes a man bustle thro all difficulty, and foil all opposition. . . . Fortune may make a Lazy Fellow great: but he will never make himself so. Diligence gives Wings to ambition by which it soars up to . . . the highest pitch of advancement. These Wings Inamorato wanted, as he did constancy, which is another ingredient to raise a great Fortune. To What purpose is it for a man to be always upon the wing, if he only fly backward and forward. He must go right out or else he will never go far. He shou'd fix one certain end in his own thoughts, and towards that all his designs, and all his motions shou'd unalterably tend. *But poor Inamorato had too much mercury to fix to one thing. His Brain was too hot to jogg on eternally in the same dull road. He liv'd more by the lively movement of his Passions, than by the cold and unromantick dictates of Reason. This made him wavering in his Resolutions, and inconstant after he had taken them. He wou'd follow a scent with great eagerness for a little while, but then a fresh scent wou'd cross it and carry him as violently another way.*[10]

Byrd thus identifies what he perceives are the two principal weaknesses of his character: a reluctance to commit all his supply of energy to any project, no matter how important its success might prove to be for him, and a recurring flightiness of resolution. He was willing to acknowledge that without the strength of resolution he knew he needed he would continue subject to the general condition of frail humanity, "the Jest of Fortune, the Emblem of Inconstancy, they Prey of Time, and the Shuttlecock of Envy & compassion" (§276).

For anyone to lead a strong, productive life, self-knowledge is required. Therefore, according to the ancient moralists, flattery is particularly dangerous, because it fosters an inflated self-regard and vanity is always dangerous.

---

10. *ASD*, 277 (italics in *ASD*). In §317, Byrd records a saying attributed to Socrates: "Hope is as barren without Industry, as is a woman woud be without the assistance of a man."

All men are soothd by handsome Flattery, yet at the same time we know, that tho' the bait appear tempting, yet there's a deadly hook under it. And the truth is, to flatter a—man is no better than to poison him with sugar plumbs, to hang him up in a silken halter, and cut his Throat with a feather. We stil love the dear enchanting sound; tho' we are convinced t'is a Syran that makes it, that charms with no intention but to devour us. (§231)

Flattery is a recurrent topic in the commonplace book, which represents the practice as universally detestable and stresses at the same time that the grateful reception of honeyed words necessarily involves an element of self-deception. The presence of these warnings in the commonplace book, with Byrd's statement that Inamorato could not flatter anyone (including himself) even though he lost favor, indicates clearly how important Byrd considered maintaining his guard against the dangers of flattery.[11]

Another snare Byrd wished to avoid was the temptation to talk too much, or to talk indiscreetly. Tedious volubility may stifle any interest in a speaker's conversation: "A Man of Wit may sometimes abound in words, but a man of sence never" (§161). The rational control of speech has a more serious dimension. In the commonplace book he notes, "Not only the wisest but the best men use the fewest words" (§107); likewise, in the autobiographical sketch he commends Inamorato for his ability to govern his tongue:

By talking little he is quit of a World of Folly & repentance. His silence proceeds not from want of matter, but from plenty of discretion.[12]

Hasty speech may commit a speaker to ill-considered actions and hence to a repentance that could have been avoided. One particularly offensive indiscretion of speech is blurting out a secret. The commonplace book offers this forceful admonition:

Unbosome to no mortal what ought not to be told, for how can you expect, that another shoud keep your Secret, when t'is plain you are not able to keep it yourself. (§252)

Byrd was apparently satisfied with his success in maintaining this principle; he declares that Inamorato had *"an excellent talent at keeping a secret,"* proof against the importunities of love, resentment, vanity, and lightness.[13]

11. See §30, 39, 169, 170, 230, 233–235, 278, 318, 391; *ASD*, 279.
12. *ASD*, 280–281.
13. *ASD*, 281.

Among the most serious of the many possible indiscretions of speech is detraction, which is described with fierce contempt in the commonplace book:

Twas said of a woman who was continually speaking ill of her neighbours, and casting dirt on all mankind, that her mouth had a strange looseness. (§365)[14]

Byrd did not consider himself prone to the fault of abusive speech; Inamorato, he states, "was always tender . . . of the reputation of those that were absent."[15] It was definitely less easy for him to endure detraction when it was aimed at him: "Uneasiness at an ill-natur'd Story, puts it into the Power of every paltry Lyer to make us miserable" (§552). The commonplace book provides a number of recommendations intended to make the victim of ill-natured speech proof against such misery. The first step is to recognize the contemptible motive for detraction, the "malicious pleasure" of causing others pain. This should produce a "contempt for Defamation" that will render the best efforts of the paltry liars ineffectual (§551). The ultimate victory over detractors is the knowledge that their allegations are unfounded: "The best way of being reveng'd of an adversary is to behave so unblameably, that people may wonder how any man coud be your adversary" (§174).

The character sketch of Inamorato stresses the importance of active virtue in the place of hypocritical shows. "His religion is more in substance than in form, and he is more forward to practice vertue than profess it."[16] Again, there are parallels with the commonplace book, which cites with approval the ironic strictures of Diogenes against hypocritical expatiators on virtue, who were "extreemly generous in recommending more vertue to others, than they cared to possess themselves" (§110). Indeed, as another entry cautions, the failure to put into practice what one knows and professes of virtue may produce immediate benefits, but the long-term effects are very different:

Time will unmask our Secrets, and unveil all those dark Disguises that hide Truth at present from our knowledge; and then all our Hypocrisy towards God, our Falsood to men, & our Treachery against our selves will be thoroughly laid open & expos'd, to our utter confusion. (§348)

Entries such as this might have reminded Byrd that maintaining a substantial rather than a merely formal religion is an unending task, requiring constant vigilance to avoid falling away from active practice of virtue into empty profession.

14. See also §116, 170, 222, 243, 246, 247, 334, 464.
15. *ASD*, 279.
16. *ASD*, 280.

One area of his life, however, receives a more contradictory treatment in these two parallel texts. In the self-portrait, Byrd assures his reader that Inamorato *"knew how to keep company with Rakes without being infected with their Vices."*[17] He makes this appear much simpler and more easily done in this passage than in the commonplace book, which takes the issue of moral contagion far more seriously:

Tis easyer to approach Persons that have the plague with ^out catching the Infection than to converse with vicious People without being tainted with their Vices. (§158)

If a man well-inclind converses much with lewd and dissolute Persons, he'll find it much easier to suck in their Vice, than instil his own vertue, because our frail nature disposes us to receive the Infection of Evil, much sooner than of good. (§263)

After I percieve a young Fellow to take pleasure in the company of Libertines, I am at the end of my curiosity to know his character, for a man can't be much pleasd with vice in other people, without being quickly tainted with it himself. (§264)

That Byrd could write such antithetical views of the same notion can be explained by taking into consideration the purpose and audience of both texts. The character Inamorato L'Oiseaux was recorded in a letter to "Minionet," an unidentified woman to whom he wrote often in 1722 and 1723.[18] These letters are filled with pleasant bantering, compliments, literary observations, and various forms of epistolary flirtation. It is highly unlikely that Byrd would be willing to reveal his more risqué adventures in this context. The fact that he mentions the company of rakes at all suggests that he knew that Minionet was already aware of his reputation and his choice of companions, and that the character sketch of Inamorato attempts to put the best face upon it. Be this as it may, the commonplace book, intended for Byrd's own benefit, demonstrates that he was by no means as confident of his ability to keep clear of the vices around him. Once more, we can see these entries as reminders Byrd issued to himself as he wavered between urges toward libertine life and aspirations to virtue and equanimity. Nowhere was this wavering more troublesome to Byrd than in his dealings with women. He castigated himself repeatedly for giving in to his urges, for failing to find the inner strength needed to exert self-mastery. In matters of sexual appetite and romance, Byrd evidently felt himself less protected by his self-control (such

17. *ASD,* 280.
18. *ASD,* 371–380.

as it was) than in any other area. He half boasts, half confesses that Inamorato was a highly "combustible" swain; he uses the commonplace book as a site for investigating the nature (and danger) of his combustibility, a topic to which we will return.[19]

The autobiographical sketch ends with Byrd's account of the key element that makes Inamorato L'Oiseaux a worthwhile man: good nature. This rather general term indicates a kind of compassion or charity of disposition, which *The Whole Duty of Man* explains is a central requirement of Christianity:

> This Charity may be considered two ways; first in respect of the Affections, secondly of the Actions; Charity in the affections is a sincere kindness, which disposes us to wish all good to others, and that in all their capacities, in the same manner that Justice obligeth us to wish no hurt to any man, in respect either of his Soul, his Body, his Goods, or his Credit; so this first part of Charity binds us to wish all good to them in all these.[20]

This requirement is based on the Christian teaching that love of God and of one's neighbor is the paramount law: "The Top of all Religion is Obedience, & the most acceptable sacrifice to God is Charity to men, & Justice to our selves" (§349). It requires a charitable disposition toward others as well as practical demonstration (acts of giving). Following this teaching, Byrd opposed this "Charity in the Affections" to the crabbed, perverse attitude of selfish, envious ill nature.

> He always thought Ingratitude the most monstrous of all the vices, because it makes a man unfit for society, which subsists by mutual returns of kindness.[21]

The ability to feel for others, one entry in the commonplace book explains, brings people closer to resembling their creator, whose very nature is merciful (§103). Human society thrives on the mutual support of kindness; the most destructive vices are those that work against our regard for others. Envy, for instance, is an advanced form of ill nature because it inverts the charity of disposition, replacing goodwill toward others with resentment of their happiness. It is corrosive, destroying moral well-being and personal happiness alike:

> Envious persons are doubly miserable, when ill happens to themselves, & when good happens to other people. (§69)

19. *ASD,* 276.

20. [Richard Allestree], *The Whole Duty of Man . . .* (London, 1673), 342–343. Byrd owned a copy of this important book of Anglican practical divinity (Hayes 1245, A25).

21. *ASD,* 281–282.

Invidious People are knawd by Envy as much altogether as Iron is with Rust. (§71)

If compassion is necessary to knit human society together, then its absence is monstrous, a denial of what is best in humanity:

> There is not a Brute in all Affrica so Savage, as a man divested of good nature & compassion; indeed he ceases to be a human creature, who has laid aside his best Distinction, Humanity. A cruel Person saves only the figure of a man, and for the rest is partly Beast and partly Devil. (§184)

Byrd goes still further, extending the range of his compassion to *"all Brute creatures."*[22] His abhorrence of cruelty even to the beasts shows his engagement with the sensible morality of good nature, and his aversion to any tendency toward the brutishness that unfits men for the society in which they must learn to function.

The autobiographical character records a time in Byrd's life in which he continually reproached himself for lack of resolution; the commonplace book records a series of exemplary positions to which Byrd aspired while fearing he fell short. The compelling and pervasive presence in the commonplace book of such fears about his performance as a gentleman in the public sphere is wound up with powerful fears relating to sexuality, political failure, and the dissolution of power that comes with old age.

* * *

That is to say, the commonplace book will expand our understanding of both William Byrd and his world: it is one more window into the mind, even the soul of a unique American. Byrd was not an academic scholar, and it would be disheartening to see his work ultimately relegated to the provinces of specialists. But scholarship is where, after almost three centuries, one begins. Begins. So, as a bold opening interpretive sally in what will be a lasting engagement by many thinkers with Byrd, his reading, and his commonplace book, we end the Prologue with an essay by one of the editors, Kenneth A. Lockridge. The other two editors happily credit Ken with being the first cause of this volume, and they welcome the chance to here give him his voice on a revealing and even passionate relationship at the great crisis in Byrd's life. Much of what is here is already woven into this Prologue, yet in other respects each of us sees Byrd and his book a little differently, as will future scholars.

22. *ASD*, 282.

THE COMMONPLACE BOOK
OF A COLONIAL GENTLEMAN
IN CRISIS: AN ESSAY

KENNETH A. LOCKRIDGE

> *Always try to attain tranquillity. Every time that you gain an advantage over bad affections, you'll be stronger. Write out Plan fully today for certain, and write obligation to Father with answers to all objections, and make him keep you to it. . . . Learn retenue. Pray do. Don't forget in Plan: when once you're fairly at business, you'll go on.*
>
> *. . . Read your Plan every morning regularly at breakfast, and when you travel, carry it in trunk. Get commonplace-book. . . . The more and oftener restraints, the better. Be steady.—James Boswell, 1763*

In the end, the commonplace book appears to capture William Byrd in the midst of a midlife crisis of considerable complexity, one that encompassed not only sexuality and gentility but also power, old age, and identity. This event occurred in the years 1719–1726, when he was in his late forties and early fifties. It revealed his commonplace book to be more than the confining instrument of self-control James Boswell would so desperately invoke, for the larger crisis in Byrd's life was worked out in the pages of the commonplace book itself.[1] In the process the seemingly dry commonplace book became an instrument of confession and of self-realization. It became a book of the self, worthy of a place alongside diaries, literary notebooks, and letterbooks.

The revelations of the commonplace book suggest that the larger crisis in his life also rendered Byrd a changed man. The origins of the crisis began just before he started this commonplace book. In 1719, the Virginia Board of Trade had ordered Byrd home to apologize to Governor Alexander Spotswood for his attempts to supplant him. Immediately before this event, "Sabina" had declined his proposal of marriage, citing both his age and his colonial status. These defeats he interpreted as evidence of his failure to become a true English gentleman, rather than a mere colonial. In the face of these humiliating setbacks, Byrd had several

---

1. James Boswell, *Boswell in Holland, 1763–1764 . . .*, ed. Frederick A. Pottle (New York, 1952), 47; my thanks to Susan Manning for drawing this to my attention, in "Boswell's Pleasures, the Pleasures of Boswell," MS, 1995, Newnham College, Cambridge University.

times in 1719–1720 felt himself on the brink of madness. Insomnia, dreams of personal annihilation, and wistful dreams of being rescued from disgrace by the intervention of the king himself haunted Byrd all through the months of his brief, apologetic visit to Virginia. He felt no confidence in Spotswood's forgiveness. Had the governor decided to punish his would-be rival, he would have destroyed Byrd's political career and stripped him of his official income. Fears of retribution sent him fleeing back to England in the summer of 1721.[2]

But by 1721 Byrd was showing the beginnings of a new self-awareness. While in Virginia he had been more kind and flexible than ever before in his relationship with other political figures, with neighbors, and with his slaves. Then, in an uncharacteristic burst of honesty, when he returned to England in 1721, he actually sent his earlier, self-critical autobiographical sketch, "Inamorato L'Oiseaux," to one of his prospective brides. In that same year he finally abandoned his attempts to manipulate Virginia's relationship with the imperial bureaucracy to his own advantage, resigning a campaign that had brought him only disaster. He had not changed completely, of course, for as late as 1722 he was still smarting from his political defeats and was still seeking a wealthy and well-placed bride who could give him the place in the English social landscape he had so long sought. Yet by 1724 he would settle for a modest marriage to Maria Taylor, and in 1726 he would return to Virginia, boasting of his "new prudence." Almost immediately thereafter he would reconcile himself happily to this lesser field of ambition. Here he would enter upon the most mature and productive phase of his life. Within the next twenty years, operating within the limits of his personality and culture, he would become a great Virginia gentleman, politician, and writer.

William Byrd's sole surviving commonplace book, most likely assembled in 1721–1726, was created in the midst of this accelerating transition from failure to maturity. To one who knows the man and the book, it is unmistakable that in the commonplace book Byrd seems to be reflecting on the failure of his project to be fully accepted in England and on the furies this failure evoked in him. He appears to be reaching for a new self, the self that would make possible his eventual contentment and maturity in Virginia. The commonplace book can be seen as both mirror and instrument of this transition.[3]

2. See the discussion of this period in Lockridge, *Diary, and Life.*

3. Modern works on William Byrd that provide background for this description of his life and self-fashioning include Lockridge, *Patriarchal Rage,* which takes up at greater length the question of the voicing of a particular passage in Byrd's commonplace book, and of similar passages in Thomas Jefferson's early commonplace book. Many theoretical works underlie this treatment of Byrd's life, in its larger sociocultural context, such as Stephen Greenblatt's *Renaissance Self-Fashioning from More to Shakespeare* (Chicago, 1980); Norbert

*   *   *

It may seem surprising that a commonplace book can be seen an instrument of personal change. In the literature on this genre, the potential uses of commonplace books range from the ridiculous to the sublime, and certainly before it ended William Byrd's own book was to partake of both potentials. On the one hand, the humanist project for these books easily degenerated into the dry assemblage of purportedly authoritative fragments of quoted "knowledge," valued mostly for their rhetoric and without wider context or possible discursive engagement.[4] By the beginning of the seventeenth century, frustration with this stilted form of "knowledge" had already led Francis Bacon to complain that, in commonplacing, "men have aimed rather at height of speech than at the subtleties of things." Bacon called for replacing this genre with "real and solid enquiry according to the laws of nature, not of language." By the middle of that century, René Descartes and others had offered similar opinions urging that epigrammatic knowledge be replaced by discursive reason. Descartes in fact was quite contemptuous of isolated commonplace entries as a form of knowledge, and his and others' new emphasis on articulated reason soon rendered the epigrammatic knowledge of commonplace books epistemologically archaic. During the ensuing century the relentless light of reason, systematically applied, slowly outshone the tiny candles of commonplaced rhetorical knowledge. As rational illumination spread from the physical sciences to all realms of human discourse, the Enlightenment became an accomplished fact. As we shall see, then, in practicing commonplacing as late as the 1720s, William Byrd was making a somewhat archaic use of an increasingly archaic genre and epistemology. It was at about this time that the genre had begun to be subjected to public ridicule.

On the other hand, commonplacing as a genre plainly had uses other than as a source of outdated, cryptic knowledge, and these other uses explain why such

---

Elias's trilogy on *The Civilizing Process* (trans. Edmund Jephcott: *The History of Manners* [New York, 1982], *Power and Civility* [New York, 1982], *The Court Society* [New York, 1983]); Peter Stallybrass and Allon White, *The Politics and Poetics of Transgression* (London, 1986); Homi Bhabha, "Of Mimicry and Man: The Ambivalence of Colonial Discourse," *October,* no. 28 (Spring 1984), 125–133. They are discussed by Lockridge in "Colonial Self-Fashioning: Paradoxes and Pathologies in the Construction of Genteel Identity in Eighteenth-Century America," in Ronald Hoffman, Mechal Sobel, and Fredrika J. Teute, eds., *Through a Glass Darkly: Reflections on Personal Identity in Early America* (Chapel Hill, N.C., 1997), 274–339.

4. Ann Moss, *Printed Commonplace Books and the Structuring of Renaissance Thought* (Oxford, 1996), esp. 270–281, for her conclusions, which form the basis for the ensuing remarks and quotations.

gentlemen as William Byrd kept on writing in their commonplace books. We have seen some of these uses in Byrd's own pages, for his commonplace book kept the Greek and Roman classics relevant to his life, and it also prepared him to shine in a high English society that, in oral discourse, never entirely abandoned the epigrammatic as a form of distinction. Beyond these desirable functions there was a further initial function to the commonplace book that the humanists and their Cartesian critics alike had missed. Michel Foucault later perceived this highest use of the genre. Shortly before his death, when Foucault was asked what he would like to study next, he replied that he planned to examine the ancient practice of keeping copybooks of quotations. The reason was that to Foucault such acts of assemblage were "works of the self, not imposed on the individual," but rather works created by means of a series of choices made by the individual. "People decide whether or not to care for themselves," he concluded, as cryptic and imaginative as ever. In the largest perspective, what Foucault was saying was that both ancient and later commonplace books, like eventual confessional texts and diaries, were all varying modes of achieving an autonomous self. Commonplace books were profoundly books of individual choice, of self-arrangement, and so were modes of seeing or making the self. It is exactly this most daring of all projects, the construction of the self, that William Byrd was embarked upon in selecting the entries for his commonplace book and that can be seen most dramatically in the personal crisis embodied in the entries of that one surviving book. What Foucault was saying as well, and this is obviously true of William Byrd, is that commonplace books are in some sense authored by their keepers and not by the writers who are excerpted in them. Like any keeper of such a book, William Byrd was authoring his book and himself simultaneously. In Foucault's language, he was "caring for himself."[5]

*   *   *

To be sure, it takes a Michel Foucault and a panel of sympathetic biographers and editors to see such a profound use of the genre beneath critics' usual response that commonplace books are a tedious and archaic genre. Simply to look at it, William Byrd's commonplace book *can* seem to have no depth at all. At first glance, it seems unlikely that an enigmatic book made up of brief excerpts from the writings of others could be an instrument of reflection, let alone of personal crisis or resolution. Even at second glance, this little book is neither discursive

5. Stuart Sherman, *Telling Time and English Diurnal Form, 1660–1785* (New York, 1996), 294 n. 22 (Foucault); Martha Woodmansee and Peter Jaszi, eds., *The Construction of Authorship: Textual Appropriation in Law and Literature* (Durham, N.C., 1994), esp. 1–56.

nor deeply revelatory. The 573 entries seem to be primarily a moral lighthouse, providing brief flashes of anecdote that illuminate persons ancient and modern in poses of virtue, vice, and wit, with epigrams emerging from their mouths. Recipes and practical knowledge occasionally fill in the spaces between such entries. The William Byrd of the commonplace book sometimes seems a disappointingly familiar fellow, often participating in a rather rigid exercise in moral learning using an ancient, epigrammatic form of knowledge, one so fixed as to be nearly preceptual. Descartes would not have been pleased.

Moreover, this mentality of gathering and framing small bits of moral knowledge means that Byrd's entries sometimes reflect a similarly limited and slightly archaic use of his magnificent library.[6] Byrd seldom identifies his sources, but, as noted, some probable ones have been found and are cited in the Commentary to the commonplace book, below. The possible ancient sources at first strike one as classics, including as they do Diodorus Siculus, Diogenes Laertius's *Lives of Eminent Philosophers,* Sir Thomas Elyot's beloved Plutarch, Quintus Curtius's *History of Alexander,* and Josephus. Yet on closer scrutiny most of these are what might be called secondhand works. They are not all written by the great philosophers, historians, and soldiers of ancient times but are, above all in Diogenes Laertius and in Plutarch, collections of stories *about* such men, stories then repeated after the turn of the sixteenth century in numerous collections of commonplaces, such as Erasmus's *Apophthegmata* and *Adagia,* Bacon's *Apophthegmes,* and Elyot's *Boke Named the Governour,* of which Byrd's library contained many examples. Byrd's possible modern sources appear to be equally disappointing collections of stories about more or less contemporary famous persons, including perhaps such collections as Sir William Temple's *Miscellanea* and the marquess of Halifax's *Miscellanies,* John Aubrey's *Gentilisme,* John Bodenham's *Wit's Commonwealth,* and definitely the *Spectator* and its successors.[7] Thus, while Byrd's remarkable library held at least three thousand titles, of which he had a good number in London with

6. For "gathering and framing," see Mary Thomas Crane, *Framing Authority: Sayings, Self, and Society in Sixteenth-Century England* (Princeton, N.J., 1993). Byrd's sources, listed here, can be found in his library (Hayes).

7. The works referred to here are identified where they might have been sources for specific entries in the text of the commonplace book. See, for example, §215, 288, 343, 346. It is, of course, uncertain whether the subtle rephrasing and shifts of emphasis in Byrd's versions are the result of an intervening translator or collector assembling tales from the same classical sources as Erasmus (such as Diogenes Laertius or Plutarch), retranslating Erasmus's Latin versions of these, or Byrd's own translation or rephrasing of the original classical sources or Erasmus's versions.

him in the 1720s, and included works by Plato, Thucididyes, Bacon, Hobbes, Locke, Dryden, and Pope together with scores of serious works of history and on public policy, his commonplace book often draws on what today would be considered the gossipy ephemera of that library—collections of epigrammatic and often witty or gossipy stories about famous persons. Those that were not entirely in this vein, such as Quintus Curtius's *History of Alexander,* Byrd (or the secondhand source he relied upon) mined solely for their epigrams. Byrd's dependency on ephemera is inevitable, given the form of knowledge embodied in a commonplace book. Where else can emblematic moral knowledge be found? Such knowledge could have genuine moral resonance, but initially it seems to lack the sustained discursive engagement the modern age claims to find in great books.

None of this at-first-glance rather limited use of the archaic genre denies that Byrd's commonplace book, beyond being a way of moral knowing and being, was also a way of social knowing and being. By means of its enscribed gossip from the past and present courts of Europe or from the lower orders beneath, he found his own level in the continuing frieze of witty as well as moral poses; he found his place, as it were. Byrd added to this function a love of tasty gossip, and this is a clue to a further, a public, dimension of this seemingly so private book, though still not a dimension that, in Byrd's hands, greatly expanded its discursiveness. For, in truth, by the 1720s it was well accepted that witty and informed *public* conversation was one of the essential appurtenances of the gentleman. Byrd seldom shared dinners with persons of note, but he frequently attended the theaters and coffeehouses of London, the most public venues within the emerging public sphere of discourse, and so he had need of fine conversation with which to craft an appropriate public self. In this sense, we must see the rewritings to which Byrd sometimes very clearly subjected his sources—sometimes offering what are, if they are his, quite elegant and thoughtful rewritings—as something that goes a bit beyond the personal appropriations Erasmus recommended. We must see these rewritings also as what David Shields has called "rescriptings" of bons mots for imminent use in coffeehouse conversations and in letters, as part of a nascent public sphere rapidly expanding beyond anything Erasmus had conceived. But, and it is a commentary on the new public sphere at least as Byrd perceived it, what was required was still chiefly epigrammatic wit and wisdom, with an admixture of the curious, and it was still most often found in long-past events. So Byrd's adaptation of the Erasmian commonplace to fit the needs of the vast public conversation in which "society" was increasingly engaged was nonetheless a relatively subtle one that in his eyes did not require direct or deeply discursive engagement with the major works of thought, knowledge, and poetic art available to him.[8] Whatever the reasons, then, Byrd's use of his library for purposes of his commonplace book was not intellectual by the emerging Enlightenment standards of his own time.

Indeed, Byrd's use of his library and of his commonplace book might have been just a bit *more* stilted than most. Possibly his commonplace book had no topical headings because it was essentially a book of poses, not of topics. In contrast, by the seventeenth century, religious commonplace books had already shown a reflective engagement with the devotional literature they cited. By 1720, Locke and many secular gentlemen of equal reflectiveness had also gradually deepened the sources and topics of the commonplace book tradition into something implying more elaborate thought, something Jefferson was to do as well. Locke indexed his book by subject, so he could assemble systematic knowledge on every topic. Presumably, the public conversations of such gentlemen acquired proportionate substance. If so, then the friezelike series of poses found in Byrd's version might have placed him closer to the archaic—or to the rigid absurdities of Martinus Scriblerus—than was comfortable. In this perspective it is impossible to forget that Byrd was also not only the keeper of a deeply codified, unusually rigid diary but was one of the few eighteenth-century gentlemen who seems rigorously to have kept the two classic genres of self-fashioning, his rigid diary and a slightly archaic form of the commonplace book, throughout most of his long life. It seems possible that his colonial peripherality supplied the imperative that drove him to such preceptual behavior.[9] In this per-

---

8. The preceding passage grows out of a critique by David Shields, and I thank him for these insights and references as well as for his support and help in general. The underlying theory is, of course, from Jürgen Habermas, *The Structural Transformation of the Public Sphere: An Inquiry into a Category of Bourgeois Society,* trans. Thomas Burger (Cambridge, Mass., 1989). For an additional insight into the functions of the coffeehouse, see Stallybrass and White, *The Politics and Poetics of Transgression,* 94–100. See also Lawrence E. Klein, *Shaftesbury and the Culture of Politeness: Moral Discourse and Cultural Politics in Early Eighteenth-Century England* (Cambridge, 1994).

9. John Locke, in *A New Method of Making Common-Place-Books* (London, 1706), gives examples of his own entries; Jefferson's can be seen in Thomas Jefferson, *Jefferson's Literary Commonplace Book,* ed. Douglas L. Wilson (Princeton, N.J., 1989). The comparisons with other commonplace books, implicitly made here, are based on extensive research in such books in England and America circa 1550–1880, discussed explicitly in Lockridge, *Patriarchal Rage.* The senses in which Byrd's and Jefferson's uses of such genres as the commonplace book, and their attitudes toward themselves and toward women, might have been shaped by the particular dilemmas of self-fashioning in the colonial context are discussed as well in that book.

spective, in its *emotional* dimension, for William Byrd as for another peripheral gentleman, James Boswell, the commonplace book at first *seems* hardly eligible to be much more than an instrument of self-control.

* * *

Yet, just as Byrd's diary need not be read as only the enscribed routines of a peripheral gentleman, so the commonplace book need not be seen only as an archive of rigid social templates. The epigrammatic world of the genteel commonplace book *was* full of genuine cultural resonances that *had* an implied discursiveness, and, above all, like the diary, the commonplace book was also an intimate personal document, a constant and a changing companion involving, in the entries selected, the exercise of expressive choice as much as self-control. It is this intensely personal, almost psychoanalytical use of the genre that is the most striking aspect of William Byrd's commonplace book and that confirms Foucault's great insight about the potential of such instruments even in their archaic form. The book offers us access to the deepest conflicts entailed in William Byrd's acts of self-creation and to his efforts to remodel and to accept himself at a crucial moment in his life.

Intimacy, reflection, and personal expression were involved in the very creation and use of the document. If the more than five hundred entries in it were made in the years 1720–1726, to offer one example, and Byrd wrote five entries each time he took up the book, then he would have written in his commonplace book something like sixteen times a year, or more than once a month. Such regular, rather long encounters, including the time needed to read previous entries, to assemble little memos from his reading, or to look passages up in his library, would suggest an intimate relationship with what at first glance is not an intimate genre. On still other occasions Byrd read in the commonplace book in a yet more unstructured encounter. Inevitably in the course of such encounters the commonplace book interacted with William Byrd's changing self. The absence of a fixed set of topics, alphabetically organized and each with its own blank pages waiting to be filled, often meant that what was entered followed a free association of ideas, with each entry in some way conditioned by those before it and each conditioning in turn the entries that followed. Selection and personal engagement were intensified in the simple fact that the field of possible selection was immense, and this is Foucault's central point. The sources and compilations Byrd used contained literally tens of thousands of possible bits of epigrammatic knowledge. Byrd responded to only five-hundred-odd of these. He sought out entries by selecting some books while rejecting others, by hunting through the books he did select, skipping far forward and sometimes back again, and rewriting the texts of the anecdotes his chosen sources made available to him, possibly resorting also to notes made earlier in the same restless, curious, personal searches. It is the very freedom of Byrd's personal interaction with this repository of an otherwise archaic and rigid form of knowledge that makes it most revealing. But one has to know William Byrd to see this happening.

Even read as isolated epigrams, some entries can be startlingly evocative of the man's life in general:

> Democritus often said, that the good Example of a Father is the best Lesson he can set his Children. For of all instructions those that are liveing & practical are the most insinuateing & perswasive. A child will be silently inveigled into an Emulation of those Vertues it sees practiced constantly before its Eyes. For tis a settled truth, that naked Example without precept is more instructive, than the most edifying Precept can be without Example. (§355)

Had it taken him this long to realize that he had suffered the lack of a father's example after he was sent to England, to Felsted School, at the age of seven in 1681? Would he now seek an example?

Or, another entry:

> A man must be very hard-hearted that feels not some concern for the death of a Wife notwithstanding she may have had some failings, for an Ox will weep when his yoke fellow comes to dye, tho' he may sometimes have pull'd against him, and perhaps have galld his neck by his restiveness. (§309)

Did he remember his wife Lucy, similarly galling, who in 1716 had died of smallpox after joining him in London, to which he had returned in his obsessive pursuit of the governorship of Virginia?

Still another:

> Pericles had a fine Daughter that was addresst by two Lovers, one a Booby with a vast Estate, the other a man of parts and honour of a moderate Fortune. The wise General generously preferrd the latter, saying, he had rather his Daughter shoud be marryd to a man, than to an Estate. (§112)

He certainly seems to have remembered his recent rejection by the wealthy Sabina and her subsequent marriage, in 1719, to the man he had called a "booby," Sir Edward Des Bouverie.[10]

On the largest scale, however, the personal revelations of the commonplace book do not come in single epigrams; they come from the weight of 573 entries

10. For biographical details, see Lockridge, *Diary, and Life.*

reflectively remembered or searched out of Byrd's library as he used this book when he felt the wish or the need, during a time of great crisis in his life. These entries often followed one another in an order best known in his own mind and quite possibly sustained across several sessions of writing as he read and reread previous entries, selected and rewrote new ones. Several hundred epigrams, comments, and bits of factual knowledge often assembled in this way slowly reveal another familiar William Byrd, this one the troubled man emerging from the defeats of 1719–1721, or, rather, from a whole series of defeats and losses, from his wife's death earlier as well as from his rejection by Sabina, from his ignominious failure to persuade the Board of Trade to make him governor of Virginia, and from a further and very recent rejection by another wealthy English lady, "Charmante." At this moment in his life, Byrd's choices of entries are such that rage, vengeance, humiliation, and sexuality constantly strain against the witty rhetorical surface of the genre.

As noted, more than fifty scattered entries show a contempt for women so profound as to suggest fury. The work also exudes a subtle conviction that virtue is apt to be ignored by those in power. This rises to explicitness in only a few entries but is implicit in many and is the implicit ground for a related theme, which nearly a hundred entries make totally explicit: that in the face of such rejection the wise man must adjust to lesser ambitions and circumstances and must look within himself for tranquillity. Variations on these themes abound. Byrd reveals a fascination with Alexander the Great, a man notorious for striving to surpass his father. Alexander becomes the most frequently recurring protagonist and alter ego of the work, yet Byrd also grows steadily more aware that Alexander's overwhelming ambition made him repulsive. Alexander, he seems to see, does not fit the dominant mood of this commonplace book, which is adjustment. More surprisingly—yet not, considering that Byrd was in his late forties and early fifties at this time—there are scores of quotations urging a successful adjustment to old age that weave in and out of the larger themes of acceptance of reduced ambitions and powers. Two-thirds of the way through the work this theme grows into an explicit concern with declining sexual and progenerative powers, which dominates page after page before ebbing. Both sexual desire and its waning concern him greatly. In this volume, a defeated William Byrd is coming to terms with middle age.

These themes are so tangled with one another—in Byrd's mind as within entries, or through what seem to be whole sequences of thought, as indeed across the entire book—that counting entries that reflect individual strands of thought almost misses the point. The point is the tangle itself, the obsessive returning to issues, the stuttering sequences of anger, adjustment, wit, self-control, and again adjustment in which William Byrd is working out his fate. In one powerful sequence his coruscating view of women was intermixed with thoughts of money and followed by images of prudence and self-control, then pursued in turn by criticism of ministers of state and by adjustment to reduced circumstances, to old age, and to failure (see entries §81–92). Two pages later he is back to troublesome women and to old age.

In another sequence, Byrd virtually recapitulates the breakdown of his romance with Sabina, then seems to throw in a touch of his subsequent political failure in an oblique reference to his colonial status, and then returns to the most recurrent theme of all, that of adjustment, in this case defined as achieving virtue through the cultivation of self-knowledge.

> Nothing proves the unaccountable power of the Fair Sex so evidently as old Fumblers, who continue to pursue the dear Sorceresses in spite of their aversion, & their own Impotence. This preposterous Inclination in men of an advanct age, is a kind of Tenesmus of the cod piece, which makes 'em fancy they've great need of a woman, and when they come to the point, alas! can do nothing. (§146)

> Old Fellows are often so short sighted they cant discern the danger of marrying of young women. For besides the great improbability that Bloom can have any likeing to Decay, tis very natural to guess, an old Gentleman can only teaze a young wench into Desires that must be satisfyd by Somebody else, and start a Hare for an abler Huntsman to catch. (§147)

> A worthless Fellow being Vain of his Family was told by a man of good understanding, that those Persons were most apt to boast of their ancestors merit, who had none of their own. (§148)

> An honest Scythian had the Barbarity of his country cast in his teeth by a worthless Athenian, and being provoked at so senceless a Reflection, said thus to him, t'is better my country shoud be a Reproach to me, than that like you, I shoud be a reproach to my Country. (§149)

> The nearest way to know other People well is to get intimately acquainted with our Selves. This is a piece of knowledge we Seldome think of tho' it be of the highest consequence to our vertue, and our happiness. (§150)

Exactly where such sequences of thought begin and end is not always easy to tell. Possibly they were created by Byrd's rereading of previous entries and extending the sequence of associations when he added others. What is clear is that, in full flight, his rather freely assembled entries often closely embroiled politics with women. In a preceding sequence, "Crocodiles" (women) gave way to a "hare braind Minister of State," and, in the example above, "Sorceresses" who evoke "aversion" are followed by the peripheral perspective of an "honest Scythian" on the corruptions of empire. Indeed, success or failure with women, itself contingent on their sexual expectations and on their reported capriciousness, is so interwoven with aging, with politics, and with Byrd's personal quest for tranquillity, that it is impossible to say that gender was a separate issue for this man. Women and power of every sort are a single issue in this chagrined mind reaching for peace.

In this mix Byrd's political emotions seldom achieve as frank an expression as his feelings about women, or as open a reference to his own history of failure. Still, his political stance is almost always with the honest periphery and against the imperial center. Favorable references abound to solid "Scythians" or to wise Spartans and to republican Rome. Occasional sarcastic references to the luxuries and vice of imperial Britain break through (see §120, 121). Some very pointed excerpts leave little doubt, however, that Byrd's own history of political failure lies behind the views he records:

> A man of abilitys was turnd out of a good Place to make room for one who had no other merit but a handsome Daughter, and when the good Man was condoled upon this misfortune, he only said, no wonder I am hardly treated, for God help me I am a poor daughterless, and sisterless Fellow, without any other Friend than truth and Honesty, who have no Interest at all at Court. (§31)

It was Byrd himself who, on the boat to Virginia in 1719 after his political rejection at the hands of the Board of Trade, had begun to dream himself daughterless and who, save for his patron duke of Argyll, had had no interest at court. In "Inamorato L'Oiseaux," his earlier self-portrait, Byrd had blamed himself for his failure to attain high office in England; but in selecting, or creating, such passages as the one above he now implies that the system is at fault for his current failures.

*   *   *

His agitation notwithstanding, the dominant theme of the commonplace book really is Byrd's overriding search for inner peace. Both of the sequences mentioned above—that beginning with crocodile women and that with old fumblers pursuing sorceresses—contained threatening women and indirect references to political failure, yet both sequences led to reminders of the need to accept reduced circumstances in order to find tranquillity. Throughout the early part of the commonplace book there is a continual returning to this theme, as if the book were composed in the form of a rondo. Troubling issues—Byrd's failures, really—pour out in brief or larger bursts of pointed stories, quotations, and epigrams; these are followed again and again by still other citations that testify to the man's attempt to adjust his self-image to harsh reality, to reach peace with himself, and therein to find true virtue. The persistence of the effort defies description; the only way to demonstrate it is to read the entire commonplace book. Cumulatively the agitation and reflection embodied in these recurrent alternations comes to sound very like the "adjustment" a modern psychiatrist would seek for a patient. Cast though it is in terms of little "places" of preceptual knowledge and never losing its witty veneer, the commonplace book is nevertheless an exercise in self-analysis.

Byrd's search for inner peace frequently expresses itself in excerpts that imply that adjustment entails not only therapeutic resignation but the deconstruction of a former self and the construction of a new one, complete with a revised emotional makeup and a fresh sense of humanity (see §132, 182–184). The self must give up the notions of vice, desires, and pride and accept that it must live within the bounds of virtue and humanity. Briefly, as Byrd contemplates the topic of "sleep," these thoughts of reducing himself to nothing or to mere humanity slide over momentarily into thoughts of death (see §189, 190). Ultimately it is, not resurrection from death, but an active reconstruction of the living self that is at stake, and thoughts of lesser station seldom lead to their ultimate implication of death. Quietly, firmly, in a later extended reflection Byrd rejects his former self while accepting with joy his new, if lesser, state.

> A wise man may be distinguisht by the probability and attainableness of his hopes; while the expectation of a Fool is commonly unpracticable and Visionary. (§320)

> Socrates usd to say, that the way to be rich in purse, is to keep your passions poor, and the ready road to be great in the Esteem of others, is to seem little in your own. (§329)

> The character of a wise man, is not to be without passions, but to keep them, as he ought to keep his Wife, in due Subjection, else like her, they will make him do abundance of very foolish things. (§330)

> S\(^t\). Chrysistome usd to say, t'was impossible to be a Saint or a Hero without strong passions, but then those passions must, like a high-mettled Horse, be brought to the manage, Else instead of a Saint, the owner may prove a Devil, and instead a Hero, a Tyrant. (§331)

Conformable to this notion, Pythagoras was wont to to inculcate, that no thing is so tyranical as our Passions, when they have dethroned Reason, and usurped the government of our actions; very like the tyrany of Slaves, who exercize the most insolent dominion over their natural Lords, and never fail to add cruelty and injustice to their usurpation. (§332)

The most agreable Companions in the world are a good conscience, & a cheerfull spirit, and to those who are so happy as to injoy them every Fast is a Feast, & every day a Holiday, all their greif is joy, and their pains are ᵐᵉʳᵉ titelations. (§333)

Byrd has here implicitly reassembled himself into a modest, cheerful soul utterly unlike the brittle, preceptual striver of his young manhood in Virginia. At moments he is also constructing a simpler world in which true virtue reigns. So far, it existed only in the pages of his commonplace book.

*   *   *

Byrd's treatment of Alexander the Great becomes a focused picture of the entire process at work here. Alexander begins as Byrd's hero, but Byrd's view of him undergoes a metamorphosis possibly parallel to Byrd's own. As Byrd well knew, Alexander was by all accounts passionately intent on surpassing his father, Philip of Macedon. The old man's successes caused such resentment in him that Alexander nearly became a parricide. This theme of simultaneously surpassing and resenting the father emerges in several of the earliest favorable references to Alexander in the commonplace book (see §29, 219). The latter entry, setting Alexander above his father, is one of the rare references that Byrd later repeats, and in this case he is either creating or selecting a version of the tale that emphasizes Alexander's competition with his father and raises the stakes to "immortality." Whether Alexander's braggings about his tutor put a shiny gloss on Byrd's exile to Felsted is uncertain, but these and other citations leave no doubt that Alexander, who so spectacularly transcended his father, is Byrd's model of the hero.

And, at first, Alexander's virtue is not questioned (see §223). Yet *heroic* virtue is not really the theme of this volume of the commonplace book, so Alexander does not sit comfortably among all the restrained Spartans and Romans who conquer, not worlds, but themselves. As if aware of the incongruity of the Alexander stories, Byrd increasingly selects from Quintus Curtius and from Arrian— or, again, from later compilations of these—tales that expose Alexander's vainglory, a more conventional view of the man closer to Byrd's real purpose in the commonplace book (see §225, 325). Byrd also becomes more impressed by Alexander's occasional ability to bridle his arrogance (see §278). By the end, Byrd's loyalty has shifted from Alexander to the older, wiser Philip (see §421). Perhaps a new, yet also older and wiser, Byrd was signaling to himself that he was now prepared to relinquish his struggle with his image of his father's greatness.

*   *   *

By the midpoint in the commonplace book, Byrd's adjustment to a lesser political role is proceeding nicely. Quotations reflecting political rage and thoughts of vengeance are fading into calm acceptance of the self. But Byrd's parallel adjustment to his unsuccessful relationships with women remains involved with related issues, with old age and with declining sexual powers, and here the process of adjustment becomes more traumatic.[11]

From the very beginning of the commonplace book, Byrd has been trying to come to terms with impending old age (see §44, 49). He proves unable to accept the lessening powers that go with age. This issue continues to agitate just beneath the surface of his efforts at composure until suddenly, about two-thirds of the way through the manuscript, declining sexual and generative powers overwhelm Byrd's thoughts in a way no other issue has. His preoccupation with female desire, and with his own fear of declining powers, comes to dominate his crisis of identity in a long set of quotations in which female desire and female power appear particularly threatening. His calm threatened by a question he cannot leave alone, he raises, leaves, then returns repeatedly to these laden issues. He covers a dozen pages with tales of animal sexuality, female sexual hunger, sexual anatomy, sexual technique, blood, and procreation. Fear and envy of female power run all through these pages. His concerns are now reduced to gender and power in their purest forms. In the ensuing passages, as noted, he begins drawing chiefly from Nicolas Venette's *De la génération de l'homme, ou tableau de l'amour conjugal* (listed in his library as *Tableau d'Amour*), but is ranging selectively through this encyclopedic work, resequencing and rewriting widely scattered entries and adding quotes from other sources that underline the points he, Byrd, wishes to emphasize. Carefully examined in sequence, these entries reveal his most disturbing weaknesses and fears at this time in his life.

In his initial outburst, animal sexual power seems to run together with female lust, which in turn merges into the subject of menstrual blood, and the blood itself becomes a symbol of women's almost excessive procreative powers (see §437–439). The entry immediately following implies that female blood and so female sexual and procreative power can be appropriated by men. If men fail to

---

11. The following episode is analyzed more fully in Lockridge, *Patriarchal Rage*.

do this, the next entry suggests, ravening women will drink *men's* blood and leave them dead. Women in this guise are instruments of the devil (see §440, 441). The very next observations literally put women in the submissive position, to be entered from behind. Only submissive women will procreate successfully (see §442, 443). But men's rule is threatened, as women always want to wear the breeches (see §446). Whether or not they wear breeches, women already possess something very like a penis, a circumstance which, as the immediately following entry suggests, is threatening to aging men with shrinking privates (see §469, 470). Aging men have their resources, however (see §476).

In this vein he continues for many pages, suggesting (in a citation from "Plato" that is really from More's *Utopia*) that men and women should see one another naked—indeed, even drunk, as in Muscovy—so that all dark secrets might be known before marriage. He adds that, while women's privy parts can be sewn up to ensure their virginity, yet "some women have been got with child without looseing their maidenhead" and indeed "some women have had milk in their Breasts who had never had amorous Commerce with man." Women's reproductive and sexual powers are, it seems, hard to contain (see §474, 481–484).[12] Man's virility counts for little in such a context, and old men have it worst (see §488). Yet as two lengthy and consecutive reflections suggest (see §497, 498), neither young men nor fecund philosophers can match women's sexual power; women's sexual voracity, as in the cases of Messalina (§498) and Cleopatra (§498), is overwhelming and, as Semiramis (§495) demonstrates, deadly to men. In the end, female lust dissolves male desire into chaos and disorder. Men must take hemlock in order to suppress desire and so avoid women (§501), leaving unanswered the question of how men are to reproduce themselves.

Several further and rather conventional epigrams on the war between the sexes follow, and then the long sexual agony is broken off by the sudden inter-polation in the manuscript of four leaves—eight sides—in the same hand but covered in love letters sent to one Charmante in 1722, with an appended com-mentary by Byrd (§503–508). These four leaves are a puzzle. A number of pages of these transcribed letters seem to be missing, as the first interpolated leaf begins suddenly in the middle of a letter to Charmante. The handwriting is by the same person but at first slightly clearer and the lines more slanted than in the commonplace book pages preceding and following. Further, after these four

---

12. Byrd's observations on the resemblance of female to male anatomy and sensitivity to the danger posed by women who become or replace or displace males (here and below) follow nicely from prevailing attitudes of the day; see Thomas Laqueur, *Making Sex: Body and Gender from the Greeks to Freud* (Cambridge, Mass., 1990).

leaves, the commonplace book resumes on a new leaf exactly as it should if no interpolation were there and evidently with a few last references to fear and to women. The transcribed letters are clearly an interpolation.

It appears that the Charmante letters belong at this point in the sequence of the commonplace book, that they were intentionally inserted there by Byrd, and that they and his following commentary on them deliberately expose the cause of the sexual turmoil imprinted on his commonplace book in the previous pages.[13] For what he enters after the record of those love letters to Charmante is a lengthy commentary on the lady and her rejection of him. Byrd here initially blames the loss of Charmante primarily on her fascination with another man's wit, but, if he is here making a leap from the profound sexual insecurity of previous passages in the commonplace book to his sudden insertion of the letters to her and to his now confessed uncertainty over the reason for her rejection of him, there can be little doubt that in his mind a lack, not of wit alone, but of sexual power as well is also associated with this failed romance. It would appear that this failure of sexuality was one of pure power also, since Charmante had been perhaps his last chance at a truly distinguished English marriage. His failure to win her favor had gnawed at him in the years since she had rejected him after 1722. Self-doubt had grown into his fulminations in the commonplace book against women's power and men's, especially old men's, weaknesses. Then, after these confessions, he had finally been able to enter in the same record his actual letters to Charmante and his own earlier commentary on her rejection of him. It was the last failure with a woman he would have to confess, for by this time—whether in 1725–1726 or later—he had married Maria Taylor and fathered the first of his children by her.

Whatever the message of the letters to Charmante, in the preceding pages of the commonplace book William Byrd had already confessed his worst fears about women. The effect was certainly confessional, and perhaps cathartic. With the exception of a few attenuated references in the next page of the true commonplace book (that is, after the inserted letters) and of "The Female Creed" written at about this time, probably in 1725, Byrd would never again show the streak of barely suppressed misogyny which reached a peak in the preceding pages of the commonplace book.[14] Even "The Female Creed" is already marked by a superficially gentler condescension toward women, and that tone itself was seldom used thereafter. Perhaps through his commonplace book William Byrd had come to terms not only with the power other men wielded over him and

13. See "A Note on the Placement of the Charmante Letters," below.
14. "The Female Creed," *ASD*, 450–475.

with his own peripherality to that power but also with the power women could wield over men in desperate need of sex, reproduction, resources, and control.

*   *   *

Nevertheless, in the case of women, it is still unclear exactly what these terms of Byrd's new acceptance were. The very depth of his fears of women revealed here in the commonplace book renders the issue of his attitudes toward women for the rest of his life resistant to closure. The book leaves the reader wondering whether the fierce "she-males" of his jottings, women able to dominate, consume, and replace men at every turn, did not return to haunt him occasionally. His second marriage, to Maria Taylor, was characterized in his diary as a distant though affectionate relationship.

In this context it may be relevant that fears of incursions by transgressing "others" had long lurked around the edges of Byrd's view of race as well as of gender. Both in his paper before the Royal Society in 1695 and now in the commonplace book itself (§173) Byrd had taken up the idea that persons of color might become white. In the first case the evidence suggested that it could happen spontaneously, but in the latter case—the anecdote in the commonplace book, in which a white father married to a black woman bred with his own daughter and granddaughter to produce white offspring—it was emphasized that whites must establish patriarchal (and incestual) dominance over any proposed transgressions into the "white" by black persons. The following entry was on the subject of revenge! Likewise in his later observations on class, in his *History of the Dividing Line betwixt Virginia and North Carolina,* Byrd would ridicule the feckless North Carolinians while revealing a corrosive fear that such rural clowns—whom he elsewhere called "Goths and Vandals"—might sweep aside his own class by usurping their lands and authority. Here, too, an imposition of leadership and control was the solution. At many times in his life, then, women, persons of color, and the lower orders all threatened to seize part or all of William Byrd's white male gentry status. For this reason we cannot finally say whether his fears of women in particular rested peacefully in the place he had put them after confessing his fury at Charmante.[15]

15. Again see Lockridge, *Patriarchal Rage,* for a deeper exploration of Byrd's relationships to and with women, as also Lockridge, "Colonial Self-Fashioning," in Hoffman, Sobel, and Teute, eds., *Through a Glass Darkly,* 274–339. The Royal Society paper is "An Account of a Negro-Boy That Is Dappel'd in Several Places of His Body with White Spots," Royal Society, *Philosophical Transactions,* XIX (1695–1697), 781–782 (reprinted in *Works,* and above, Chapter 7). The entry in the commonplace book is, again, §173, and I thank Kathleen Brown for calling my attention to it. *William Byrd's Histories of the Dividing Line betwixt Virginia and*

∗   ∗   ∗

Byrd's commonplace book, then, which appears at first glance to be a random collection of sententious epigrams designed to position him in society, or at best a potential means of self-control, became much more than this. Always possessing deeper resonances than superficial readings indicate, it seems above all to have become a disguised instrument of self-expression, of self-realization, and of incomplete self-transcendence in the midst of a personal crisis. It is difficult to sort out the surface sheen of the genre, with its elements if not of stereotypicality then of typicality, from the subtexts that make the work so intensely individual, but this masking is what the early eighteenth century required of its modes of self-expression.

In his commonplace book Byrd had drawn on a conventional literature of ancedote richly represented in the publications of seventeenth- and eighteenth-century England. Within his own library, this vast literature was evinced not only in Plutarch, Diogenes Laertius, Erasmus, the *Spectator,* and so forth but also in such now-forgotten titles as Temple's and Halifax's respective miscellanies, Samuel Butler's *Hudibras,* a book identified only as *English Worthies,* Thomas Stanley's *History of Philosophy,* John Ray's *Proverbs,* something labeled *The Polite Gentleman,* of course Venette's *Tableau de l'amour conjugal,* and so on and on. He had selected items from this floating world of tens of thousands of apposite anecdotes on every conceivable subject, according to his own rather loose interpretation of the roles of the subgenre in which he was participating, which we might call the anecdotal, positional gentleman's commonplace book. As he reached into this grab bag for epigrams to repeat, most of what he pulled out was conventional if rather archaically frozen wisdom. Much was evidently culturally resonant, and much was rephrased, some quite nicely, but was intended primarily for a self and a personal social sphere still resistant to extended intellectual engagement.[16] What is truly unique about Byrd's commonplace

----

North Carolina is found in modern dress by Dover Press (New York, 1967). The reference to "Goths and Vandals" is in Richard Croom Beatty and William J. Mulloy, eds., *William Byrd's Natural History of Virginia; or, The Newly Discovered Eden* (Richmond, Va., 1940), xxi–xxii. For an interesting mirror image of Byrd's use of his commonplace book to work out his problems with gender and sexuality, see Catherine La Courreye Blecki and Karin A. Wulf, eds., *Milcah Martha Moore's Book: A Commonplace Book from Revolutionary America* (University Park, Pa., 1997).

16. Byrd's library is included in the shelflist taken in his son's time and reproduced with some omissions in John Spencer Bassett, *The Writings of "Colonel William Byrd of Westover in Virginia, Esqr."* (New York, 1901), appendix A. The titles cited here are shelf titles, and so

book is the juxtaposition—amid these typicalities—of his own known personal traumas with the profile of the five-hundred-odd anecdotes he has selected from among the tens of thousands available.

Nothing in the genre or in his dozens of volumes of ephemera made him devote the greater part of his commonplace book to an obsessive round of misanthropy, of politics seen from the periphery, and of adjustment to failure, to a maturing view of Alexander the Great, and to a score of pages of passages collectively overwhelmed by the power of female sexuality and with the feebleness of men, especially aging men. Within the climate of his age and the range of anecdote available, for example, Byrd could have delighted in science, extolled or condemned religion, praised the uses of a suitably tempered ambition, or, alternatively, added Caesar to the arrogant Alexander as a hero. While mixing in sexuality with power, he could have indulged more in the gentler and far more woman-friendly witticisms of the sixteenth-century French courtier Brantôme. For that matter he could, as many of his contemporaries did, have followed Locke's scheme and subordinated all his entries under conceptual categories, thereby collecting his personal thoughts under categories but fragmenting their larger, personal unity. Other writers of commonplaces took these options more frequently; decidedly Byrd did not. He did not let the Lockean Enlightenment destroy what Michel Foucault would later see was really the principal function of this genre: self-construction.

William Byrd's particular choices explain why among the one hundred-odd commonplace books at the Bodleian Library at Oxford, in the American Antiquarian Society in Worcester, and in the Virginia Historical Society in Richmond, his is unique.[17] Like diaries, each commonplace book is in some senses typical, yet each is in other senses unique and personally revealing. This fact suggests in turn that all commonplaces shared a further feature, one that Foucault was unwilling to assign to classical commonplacings, at least, or implicitly to all: they were a disguised confessional literature. Such books were confessional in the sense that the early-to-middle eighteenth century could tolerate; beneath the surface roles of a formal genre lay a process of selection by which the genre became resonant with the needs and memories of each participant. Freud would later identify a process called "transference," in which the subject replays in a safe context that which is most disturbing. Foucault called it self-care.

---

the actual edition is usually unknown, but, for as complete references to these books as we have, see Hayes.

17. Brantôme and the commonplace books referred to here are identified and discussed in Lockridge, *Patriarchal Rage.*

Even Byrd's worthy successor in this unstructured form of the genre, Thomas Jefferson, was to use his own somewhat different version of the genre in a remarkably similar fashion, as a confessional, a counselor, and an arena for constructing the self. Modern scholarship has been able to date Jefferson's excerpting very precisely, and it reveals that many of the emotional crises of his youth and many of his changing images of his self were played out in the passages he selected to enter into in his commonplace book. Defiance, rebellion, loneliness, romance, death, and efforts at self-control spill out onto his copybook's pages just at the times when, as is known from other sources, these became vital issues in his life. (The two books also resemble one another in one exact peculiarity. In their self-shapings, both men had to deal with women as well as with power, and misogynist rage marks Jefferson's early commonplace book as profoundly, and unusually, as Byrd's late one.) Jefferson's commonplace book also "reveals the early directions and tendencies of Jefferson's inner life as no other document is able to do—its fantasies, its posturing, its varying attempts to find, in the situations and utterances of [historical and] imaginative characters, suitable images for the self."[18] While Byrd's form of the genre was slightly more archaic than Jefferson's, full of rhetorical poses instead of lengthy and discursive excerpts from fiction and from political philosophers, both men found in these books a place where the self could be expressed, consoled, and recreated, Byrd perhaps even more than Jefferson.

What is fascinating—and significant for William Byrd's personal development—is that in its final pages his commonplace book also came to resemble Jefferson's even in the modern form of knowledge it embodied. In this may lie one key to Byrd's eventual rebirth as an effective human being, the Virginia planter, statesman, and author of the years 1726–1744. For the commonplace book, which had already begun to change before Byrd's great outburst of sexual fear and of fear of women, was to change further thereafter. Possibly this continuing change came about because its creator was the better for all his purgative exercises or, in the case of women, relieved by his attempted exorcising of them. First political bitterness fades completely from the pages of this book, then by the end women, sexuality, and old age virtually disappear. Even the constant refrain of philosophical adjustment evaporates. The remaining surface of witty epigrams becomes largely mere court gossip, and it is increasingly displaced by a

18. See Lockridge, *Patriarchal Rage,* and the judgments and quote here are from Wilson, ed., *Jefferson's Literary Commonplace Book,* 15–20. Jefferson later added structure and organization to his commonplace book, in effect modernizing it retrospectively; but, thanks to Wilson's dating of his various handwritings, the original can be more or less reassembled.

use of the commonplace book as a record of scientific information and even of intellectual speculation. In this change there may be a hint of a new mentality as, from being a tortured self-analysis hidden within an archaic form of knowledge, the commonplace book becomes a tentative searching for the meanings of the Enlightenment.[19]

Extended entries lay bare human anatomy in the perspective of the new discoveries of the seventeenth century. Blood and its circulation are delineated, as are the bones and the digestive system. Byrd is making the body's systems visibly transparent, looking deeper with the eye of reason than he has in his previous explorations of his own psyche. The nature of the rational faculty itself is explored at some length. Zoology, language, and astronomy follow on the heels of anatomy, albeit not explored so deeply, and in a fashion that flirts with yet avoids the antiquarian. Then, in the extraordinary entry that is the longest in the book, Byrd writes a précis that in this context amounts to a reflection on the Reverend Doctor William Wollaston's *Religion of Nature Delineated,* first published privately in 1722 but widely available, reviewed, and discussed in other prints by 1725.[20]

Byrd's implicit reflection reveals more than simply his attitudes toward religion, for, while Wollaston was primarily a devout Anglican, Wollaston's work (according to Norman Fiering) was also a landmark in the application of the Enlightenment principles of reason and of God's rational design of nature *to* the problems of religion and of ethics.[21] And rational, systematic knowledge is precisely where the commonplace book is already going. To quote Byrd's entry on Wollaston:

> He condemns all . . . vices by being violations of Some plain Truth, and
> consequently against all the Rules of Reason, and our own and other People's

19. Thus, comparing pp. 22–50 (§131–348) to pp. 94–108 (§515–573) in Byrd's commonplace book yields, respectively, 26 commentaries on women, most hostile, in the earlier pages and virtually none in the latter; 111 anecdotes on virtue and vice, often political, in the former pages as against only 18 in the latter; and 49 references to adjustment and to old age in the first pages as against only 2 at the end. Information—usually scientific—and ideas, on the other hand, are found in only 6 entries in pp. 22–50 as compared with 24 entries in the shorter compass of pp. 94–108.

20. These entries are in the commonplace book, §515–526. Wollaston's book was published in London, 1722, 1725, and later editions. The reference to Wollaston is in the commonplace book, §526.

21. See Norman Fiering, "The First American Enlightenment: Tillotson, Leverett, and Philosophical Anglicanism," *New England Quarterly,* LIV (1981), 307–344, esp. 331–337; also *Dictionary of National Biography,* s.v "Wollaston, William," and Hayes, pp. 87–88.

happiness. and that we may not plead Ignorance, what things are true & what not, the author of nature has endued us with Reason, which if duly attended to, will be our Sufficient Direction. Upon this Foundation all Natural Religion is built, according to our author, and the light by which any Person of common understanding may clearly discern the distinction betwixt moral Good & Evil. (§526)

In short, Wollaston supplemented the necessity for a transcendental imperative from God as the source of all ethics by grounding Christian ethical behavior also in the rules of a logically consistent sense of natural truth, which itself was divinely granted. To violate that sense of truth was to be immoral. God thereby became in part a distant helper to ethics in the sense that, outside his immediate voice in revelation itself, he had shaped the logical consistency of nature's observed facts and given men the intelligence to perceive this consistency. To lie, to misrepresent nature's logical consistency, known as truth, was a chief form of sin. Without abandoning his religion at all, Wollaston was applying a version of Newton to Christian ethics.

Byrd often superimposes his own words (and his own temptations) on the structure of Wollaston's argument. The significance of this reframing lies in the promise of aid that rational Christianity could provide Byrd in his battle to contain his passions and desires. Some of the exemplary and epigrammatic entries distributed throughout the commonplace book already point to the power of reason to disarm the enemy (to answer doubts, to moderate the passions, to expel fears) and thus to work toward contentment. But, significantly, for the first time in the commonplace book, the wisdom to be found in Wollaston was not also contingent upon the ethos of the author or central character of the narrative excerpted. Wollaston's personal courage, moral stature, and wit were irrelevant to the ideas he set forth in his book—his contribution was enacted, not in speech, but in print. It operated on a different level from most of the other, more fragmentary entries in that it represented an open, rational discourse. Byrd found himself able to engage with the steady, logical process of the argument, to adapt the argument to his own circumstances, and to find some answers, some comfort in the way his own reason could work to clarify his spiritual and emotional situation.

In his reframing of Wollaston, we can see for the first time the possibility that Byrd as a reader could engage fully in dialogue with a text he had read. The fragments of moral wisdom and the idealized social positions outlined in all the exemplary and epigrammatic extracts might have given him encouragement. He might have tried (and failed) to live up to these traditional standards. He might have used the assemblage of extracts articulating his fears and doubts in order to contain and overcome them. But, in his précis of Wollaston, Byrd demonstrates his understanding that a happy, virtuous life cannot merely spring from the emulation of great lives—it can only come about when reason is in control, when matters are thought out as they are enacted rather than regretted afterward.

It might have been that this flash of effective rationality stood for a larger, liberating process taking place in Byrd's mind during these years. During this very period he symbolically relegated superstition, magic, spirits, portents, goblins and all, to credulous women, in "The Female Creed." The catharsis on gender relations he reached during the commonplace book period might not have been complete without depositing the world's outmoded credulities condescendingly upon the opposite sex (as well as ridiculing them in other ways in the course of the satire), but in doing so he nonetheless left behind magic to move toward the Enlightenment as it was then construed. Byrd's belief that rational men could improve the world through the power of reason seems to have been confirmed by events. Later in his life he was to be above all else a man of projects, and some of them were realized. The ironic stance of the *Dividing Line* histories also reveals a writer intent on defending colonial civilization against the chaotic influence of men whose passions are unregulated by reason. Perhaps the culmination of Byrd's Enlightenment views occurs in 1736, when he set forth with compelling discernment the evils of slavery with a reasoning his successor Thomas Jefferson could not have surpassed.[22]

This is not to say that Byrd became an Enlightenment thinker, or that he was entirely absorbed into this new cosmology by a spate of scientific detail followed by a single, albeit long and fascinated entry on rational but still Christian ethics as espoused by a devout Anglican, all placed at the end of a changing commonplace book, or even that a conversion is demonstrated by the series of subsequent "enlightened" phrases and actions chronicled here. For him as for most persons of the late seventeenth and early eighteenth century, credulity and reason, superstition and "enlightenment," positional knowledge and elaborated, the role of revelation, of power, and the faith in the reason of all human beings continued to blend in their minds. But in the last pages of his commonplace book, as soon enough in other sources, we can see him *entering upon* a new

---

22. Again, "The Female Creed" is in *ASD*, 445–475; a key 1726 letter identifying himself "first mover" of his plantation world is Byrd to Charles Boyle, earl of Orrery, July 5, 1726, *Correspondence*, I, 354; and the 1736 critique of slavery is Byrd to John Perceval, earl of Egmont, July 12, 1736, *Correspondence*, II, 487. See also Hayes, pp. 58–61.

cosmology and a new epistemology. Further, the Enlightenment mentality was perhaps more liberating for him than for some others. The record of his life thereafter, its growing effectiveness and indeed fruitfulness, may derive as much from his tentative approaches to the new mental world of the Enlightenment as from his earlier exercises in self-analysis. If facing his fears in thinly disguised form in the earlier pages of the commonplace book was a healthy substitute for the tyranny of his nightmares, and indeed he was to record only two more, both taken philosophically, then a second liberation surely lay in learning to trust, not only divine imperatives to "improve," but also his own reason.

*   *   *

It was this William Byrd who, in 1726, exited the pages of his commonplace book and permanently entered Virginia's history as a fruitful and effective agent. He abandoned an earlier lifetime of hopeless provincial ambition, rigid self-control, and stifling precept to become the reflective colonial planter, political thinker, and essayist who reconceived the role of his class in American history.[23] That he had still not fully resolved his views on women and that the Enlightenment was in some sense also yet another tool for genteel masculine self-construction cannot entirely obscure his achievement. Soon, old age would do more to mellow this man than either his consoling commonplace book or his new faith in reason. In the end personal history became not epistemology but gerontology.

A Note on the Placement of the Charmante Letters

One theory concerning the letters to Charmante says that William Byrd did not in fact place them at the present point (after §501) in the order of the leaves of the commonplace book. True, the binding that held the pages of the commonplace book loosely together when it was finally purchased by the Virginia Historical Society appears to have bound these peculiar leaves among the others at this point, but there is no absolute evidence that this was Byrd's original binding. Similarly, while Byrd has just referred to "this island" in the immediately preceding pages of commonplace book entries and so is probably still in England after his brief visit to Virginia in 1719–1721 and writing before his final return to Virginia in 1726, there is a potential reference to 1731 in the commentary appended to the Charmante letters. If the apparent reference to events in or after 1731 were valid, it would raise the question of how Byrd could have stopped using his commonplace book shortly before 1726 and resumed only after adding these letters after 1731 and then resumed the entries in the commonplace book with the same theme, fear and women, with which he had left off and in the

23. See Lockridge, *Diary, and Life;* Margaret Beck Pritchard and Virginia Lascara Sites, *William Byrd II and His Lost History: Engravings of the Americas* (Williamsburg, Va., 1993); Susan Manning, "Industry and Idleness in Colonial Virginia: A New Approach to William Byrd II," *Journal of American Studies,* XXVIII (1994), 169–190.

identical hand as five or more years before! Perhaps a later owner, who also possessed Byrd's letterbook, inserted these letters and Byrd's later (1731 or after) commentary on them, in the commonplace book at this point. Or, what could have happened instead, if the 1731 date is valid at all, is that sometime after that date Byrd inserted these old love letters, and added a commentary, on blank pages remaining at the end of the completed commonplace notebook. Then, if after his death the later part of its binding disintegrated, at least one of those last leaves could have disappeared and the others got inserted and rebound at an earlier point in the sequence of leaves and so in the midst of the commonplace book entries. In that case these four leaves of letters to Charmante might still be Byrd's commentary on his commonplace book, but on exactly which part would be less clear.

But a more persuasive theory says that, while there may be pages of the transcribed love letters missing, these copied letters nonetheless belong at this point in the sequence of the commonplace book because they were intentionally inserted there by Byrd either before his return to Virginia in 1726 or later. He could have inserted the letters in the commonplace book at the earlier date, before 1726, if the "reference to 1731" in his commentary is in fact invalidated. It probably should be, since it is said to refer to the death of his erstwhile lover's child by a successful rival for her hand, when in truth this child of 1731 to whom he is said to refer did not die and so the whole series of identifications on which this date is based seems to be wrong. Alternatively, Byrd could have inserted the letters either at this earlier date or later, and the reference to 1731 could have been valid, if he copied over the entire commonplace book sometime after 1731—something his own practices and its homogeneity of handwriting suggest is possible—and when he did so added at this point in its sequence either his commentary on the already-inserted letters or both the transcribed letters and his commentary.

If these transcribed letters were deliberately inserted by William Byrd at this point in the commonplace book either before 1726 or after 1731—and possibly even if he added them instead at the very end of the commonplace book and they were later rebound here by accident—he may be exposing the precipitating cause of his preceding sexual agony.

The problem of the possible-yet-dubious reference to events in and postdating 1731 in the "Charmante" letters is explained in *Correspondence*, I, 332–333n.

The Commonplace Book

[1] [/1] [. . .] the tread of a man at his [. . .] dos [. . .] happend to be out of the way. She cryd out, whos there? [ ] you, Madam, said the man, in the tone of [. . .] not believeing her own Ears, She hollowd out a [. . .] who's there? and he made the same reply, one that [. . .] for you. Come in then said she, & shew your self that I may see whether your [. . .] doubting but some fine Lover woud make his appeara[nce] but instead of that, to her sad disappoint[m]ent in came a dirty Dyer, with an old Gown & Petticoat, to which he had been orderd to give some new Coulour

[2] A formal Fellow, who usd to pronounce all his words very distinctly, came to inquire for a Gent[leman] whos name was Owen. When the Servant came to the door [. . .] O:N [. . .] said this <u>distinct Fop</u>, [. . .] the Servant made answer very humourously, N:O.

[3] A Sturdy Custome-house officer [. . .] came in a canoe, with only one Negro to paddle it [. . .] one of the Kings Ships of 50 guns which he suspected [. . .] demanded of the Captain to Secret [. . .]. But he not [readily] submitting to that demand why then S[ir] the old Pudhean, I must do it by force and as the [. . .] if any [. . .] bloud shoud happen to be spilt, captain, you must [. . .] it.

[4] A Judge in France, whose Integrity was [. . .] together [. . .]able, was [. . .] to be a fine Lady to [. . .] her Husband, cause His Lord<u>p</u> told her, she carr'd [. . .] about [. . .][1]

[5] [/2][2] [. . .]of ingrafting or inoculateing the small[pox was fir]st brought out of the northern part of Ne[. . .]a into Turky, where it has now been in [use] about 70 years. At first they kept a Register [at Con]stantinople of all Persons who under went Inoculation, and out of all that number, there was only one old woman miscarryd by being very disorderly and ungovernable, and now this practice is grown so universal in Turky, that they have left off keeping any Register of them.

[6] Goats milk is accounted better than Asses milk in a consumption, and a wholesome womans milk better than either.

[7] Alexander among the rest of his Freaks, woud needs make his friend Ephestion a God. After his death, therefore he orderd divine honours to be paid him and made it very penal for any body to behave disrespectfully to this new Deity. All nations therefore built Temples, and erected Statues in honour of him, and Alexanders Flatterers made their court to him in proportion to their zeal for this ridiculous adoration. But Agathocles one

1. The rest of the page is very faint, illegible and torn.
2. The corners of page 2 are missing.

of his captains thought it too gross, after complementing Alexander with being the offspring of a God to allow him also to be a God-maker,—and therefore when he past by Ephestions Tomb, he coud not refrain tears, at the thoughts that he who was scarce a man when alive, shoud be accounted a God when he was dead. But this brave man had like to have been thrown to the Lions for [unseas]onable Tears, and was obligd to a Stratagem of his friend Perdiccas, who Swore to Alexander by all the [G]ods, & Ephestion among the rest, [that] Ephestion appeard to him, and strictly chargd him, to tell [the] King, twas [his] pleasure Agathocles shoud be acquitted [. . .] proceeded from no other cause, than the R[. . .]³

[8] [3/3] An ill breath is enough to blow out Loves Goo[d] [. . .] the livid Flame of hatred and aversion.

[9] Attention and diligence were accounted by the old R[omans so] much the duty of a Senator, that the Censors once degraded o[ne of] that order for yawning at a debate that concernd the Safety of [. . .] Common-wealth.

[10] Upon the defeat of the Roman army by Hanibal, There [. . .] several of the Senate moved for deserting the city, upon which Scipi[o] standing up said, he woud as freely draw his Sword against those who shoud offer to abandon their Country, as those who offerd to invade it.

[11] The Duke of Rohan had renounc't the Protestant Religion in complement to Harry the 4ᵗʰ of France, who thereupon made him a mareshal and being askt afterward by that Prince, which he thought best the Popish or the Protestant Religion replyd without hesitation, the Protestant. For your majesty has given me a Mareshals staff and Popery in exchange for it, that I might be no looser by the Bargain.

[12] The late Marquess of Halifax usd to say, whoever woud bri[ng] himself to swallow a Dagger, must begin to swallow a Penknife, as [Milo] began with a Calf, before he coud carry an Ox.

[13] Things are not always valued according to their Bulk, but their Rarity, as a cow is as cheap at Fort Sᵗ George as a Rabit, and may b[e] had for 8 or 9 Shillings.

[14] The Poet Polemon dyd a merry death, for being on a couch reposing himself he saw an Ass Slink into the Room and gredily dev[our] a Plate of Figgs provided for his own dinner. This threw him into so violent a fit of laughter that being 97 years of age he dyd upon the Spot. And Sophocles the Tragick Poet was choakt with a grape kernal Many have dyd by the Juice of that Fruit but none before of the kernal.

---

3. Illegible, rest of page torn.

[15] A Souldier of the Guards had a wife very much given to discourse, who usd to come to him when he lay encampt at Hide-park. She pigd in with her husband, in the same tent where he lay with 3 of h[is] fellow Souldiers upon clean straw, and was not content to streighten their Room, but woud also keep them awake by crying without ceaseing dow[n] with the Rump. The souldiers made her no other reply but in their [/4] [. . .]age said up with your filthy Rump. This provkt [. . .] best part about her Vilifyd, and made her reply [. . .] of her Soule, my Rump is cleanlier than your Squabb [. . .] from H . . . r. The Husband upon this thought it [. . .] to give her a little camp-discipline, and told her, she woud [. . .] have done with her damnd Politicks, til she had [. . .] him out of the Guards with marks of dishonour.

[16] Some Gentlemen of South Britain were traveling for improvement into Scotland, and being at dinner in a publick house they observd the lad that waited, had a scald head, which did [. . .]d much to the keeness of their Stomachs. One of the compa[ny] told the Fellow he shoud put something on his head to hide [. . .] foul prospect from their Sight. that I usd always to do, said [. . .] only to day the cook borrowd my cap to boil the Pudding that is for your Hon[rs] dinner.

[17] Another English man whose curiosity carry'd him into [North Bri]ttain came to an Inn in the County of anandale, and after he had made a cleanly dinner, being a little tird with his Journey [he] went to lye down on a bed in the next Room. But before he [. . .] extended his Person, he felt something that hurt him, and [turn]ing down the Bedcloaths he found a joint of lean mutton [. . .]dy dishd, and not quite cold. The Surprize of this discovery [. . .]de him inquire of the woman of the House how that meat [ca]me there? In truth said she I set it there to keep warm for my [. . .]d mann's eyn dinner.

[18] A Cobler was surprizd in the fact of chastizeing his wife with his Strap and being reproacht for it, he humorously answerd, that he lovd the Jade very well, but did not care to let her know it.

[19] When a fruit Tree is cankerd rub off the canker, and then apply tar and Greese to it and twill recover it self again.

[20] Burn that part of a Post that is to stand in the ground [. . .] then tarr it well over and twill last many years without rotting.

[21] [5/5] Sir William Davenant was a man of loose mor[als,] [. . .] been a sufferer by the love of Women to that degree, as to ha[. . .] less than he had. However this disaster was so far from recla[iming] him, that he disgraced his Grey hairs, by continueing [. . .] despite [. . .] nature. One of his friends

gravely rebuked him for it, and [. . .] to leave off such unbecomeing pleasures. How, replyd Sr William, [. . .]sleing, woud you have me leave off a looser? Yes, said his [. . .] when tis impossible for you to win back what you have lost [. . .] probably if you play on that you'll loose all you have about you.

[22]   John Bazilowitz had amongst many other wanton methods; of oppressing his Subjects, this unmercifull way of raiseing Taxes. He woud send to a Town or Country for something he knew they coud not supply him with, & then woud amerce them for disobedience. as once he sent to Moscow for a certain measure full of ᵗᵛᵉ Fleas for a Medicine, as he pretended. They returnd His majesty word, that the thing was impracticable, and if the Quantity were to be got, they coud not fill the measure with them because those nimble Vermin woud be always leaping out. Upon this he set a mulet upon them of 7000 Rublis.

[23]   A Country man complaind to General Kirk that his Souldiers (which he calld his Lambs,) had plunderd him of all he had in the world. Thou art a happy Rogue says the General for then thou art certain of being plunderd no more.

[24]   The Pope buys up all the Corn of St Peters patrimony at 5 Crowns their measure, and in selling this out, the measure is lessend a fifth part, and the price of the whole is doubled, so that what corn he bought in for 5 crowns, he sells out for 12, and all Bakers & others must take their Corn of his Holiness at this unconscionable price, and of nobody else under a severe pena[l]ty. These and many other such Exactions make the Inhabitants of this Rich Country, live abundantly more miserably, than upon the mountains of Switzerland, where they labour for themselve[s] and not for an Inhumane Tyrant.

[25]   [/6] [The Q]uality most in Esteem in any Country is there calld [by the] general name of vertue. In old Rome courage was calld [vert]ue, and whoever had that happy Quality in any degree [w]as calld vertuous. But in modern Rome the case is alterd [. . .]nd a Superiour Skil in antiquity, and in the Polite arts is calld [v]ertue at this day. As courage formerly denominated a man vertuous at Rome, so tis usd have to betoken a man of Honour, tho he want all other good Qualitys. So if amongst the Ladys a nymph is but chast, we allow her to be vertuous, tho she ᵇᵉ ⁿᵉᵛᵉʳ so proud so peevish so disorderly and backbiteing. So that in truth the Honour of a Woman consists according to this fashion, in not being a Harlot, as a mans dos in not being a coward. And therefore a Lady may with the Same good grace ᵒᶠᶠᵉʳ ᵗᵒ perswade a man to be ᵖᵃᵗⁱᵉⁿᵗˡʸ kickt & cufft, as he perswades her

to prostitute her chastity because both are by those means perswaded to part with that which the world is pleasd to call their honour.

[26] The medals struck in the time of the old Romans was their currant mony which was an effectual way of spreading and perpetuating the great actions of their Emperours. On the reverse of these Medals, was the Devise and the Legend, expressing [i]n very smal compass, some great Vertue or action of the Prince. The Gold & Silver medals are much more rare than the brass or copper ones, because the first have been melted downe by the Ignorant People that had them who thought their value lay all in the metal. The nice Virtuosi in Medals pretend to judge of the antiques by every one of the Sences, by the sight, by the hearing, (when they ring them) by the touch, by the smel, and tast, which in Corinthian brass is very different from what it woud be in the modern. Medals serve to illustrate History, settle disputes in Chronology, to assist Poetry wth Images, and painting ^with the figures of imaginary Beings. They give us some impression of the features of great men, and enable us the better [to] judge of the goodness & antiquity of Busts, & Statues. They give [7/7] us the Plan of some old pieces of Architecture, which we [would] otherwise have known nothing of, and so it dos the figure of [Ma]chines, Engines, & instruments of War, vessels of Sacrifice, comm[on] utensiles, and of the habits of men & women of every rank, age, and profession. All these considerations make the Study of Medals no[t] altogether so triffleing & impertinent as some Wise People think, tho in this science as in all others there are some Visionarys, that by their foppery bring it into disgrace and Ridicule.

[27] Some Jesuitical Disputants manage in their arguments as Watermen do in their boats, look one way and row another as the impious Vannini put out a ridiculous Treatise to prove the Being of a God, with a wicked design to make it evident that there was none.

[28] A wise General will always endeavour to have a corps of Forrein Troops in his army with design to lay the fault on them in case the Enimy shoud get the better of him. This is an old Strategem and was not first usd by our Generals in Spain & Portugal.

[29] Alexander declard he owd more to his Master Aristotle, than to his father Phillip, because he only made him live, but the other made him live with glory and reputation. His father gave him mortality, but his master immortality.

[30] Demetrius advisd Ptolemy to converse with Books rather than men, because said he, Books will tell you the truth, while Men will only flatter and decieve you.

[31] A man of abilitys was turnd out of a good Place to make room for one who had no other merit but a handsome Daughter, and when the good Man was condoled upon this misfortune, he only said, no wonder I am hardly treated, for God help me I am a poor daughterless, and sisterless Fellow, without any other Friend than truth and Honesty, who have no Interest ᵃᵗ ᵃˡˡ at Court.

[32] Dry walnuts 24 hours in an oven or other gentle heat and when you have a mind to eat them, crack the shell, & steep the kernel 24 hours more in cold water, shifting the water every 6 hours, and theyll eat as well as if they were just taken off the Tree.

[33] [/8] The way to make a Ham eat in perfection, is to steep it [. . .] in Milk and water, and then let it only simmer for 5 hours [in wa]ter just ready to boil, which is better than Boiling, because that is [. . .] drive the salt into the meat, while simmering will draw it out.

[34] A man was boasting he had an ingenious Wife who [kne]w when to speak, very probable said his friend. but do's she know when to hold her tongue?

[35] A man who had been marryd 6 weeks was talking about crying Sin of Self murder, I cant tell said he how it happens, but I never in my whole life thought of hanging my self, before I was marryd, but the Devil has put it into my head a thousand times since. In fact it has been observd that most of the men who have made away with themselves, have been marryd, & most of the Women have been single. What ungallant inference may be drawn from hence I leave to the marryed People to determine.

[36] The Virtuosi who Study the nature of their Fellow creatures affirm, that a mule cannot only carry a great deal upon his back, but also a great deal in his head, for not Quantity of strong drink will make him drunk.

[37] A Parson who practiced not so well as he preachd, was reproved for it by a grave Justice in his Parish, who askt him with some concern, why he woud not follow his own wholesome doctrine? Because, replyd the Parson, when a man has lost his way, I'm a good Guide ⁱᶠ I direct him into the right Road, without being obliged to go the whole Journey along with him and he woud be a little unreasonable to desire it.

[38] In Spain the Jews are obliged every year to go to church and hear a sermon preacht in proof of christianity against themselves.

[39] The hearty acknowledging of one kindness is always ᵃ Bawd for another, said Thales.

[40] The 2 things in the world that: the soonest grow stale upon our hands, are ᵃ kindness receivd, & a wedded Wife.

[41] [9/9] Epaminondas was not in the least elated with the glorious Victory he

obtaind over the Lacedemonians at Leuctra, so that he gaind a [...] advantage over the Enemy by his moderation, than by his conquest, [...] that he was heard to say about it, was, that it was not so great a pleasure to him that he had won the day, as that his dear Parents were both liveing at the time, that they might have the joy of seeing their Country savd by their own Son.

[42] Pittacus being chosen Umpire in a Controversy betwixt a Father & a Son, before hearing the Cause he told the son, that in case he said any thing to his Fathers disadvantage he woud condemn him, and in case he said any thing to old Gentlemans—advantage, he woud condemn himself.

[43] Cato usd to say, that for his part he had rather go without his Reward for doing well, than without his punishment for doing ill, because a man's never in so bad a way as when he may transgress with impunity.

[44] Old age is a very desirable dish if it be tosst up with good sauce, and the best Sauce to that dish is a proper mixture of vertue & good nature, relisht with good Breeding.

[45] Lord Somers being askt how he coud arrive at such a charming excellence in Speaking? replyd by useing more wax than Honey. In imitation of Demosthenes, whose answer to that question was, by useing more oil than wine.

[46] Rage differs from madness in nothing but the length of the Fit, & so dos Love from Folly.

[47] Women love those best that gave them the first Pleasure & the first pain, their first Lover & their first child.

[48] The Richest man in the world is He who is the most intirely contented, for he wants nothing, while all the Princes of the Earth are poor enough to want Ten Thousand things. And their avarice encreases with their possession as the thirst of the Dropsical man dos with drink.

[49] [/10] Not He, who has seen many years, but He who has sufferd [m]uch decay, is old as a pair of shoes that are wore out in one week are older [th]an a tough pair, that are stil perfectly serviceable tho' they've been made [m]uch longer.

[50] There's nothing in this world so pleasant & delightfull, but cloys and Surfeits by constant useing, which ought to instruct marryd people, tho' they love never so affectionately, to make Raritys of one another, as much as custome & decency will permit.

[51] The desire of more always Spoils our Tast for what we have already. and when we woud carve for our Selves, we loose all the Enjoyment of what Provdence has thought best to carve for us.

[52] In the begining of any acute distemper Evacuations are proper to assist nature, but after it has weakend our Strength by continueing upon us any

time, all strong Physick not haveing any assistance from nature will join with the distemper & only help to oppress and destroy us. Says Hypocrates.

[53] Lysander was a great Lover of Stratagem, and woud rather get the better by art than by violence, to justify which he usd to say, that Hercules himself, where the skin of the Lyon was scanty used to help it out with that of the Fox.

[54] Bias usd to say, twas better being Umpire betwixt 2 Enimys, than betwixt 2 Friends, for in the first case you will make one of the Partys your Friend: but in the last you'll be in danger of makeing both your Enimys.

[55] General Seymour never coud speak a Word of French tho' he was bred up in the army. However after the Peace he went over to Paris, where he spent his time but awkwardly for want of the Language, and the rather because he coud not ask for the common necessarys. An Instance of this he gave one day when he had great occasion for a House of office. He inquird of his Landlord where he coud ease himself? [/11] but he not understanding the Generals English, coud make him no [sa]tisfactory answer. At last Mr Seymour was forced to make an an unseem[ly] sign to the man, which he readily apprehending pointed up stairs, & all round the court yard, adding partout Monsr ou il vous plaira. Damn you Partout, replyd the General. I must own you French are a very happy people, when all the liberty you have left is to Sh——t when you please.

[56] At Thebes the Statues erected in honour of the Judges were without Eys, & without hands, signifying that Judges ought never to have Respect of Persons, or to receive Bribes to byas their Judgment in any case.

[57] When Bias pronounct sentence of Death upon an unhappy Person he coud not refrain from Tears. One of his friends observing this tenderness, ask't him, why he woud not save himself that concern by acquitting the Criminal? replyd, that tho' he was obligd to fullfill the sentence of the Law, yet he was not obliged to cancel the sentiments of nature.

[58] A Common Swearer as often forswears himself as other People lye, because swearing is his manner of affirming & denying, and is only usd as an ornament of Speech and not as confirmation of the truth.

[59] All wit and knowledge except it be accompanyd with honour and Justice, degenerates into paultry Fraud & cunning. These are the more contemptible qualifications in men of parts, because they have them in common with Fools & Blockheads.

[60] Heraclitus usd to say, that men shoud be more Vigorous in defence of their Laws than in defence of their Walls & fortifications because without Laws no Town coud subsist long, but without Walls it might.

[61] Archisialaus usd to observe, that as there were most Deseases where most Physick was stirring, so where there are most Laws there never fails to be most injustice.

[62] [/12] Alexander usd to say, that a Wise Prince shoud keep his Friends by his Liberality, & gain his Enimys by his clemency and forgiveness.

[63] Agathon usd to say, that Princes woud do well to remember 3 things. 1st that they are to govern men, 2ly that they are to govern by Law, and 3ly that they are not like to govern always.

[64] The Death of an old man is like a ship's peaceable arrival at her Port, but when a Young man dys, tis like a ships being cast away by stress of Weather.

[65] Pindar haveing made humble supplication to the Gods, that the best thing in this world might befall him, He instantly sunk down and dyd in the arms of his Friend Theoxenus.

[66] Cleanthes usd to say, the certainest way to be rich in circumstance, was to be poor in Inclination.

[67] Some Souls & Bodys are as ill joind in constitution as some Husbands & wives are in Matrimony and are eternally plagueing one another.

[68] Somebody inquird of Denis the Elder if he was at leizure? God forbid said he, that ever a Prince shoud be at leizure from studying the happiness of his People.

[69] Envious persons are doubly miserable, when ill happens to themselves, & when good happens to other people.

[70] Envy follows a Man in prosperity as close as the shadow dos a Body in Sun-shine.

[71] Invidious People are knawd by Envy as much altogether as Iron is with Rust.

[72] Bion observeing an Envious man far gone in the vapours, askt him whether any ill had happend to himself, or any good to [o]ther People?

[73] [13/13] A Presbeterian Parson was complaining amongst the [. . .] that the Gospel at that time had not free passage. Yes it has said one of the Company a very free passage, for it gos in at one Ear and out at t'other.

[74] Colo Froud had marry'd a very tarmagant Wife, who usd to reprove all his misbehavior. This unhappy man was in company with a great Joker, who seeing the Colonel had no Ruffles, told him he observd that all men who were dutifull to their dear Wives, wore no Ruffles in token of subjection. As to Ruffles replyd the Colonel I cant say: but if I were not dutifull I am sure I shoud have Cuffs.

[75] In the sacrifices made to Jupiter the whole ceremony was performd with a most awfull & profound Silence: but in those paid to Juno the place rang

with the noise of Rattles ^{Timbrels} & Kettledrums, to betoken vocality of one sex and the Reserve of t'other.

[76] When 2 Beggers marry in France they call it a Match betwixt hunger & thirst, or between Famine & nakedness.

[77] In the Island of Zeylon in the East Indies they have Elephants Milk White, and some of them 18, & some 22 feet high. In Spain they have Asses that are 15 or 16 hands high.

[78] In the Island of Madecascar the Parots are as black as Crows, & they as well as all other Parots are very good to eat, not being Birds of Prey, but feeding only on grain and the kernels of fruit.

[79] Col° Groves so soon as he has lain with any Harlot makes use of the following Injection. He dissolves a Small piece of Allom in a pint of fair water, & puts in one spoonfull of French Brandy. This he injects morning & evening to prevent a Disaster, and oftener to cure one. Another man when he lay with any suspected nymph, usd to drink 2 Quarts of Epsome Water next morning, & then feard no ill consequence in the world, tho' [/14] [. . .] nymph was never so common or dangerous.

[80] At Moscow and other great Towns in Russia, they carry Houses to market as well as other Comoditys, & set them there as they ought to stand. They are taken in pieces again when they are bought, & carryd to the buyers land, and set up there in a very little time.

[81] Naturallists assure us that Crocodiles have no Tongues in which particular they are of so exact Emblems of Women as they are in the counterfeit Teers they shed to Surprize their unwary Prey.

[82] We are told that in the dark vaults of the Seraglio prodigeous Treasures of Gold & Silver lye buryed to the Value of more than 30 Milions Sterling, and much more in the Hideing Places of the Great Mogul.

[83] A Fine Woman that spends most of her time in adorning & admireing of her self, is at the same time both the Idol and the Idolater.

[84] Most Ladys allow discretion to be a fine Ornament, but few are fond of putting it on, because it gives 'em an old look: but giddiness & folly are much more their Favorites, because they make them appear young & lively, tho' age has set his broad O upon them.

[85] The great misfortune of giddy & inconstant Persons, is, that they act by humour & passion, and seldome by Good sence, which is always uniform, always the Same.

[86] How much more prudent it is to think with caution of a Business before hand, than with concern of it afterwards.

[87] A hare-braind Minister of State is by so much more pernicious than a Guide that is blind, or a Pilot that is drunk, by how much the mischeif he occasions is more general and extensive.

[88] [15/15] Young People have little prudence, and need much, to ballast the exceeding Levity of their Tempers, and steer them safe thro' the [. . .] tempest of their Passions.

[89] Aristotle observes very justly that Rich men are not so compassionate as the poor, because they are less acquainted with the distresses of want & calamity.

[90] T'is less trouble for a man to be Rich by contracting his desires, than by enlarging his Estate.

[91] Age ought not to be computed by the number of our years, but by the decay of our Persons, as a Building is not properly old that has stood a great while, unless it be grown ruinous and out of repair. Indeed Time will wear out every thing at last, but some antidiluvian constitutions with the help of temperance & regularity, will hold out a great while. Nobody woud have calld one of the Patriarchs old at 500, because at that age he was in truth hardly the worse for wearing, but was in the bloom of his beauty, and full vigour of his youth. A man was not then reacond at the years of discretion before a Hundred, nor a Woman before a Hundred and fifty. It was then Felony by the Law to have carnal knowledge with a Miss under four score, which was then the time of puberty, when her breasts began to swell, and her Fancy to figure all the Joys of Woman. In those happy days boys went not into breeches til 40, and Girles continued in hanging sleeves til 50, and after that were content to play with their Babys til three score. Age shoud therefore be dated from the declension of our Vigour, and the impairing of our Faculty, rather than from the time we have livd in the world, otherwise a batterd Debauchee that is fairly worn out at 40, woud be calld as young as an orderly Heart of Oak, who long after that retains all the strength and gaity of youth, and as able to do the Ladys very handsome Justice.

[92] Most People bear adversity with a better grace than they do Prosperity, the last is apt to make them insolent, but the first makes every Creature, but a French Man, humble. Distress in spite of our talk will make us wise, but success most commonly makes us foolish. This transports us out of our Sences, but that brings us back to our selves again. This Swell us into Gods: but that shrinks us into something less than Men.

[93] [/16] A yorkshire squire was commending the quick growth of the grass in

his County and to prove it affirmd to a North Britain that if a hare went overnight into a feild newly mowd you coud not see it in the morning. That's no such wonder replyd the honest Scot, we have feilds in Scotland where if you put a Horse over night youll not be able to find it in the morning.

[94] Paulus Æmilius for his mighty Victorys was honourd with a Triumph: but unfortunately one of his 2 sons dyd 5 days before, and the other 5 days after that solemnity. Under this affliction his Friends came to condole with him, to whome he said, he thought himself very happy, that Fortune was pleasd to accept of the dearest sacrifice he coud make her, for all the glorious successes she had heapt upon his country.

[95] The Spartans sufferd not their citizens to ramble into other Countrys, lest they might, according to the modern custome, import more of their ill customes, than their good. They likewise discouraged Strangers from comeing to Settle amongst them, for fear of bringing in Luxury along with them, and tainting their honest Spartans with Vice, and good breeding. Nay they deprivd their own Countrymen of all their Priviledges, unless they agreed to to train up their children in the Spartan discipline, and in their Stead, enfranchizd Strangers who woud submit to it.

[96] Instead of dedicateing Holidays to acts of Piety to God, & beneficence to man, we commonly profane them with intemperance & every kind of Disorder. Just as if we thought it the properest way of doing honour to the Saints, to make Devils of our Selves. Thus at a time when we ought to be thanking God for mercys past, we are fixing a Barrier against those that are to come, and instead of blessing his name, we are blaspheming it, & blotting out his Image in our Souls.

[97] General Kirk had a Present made him of a suit of Armour, of which he made no use himself, but when any of his Servants disobligd him, he made him put on the armour, and do all his business in it that day.

[98] [17/17] Along the Coast of Barbary if any Christian lye with a Moor Woman, he may take his choice whether he will turn Mahometan or be burnt alive.

[99] A Bishop was gravely reprimanding a loose clergiman for too great a passion for the Female-sex, and askt him why he woud not take a Wife? For a very good Reason, my Lord, said he, because I cant perswade any Husband to part with Her.

[100] When a young woman is to be marryd in Barbary, great care is taken to fatten her up against the wedding, and for that purpose they dont only

cram her adays, but 'wake Her 6 or 7 times anight, and stuff her with a kind of dumplin made of the heart of wheat, which is very nourishing.[4]

[101] A Bishop was argueing with the Earl of Peterborough against a standing army, God said His Lord^p I dont think souldiers the worst sort of men in the world; however I will venture to agree, that if you'll disband the Blackcoats, we will disband the Red, because there will then be less need of them.

[102] Compassion is a tender Passion that like deflowring tickles at the same time that it tears, and pleases at the instant it gives pain.

[103] Pity is one of those gentle wounds that bring its ^{own} balsome along with it. It is a disposition of the heart, which Saints delight most in, and the more we poor creatures partake of it, we more we ressemble our maker. For Compassion is inseparable from the Deity and seems to be an argument against the Eternity of future punishment, because in that case there will be no room for this sweet and heavenly frame of mind. The Blessed will certainly need it no more and the Damn'd will be utterly incapable of inspireing it so long as $^{their\ doom\ is\ everlasting}$.

[104] A discreet Person advisd his Friend how to behave in domestick life in these terms, never beat your Wife, said he, because she is by no means your match, nor don't scold with Her, because there you are not hers.

[105] [/18] There are 2 things which men passionately desire, & when they come are extreemly troublesome, a Wife, and old age; the first he may get the better of by her death, of the other only by his own.

[106] Most men, said old Socrates, are like Silly Fish, which are uneasy to get into the net of Matrimony, & undone (God knows) if they dont get out again. To the same purpose our own Chaucer sang, marriage is like a Revel-rout, those who are out woud feign get in, & those who are in woud feign get out.

[107] It was an observation that not only the wisest but the best men use the fewest words, and if it hold true in men, it certainly do's in women.

[108] Musicians are commonly a very Vile and dissolute kind of People, which made Diogenes say, that Lovers of musick had a great deal of harmony in their heads, & none at all in their hearts, and that they were the most reasonable people in the world, because they'd take Sound in payment instead of Sence.

[109] This Philosopher gave Astrologers as little Quarter by saying that while

4. Coded marks follow this entry.

they were with an impertinent curiosity peeping into the ^{stray} motion of the Planets ^{above} they knew nothing of the stray motions of their wives below.

[110] And of the Orators of his time, he said what we may justly say of ours, that they were extreemly generous in recommending more vertue to others, than they ^{cared to} possess themselves.

[111] Pittacus askt an old fusty Batchelor, why he never took it in his head to marry? because, said he, if I marryd a handsome woman, other men woud pretend to share in her charms: but if I marryd a homely one, I shoud be forc't to keep all her deformity to my self.

[112] Pericles had a fine Daughter that was addresst by two Lovers, one a Booby with a vast Estate, the other a man of parts and honour of a moderate Fortune. The wise General generously preferrd the latter, saying, he had rather his Daughter shoud be [19/19] marryd to a man, than to an Estate.

[113] Democritus usd to say, whoever marryd his Daughter to a good man had 2 children: but he that marryd her to a Fool or a Brute ^{woud soon} have none at all.

[114] The best Guard against the contempt of other People is to think, and Speak meanly of ^{our} selves.

[115] Next to a man's being governd by his mistress, the greatest Reproach is to be governd by his Wife.

[116] The only way to be spoke well of by all mankind is [. . .]⁵ all occasions to treat them with good nature & good Breeding.

[117] A mans Temper may be discoverd by his Conversation and his discourse will lead you to his real Inclinations, tho' he be able to out dissemble a Lover or a Statesman, or even a Jesuit or a Quaker.

[118] Romulus usd to observe, that you may judge of men as well of mettals by their Sound.

[119] Reason and good Sence are not so powerfull in the art of Perswasion as a sweet Pipe, and an Engageing action.

[120] An Athenian Coquet was boasting to Phocions wife of her Jewels, and the other ornaments of her Person (which by the way had been the Presents of a Husband who had enrich't himself by the Spoils of the People) my greatest ornament, replyd she, is, that I am the contented wife of a Husband, who after haveing commanded the army 20 years remains stil as poor as an ^{English} Poet, or a German Count. The D. of M . . . ^{poor woman} might make the same reply in our days.

---

5. The manuscript is torn and illegible at this point.

[121] King C. 2. of pious memory was over a bottle giveing him Self ayrs what Feats he was able to perform in the Feild of Love, and how oft he coud gratify a Lady in one night. Sir said the bashful E. of Rochester, I must not pretend to perform my Exercizes so many times as your majesty, but I believe I have a Sister that can.

[122] A Teeming Gentlewoman that had often been very whimsical in her Longing, took it into her head to long for One Inch only of a young Fellows Virility, who usd to come to the house. The Husband good man, apprehending the danger of crossing a Females inclination in her circumstances, _____ perswaded the man to [/20] [. . .] the longing of his Consort, by giveing her a Single Inch and more. He was to too good-naturd to refuse his friend that very small Request, and so Deary carryd him without loss of time to his Wife, but desird however, that he might be present, to see that the Knave gave her no more than she longd for. The Woman instantly put herself in guard, and the man made a Thrust, but unfortunately it proovd a home one. This made the Husband cry out with some concern, my Dear I'm affraid at this rate instead of an Inch you take an Ell. no—no—no Sweetheart, replyd she, the Inch I longd for is that [n]ext his—Belly.

[123] An Irishman by dint of modesty and good understanding, had prevaild with a Widdow to accept of him for her Lord & master. When the ceremony of the Stockin was over, and the candles carryd out of the Room to save the Relicts blushes, Dear Joy now, said the modest Bridegroom, will you choose to have your **Procreations** before you sleep or after? Both my Love, said she, if you please. Not both, replyd Tiperari, for I made a vow to St Patrick haveing once put a poor Female to death that way, never to mount the Guard more than once in a night. Very well answerd she, than my Dearest may please to rest in the Saddle all night, for you know twoud be—very wicked to break so solemn a vow.

[124] Alexander once sent honest Phocion a Present of 100 Talents: but he good man not understanding how he coud fairly merit so much bounty, askt the Person who brought the mony, how it came to pass, that he of all the Athenians came to be so high in his Majestys favour? T'is without doubt, replyd he, because he takes you to be a worthy honest man. I beg then said Phocion, that he'll please to suffer me to continue so, and so dismisst the ambassadour without takeing one penny of the mony.

[125] Epaminondas the brave Theban General receivd a complement from the King of Persia by the hands of one of his ministers, who in his masters name, intreated him to accept of a small present of one hundred Talents.

The rough General, instead of receiveing the mony, reproacht the Minister with the base intention to corrupt his Fidelity, adding at the same time, that if the King had any designs for the honour & interest of Thebes, he woud be his Friend for nothing: but if other wise, all the wealth of the East shoud not buy him off from [21/21] being his Enimy. glorious Integrity!

[126] A merry Priest to shew he did not think Matrimony a sacrament, & consequently that he was no Roman Catholick, usd frequently to joke on that holy Ordinance. Particularly once haveing marryd a Couple not very conspicuous for their vertue he gave them the following certificate in Metre

> This tenth of March in Stormy weather
> I joind this whore & Rogue together;
> And none but he that rules the thunder
> Can part this Rogue & whore asunder.

[127] Georgias when he was Old and infirm, was taken with a dangerous illness, & being askt by one of his Friends, if he was willing to dye? yes, said he, as willing to dye as I shoud be to run out of a ruinous old house, that was just tumbling upon my head.

[128] Plato being askt by one of his Disciples what might properly be accounted a Competency? replyd, Just as much as suffises to set a Man below Envy, & above contempt; or Enough to maintain him handsomely in the Port of his Education.

[129] The Earl of Portm . . . haveing a nestling in his gate & being newly honourd with the Green Ruban, his movement grew still more niggleing & convulsive than ordinary. Hereupon a Wagg being askt, where my Lord carryd his Thistle, made answer that by his motion he believd he carryd it in his A . . . e.

[130] When my Lord N . . . by a wound he had receivd in his arm, was obligd to cut it off, he sent it about with great Pomp to all the Officers of his Regiment, to shew 'em how much he had lost for his country. At the sight of this odd Shew, an officer being under the smart of his own wounds, coud not forbear saying, If my Lord woud shew us a Sight of terrour indeed he shoud send us his Head.

[131] The same Lord N haveing not so much Sweetness in his countenance, as he has in his Temper, took the Liberty of an old acquaintance with Brigadier Sutton (who had assurance enough for a Lieutenant General,)

and said to him, where dos your Modesty dine today? Why faith replyd the Brigadier, my modesty cant keep safer [/22] Company my Lord, than with your Beauty, and therefore I'll e'en dine with you.

[132] To a man, who inquird of Cleanthes what Person was the Richest among all his acquaintance, he made answer, He that knows how to contract his Wants to the Size of his Income: because if a man has no needs, he is certainly more at his Ease than that if he had both the Indies to satisfy them.

[133] Agreably to this Socrates usd to say, that man was the richest, who was content with the fewest Enjoyments, content being a natural wealth, of which we can neither be robbd nor defrauded, either by the great Villains of the World, or the Small.

[134] Sʳ R . . . S . . . haveing learnt in Turky to prefer the pleausres of the male sex, to those of the Female, reprovd his Brother the Br . . . r, for getting drunk continually & runing after vile Harlots, to the imminent danger of his health. Your concern is very obligeing Brother, said the Br . . . r, but my Carcase is very safe, for I never attack the Strumpets in Front, but in Rear. I'm very glad to hear that, replyd Sʳ Robᵗ, for no harm can follow from a tast so innocent and refind as that is.

[135] The Promises of Princes are made on a supposition of the things being just, and therefore an officer urging a promise made to him by Agesilaus King of Sparta, of something very unreasonable & unfit for him to do, into which he had been surprizd, the King told him he had only ac-quiesced, and not promis'd. For tho' a Prince shoud make good his very nods, where the Petition is just; yet where t'is either unrighteous or misbecomeing his Dignity, t'is a much greater crime to desire a Promise, than to break it.

[136] When a Man obtains a Promise of any thing that is impious to God, or unrighteous to man, the performance of that promise woud be a crime, and he ought to reproach himself for surprizeing another into a Promise, which he is bound by a higher obligation not to comply with.

[137] It was the advice of that good man Phocion, let your Promises be very moderate, that like the Gods you may be always found better than your word.

[138] [23/23] Heaven is the never failing confederate of a State that acts up-rightly, in which happy situation, as its Neighbours will have no provoca-tion to attack it, so if they do, they must not hope for success, because the arms of the almighty will fight against them.

[139] Cato usd frequently to say, t'is more happy for a man to meet with no Reward for his good actions, than no punishment for his bad, because nothing betrays us into such a train of mischief as Impunity.

[140] Bias was so good-natured, that he coud never pronounce sentence of death against any Criminal without Tears. One of his Friends observing his tenderness on that occassion, askt him how he coud find in his heart to condemn any Person he thought worthy of so much commiseration? Because said he, I pity the unhappy Wretches for their own sakes, but I punish them for the sake of the publick. However tho' I must put the Laws of the land in execution as a Judge, yet I cant repeal the Law of nature as a man, who is never so much the Image of his Maker, as when he is compassionate.

[141] Whenever the Emperour Trajan appointed a New Captain of his Guards his way was to gird him with a Sword, and to address him with this re-marquable Speech, Here wear this Instrument of Justice, & in case I gov-ern well, use it in my defense: but if ill, then draw it for my destruction.

[142] Bias often said, He had much rather be an Umpire betwixt two of his adversarys, than two of his Intimates, because in the first case He gaind a Friend but in the last he was sure to make an Enimy.

[143] Plato usd to teach his Disciples, that Vengeance continually waits on Gods right hand, ready to execute his Pleasure on all that presume to violate his sacred Laws. And if offenders are not immediately chastiz'd, yet their punishment, like a debt at Interest, will increase by forbearance.

[144] The same said frequently, that the vengeance of the Almighty, like his Providence, never nods, but grasping the glowing Bolt, is always ready to hurl it at the workers of Impiety.

[145] Divine Vengeance is drawn by Micaelangelo in the shape and Equipage of a young man, in the full Vigour of his strength, looking wth concern and Rage in in his countenance and pointing the blue lightening at Wicked & impious men. All around him are Furys and Harpys forging of Racks and wheels and other machines of punishment of every kind, and leading Plagues and Torments in [. . .] hopes to punish the Various trangressions of Mankind.

[146] [/24] Nothing proves the unaccountable power of the Fair Sex so evi-dently as old Fumblers, who continue to pursue the dear Sorceresses in spite of their aversion, & their own Impotence. This preposterous Inclination in men of an advanct age, is a kind of Tenesmus of the cod piece, which makes 'em fancy they've great need of a woman, and when they come to the point, alas! can do nothing.

[147] Old Fellows are often so short sighted they cant discern the danger of marrying of young women. For besides the great improbability that Bloom can have any likeing to Decay, tis very natural to guess, an old Gentleman can only teaze a young wench into Desires that must be satisfyd by Somebody else, and start a Hare for an abler Huntsman to catch.

[148] A worthless Fellow being Vain of his Family was told by a man of good understanding, that those Persons were most apt to boast of their ancestors merit, who had none of their own.

[149] An honest Scythian had the Barbarity of his Country cast in his teeth by a worthless Athenian, and being provoked at so senceless a Reflection, said thus to him, t'is better my Country shoud be a Reproach to me, than that like you, I shoud be a reproach to my Country.

[150] The nearest way to know other People well is to get intimately acquainted with our Selves. This is a piece of knowledge we Seldome think of tho' it be of the highest consequence to our vertue, and our happiness.

[151] True nobility consists in pleading noble Acts, rather than noble ancestors, and tis the foulest Reproach for a man to derive himself from a good Family, that is debased and disparagd by his Vices.

[152] A man of great Rank & merit in Antigonus's army, had a son that degenerated from the Vertues of his Father. He had however so [g]ood an opinion of himself, as to apply to the King for his Fathers places. But Antigonus soon gave him to understand, he never preferd People for their Fathers merit, but their own. And if ever he intended to receive any favours from Him, he must first take care to deserve them.

[153] One of Denis's courteours askt him with great Respect if he was at leizure? A Prince shoud never be at leizure, said he, from the noble work of makeing his subjects happy.

[154] [29/25]⁶ [. . .] of my countrymen, very weak and very windy.

[155] When Anaxagoras refus'd to tell an untruth to save the state, he was reproacht with haveing no regard or affection for his Country. You mistake said he, yonder is my Country, pointing up to Heaven, and tis but fair I shoud prefer the Place where I expect to live, to that where I am sure to dye.

[156] When Sylla had taken Preneste by storm, he order'd his Souldiers to put all the Citizens to the sword: but excepted out of this bloody order a Person from whome he had formerly receivd much civility. Yet this brave

6. Intervening pages missing.

man disdaind to owe his Life to the Destroyer of his Country: but rusht into the Throng of his unhappy Fellow Citizens, & mixt his Blood with theirs. When Sylla came to understand this, Im glad my Friend has had his humour, said he & has made himself remarquable to Posterity for publick Spirits. He is certainly beholden to me for giveing Him Fame, tho' he woud not let me have the pleasure of giveing him his Life. I am satisfyed to have shewn my gratitude to him his own way.

[157] Socrates usd to say that Perswasion was the sweetest Violence in the world, and that women know how to use that violence the most effectually, not only [with] their Words, but even with their Eyes, their Tears, and most of [all w]ith their Submission.

[158] Tis easyer to approach Persons that have the plague with out catching the Infection than to converse with vicious People without being tainted with their Vices.

[159] A Friend told Diogenes, that he was very ancient and for that reason shoud not fatigue himself so much as he did. How, reply'd the Philosopher, woud you have me lagg towards the end of the Race, when I ought to press forward with my utmost Speed?

[160] Simonides was askt whether he thought it better to be rich or ingenious? how can you ask that question, said the Poet, when you see the Wits pay much greater court to the Wealthy, than the wealthy do the Wits.

[161] A Man of Wit may sometimes abound in words, but a man of sence never, because he knows how to proportion his expression to his Subject. Most things may be comprehended in very few words, without abuseing the patience, and offering Violence to the Ears of the Audience. A long discourse rather tires than instructs, and looses all that force and Spirit, with which a Natural Brevity abounds.

[162] [/26] To be Subject to an arbitrary Prince is a more honorable Slavery, than to be Subject to his own more arbitrary Passions.

[163] When Agesilaus was upon his death-bed, he left it in charge with those about him not to suffer any Statue or other monument to be created to his Memory, for said he, if I have been so happy as to perform any great & good actions, I shall be best rememberd by them: but if I have behaved impiously to the Gods, or insolently to men, tis best I shoud be forgot, my Statues will but reproach me.

[164] When Demetrius was told that the Athenians had had the Confidence to demolish his Statues, he said with an air of contempt, my Comfort is, they cant demolish the Merit for which those Statues were created.

[165] A good understanding without the guidance of good Principles, is in danger of dengenerateing into ᵖⁱᵗⁱᶠᵘˡˡ Fraud, & Cunning.

[166] Diogenes usd to observe of the Astronomers of his time, the same thing that may be observd of Ours, that ʷʰⁱˡᵉ they affected to know abundance of the worlds above, they knew nothing of this below, & while they studyed the Courses of the Stars, they took no sort of Care of their own.

[167] Of the Orators he took the liberty to say, what has since been said of K. C. 2, that they seldome said a foolish thing, but never did a wise one. And he was so free with his brother Philoˢᵒphers, as to give it as his opinion of them, that their vertue commonly reach't no lower than their Beards.

[168] Duke Hamilton was kept out of his Estate by an unmercifull old woman, that had a monstrous Jointure out of it, til he was near Sixty years of age. So soon as this long-livd lady was dead, he said, twas a little hard upon him, to want bread til he was three score, and afterwards want Teeth to eat it.

[169] Clemenes usd to say, that the best way to hunt down Deer was with Hounds: but the best way to hunt down Females was with Flattery.

[170] The same usd to observe that sincere Scandal was not [ne]ar so abusive, as counterfeit Commendation.

[171] [31/27] Demosthenes being askt, wherein lay the great force of Rhetorick? returned for answer, in addressing your Self to the Eyes of the audience by gracefull action and to their Ears by harmonious sounds, rather than to their understandings by Solid argument.

[172] Tho' Demosthenes had a strong ambition to excell in Eloquence, yet he had at the same time a great Byas to pleasure. It was therefore necessary for him to get the better of this last inclination, that he might have leizure to apply himself more intirely to the first. But that he might be able effectually to shut himself up from runing after the gaitys of the Towne, he cut off one Side of his hair. This made him to ridiculous a Figure ᵗᵒ ᵍᵒ to Phryne's lodging, or any other place of diversion, til it grew again, which woud be some months, and in that time he hoped to have weend himself from hankering after Pleasure, which clouds the understanding, and cloggs all those Talents, which might otherwise distinguish us from the rest of of our Neighbours.

[173] A wicked West Indian boasted that he had washt the Black [. . .] White, and being askt by what art, he did it, he replyd, that in his youth he had an Intrigue with an Ethopian Princess, by whome he had a Daughter that was a Mulatto. Her he lay with, believeing no man had so good a right to gather ᵗʰᵉ Fruit as he who planted it. By this he had another Daughter of

the Portuguese complection ᵃⁿᵈ When she came to be 13 years old he ᵃᵍᵃⁱⁿ begot Issue Female upon her Body, that was perfectly white; and very honourably descended.

[174] The best way of being revengd of an adversary is to behave so unblameably, that people may wonder how any man coud be your adversary.

[175] When a woman can stand an obscene story without recoiling, can be tickled with lewd Images, & make the most of a double meaning, her Imagination & her Soul are already debauch't, and if she don't prostitute her Body too, she won't owe it to her modesty, but to her Pride or her Politicks.⁷

[176] Twas a standing observation of Isocrates, that Truth & Justice are the stedyest Allys any State can possibly have: because they never fail to bring the Auxiliarys of Heaven into the Feild ᵃˡᵒⁿᵍ with them.

[177] Sᵗ Chrysostome laid it down for a Rule, that whoever Sins much, & is not presently chastizd for it, has terrible things to fear from [32/28] the Divine Justice, which will never suffer to escape unpunish't the abuse of Gods patience: but He to whome vengeance belongs, will at last repay our Crimes with interest upon interest.

[178] The Divine Plato usd to teach that Justice always attends upon the Throne of the Almighty, to be employ'd as the last Remedy to reclaim Sinners, after all the gentle Methods of his Mercy have provd unsuccessfull.

[179] Lycurgus pronounc't it as good law, that when any Crime has been committed, til it be brought into Judgment, the guilt rests wholly on the Criminal, but if he be afterwards convicted, and the crime forgiven, then the guilt will be transferrd on those, who procure and grant the Pardon, & sooner or later the Divine Justice will require it at their hands.

[180] God is pleasd to punish some notorious Sinners here lest we shoud distrust his Providence in this world: but he dos not punish all lest we shoud disallow his Judgment in the next.

[181] The great Bands of Humane Society are Rewards & Punishments, without the first, Vertue will sicken, & without the last Vice will triumph; & in whatever State, these are not duly dispenc't, without respecting either Persons or Partys, Violence & corruption will shortly overturn it.

[182] That man certainly knows himself best, who thinks himself nothing, or worse than nothing.

[183] God coud have made this world without calamity, but then there coud have been no such vertues as Charity & compassion, no such thing as

7. This entry is followed by coded marks.

Invention & Industry, which depend upon our wants; Patience and Fortitude woud have had no being, and the world wou'd have sunk into Vice
and inactivity. Nay without the notion of Pain, tis a question whether we
shoud have any quick tast of Pleasure. At least not quite so lively a Tast as
we have at present, for as we are now formd, all our Enjoyments are
heightend and improvd by opposition.

[184] There is not a Brute in all Affrica so Savage, as a man divested of good
nature & compassion, indeed he ceases to be a human creature, who has
laid aside his best Distinction, Humanity. A cruel Person saves only the
figure of a man, and for the rest is partly Beast and partly Devil.

[185] [33/29] If the Delights of Heaven are capable of improvement, they will
be heightend, by the dismal prospect we shall have of the miserys & pains
we have escaped, which lye on the other side of the Gulph.

[186] Tis said of our Saviour, that he never was seen to laugh, the same has been
since observd of the Duke D'Alva: but tis recorded of Phocion that he
never was known either to weep or laugh.

[187] Arcesilaus was askt how it came to pass, that very many Disciples revolted
from the other sects of Philosophers, and went over to Epicurus. For the
self same reason replyd he, that many men dwindle into Eunuchs, but no
Eunuchs ever improve into men.

[188] Tis Strange that the Devil shoud be fobidden to attack us by open force,
and at the same time allowd to insnare us by Fraud & cunning. He
overmatches us as much in the last as in the first & without the divine
Protection we are equally liable to become his Prey in both cases. He is an
old Souldier and turns our own cannon against us, by subdueing us by
our Passions & inclinations.

[189] Sleep is dying for a time a Death of Short continuance, from which we
rise again every morning. And when we really give up the Ghost, we shall
only take a longer nap til the day of Judgment, wch perhaps will seem
much shorter than one single night dos now, because where there is no
thought, there can be no succession, no reasoning of time: But the moment of our Resurrection will seem to follow immediately the moment of
our Decease. We shall then be apt to call the time of our Expireing by the
name of last night, so short will seem to be the space of our Repose in the
Grave. And perhaps it was with relation to this seeming shortness of time
betwixt our Death & Resurrection, that our Saviour told the Theif upon
the Cross, that he shoud be that night with him in Paradise.

[190] We may justly pronounce, that Sleep is the Picture of Death in miniature,
and our riseing again the next morning the shadow of our Resurrection.

[191] Sleep pays us in Dreams for the large portion of time it takes from our lives, and they busy most of us as profitably, when we are asleep, as we busy ourselves when we are awake, and generally too with more Innocence.

[192] Some Sages are of opinion, that the Dead only dream in their Graves til the day of Judgment. Those who have livd well dream of all the pleasures of Paradise: but those who have been wicked of Furys, Harpys, and all the torments of Hell. Thus also the Theif upon the cross might be said to be that night with our Savior in Paradise; [34/30] because he woud soon be dead, and dreaming of all the Joys of [t]hat delightfull Place.

[193] A man was foul of his Friend for suffering his Wife to spend so much of her precious time in Sleep. Alas replyd the good man, twoud be well for me and her too, if she woud sleep til the Resurrection, that being the most innocent & peaceable part of her life.

[194] Plato was wont to tell his Disciples, that too much sleep, as well as too much labour woud blunt the sences, & stupify the understanding.

[195] He that believes in dreams is superstitious, but yet not near so superstitious as a Roman Catholick. For the first believes only in conceits, but the last in Contradictions.

[196] Georgias dozeing not long before his death his officious Friends woud often wake him to take such slaps as were thought necessary. After being tear'd in this manner for some time I beseech you said he suffer me to depart in peace, and dye a natural Death.

[197] The Emperour of Morocco keeps people constantly looking out upon an Eminence near Tangier, to discover when any ships of War pass thro' the straights into the Mediterranean, who send an Express away immediately to Mequinez to give the Emperour notice of it. Upon this intimation he causes proclamation to be made, signifying that tis by his Royal permission such Ships have passt into his Sea, of which he pretends to keep the Entrance. And he has his Ends, for his Subjects are generally stupid enough to believe it, & those few that know better only laugh in their sleeve and dare not disabuse their Neighbours.

[198] Alexander being advisd by some of his wily Generals to surprize the Enimy in the night refusd it with scorn, saying a brave man shoud disdain to pilfer a Victory in the dark. What a Triumph shoud be for Alexander to cut his Foes to pieces in their sleep!

[199] Conquest in any of the Viler arts is more disreputable than a Defeat in [...] more [. . .] So to excell in the meaner accomplishments is unhappyer far than right down Ignorance, and to hope for Credit by them, is paltry Vanity and a most pitifull amibition.

[200] When any person spake ill of Epictetus for any particular fault, instead of justifying himself, he only told him very [. . .] happy for him he knew not his other Infirmitys, for then [35/31] he had spoke much worse of him.

[201] As the Gout is commonly the distemper of an unexercisd Body, so Love is the Distemper of an unexercized Mind.

[202] Love is a longing desire to injoy any Person, whome we imagine to have more perfections than she Really has. It is a kind of Natural Idolatry, by which our Fancy sets up an Imaginary Deity, and then we falls down and worships it. Fancy will needs have a Woman to be an Angel, when perhaps, if Reason might have leave to speak, twoud tell us she was a Devil, and many a misguided marryd man knows this to be wofully true. If men woud therefore please to make a little use of their understandings when they judge of Females, or even of their Sences, they might discover in them so many imperfections of mind, so many impuritys of body, & so much perversness of Temper, that they woud never agree to sacrifice their Innocence, their character, their health, their Quiet, and Estates to injoy them.

[203] Poets and mad men tell us there is no Remedy for Love, but Experience that wont impose upon us, is positive there are two very sure ones, marriage and a Halter.

[204] There is nothing upon which grave advice is so much thrown away as upon Love. You may as well preach to a Tempest, or parry the Lightening, as perswade a Lover from his Inclinations.

[205] Socrates advises very sagely to avoid the kisses of a beautiful Woman as you woud the bite of a deadly Serpent, this may putrify your Body, but that will prison your Soul.

[206] Expose your Self only to those Dangers where in t'is gracefull to suffer, and glorious to perish said Demosthenes; to the same purpose was the advice of Socrates, never to engage in those Disputes in which twas infamous to get the better.

[207] A man never begins to be Wise, til he has first found himself out to be a Fool.

[208] Merit, like a Virgin blushes, stil most discovers it self when it labours most to be conceal'd.

[209] Excess of Desire is Love, and excess love is madness, and there fore when it pushes a man upon breaking the Laws, it ought like other acts of Lunacy to be forgiven.

[210] Love within decent Bounds, makes a bold man bashfull: but Love in extreams, makes a bashfull man impudent.

[211] That Love that enters at the Ears takes faster hold of our heart than that which enters in at the Eyes.

[212] [36/32] The certain way of recommending your self to any Persons freindship, is to shew him good will, and do him good offices.

[213] To true Friendship 3 things seem absolutely necessary, Mutual agreableness, a Mutual Endeavour to oblige, and Mutual Faith. Without the first no Friendship can begin, without the 2^d no Friendship can grow, and without the last no Friendship can continue.

[214] Never go to partake of your Friends good ^cheer without invitation: but go uninvited to partake of his afflictions.

[215] Aristotle being askt what Friendship was? said it was one soul animateing 2 bodys, so much ought friends to be animated with the same sentiments & inclinations.

[216] In the Province of Kuei Chu in China there is a Bridge 120 feet long, & 18 feet broad, all of one intire stone. The 2 Ends of this unweildy mass is placed upon a strong stone-Wall on each side the River, which makes it very wonderfull, by what machinery they—coud raise this prodigious stone upon it.

[217] A man was discoursing with some learning and much assurance, concerning the distance and nature of Heavenly bodys, Pray, good Sir, said Diogenes, you wou'd seem to be very knowing in the affairs above, how long may it be since you came from those Parts?

[218] Alexander being askt by his Father Phillip, why he, who was so swift of foot, woud never run at the Olympicks? because said he, I shoud disdain to get the better of any Competitors but Princes.

[219] Every Victory obtaind by Phillip broke the heart of his son Alexander, which his freinds observing, askt him why his Father's Successes gave him so much concern? Because, said he, if this old Fellow go's on at this ^mad rate, he'll ^leave nothing for me to conquer, & What joy can it be to a generous Mind, to owe all to his Father, & nothing to himself?

[220] [37/33] Cæsar once travelling over the Alps, and stopping at a little Towne as filthy & ^as poor as any in Scotland, told one of his Friends (who was saying that in such a Hole, surely there coud be no competition for Places) that he had himself rather be the first man in power there, than the Second in Rome.

[221] Aristotle once observing a Female too conscious of her own dear charms, & prideing her self in the richness, & good Fancy of her—dress, said, behold one Insect bloated with the gaudy Spoils of another.

[222] A foul-mouthed Fellow was once saying Scandalous things of Plato, in the hearing of Diogenes. The Cynick resenting the ill treatment of his Friend, forbear, miscreant, said he, for thou willst no more be believd, when thou speakst ill of Him, than he woud, if he spake well of Thee.

[223] One of Darius's captains put a Souldier to death for speaking unworthily of Alexander, telling him, that he recievd his pay, to fight against the Enimy like a man, & not to chatter against him like a Woman.

[224] Anaxagoras reading to Alexander a Lecture about a plurality of Worlds, the tears were observd to run down the kings cheeks. One of his Favorites askt him why he shewd so much concern? because said he, tis Vexatious to think, there are so many worlds, & we have not masterd one of them yet.

[225] Alexander desird the Lacedemonians to inroll him in the number of their Gods, to which old Damis returnd this answer, Let him be a God since he has a fancy for it tho' tis the humblest request he ever made in his Life. Henceforth he must own us his Superiors, it being much greater to be a God-maker, than a God.

[226] Croesus being cloathd in his Robes, with all his Pomp of Roialty about him, askt Solon, if in his whole Life he had ever seen so fine a sight? never sir said he, except only when I saw a Parrot, or a Peacock.

[227] In the time of your Prosperity pay your adorations to God the author of all your happiness, that so haveing made him your Friend, you may with Confidence fly to him in the day of adversity, when all other Friends are likely to abandon you.

[228] [38/34] It was a saying often usd by Xenophon, That the Gods delight to raise great things out of small, and produce small things out of great, that no good success may swell us up with too much confidence, nor bad affect us with too much dispair.

[229] The Athenians applauding Pitho[. . .]rius for some great Feats he had performd, Rob not the Gods, said he, of the Glory due to them, by imputeing this atchievement to me. It was their almighty hands that wrought it, while I alas was only the Vile Instrument they were pleasd to use for your service.

[230] Diogenes was askt which of all the Vipers was the most poisonous? To which he answerd, The Basilisk of those that are wild, but of the tame the Flatterer. one destroys wth the look, the other with the Breath.

[231] All men are soothd by handsome Flattery, yet at the same time we know, that tho' the bait appear tempting, yet there's a deadly hook under it. And the truth is, to flatter a—man is no better than to poison him with sugar

plumbs, to hang him up in a Silken halter, and cut his Throat with a feather. We stil love the dear enchanting Sound; tho' we are convinced t'is a Syran that makes it, that charms with no intention but to devour us.

[232] An Extraordinary Prude usd to stand in it, that People in love were exceedingly impudent; because they desire to be doing the lewdest thing in the world.

[233] He that reproves you with Reason is your Friend; because he seeks your good: but he that commends you without reason, is your Flatterer, & Seeks only his own.

[234] A Flatterer is in all respects a detestable character, & resembles the great Enimy of Mankind, by applying to our passions & our Frailtys, & never to our understanding. From thence we may fairly conclude, his intent is to surprize and deceave for his own advantage, and our undoing.

[235] [39/35] Of all the Flatterers in the world, said Thales, be sure to avoid Him that is the most dangerous & most difficult to guard against, Your Self.

[236] Mr Pope understanding Mr C . . . was listing himself amongst the Wits complemented him with the following extempore verses,

> C . . . y pretends to be a Wit,
> For what?
> Is it because he has writ?
> No, because he has not.

[237] You had much better become a Prey to Vultures than to Parasites, for they will only devour you when you are dead: but these while you are alive.

[238] The 3 things in the world that ever were found out to gratify the nicest palate, were the Trunk of an Elephant, the tail of a Beaver, and the paw of a Bear, & all three of 'em woud be a Feast for the Sophi of Persia, the Great Mogul, and the Emperour of China.

[239] Bias being askt by a young Debaucheé what vertue was? made him no answer, and being farther askt the reason of his silence, told him, t'was because he inquird after things that did not belong to him.

[240] Tis for the Gods only to do as they please, said Aristotle, but for poor man, he must do as he's bid.

[241] Amongst the Jews t'was a Custome to give wine mixt with myrrhe to such persons as were going to dye—a painfull & violent death, with a belief that it gave them spirit and made them suffer with more fortitude, & less sence of pain. So far we find they woud have favourd our Saviour just

before his crucifixion: but he refusd it, as haveing the much greater Support of Innocence, & a firm Reliance upon Gods mercy.

[242] The Jews also fancyd that Vineager woud revive and collect the Spirits of one going to expire, and prolong his life for some moments, for which reason they put some in a Sponge, and offerd [41/36] it to our Saviour upon the cross, to give him time to see if Elias woud come and rescue him.

[243] A Foul mouthd Fellow fell upon Demosthenes once in a Publick Place, and said a thousand injurious things to him. To all wch he made no other Reply but only this, Be easy Friend, I yeild you the Victory, neither shall I engage in a Quarrel, wherein it woud be scandalous to get the better.

[244] After Alexander had defeated the Persian Army, some of his officers told him, how charmingly handsome the Queen & Daughters of Darius were, & presst him to see them. The King refus'd, because they were so dangerously beautifull, ading, we shoud make a mean figure, if after haveing got the better of the men, we shoud suffer the women to get the better of us. However he did venture to see these fine Ladys after wards, & got as much glory by vanquishing his Passion then, as he had by vanquishing his Enimy before.

[245] As the man that eats much, is not the healthier for it unless he digests what he eats: so neither is he that reads much one whit the wiser, except he digests what he reads, and as the stomach of the one, so the head of the other will be filld with Cruditys.

[246] Phillip being urged by his Friends to banish a Scandalous Fellow, who had utterd vile things of him; By no means reply'd he, that woud be the way to have the Villain go and abuse me all the world over. No, Ill take a handsomer Revenge, and behave in such a manner as to prove him an infamous Lyer to all mankind.

[247] An honest Greek was told as great news, that an abusive Fellow had spoke well of him; Surely said he, the Rascal had heard I was dead, for he never spoke well of any man liveing.

[248] A Spartan Dame had losst her onely son in a battle fought for the Liberty of Greece,—and being condoled upon it, you shoud rather give me joy, said she, for my Boy has gloriously performd the Deed for which I brought him into the World, he dyd in defence of his dear country.

[249] [42/37] Aristotle being askt how it came about, that he whose Teeth were so good, came to have a stinking breath? because, said he, abundance of secrets are shut up in my mouth, and corrupt.

[250] A man of distinction haveing invited a Lawyer to dinner was surprizd at his silence, & reproacht him that he whose Trade was speaking, shoud take that occasion of holding his Tongue, since talking is my business no wonder I shoud hate it, reply'd he, besides you are to understand that the most difficult Rule in the art of Speaking, is to know when to be silent.

[251] A Lady desireing to learn Rhetorique, sent for Isocrates, who was so ungallant as to demand twice as much as he had for teaching the men. But she asking the Reason of such an Imposition, the oratour let her know, that he was not only to teach her the art of Speaking, but also the art of holding her tongue.

[252] Unbosome to no mortal what ought not to be told, for how can you expect, that another shoud keep your Secret, when t'is plain you are not able to keep it yourself.

[253] A Female that is hard to be tempted to frailty her self, is not so ready to suspect her Neighbour; Innocence is ever less uncharitable than guilt, which takes every appearance by the worst handle, & construes every look, every motion, & every word in the most ill-natur'd sence, as knowing by fatal Experience the full Extent of Human frailty.

[254] A certain Prince inquireing of Alcamenes, how he might best preserve the Empire he had gaind? was answerd, by governing your Subjects in such a manner, as may give them an opinion, that no other Prince coud govern them better.

[255] Whatever you woud desire your Subjects to do, said Dion, be sure to practice your self, because men have naturally more regard to the Example of their Soveraign, than to the penalty of his laws.

[256] The first Lesson in the art of governing well, is to have learnt thoroughly to obey, because that man will [43/38] certainly make the best Soveraign, that knows how to make a good Subject.

[257] A Bachelour unknowing in the cloying charms of the Female Sex, was asking a marryd man what was meant by a man & his wife's being one Flesh? Oh say's the Husband when you come to be marryd you'll find out the reason, for when you lay your hand upon your wives Belly, twill give you no more disturbance than if you laid it upon your own. But to make you amends youll find, that tho' you are but one Flesh, you will be 2 Spirits.

[258] The only way to gall—an Enimy to the Soul is to behave your self without reproach, and every body will speak well of you in his Hearing.

[259] A merry man was upbraided for spending his Estate, why said he twas better I shoud wast my Estate than that that shoud wast me. for had I kept

it, I shoud either have bloated my self with luxury, or pind away with carking cares & covetousness.

[260] A Reverend old Gentleman being askt why he wore his Beard so long? replyd, while I carry my grey hairs in sight, I shall be admonisht to commit nothing misbecomeing of them. thus a wise man stil catches at every thing that may be an incitement, & invitation to Vertue.

[261] T'was the advice of honest Cato, that since the unavoidable Inconveniences of Old age are but too many, to take care, how we add to them the Reproach that comes along with Vice, and the and the Distempers that come after it.

[262] Gorgias being askt by what Rules it was he arrivd at so advanc't an age, made answer, by indulging neither my Ease, nor my appetite

[263] If a man well-inclind converses much with lewd and dissolute Persons, he'll find it much easyer to suck in their Vice, than instil his own vertue, because our frail nature disposes [44/39] us to receive the Infection of Evil, much sooner than of good.

[264] After I percieve a young Fellow to take pleasure in the company of Libertines, I am at the end of my curiosity to know his character, for a man can't be much pleasd with vice in other people, without being quickly tainted with it himself.

[265] Somebody was calling Calisthenes a very happy man before Diogenes, for that he was distinguisht so much by Alexander, as to be askt to eat at his own Table, & be always near his Royal Person. An arrant slave, said the Cynick! who must neither dine nor sup but just when the King pleases.

[266] As a good Sailor knows how to shape his sails to every change of wind so dos a wise man know how to suit his Inclinations to every turn of Fortune.

[267] Tis a most excellent frame of Mind in any Person, the more highly he is exalted in his Fortune, to be the more lowly in his behavior, and to esteem the good things of this world to be only lent, and not given him by Providence, because he must be accountable for the right employment & disposition of them.

[268] The Path of Fortune is a slippery Path, wherein it concerns a Man to take great heed to his going, said Dion, for as it is difficult to keep ones feet in one, so tis to keep ones moderation and equality of mind in the other.

[269] Tis a great objection to the building a fine house, and makeing fine gardens, that we dont foresee who will dwell in the one, or eat the fruit of the other, for as to our Selves, we know not whether our Lives or our Fortunes will hold out til they are finisht, and then who can tell but our mortal Enimy will enjoy them

[270] Tho' the Invention of Condums has an air of Lewdness in it, yet since mankind are so mad after Women, that they cant forbear ventureing all for them, the great mischiefs they prevent seem to render the makeing of 'em not only lawfull, but meritorious. For this reason the nuns in Portugal make them, for the service and preservation of those who have not vow'd perpetual chastity, and with the pious design too, that while men are under the delay and preparation of puting on these Guards, [/40] they have leizure to bethink themselves, and be diverted from their wicked purposes.

[271] How easy and resignd ought mankind to be in every change of Fortune, since tis not doubted but all Events are directed by infinite Wisdom prompted by infinite goodness?

[272] If the angels were not so good naturd as to pity us, they woud be extreemly diverted with our grave impertinence, which is commonly most ridiculous, when it woud appear most wise, and most considerable.

[273] The world is now come to that degree of charity, as to think him a good sort of a man that is not monstrously and diabolically wicked.

[274] Socrates had a modesty which woud much better become most of our modern Authors, for being asked why he woud not oblige the World with some of his works, replyd, t'woud be a pity to spoil so much paper.

[275] Whoever reflects how wretched a Creature man is, will not be surprizd at any foolish thing he do's, or any frightfull thing he suffers, said Isocrates.

[276] Aristotle had a despicable opinion of humane Nature, by saying, that man was the very center of Fraility, the Jest of Fortune, the Emblem of Inconstancy, they Prey of Time, and the Shuttlecock of Envy & compassion, and for the Rest nothing but Flegm and melancholly.

[277] Approach not the tremendous Throne of God wth with any petition for Prosperity, but pray for such a portion of grace & wisdome, as may enable you in all conditions to behave in a manner suitable to the Dignity of your nature, & the firmness of your dependence.

[278] The compliment most in fashion in the Court of Alexander, was to treat him as a God. He encouragd this monstrous Flattery for politick Views, and in some sort too, to gratify his own Vanity. However being afterwards wounded in the Leg, and a great flux of bloud issueing at the wound, he pleasantly told his Flat-terers, [/41] they had been excessive in their Complements, for twas mere bloud that flowd from his wound, and nothing like that same Ichor, which was said to circulate in the Veins of the immortal Gods.

[279] However his Mother Olympia, observing that he swallowd greedily

enough the notion of being descended from Jupiter, desird him not to make a ^{needless} Quarrel betwixt Juno & her, nor for the pleasure of exalting himself into a God, make a whore of her, and a Cuckold of his Father. Therefore pray, dear Son, said she, condescend ^{for once} to be a man in ^{pure} pity to your Relations.

[280] Peace & gaiety of mind are so necessary to our happiness, that health of Body is hardly a Blessing without cheerfulness of Spirit. This continual Feast, as Soloman justly calls it, is rarely to be had without Temperance & Exercize, the 2 great Instruments of all our vertue & felicity. This made Democritus say that whoever is lazy or intemperate, is a Traytor to his own happiness.

[281] A Life of Business without diversion is as tiresome as a Long Journey without an Inn, & baiting by the way is not more necessary in one case, than Recreation is in the other. Thus Plutarque usd to say, that Pass-time is the Sawce to make labour and fatigue go downe. And as the Strings of a Musical Instrument are screwd up & down to make them more harmonious, so must the Facultys of a man be, to render them more Vigourous & sprightly.

[282] Gellius was entertaind at the house of a Gentleman, who was infamous for treating his servants with Severity, and even grutch't them time sufficient for their natural Rest. In return he invited this hard hearted master to his house, where after dinner he calld in his young Fry of Slaves, who danct merrily before him. His Guest inquireing how he came by so great a number of young slaves? My servants divert themselves with getting these ^{said he} while yours are set to work about something not half so pleaseing to them or so profitable to their master.

[283] Plato surprizeing one of his Disciples at Hazard, reprovd him smartly for it. The young man excusd himself by assureing him he playd but for a Triffle. That may be, replyd the Philosopher, but the Itch of gameing is a Distemper that will grow upon you, and Habit is a Downhill path, in which you will not be able to stop your self when once you are set a runing, til you come to the bottom of your fortune.

[284] [/42] The character of Wisdome is to think of every thing just as it is, and esteem it as it deserves. If men shoud be tryd by this Rule, how few will merit the Reputation of being wise? For most of us, God knows, are over fond of triffles and trumpery, and undervalue things of the highest worth and concern.

[285] Men may properly enough be divided into 3 classes, The Fops & the Fools who excite our mirth, the cruel and the criminal that provoke our hatred,

and the painfull and unfortunate that move our Compassion. None stir up our Love, and admiration but our selves.

[286] A Gay man who had Spent the best part of his life in the fashionable pleasures of the World, began to reflect upon the wrong courses he was in very seriously. His companions inquird of him why he, who usd to be all joy and good humour, was of a sudden grown so reservd? To this he replyd in this manner, I have long enough made you Rakes merry here below by my follys, I will now go and make the saints above merry by my Repentance.

[287] Accustome your self by all means to practice the most desirable Qualitys, for tho' they be never so difficult & disagreable in the begining, yet **Habit** will soon make them both easy and delightfull.

[288] Socrates once harangd the Mobb in a manner that pleasd them extreemly: but their applause was such a Surprize to Him, that turning about to his Friends, surely, said he, I must have been talking very foolishly, else I shoud never have been thus honourd with the approbation of the multitude.

[289] In like manner when Antisthenes was told how great a favorite he was with the Common People, God grant then said he that I have not done something exceedingly wrong.

[290] Archesilaus was askt how it came to pass that Philosophers of every sect revolted to Epicurus but none of his Disciples revolted to them? Because said he men frequently become Eunuchs but Eunuchs never become men.

[291] St Basil usd often to say, that the Devil baits his infernal hook with Pleasure, to catch the Silly Gudgeons of mankind.

[292] [/43] A Lady of Sparta upon the news that her son had scandalously turn'd his back upon the Enimy wrote this concise Billet to him, Either purge your Character or poison your self and hide your shame forever in the grave.

[293] Anacharsis was in Company where the Conversation ran upon ambition, & after every body had declard what Empires he woud choose to be at the head of, he told 'em for his part he was so reasonable he desird to extend his Command only over 3 Single Subjects, his Tongue, his Belly, and his Codpiece.

[294] The best way for a man to be easy, and preserve his good humour & his Quiet, is, not to set his heart upon the perishable Things of this life, which will be sure to leave him in the lurch, said Democritus.

[295] If you perform a handsome action with labour, the labour soon disap-

pears and the vertue remains; but if you do a Vile thing for the sake of Pleasure, the Pleasure will vanish, but the Infamy stick by you even in the Grave.

[296] St Basil tells us, that pleasure as beautifull as it appears to be in the Eyes of young People, has nevertheless a very monstrous Posterity, for t'is the own-mother of Sin and the Grandmother of Death and Damnation.

[297] Tis a more noble conquest to get the better of what we love than of what we hate: For what we hate, if it do its Worst, can but destroy our Bodys, but what we love, may destroy both Body and Soule.

[298] A Gross Body is very rarely the habitation of a great Soul, for she is mired in that foul situation, and can never exert her sprightly Facultys. She is heavy, she is cloudy, and Sympathizes, with her unweildy organs. From hence t'is observd, that a Spare Body is most commonly the Lodging of a Sprightly mind.

[299] Recreation recruits the Spirits of young people as much as sleep, while too intense an application exhausts the Vigour of the mind, as well as of the Body. And tis an observation as old as Democritus, that a Bow, a Violin, and a Boy are the better for being sometimes unbent, relaxed, and unbraced.

[300] [/44] The Oracle pronounc't Socrates the wisest of Men because he had the penetration to find out, and the humility to own that he knew nothing.

[301] T'was observd by Bion, that God dos not give, but only lends the good things of this world, & by no means has conveyd the property of 'em to us, but only the use.

[302] Socrates usd to say, that as discreet Mariners are provided against every change of weather, so ought a wise man to be provided against every change of Fortune, for tho' the Sun shine bright, the wind blow fair, and all nature seem to flatter, yet we shoud have every thing in readiness to defend us against a Storm, whenever it descends upon us.

[303] Voluntary labours make those easier that are involuntary; so the wants & mortifications we chuse to undergo our selves, are usefull to make us support those which Providence has alloted for us.

[304] A Beggar thought to move the more compassion by saying twas the first time he had askt Charity. God forbid then, said a Gentleman, that I shoud enter you into so vile a Trade, by giveing you the first handsel.

[305] Some inquisitive person askt Diogenes why men were so forward to bestow their Liberalitys upon Common Beggers: but woud give nothing to a poor Philosopher, T'is because said he, men don't know but it may

come to be their own case to be lame and blind and needy, but they ^{are}
secure enough of never comeing to be Philosophers.

[306] There are 3 degrees of Charity ^{the} first when we relieve those Persons who
suffer for Righteousness Sake, or whose vertue has been the cause of their
distress. The 2^d sort is, when we are bountifull to such as have been
impoverisht by unavoidable misfortune. But the 3^d and lowest charity is,
when we are good to those whose Vices or Indiscretions have reduced
them to a necessitous condition. In all competitions for our Generosity
we are [/45] obliged to preferr the first or the Second, and put them in the
place of our Benefactors.

[307] An impudent Begger modestly askt a young Spendthrift to bestow a
Talent upon a poor man in great want. Art not thou an unconscionable
Dog, said the Gentleman, to ask a Talent from me, when you ask only an
Obolus from other People. Very true an't please your Hon^r replyd the
Begger, but then I hope to receive more from them another time: But you
are rideing full speed thro' your Estate, and I fear twill be the last time I
am like to tast of your charity. For this Reason I ask for as much as may
enable me to relieve you, when you have brought your self into my
Condition.

[308] Solon amongst many other good Laws enacted one, prohibiting any
orator under a severe penalty, from useing any gracefull action or other
ornaments of Speech, to captivate the affections, and surprize the Reason
of the audience. It was likewise a standing order of the Court of Areo-
pagus, for the Lawyers to use neither Exordium nor conclusion in their
pleadings, for fear of perverting the Judges and casting a mist before their
understandings. This Law prevail'd among the Arabians likewise, who
woud not suffer their oratours to make use of any Flourishes in their
publick discourses for fear of imposeing upon the People.

[309] A man must be very hard-hearted that feels not some concern for the
death of a Wife notwithstanding she may have had some failings, for an
Ox will weep when his yoke fellow comes to dye, tho' he may sometimes
have pull'd against him, and perhaps have galld his neck by his restiveness.

[310] If in publick Communitys custome obtains the force of a Law, Habit in
private Persons is more arbitrary, & rules as absolute as a Tyrant.

[311] There is this advantage in habit, that if we are so happy as to accustome
our Selves to great & vertuous actions, tho' they be difficult and disagreable in the begining, yet habit will make them in a little time both easy &
delightfull, and by use we shall grow as fond of 'em as of Coffee &
Tobacco.

[312] [/46] Alexander being ᵃˢᵏᵗ to which he thought himself most indebted, to Phillip or Aristotle? to the latter said he, for my Father only gave me life, and made me a King: but my Tutor gave me Learning, and made me a Hero.

[313] The greatest Title that ever was given to Man was first given to Cicero, that of Pater Patriæ, the Father of his Country than which ambition it self cant form a character more desirable.

[314] Q. Ligarius was accusd of haveing sided with Pompey against Cæsar, which made that great man determine to punish him. However Cicero venturd to undertake his defence, and Cæsar very desirous to hear what he coud say in so bad a cause, came to hear him, with a Fixt Resolution however not to be movd by his arguments. But that charming Oratour toucht the passions of the Hero so powerfully, that he let the Paper containing the Condemnation of Ligarius drop out of hand, and was forct in spite of all his Resolution to pardon him. So great is the enchantment of Eloquence, and the sweet art of Perswasion.

[315] Some Rules for preserving health.

1. Use as much exercize as will invigorate the Spirits, and not wast them excessively, as much as will make you perspire, but not sweat.

2. Never eat when you have fatigu'd your self with too much exercize, because then the Spirits flag, and are more unfit to to carry on the necessary business of digestion.

3. Never eat til hunger calls upon you, and leave off before your appetite is fully satisfyd; eat rather often than much at a time.

4. Eat of no more than one thing at one time, and let your drink be only water, or at best but wine & water.

5. Either eat no Supper at all, or something very light and cooling, at 3 hours distance from the time of going to bed.

6. Spunge your self all over with cold water every day to prevent takeing cold, and haveing so hardend your self, open your windows whenever the air is dry, because nothing is more wholesome than the open air, if it be not too much cloggd with moisture or tainted with ill smells. and because air is so beneficial, never draw the curtains close about you when you lye in bed.

[316] [/47] Aristotle usd to say, that **Hope** was the dream of a wakeing man, and happiness the dream of a man sound asleep.

[317] Socrates said, that hope is as barren without Industry, as is a woman woud be without the assistance of a man.

[318] Hope is a Harlot that's common to all Mankind, & like a Harlot flatters & deceaves all that have any commerce with it.

[319]   Hope is the last comfort & Cordial of the Afflicted in this world, who have always that Refuge left: while tis the peculiar misery of the damn'd, that their case is utterly desperate.

[320]   A wise man may be distinguisht by the probability and attainableness of his hopes; while the expectation of a Fool is commonly unpracticable and Visionary.

[321]   As a wise Mariner never trusts himself to Sea with one Anchor only, & as an experienced Merchant ventures not all his Effects in one bottom; So ought a Man of Sence to take care, never to center all his hopes in a Single Event, that by miscarrying may leave him without Resource, said the divine Socrates.

[322]   At Sea, have all things in readiness in fair weather, that when it comes to blow, you may the better ride out the Storm: and at land, in the years of Plenty make provision against a Famine, and in Success prepare against adversity. In youth lay up a Store proper for old age, and in health make all ready against sickness, for every thing is liable to change in this unconstant world.

[323]   A man that is frugal and industrious can have few other wants, than such as he imposes on himself, and no want that is voluntary can be very unfortunate.

[324]   When Diogenes found by the Bill upon the door that the House of an idle Drunkard was to be sold, I thought, said he, that after so many Debauches he woud come to vomit up all he had.

[325]   A conquest the most difficult, as well as the most glorious any Hero can obtain, is over his own unruly Passions; & this is the only conquest of which a good naturd man woud be ambitious, because tis beneficial to others, as well as to himself. And thus it is a man may be a Conquerour without being a Robber and Destroyer of mankind, like Cæsar & Alexander.

[326]   [/48] Diogenes being askt what sort of Wine he liked best, that, said he, which I drink at free-cost, which woud have become a Parasite better than a Philosopher.

[327]   Asses are very lustfull Creatures, and the best provided for makeing Love of any animals whatsoever, and in that affair at least they are not sloathfull. In hot Countrys t'is very common for one Horse-ass to caress another with as much gusto as the most refin'd Gentleman, and with much more Vigour. So that man can by no means boast that he's the only Brute of the creation addicted to male-venery: but in that the Dull ass is both his Rival & Superiour.

[328]   Women have so much regard for their good looks, that they will undergo

more fatigue & Self denyal to appear charming, than for any other consideration. And some amongst that dear Sex there are, who take a Clyster every night, & keep several Issues runing about their sweet persons, for the sake of their complexions. and none of em I beleive will say, they suffer all this to please themselves; or one another.

[329] Socrates usd to say, that the way to be rich in purse, is to keep your passions poor, and the ready road to be great in the Esteem of others, is to seem little in your own.

[330] The character of a wise man, is not to be without passions, but to keep them, as he ought to keep his Wife, in due Subjection, else like her, they will make him do abundance of very foolish things.

[331] St Chrysistome usd to say, t'was impossible to be a Saint or a Hero without strong passions, but then those passions must, like a high-mettled Horse, be brought to the manage, Else instead of a Saint, the owner may prove a Devil, and instead a Hero, a Tyrant.

[332] Conformable to this notion, Pythagoras was wont to to inculcate, that no thing is so tyranical as our Passions, when they have dethroned Reason, and usurped the government of our actions; very like the tyrany of Slaves, who exercize the most insolent dominion over their natural Lords, and never fail to add cruelty and injustice to their usurpation.

[333] [/49] The most agreable Companions in the world are a good conscience, & a cheerfull spirit, and to those who are so happy as to injoy them every Fast is a Feast, & every day a Holiday, all their greif is joy, and their pains are mere titelation.

[334] Many things are hard to get, as a good Friend, & a good Wife: and many things are hard to keep, as a good name, and a good husband.

[335] Never do a shamefull thing with the hopes of keeping it a Secret, because tho' it may escape the knowledge of Men, yet you can never conceal it from God, & your own Conscience; and if it shoud remain a Secret in this world, yet it will be exposd, & made very publick in the next both to men & angels.

[336] No Man is so qualifyd to undergo the tyrany of an arbitrary Prince, as he who has been accustomed to be a Slave to his passions. This is the true reason, that private Vertue is the safest Guard of publick Liberty, witness the Commonwealths of Greece and Rome of Old, and of Switzerland & the Seven Provinces in Modern Story.

[337] Mortify your Passions continually, said Isocrates, or sometime or other they'll mortify you.

[338] A Grave man askt Philoxenus the Poet, why he never introduced any

Women into his Plays, but bad, since Sophocles had introduced none but good? The reason's plain, said the Poet, because Sophocles shewd women as they shoud be: but I follow nature, & shew them just what they are.

[339] Somebody brought word to Socrates, that his Wife had hang'd herself upon an apple tree, I protest said the Philosopher, that's the very best bearing Tree, I ever knew in my life.

[340] Aristippus advized an intimate Freind of his never to marry, for said he, in case your Spouse be handsome, other men will be apt to Share in her Charms, but if she be ugly, you'll be forced to keep all her Deformity to your self.

[341] There are 2 things for which t'is impossible to find any Remedy on this side the Grave, Old Age, & a bad Wife.

[342] [/50] The Ægyptians of old never allowd their Wives any sandals, because they had no business to gad abroad, but to stay at home & take care of their Familys. For the same Domestick reason, the Chinese make the Feet of their Women so smal by binding them up, that they are not able to walk without help, but need the aid of a Go-cart like Children. According to this notion Hyperides usd to say, a Woman shoud not appear out of her House, til she is old enough for people to enquire whose Mother she is, & not so young as to have it askt, whose Wife she is, or whose Daughter?

[343] When a Wife dresses to stay at home, tis to engage the affection of her Husband: but when she only dresses to go abroad, it may be suspected, that she dos it with a traiterous intent to tempt other people.

[344] After Paulus Æmilius had divorced his Wife Papyria, his Friends expostulated with him, for parting with so prudent, so beautifull, & entertaining a Lady. To all this He made them no other Reply, but holding out his foot, look ye Gentlemen, said he, is not this a handsome shoe, is it not fashionable, & the Seams neatly wrought, yet it may pinch me damnably for ought you know?

[345] There is a **Critical Minute** in which almost any thing may be brought about: but the great Secret lys in nicking it exactly. It requires penetration & vigilance to discern times & seasons, and Resolution to use them effectually when they offer.

[346] We all reason the time of Life very Short, and yet squander it, as if it were never to have an End. But I must put the Ladys & fine Gentlemen in mind, who lavish theirs at best in sleep and Triffles, that loss of time is the unhappyest Loss in the world, and hath this peculiar Ressemblance to the loss of our Souls, that t'is never to be repair'd.

[347] The Labours & sufferings of a Christian are only for a short time, but his

Reward is for a long Eternity. Those below our concern, this beyond our Expression. Vast disproportion!

[348] **Time** will unmask our Secrets, and unveil all those dark Disquises that hide Truth at present from our knowledge; and then all our Hypocrisy towards God, our Falsood to men, & our Treachery against our Selves will be thoroughly laid open & exposd, to our utter confusion.

[349] [/51] The Top of all Religion is Obedience, & the most acceptable Sacrifice to God is Charity to men, & Justice to our Selves. God is so good as not to regard the price of the gift, but the purity of the heart. Licurgus therefore instituted Sacrifices of small value, that his Spartans might not be deter'd by the Expence of the Offering, from the constancy of the duty: but that they might compound for the cheapness of the Service, by the honesty of the intention.

[350] Solon usd to call that a happy Government, where the People reverence the Magistrate, & the Magistrate the Laws.

[351] A Young Fellow that had many Qualifications for Intrigue, was at first setting out discouragd from it by two very unlucky accidents. He had taken abundance of pains wth a Young Gentlewoman to bring her to listen to his passion, and at length perswaded her to a Rendevous. The Time and place were agreed upon, and just as our Gallant was approaching the Scene of joy, a very unsavory shower descended from a window upon his head, which made him ^utterly unfit at that time for the Embraces of a Mistress, and the ^first disappointment was ^so unpardonable he never coud perswade the Dear nymph to run the risque of a Second. This was for some time a check to his Inclinations, but at last he ventur'd to make love to another Princess. After a great deal of Sighing and protesting he ^likewise made some impression upon her gentle heart. She promisd to let him in to her Lodging at a certain hour and he was to mew like a Cat for the Signal. He was as punctual as the intriguing moon & no Grimalkin coud mew more naturally than he did. But by ill luck for the poor Lover, a Colonel happend to come by at the moment who had a mortal aversion to a cat. And tho' in the dark, yet observing narrowly from whence the hatefull sound came, he took up a stone, that he happend to kick with his foot, and threw it so exactly, that he hit the unhappy Gallant on the head, and laid him sprawling on the Pavement. In a little time he recoverd his Sences, which told him he had more occasion for a Surgeon than a mistress. This sad reflection made him grope his way home again, full of Vertuous Resolutions never to engage in any other amour but an honest one, the lawfullness of which might make the Disasters of it Supportable.

[352] [/52] Wine has the Same effect upon our Wit, that water has upon Fire, a little makes it flame higher: but a great deal puts it out.

[353] Socrates being askt, why the life of man was seldome sufferd to exceed one hundred years? replyd, because in that interval there happens all the Variety of Events, that makes up the History of ages. Therefore to live longer wou'd be to loath Life, because we shoud only see the same things over & over again. Nay Providence is generally pleasd in its great goodness, to impair the memorys of ancient People, that the returning accidents of Life may appear a little new to them. This Forgetfullness restores the pleasure of Wonder & Surprize, which old people of sound memory have totally lost. For after all the Present is only the Picture of the past, and the Past the Sample of what is to come, and is little more than pulling on our Cloats, & pulling 'em off again.

[354] The Proverb tells us, that bought wisdome is best, but then it shoud be bought at the Expence of other People. At least those are wiser at first setting out, that take warning by the harms of their neighbours, are made better by their false steps, and more prudent by their Inadvertency. One very great happiness we have at least, that we are like never to want lessons of this kind to instruct us, if we are disposd to make our best advantage of them.

[355] Democritus often said, that the good Example of a Father is the best Lesson he can set his Children. For of all instructions those that are liveing & practical are the most insinuateing & perswasive. A child will be silently inveigled into an Emulation of those Vertues it sees practiced constantly before its Eyes. For tis a settled truth, that naked Example without precept is more instructive, than the most edifying Precept can be without Example. And really a man is like to make very little impression tho' he talks like an angel, if at the same time his behaviour give his words the Lye, and he act like a Devil.

[356] The great **Secret** of thriveing, and being happy in this world, is to keep some worthy & profitable End in view, and after that to find out the properest means of attaining that End. However great nicety shou'd be usd, that we employ no other means but what are consistent with honour and a good Conscience. For an Empire purchasd at the price of these, woud be much too dear bought, and prove a Bubble bargain in the end.

[357] [/53] Tis the grave advice of Isocrates, never to consult any Person in your affairs, that have been ill managers of their own: Else tis not impossible but you may consult a Prodigal about Oeconomy, and a Bawd about the Education of your Daughter.

[358] Antisthenes was ask't the reason why Philosophers always make court to the Rich, and the Rich never to the Philosophers? Because said he, Philosophers are sensible of their wants, and Rich men are not.

[359] A Wise Man has 3 very troublesome things to do, he shoud call to mind the times past, make the most of the Present, and provide against that which is to come.

[360] A Vile Person when he finds his profit in any Proposal, asks no more questions: but an honest man is so troublesome as to inquire also whether it be lawfull and expedient.

[361] Solon said often, that prudence made the same Figure among the Vertues, that the Sight dos among the Sences, that all was dark & comfortless without it.

[362] Be slow ᵃˢ ᵃ ᴳᵉʳᵐᵃⁿ in deliberateing what is fit to be undertaken, but Swift as any Frenchman in the Execution, that so your mine may be sprung, before t'is so much as Suspected.

[363] The way to be highly esteemd by God and man, is to think lowly of our Selves for. tho' humble People may not be good in other Respects, yet they are very capable of being so: but the proud and high-minded are incorrigible. This was the difference between the Publican and the Pharisee.

[364] When a man is attackt by any Temptation tis brave to run away, because the odds are so great and unequal against us, that we have ˢᶜᵃʳᶜᵉ any chance for victory if we stand our ground.

[365] Twas said of a woman who was continually speaking ill of her neighbours, and casting dirt on all mankind, that her mouth had a strange looseness.

[366] A Humane Body justly proportion'd ought to be just 4 times as long as tis broad at the wast, & Homer describes the vast proportions of Otus & Ephialtes to have answerd exactly to that rule.

[367] A Christian Renegade was summond before a Cady or magistrate ᵃᵗ ᴬˡᵍⁱᵉʳˢ for haveing profand the Rights of Mahomet, by solemnizeing them at the funeral of a Favorite Dogg. The case was too plain to deny it, and [/54] therefore since Innocence coud not plead for him, he carryd a purse of one Hundred Chequins to convince the Cady, that what he had don was no more than a Joke and a Frolick. At the first appearance of the Prisoner the good Magistrate calld him impious & abominable, for haveing paid those Religious honours to a Dog, that are paid to a true Mussleman. May it please your Honʳ said he, I was surprizd into this harmless ceremony, by a thousand good Qualitys wᶜʰ my poor little Dog possest. He was fond of me all his life, and was a generous Curr to his friends at his death, and

amongst the rest, S^r has bequeathd to your honour a Legacy of one hundred chequins, which he orderd me to deliver with his last Respects. The Magistrate made no scruple to take the purse, and told the Prisoner he had paid very just honours to an honest Favorite, who shewd so much distinction to people of worth.

[368] In the time of the Heros Robery and Pyratical Excursions were not lookt upon as acts of Injustice, but were instances of Bravery, that gave men Reputation in the world, so there were times in England, when Deer steeling, & takeing a Purse upon the High way were only accounted signs of mettle, and lookt upon as atchievements by no means below a man of parts, & a Fine Gentleman and to this day in the Highlands of Scotland the takeing Herds of Cattle from any Person they have a grudge to, is not calld stealing but **Driveing** of Cattle. Just so the Deerstealers of old soft-end the Robbery by calling it **Driveing** of Deer. Witness Chevey Chase.

[369] The Spaniards call a short meal a Feast of St Anthony, who was a great Enimy to Luxury of all kinds, & especially that of the Belly.

[370] In the tryall of Bishop Atterbury before the House of Lords the Lord L . . . e said he was convinced by the Seals with which the treasonable letters had been signd. The Duke of W . . . n in his Reply told the House that he believd that noble Lord had not been so much convinced by the Small Seals as by the Great.

[371] The Duke of Ormond had opposd a Grant which the Dutchess of Cleiveland endeavourd to obtain of King C. 2 in Ireland. The Dutchess in a great rage told the Duke she hoped to see [/55] him shorter by the Head. To this the Duke very cooly replyd, that he hoped only to see Her Grace old.

[372] The Earl of Anglisy who is also a Peer of Ireland was shockt to see several of the Irish Lords ready to give up their Jurisdiction, & told Their Lord^{ps} in the House there, that for his part he was only a Lord by accident, that honour being descended upon Him from his Ancestors, but most of their Lord^{ps} were made noble by their own Merit, and therefore as all the Priviledges of nobility were new to them, they ought in reason to put the greater Value upon them.

[373] A Lady said that twas harder for a woman to keep a Gallant to herself than the change of a guinea, or even than a Secret. A Female needs only beauty to make a Conquest, but needs more to preserve it. She needs to be very obliging, & very agreable.

[374] A Laconick Lover usd to be very short with his Mistress, for fear of spending more time upon her than she was worth. He usd only to address her in this consise manner, my Princess, you are in beauty, I am in love,

tell me truly, must I love on or leave off. Thus ^{if} he lost his Mistress, however he lost no time, & the man was much in the right.

[375] We shoud enter upon Martrimony as we enter upon a Voyage, not look upon the dangers but the Profits of it, else no man woud either go to Sea, or marry.

[376] A drole actor who had the fortune to delight the Pit & the Gallerys, amongst other instances of his Skil, usd to act the Squeeking of a Pigg with loud applause. A Country Fellow was much offended that the audience shoud lavish their applause so undeservedly, & let them know that the next day he woud act the same part much better, if they woud take ^{the} trouble to come & hear him. They came, and the clown enter'd on the stage with a Pig under his coat. He fell down upon all four, & pulling the poor Pig by the Ear made it Squeek very distinctly. ^{However} The Gallerys preferd the action of the first actor, & endeavourd to hiss the honest Rustick off the Stage. But the man took courage, and told 'em t'was a Real Pigg they had hisst & not him, & begd off 'em to learn how to distinguish betwixt nature, and a senceless imitation. I'm affraid this Story is but too applicable to the bulk of our Spectators.

[377] [/56] A certain Queen of Egypt was very beautifull, and so generous that she wishd every Male Subject in her Dominions might have a tast of her Charms. Nay she went so far in the actual distribution of her favours that she built one of the loftyest Pyramids by requireing of each of her Lovers only one Single stone of 2 feet Square. Tis pity the name of this tender-hearted Princess is buryd in the Ruins of Time otherwise she might be as dear to us, as her character is glorious.

[378] The Spaniards that affect the genuin Spanish air wear a long Toledo with a great Basket Hilt in which they usually carry their hankercheif & gloves.

[379] The Romans usd to call a very ancient Man as old as Saturn, & that he remembers the golden age.

[380] It may be said properly of a dirty Slut that she is daggled up to the Chine, A Trapes to the Surloin.

[381] One may say of an extensive Relation that the Family is more numerous than that of King Priam, or Father Jacob.

[382] Chancellour Jeffrys Spying at the Chancery Bar a young Council with a tyd wigg, calld to him to move; the young Gentleman bowd respectfully & told his Lord^p he had nothing to move. S^r replyd the Chancellour you seemd to me to be going out of Town by your Dress, & believeing you might be in hast I desird you to move one of the first.

[383] The Tanners Bark after haveing servd all the uses of Tanning, has another

excellent use in being beat to pieces, and put into a Layhouse (that is a little house, the top & one side of which is glass) and laid so thick as to be level with the top of the pots or tubs in which any tender Southern Plants are growing. This will continue hot Several months without renewing, and needs only be turnd once in 3 months or thereabouts, (according as you shall find the heat abate) and preserve the Plants from cold, even in the most frosty weather, & will ripen common fruit in Winter. In the day time, when the Sun shines warm, you ^{may} open one or more of the Pannels of Glass to let in the Sun or warm air, keeping them duly waterd.

[384] [/57] By the help of the foregoing method Pine-apples [are] ripend in England or any Spice-tree or Coffee Tree may be kept alive in any clymate be it never so cold.

[385] The Flowers of Artichoke either fresh or dryd boild in a small Quantity of Water, give it the qualitys of Runnet, and twill turn milk in order to make curds or cheese altogether as well as Runnet, with the advantage of being much sweeter.

[386] The French say there comes a man with a Greek mien, when a man gives himself airs of Sufficiency, because that nation had a contempt for all mankind, and the softest [name] they coud vouchsafe to give them was that of Barbarians.

[387] A Commander of a ship took great pleasure in opening the saylors letters from their Wives & mistresses, amongst the rest one good woman told her Dear Triton, after entertaining him with her other Domestick affairs, I must not forget to tell you that our Tabby cat has chittend.

[388] An Antilope is a small & very beautifull Deer in Asia that is so exceeding swift, that they cant catch it with Greyhound alone: but they are forct to let fly a Hawk, which wounds the head of this innocent creature, & gives time for the Dogs to come up with it. And we are inform'd by Arrian in his 2^d book, that the ancients made use of this kind of hunting of Deer with hawks, which either drove them into nets, or else turnd them to the Hounds. And by the 22^d book of Homers Odysses we find, the ancients usd Hawks to drive the Birds into nets. I saw 2 of the Antilopes above mentiond at Mr Lenoy's at Hamersmith in the year 1723.

[389] T'is too much the Custome in France as well as at Edinburg, to throw their nastiness out of the Window into the Street. This being thought no great harm, it happend that a very pretty Wench dischargd a Pisspot on a Gentlemans head that was walking by: but at the same ^{time} had the good breeding to cry out Gard de l'eau. However this courteous warning came

too late, & his cloaths were in a [. . .]le[8] with this natural Sal Almonize. This made him run I[. . .] [/58] [. . .] in great indignation, & demanded to see the wench who had made him this unsavory present. She came immediately to him to ask his pardon: but her charms disarmd his fury, and very soon converted it into love. The Damsel woud hear of no other terms but those of Matrimony, which made the Gentleman resolve to marry her, which it seems was his way of being revengd for the injury she had done him.

[390] The character of Demosthenes's Eloquence was lively, overbearing, & impetuous. His reasoning was close, [. . .] and convincing, ever addresst to the understanding & not to the Passions. He rather ravisht his Hearers into a compliance than perswaded them. There was a flame and vigour in every thing he said, which like Lightening bore down all before it. His utterance was strong animated & commanding, & every word he pronounc't seemd to come directly from his heart. The sanctity of his morals & the integrity of his Soule gave a might & a strength to all his arguments. He was so far from flattering his audience, that he did sometimes treat them with too little ceremony. In short whatever art he had, he had the secret to make it all appear pure Genius and simple Nature.

[391] But the Eloquence of Cicero had a more agreable Turn, & tho' it might not have more force, had more enchantment. It was easy, passionate, & insinuating, full of sweetness & harmony. His Genius was comprehensive, and his knowledge universal. His person was beautifull, his address—engaging, His voice musical, his delivery just, and gently flowing. Nobody ever understood the passions so well, & knew how to touch them so powerfully. An Instance of this never to be forgot, was, when the oratour pleaded before Cæsar in favour of Ligarius. This Person notwithstanding his many obligations had drawn his sword against Cæsar, for which ingratitude he was resolvd never to forgive him. nay t'was with the utmost difficulty he permitted Cicero so much as to plead for him. His Flatterers had begd of him, not to hear that dangerous man speak because Enchantment flowd from his lips, & sweet perswasion dwelt upon his tongue. It is resolvd, said Cæsar, tho Venus & all the Graces were to interceed for the Villein I woud never [reve]rse his fate. The Orator spoke, & spoke like the first Tempter [. . .] [m]ankind. He flatterd the Hero so neatly upon his Bravery, his [. . .]sity, saying, [. . .] solis oblivisci

8. The page is torn and illegible here and through the next sentence.

risi injuria[...] [/59] that he let fall the Dead Warrant he held in his hand, and cry'd out, there's no resisting the invincible charms of this mans Eloquence, he has overcome me, & his Client must live in spite of all my Ressentment.

[392] Tho' Individuals that are just & good, may not for several wise Reasons receive their Reward in this world, yet communitys that encourage Vertue, and act uprightly must receive theirs in this, because it is here only they subsist, and will not survive the grave, and therefore if they have not their Reward upon Earth, they will never have it at all, which woud arraign the Justice of Providence.

[393] Mr Sh ... and Mr W ... l hate one another more than either Rivals in Love or Competitors in ambition, & yet whenever they meet, no Spouses are so familiar. Happening to Sit together one day in the House of Commons, now Will, said Mr W ..., I'm going to do a thing that will be agreable both to the Whigs & Torys. What can that be, Robin answer'd the other. I hope you are not going to strike such another blow as my Lord Teynam did a month ago. (when it seems that unhappy nobleman had shot himself thro' the head.)

[394] The Learned differ widely to which the Preference in Poetry ought to be given, whether to Homer or Virgil. The first carrys it by the greater numbers, but the last by the Judges of the finer Tast, which will always be the Few. But I think by the different Talents of these two great Poets, they may fairly divide the Prize betwixt them. Homer has the advantage in the heat and fruitfullness of Imagination. His Invention is more seeming, his Expression more Sublime and more flowing. His descriptions are more beautifull, and his Sentiments—more moral & instructive: But then Virgil has infinitely more Judgment, and—a more managd muse than Homer. He has a much cooler Head, a more temperate Imagination. Pegasus do's never run away with him, as he often dos with the other. He is more courtly & polite, never suffering His Hero's to be abusive or indecent, cruel or insulting. He knows better how to prune the redundancy of his thoughts, and restrain the wantoness of his Fancy. In one word Virgil has more Judgement, but Homer more wits, Virgil more art, and Homer more nature. And tho' some may believe that Vir-gil [/60] had a mighty advantage in writeing last, & (by reading the criticising of the Learned upon Homers faults) was instructed to mend them: yet the advantage that Homer had in writeing his Poems first, is at least as great, by the allowances that all people are ready to make for indecences & improprietys committed in those early days. Then arts were supposd to have

been in their Infancy, and mankind not yet advanc't to that degree of improvement, they were in Augustus his time, when without question all polite Learning was arrivd at the utmost perfection. It must be confesst indeed that Homers Heroick Poems serve Virgil for a Plan & a Model to form his Eneid upon:—yet this Imitation is not so resignd & Superstitious as to extend to his Imperfections. He follows the Excellences, & beautys of the original, but mends its blemishes, which must shew a fine tast, and perfect good understanding. But tis probable that, tho' Homer's Poems be the most ancient that are now extant, there might have been others of greater antiquity for him to follow. Artistotle in his Art of Poetry mentions a lesser Iliad, which Suidas says was written by Antimachus. By that t'is possible Homer might model his great one, which woud rob him of the honour of the first Invention. Athenæus makes this the more credible, by telling us in his 3ᵈ book, that Hegesianax had before Homer, publisht a Poem concerning the Siege of Troy. And Suidas affirms, that one Corinnus a Disciple of Palamedes, had versifyd upon the same subject long before Homer was born. These may have been great Helps to this celebrated Poet, and perhaps some part of his Reputation may depend upon his Poems haveing had the luck to Survive theirs. Upon the whole matter I must conclude with Propertius, that not only Homer, but every other Poet must yeild to ᵗʰᵉ incomparable Roman.

Oedite Romani Scriptores, cedite Græci

[395] The Country People amongst many other idle Superstitions, do fancy when a cow is restless, & wont stand at the Pail, tis a Sure Prognostick of Rain. So when the Ramms butt at one another tis another infallible Sign of wet weather. But these rural Forebodings are no more to be depended upon than a visit from the Screech-owl portends Death, or a Blazeing Star, or an Eclips dos some general calamity. I believe it may be laid down for a Rule, that all the grave People, that deal in omens, Dreams, & every other kind Divina[tion], are oftener deceivd, than confirmd in their Superstition.

[396] [/61] Dʳ Radcliff was the most eminent Physician in the Reigns of King William & Queen Ann. His Eminence however consisted not in an uncommon degree of Learning, for which he was by no means remarquable: but in a prodigious Sagacity in distinguishing the Distemper by the Symptomes. This was his great Excellence, in which no Phisician ever went beyond him. He studyd the Pulse with great application, as he likewise did the Coulour of the Urine, both which serve to give the clearest light into the distemper. He also took many hints from the look

of the Eys, the complexion of the skin, the smell of the Breath, the
condition of the Tongue, the frequency of the stools, & the temper of the
whole Body. Particularly in difficult cases, he woud consider the pulse a
long time with strict attention and sometimes make surprizeing discoverys from it. A remarquable Instance of this happend in the case of S^r
Andrew Fountain, who by some mischance receivd a Hurt in his Side. He
was dress't by an able Surgeon: but for the greater Security sent for D^r
Radcliff whose skil he thought might keep him from a Feaver. The D^r
when he came considerd his Pulse diligently for some time, & then askt
who was his Surgeon, & after Sr Andrew ^had told him, Pray send away
instantly, said he, & order him to attend me at my house an hour hence.
When the Surgeon came to the D^r, he askt him in what condition he had
found his Patient's wound? He answerd, in a very good condition. I
believe you are mistaken, replyd the D^r, for I coud almost swear from his
Pulse, that it is not far from a mortification. Go therefore & take off his
dressing this moment, & treat the wound, as if it were begining to mortify. The Surgeon ran away in a great fright, & found it just as the D^r had
judgd: but was time enough to stop the Gangreen, & made a Shift to save
his Patient purely by the D^rs skil in Pulses. This famous Physician was
very fond of Blisters, & woud apply them sooner than is commonly
orderd by others, who reserve them for the last Refuge. He was once sent
for to a Gentleman in a very dangerous small pox. It was the Flux-kind,
and none of the usual methods coud raise it. In this desperate case he
orderd his poor Patient to be blisterd on his head, & almost every part of
his Body, so that his skin was flayd near all off, & he yeilded such a stench,
[/62] that there was no endureing the Room. In this wretched condition
it was necessary to shift him twice or he must have been poisond by his
own stink. He lay struggleing with Death for about 30 days, & then
miraculously recoverd, to the immortal Reputation of his Doctor. He was
a little too much a Humorist and if he did not like a man he might perish
for him, he woud not go near him. If he was got over a bottle with
agreable company, a coach & six was hardly able to draw him ^away to any
Patient, except he happend to be his favorite and then he grutcht neither
his time nor his pains. But he was not so fond of his Friends as he was
implacable to his Enimys. As he sav'd many lives out of pure kindness, so
for variety once, he savd a man out of burning spight. When Sr Thomas
Abney was Lord Mayor of London the Towne clerk was extreemly ill,
(whose place was in his Lord^ps gift, and of very great value) news was
brought the D^r that this poor man was given over, & that his Place was

like to fall into the hands of this good-for-nothing Magistrate, who had some how or other disoblig'd him. For that reason he forgot his natural Pride so far, as to go to the sick man without being sent for, & took so much pains in studying his case, and in applying of proper Medicines, that the Man recoverd after haveing been given over by his other Physicians, & counted amongst the dead ^{by} all his Relations. And the D^r usd to boast that he had more pleasure from the Success of this case, than from all the cures he ever made in his life, tho' he had formerly the happiness to recover both his Father, & his Elder Brother. Wherever this English Esculapius found his Patients to have a strong and a lively Imagination, he had the art of working upon it, with so powerful an Impression, ^{that} he curd them with innocent ^{Physick} that by the Chymerical vertues he gave wrought upon their Fancy more than their constitution. Thus he frequently treated the Ladys who are often very fancifull, and are cured by Faith of most Distempers. The like Method he observd with Painters and Poets, whose business is carryd on by strength of Imagination. But this Practice needs as much skil in humane minds, as the common way of Quacking do's knowledge of humane Bodys.

[397] [/63] When King C. 2^d after the Restoration thought it proper to shew himself to his Subjects, he took a Progress towards the west, & passt thro' Salisbury. In that city the Inhabitants crowded to see their lawfull Soveraign, & amongst the rest an honest country Fellow had forcd his way very near his Majesty, so near that some little Black Spanels which the King kept about his Person, began to Snarl at this curious Person. His Majesty, who condescended to Speak to the meanest of His Subjects, desird the man not to come too close for fear the Spanels shoud bite Him. But ^{the} poor fellows curiosity being greater than his Fears ^{he} venturd up so near, that they really did bite him. ^{The} Extreem smart of this disaster made him cry out God bless your Majesty: but God damn your Dogs. This may serve for an Emblem to justify our dislike to evil Ministers, without the least disloialty to the Prince who by mistake or misinformation appointed them.

[398] Almost every act of Providence is an Instance of compassion to mankind, & even the Terrors of Gods Justice are Instruments of his Love, to affright us from our Sins & make us capable of his Mercy. To this purpose t'is remarquable, that when our Sins are great enough to draw down a Plague upon any city or nation, it first strikes the cattle before it reaches mankind, that they may, by so near & so visible a warning, have time to humble themselves & sue for pardon, before the full fury of Gods Ven-

geance be pour'd out upon them. And old Homer ᵂᵃˢ so sensible of this divine goodness that he tells us in the first book of the Iliad that Apollo first sent the Plague upon the Mules & Dogs of the Grecian Camp before he sufferd it to break out upon the Officers & Souldiers.

[399] Some men are so happy in their Talents & qualifications, that they have the knack of makeing the worst things in Nature agreable. Thus t'is said of Pisistratus, that he had so much address, so much eloquence, so much good breeding, & every part of his behaviour was so engageing, that he made even Tyrany, the greatest of humane calamitys, very tolerable. This charming ᵀʸʳᵃⁿᵗ ʳᵉⁿᵈᵉʳᵈ the Athenians ˢᵒ happy under oppression, by his insinuateing manner that they were in danger of forgeting the name of Liberty forever. [/64] He sweeten'd every Act of injustice, and graced his very Insolence with smiles. This made his Subjects easy under their sufferings, and ready to kiss & embrace the rod that chastisd them. How much art must that man have been master of, who knew how to draw the teeth of hunger, and to disguise pain & distress in such a manner as to ᵐᵃᵏᵉ ᵗʰᵉᵐ loose all their terrours? But this arbitrary Prince made the Athenians ample amends for all his skilfull oppressions, by causing the Iliad & Odysses of Homer to be collected into 2 intire Volumes, & brought to Athens by his son Hipparchus, they haveing before ᵗʰᵃᵗ been sung about the world only in parts, which were calld Rapsodys. Tho' others tell us the same good work had been done by Lycurgus about 300 years before: but ⁱᶠ ᵗʰᵃᵗ ʷᵃˢ ˢᵒ the Lacedemonians kept it up so close, that no other part of Greece coud reap any benefit by it.

[400] The members of Christchurch in Oxford have a very humble opinion of the rest of the Colleges & imagin all Learning confined to themselves. With his head full of such partial notions a Christchurch-man forgot himself so far as to petition in his Prayer before the Sermon, for the 2 famous universitys of this land, Cambridge & Christchurch & thought himself very submissive in not nameing Christchurch first. nay tis ˢᵃⁱᵈ ʰᵉ ʷᵃˢ threatend to be expelld the colledge for so mean a prostitution.

[401] Dʳ Stratford a cannon of Christchurch was very fat by being an exceeding good Liver, insomuch that a Wag made his Epitaph yⁿ advance before he was dead in two Lines.

> Pass gently Travellor, & dont tread hard
> For Stratford sleeps under this whole Churchyard.

[402] A Prateing Frenchman who livd in Holland was always publishing Libels against Monsʳ Louvois, in which he discoverd more of that Ministers

Secret History than was convenient. Neither did this happen seldome, but this malignant Historian was perpetually tireing him with fresh intelligence about his great Infirmitys. It grew at last so intolerable, that Monsr Louvios bribd this man's Landlord to decoy him to the Frontiers, by a large Summ of Mony, [/65] where he was surprizd by a Troop of horse, & carryd Prisoner to Paris. Monsr Louvois let him know he woud cure Him of his Itch of gaining Intelligence. For that purpose he causd a Machine like a Cage to be erected, into which he put this inquisitive Person, & placed a Centry upon him, with orders not to speak one Syllable to him on pain of death, & to shoot any other Person that shoud dare to open his Mouth to Him. Accordingly an Edict was published giveing leave to all to go to see this poor Man: but forbiding them to speak to Him, or make him any answer under the penalty of being shot dead upon the Spot. In obedience to this Edict not one of all the vast number that crowded to See him woud open his Mouth, tho' he begd, implord, & conjurd every mortal to break his intolerable Silence. In this provokeing condition the poor wretch livd for more than ten years, raveing and cursing and lamenting that nobody woud converse with Him, & for his greater punishment he was not sufferd to have any book, or any Pen Ink & Paper to amuze himself withal, or to divert the chagrin of seeing nothing but Mutes for so many years together. Tho there was some humour in inflicting this dumb kind of Punishment upon a talkative & inquireing Person, yet it was as cruel as malice, or religious Zeal & Superstition coud invent.

[403] The best way to cure the vapours in Man or Woman is to endeavour put 'em into a Passion which quickens the circulation & frisks the Spirits effectually.

[404] Two Gentlemen who pretended a wonderfull nicety in distinquishing of Wine went to a Merchant, & tasting a particular pipe, one of 'em said it tasted of Iron, & the other of Leather. and after it came to be drawn out of the Cask they found at the bottom a small kea fastend to a piece of Leather, wch shewd a very distinguishing faculty, & a great acuteness in the sence of tasting.

[405] T'is very hard upon the poor Women, that every man liveing has a kea to the greatest Treasure they have in the world, and therefore no wonder if the poor Creatures cant preserve it long very safe without looseing it.

[406] [/66] Somebody askt Buchanan why the Muses were call'd Virgins, because said he they are such poor Jades that nobody woud ever marry them.

[407] The K. of Poland when he is displeasd with his Pages makes them hold the

candles in their hand while he shoots wth Pistoles at those candles in order to Snuff them.

[408] King James the 2^d out of Zeal to the Popish Religion was for makeing all the Converts he coud, & amongst the rest he thought he shoud meet with no great difficulty in perswadeing Gen^ll Kirk to be of the Court Religion, since by his reprobate course of Life, he seemd to have his Religion stil to choose. But the Gen^ll, to the Kings great Surprize, told Him, he was sorry he was not at liberty to oblige his Majesty in such a triffle as that was: but when he was at Tangier, he had unluckily pre-ingagd himself to the Emperor of Morocco by promise, that whenever he chang'd his Religion he woud turn Mahometan, and your Maj^ty knows a Man of honour can never be worse than his word.

[409] The Duke of Villa-Medina being a very Gallant man, was askt by Q. Elizabeth if, he had not lost his heart since he came to England? Yes Madam said he, there is in your Majestys Family a Divine Lady which I adore. When the Queen askt who that coud be? the Duke replyd, that his Angel woud take it ill of him if he namd her name, but he woud send Her Maj^ty a very like Picture of her. The next day He sent the Queen a Gold Box with a a looking Glass in it which she was too Quick of Apprension not to understand, & too gracious not to forgive.

[410] Some Young Officers in Pyrrus's his army once over their cups took insolent libertys with their Prince, which he was soon informd of. The offenders being brought before the King, he askt them, if they had been so audacious as to open their mouths against their Soverain? We did, Sir replyd one of them, and possibly we shoud have talkt more treason, if we had had more wine. Pyrrus [/67] who was a generous Prince pardond them all, being himself no stranger to the mad Effects of strong liquor.

[411] A Souldier in the Trenches opend his Knap sack & askt his comrade to eat. To what purpose said he shoud a man be at the trouble to dine, when tis odds if he live to digest his dinner.

[412] A Fool of Charles the 5th had been too smart upon the failings of the Emperor, & for that Crime was condemd to undergo a Fast of 3 days; This to a Gentleman of that merry profession was a Punishment worse than capital. He applyd himself to the cook on this occasion but he was not to be intreated. In the malice of his Heart he went & naild up all the closs stools in the Palace. In which Fact when he was discoverd, he said in his excuse, That a Prince who woud not suffer his poor Subjects to eat, ought by no means to be sufferd to Sh——t himself.

[413] A Gay officer, whose Income bore no proportion to his Expence, was

broke after the war, & forc't to turn off his Servants, & part with his Equipage for what he coud get. As he was walking with melancholly reflections one day, he spyd one of his disbanded Souldiers very merry a louzeing himself under a Hedge. What art Thou doing there honest Ned said the Officer? To tell you the truth Sr replyd he, I am like my betters retrenching the number of my Domesticks.

[414] A Poor Souldier was decently retird under a Hedge to ease Himself, & unhappily the General passing that way, was offended with the ill smell. What an unsavory Dog art thou said the General to poison the country at this filthy rate? The Savour is something strong Sir replyd the Fellow but your Honr cant expect that a poor Souldier can Sh——t musk and Civet upon 6 pence a day.

[415] An honest Dyer went out of his Zeal to the Protestant Succession to Swear in the Court of Exchecquer, His hand being tinged pretty strongly, the clerk with much gravity said to Him, Friend put off your Glove. To which the Dyer made answer as gravely Friend put on your Spectacles.

[416] [/68] A Gentleman calling at a Farmers House saw 6 or 7 lusty wholesome Children. Pray Friend Said He, how comes it to pass that thy Children are so healthy & Robust, while mine are all of em meer Weeklins. Why to tell your Honr the plain truth replyd the Countryman, I take the trouble to get my children my Self.

[417] A Country Fellow makeing for the first time a visit to London spyd a fine Apothecarys Shop in which he coud see nothing But painted Pots, & guilt Drawers. His curiosity made him enquire of Mr Squirt what good wares were sold there? The pragmatical Prentice told the Fellow, they dealt altogether in Asses Heads. Good lack reply the clown sure ye have wondrous much custome for I can find only one you have left in your Shop.

[418] The Jews have a Tradition, that while Moses was in conference with the Almighty on the Mount, God commanded him to direct his Eye to the Plaine below, & he woud See an extraordinary Scene. The Prophet obey'd, and he beheld a man of rank stoop down to a Brook of water to drink. By accident he dropt a Purse of mony near the Place, which a Boy who came soon after him, pickt up & carryd off. Then came a very ancient man who being tird with his walk drank, and sat down to rest Himself. While the poor old fellow staid, this man returnd to look for his mony, & tho the other protested he knew nothing of it, yet he first reviled him, & then cut his Throat. Without doubt (the Almighty said) this appears a little unjust to shortsighted mortals, that the Boy shoud commit the Injustice, & the old man be slain for it: But I will open your Eyes

and let you know, the old Man did formerly kill the Father of that Boy, which was a debt of blood that he has justly paid to the Family.

[419] The Hotentotes in copulation approach their Females behind, lying on one side. They cut out one of their ᵐᵃˡᵉ childrens Testicles as soon as they're born with an opinion that they will run the faster afterwards. When they sit tis commonly in the posture of a child in its [/69] Mothers womb, with their head betwixt their Knees wᶜʰ they embrace with their arms.

[420] The whole Secret of teaching lys in finding out ways to make our duty agreable. Children shoud be taught those things, which will be of the greatest advantage to them when they are men or women. And not like Girles who learn those triffles, which they neglect and forget when they come to be marryd.

[421] My son follow the Instructions of honest Aristotle, said Phillip to Alexander, that he may teach you to avoid many Errors, of which I have livd to repent ~~of~~.

[422] Elephants are very furious & ungovernable when they are in lust. They couple Belly to Belly contrary to the custome of other Brutes. The Female carrys her young 12 months, and without an accident they live about 100 years.

[423] A brave Chinese defended a City very gallantly against the Tartars, so that with all their numbers they were not able to take the place. At last the Tartars contrivd to get the Father of this Hero into their power, and brought him within sight of the Besiegd, threatening to put him to a cruel death unless the Town was surrenderd in ten hours. The Son refus'd, humbly. begging his Fathers pardon on his knees, and lamenting the cruel Dilemma of giveing ᵘᵖ either his Father or his country. But since the fatal choice must be made, he was ᵒᶠ opinion, that all private duty must give place to that which a man owes his Country. The poor old man was therefore beheaded before his sons face, and gloryed in a Death which had been occasiond by his Sons publick spirit.

[424] [/70] When a Mistress wishes her Gallant every thing that is good, she excepts always good Sence, which might open his Eyes, and make him dispise charms, which owe their being to imagination only.

[425] Among the Hotentots, if any one happen to be bit by a Serpent, they fall to beating the part with a Small Stick til the bloud be all Settled about it. Then they draw off that bloud by Scarification, ~~and~~ sucking it out together with the poison.

[426] In some part of the East Indies the women possess their dear Husbands with the opinion, that they may be got with child by thinking of their

Spouses at a great distance from them. Which doctrine of being pregnant by strength of Imagination, woud be very convenient in some other countrys, if their Husbands coud be brought to that pitch of credulity.

[427] A Poor woman attended her son to the Gallows, where he was to be executed in good Company. Here lifting up her Eyes to the Tree, she cryd, alas must my dear boy hang there like a Dog, that will be a dreadfull spectacle. A merry fellow who was to undergo the Same Fate, said, be easy good woman, I shall hang there too, & then you'll have a pair of spectacles.

[428] Clemency & good nature soften gentle & generous minds into a Sence of their own misbehaviour: but hardens base men in their perverse & disobedient courses, not unlike the Sun which dissolves Wax, while it makes dirt as hard as a stone.

[429] A Gentleman had a very carefull servant, who was very usefull upon a Journey. Tom said he once going away from an Inn, have you packt up all my Things? Never fear S^r replyd the Varlet, all your things at least, & tis well for my Landlord if I han't packt up more

[430] A Fine man who had disabled himself by Luxury, coud get no children that woud live. He happend one day to call [/71] at a Poor mans cottage, and seeing 3 or 4 Robust wholesome Bearns about him, Pray honest Neighbour said he, how do you contrive to have such Strong healthy children? and please your worship said the Fellow, we poor Folk take the pains to get them our selves.

[431] A certain very ingenious Gentlewoman who was a great admirer of her own Dear Person placed a Looking-glass at the Teaster of her bed that she might see how pretty she lookt when she was asleep.

[432] And a Pretty Fellow very near akin to this Lady in understanding, said, he woud purchase a tame Crow, to see whether, as naturalists inform us, it woud live 3 or 400 years.

[433] Alphonsus the 10th succeeding very young to the crown of Castile, the Grandees advisd him to choose from amongst his Subjects 7 wise men, perfectly upright & incorrupt in their characters, to assist His Majesty in the administration. Your council is very good reply'd that Generous Prince, & find me but one single man that possesses those Vertues, and I will not only trust him with the Government, but I will also put my crown upon his Head, and Surrender to Him my whole Kingdome.

[434] The Pope asking a Prelate at his Audience what news? he answerd, there was a Report that His Holiness intended to honour him with the Government of Rome. Alas replyd the Holy Father, you are too well acquainted with Mankind, not to know, that Fame is the greatest Lyer in the world.

[435] A Prateing French man had been so troublesome to a Minister of State, that he was obligd to order his Porter never to let him in. However monsier one day found means to slip in in spite of Cerberus, at which the minister was so offended, that he threatend to discard the Porter that very minute, [/72] if the Frenchman said more than one single word to him, believeing that none of that Nation coud be so laconique. Monsr took the hint very quick, & pulling a commission out of his Pocket for a Troop of Dragoons, made a very low Reverence, & said no more than **Sign**. The Minister was pleasd with the Quickness of the mans apprehention, and did as he desird.

[436] A certain King of a certain Island was complaining very justly that his Exchequer was exceeding low, I believe I coud find a Remedy for that, replyd an honest courteour, for I have always observd whoever is at the head of Your Majesty's Treasury grows very Rich, and therefore you had best reserve that Post for Your Self, and then you'll grow rich too.

[437] T'is a Common thing for Rams to tup 50 or 60 Sheep in one night which denotes a prodigious natural Vigor especially when we consider that they Seldome miss to impregnate the Female every leap they make. how short do poor men fall of these Feats!

[438] Women are most lascivious about the time their Terms begin to flow, because of the irritation which the flux of blood & Spirits gives their **Parts** at that time: But Moses was very wise in forbidding copulation under that circumstance, because tho' the Inconvenience may be very little to the Partys themselves besides the Impurity yet if a child shoud be got at that time it woud be a miserable Weakling, that woud be hardly worth the trouble of bringing up, & tis odds but it woud come dead into the world.

[439] Nature shews by the Instinct she puts into other animals, that after a woman has once conceiv'd she shoud no more approach a man til she is deliverd & passt her time of purification. By this abstinence she woud not run so great a Risque of miscarrying, because there is some danger of that by the bloud that rushes to the womb in every act of copulation. There happens likewise sometimes a Superfetation or second conception, which hinders the Safe & regular proceeding of the first. These [/73] accidents bring women often in danger of their Lives which makes it more expedient for them to abstain from the greediness of craveing more when their Belly is full already. This piece of Prudence is strictly observd by the natives of Brasile & several other parts of America where the dictates of Nature are more inviolably observd than in the politer parts of the world where pleasure & Luxury have got intirely the better.

[440] A certain great Performer with the Sex finding his vigour begin to abate was so unwilling to part with any part of that dear Pleasure, that he causd one of his Legs to be cut off, that so the bloud & Spirits which usd to nourish that Limb, might add strength to those which remaind, and increase his abilitys with the allureing Sex.

[441] Faustina the Daughter of Antoninus Pius was desperately in Love with a Gladiator. She was sensible of the absurdity of so low a passion, & tryd all the Remedys of Prudence as well as abstinence against it. But alas all her Endeavours were vain, & had the effect that oil woud have towards extinquishing a flame. At length she consulted the oracle which told her, nothing woud calm her concupiscence but drinking the bloud of her Beloved. This she did, & afterwards hated him to that degree that she causd him to be put to death. A very cruel Remedy against Love invented to be sure by the Devil himself.

[442] Luxury has taught men to caress their wives before: but Nature woud rather teach them to caress them behind. Indeed When he attacks her before he has more pleasure, because the Lips of the Persons engag'd & several other parts of their bodys meet in this Posture, which dont in the other, & the Penetration is commonly more home. But tis however agreed by all anatomists, that the Womb of a Woman is better situated for conception, when she rests upon her hands & Knees, than when she lyes upon her Back. For in that Posture the Bottom of the womb lys lower much than the Orifice, & consequently the Seed may more easily be injected into it. Besides if a Woman expects a Husband shoud perform Duty after she's with child, twill be much safer for her to receive him behind, because the Violence of the Shock will not be so dangerous upon her Buttocks, as upon her Belly, where the tender Fruit lys reposited.

[443] [/74] Twas the advice of a man very knowing in the nature of Mankind, when a Lady enquird of him what courses she had best take to be prolifick. Eat fish Madam, said he, drink Water, & f— upon all four. She took his advice & had a child after she was **Fourty**.

[444] A Young Fellow out of the abundance of his heart, told a sawcy Dame that she was exceedingly agreable. I thank you kind Sir, said She, & wish I coud make you the same complement. You might do that Madam very easily reply'd the Squire in a Pet, if you made as little Scruple of lying as I did.

[445] A clumsey Country Justice happend to meet a Parson upon a fine Horse. Good times indeed Quoth His worship, to see the Disciple mounted on a prancing Steed, when the Master was humble enough to ride upon an

Ass. Alas replyd the Doctor, I woud feign bestride an ass too, but they have all lately been taken into the Commission of the Peace.

[446] A man & his Wife were one morning in high dispute which shoud wear the Breeches. In the midst of the Fray somebody knockt at the Door, & wanted to speak with the Master of the House. Pray friend said the good man, tarry a moment, til that matter is decided & you shall have an answer. Then he returnd to the charge, & haveing subdued His Spouse with—arguments that convinced her only of his superiority, he went back to the Stranger, & gave him audience to his satisfaction.

[447] A Gentlewoman was cheapening a close-stool, and not comeing up to the Joiner's price, pray Madam said he consider the goodness of the lock. That's very true replyd She, I had forgot, that what it is to hold will be in huge danger of being Stole.

[448] A Welshman haveing carryd cheese in his pocket, a Rat had the impudence to knaw a hole in his Breeches. This accident appearing ominous, the Superstitious Briton went [/75] away to a Conjurour to inquire what it foreboded. Nostrodamus haveing cast his figure gave his customer to understand, that since the Rat had eat his Breeches, all was safe enough but if his Breeches had happend to eat the Rat, very great misfortunes must infallably have ensued.

[449] One Mr Sampson steping into a Tavern where some of his Friends were makeing merry. Oh cryd one of them, we may rake as much as we please to night in defiance of the watch & the Constables, for here comes Sampson who will smite a Thousand of such Philistines. That I will replyd honest Sampson, provided you'll be so kind as to favour me with one of your Jaw-bones.

[450] Some young Councellors rideing the Circuit & being merrily disposd, askt a poor Carter upon the Road what made his fore-horse so fat, & all the rest so lean? The case is very plain, replyd the Carter, The fore-horse is a Lawyer, & all the rest are his poor Clients.

[451] A true born Englishman being in France, desird His Landlady upon a Fast-day to boil him a Rump of Beef. Upon my conscience Sir said she, I dare do no such thing. Why so said our country man, my Landlord 2 leagues off let me have meat on a fastday, are you more Scrupulous than he? Oh replyd the good woman, in that Towne the Innkeepers only take an oath they wont transgress the ordinances of the Church, & so may oblige their customers: but we have given Bond with security, & consequently may be undone if we shoud venture to do it.

[452] A polite Clergiman had made a fine Terace-walk in his Garden, & a

Country wit comeing to make him a visit, commended his walk extreemly, but said, D^r, I'm affraid tis too broad & too pleasant to be the way to Heaven. I fear so too reply'd the Parson, for if t'were the way to Heaven youd be the last man in the world I shoud expect to meet in it.

[453] A smart young Gentlewoman being at the Masquerade in the dress of Q: Elizabeth was accosted by a coxcomb who had more life than wit, with this ^{familiar} question. Pray did your Majesty dye a Maid, because Historians are very much divided about it? Nobody woud have calld my vertue in question [/76] replyd she, if I had met with Men no more agreable than Thee.

[454] An officer had a long time made unsuccessfull love to His Landlady's Daughter. At last when he found the force of Language coud do nothing, he resolvd to try the force of gold. And one day claping a Guinea over one of her Eys, he told her, Love was blind. Very true said she, but then tis blind of both Eyes.

[455] A blunt officer seeing the ArchBishop of Cologne march at the head of his Troops, begd him to trust his Troops to His Generals, for said he it ill beseems the meak Spirit of an Ecclesiastick to head an army. So it woud said he, but here I appear in the capacity of a Duke, & not of an Arch-Bish^p, That may be replyd the Officer: but then if the Duke shou'd happen to go to the Devil how will the poor ArchBish^p come off.

[456] Buchanan was askt why the Muses were Virgins? because said he they were such poor Sluts that they coud not get Husbands.

[457] A Pretty girle told a young Fellow that woud have perswaded Her out of her Modesty, I will yeild to all you desire, provided you'll intitle yourself to the Favour, by giveing me what you neither have your Self, nor can possibly have, & yet you can bestow ^{it} whenever you please. Meaning a Husband.

[458] If a Mahometan has ever been at Mecca he is call'd Hag or holy because all the Sins he committed before that time are supposd to be remitted and he in a fair way to Paradise.

[459] In Barbary fat women are most esteem'd & the fatter the better; while lean ones tho' never so handsome are counted little better than carrion. For this Reason when a young girle is to be marryd, her friends keep her up & feed her several times a day with a kind of Panada, and even awake her often in the night to cram her, that she may be plump & will likeing. The wenches in that country are very carefull to preserve their [/77] Maidenheads because if the Husband don't find all the Tokens of it on the wedding night, tis a legal reason for a Divorse. And the woman is so

carefull to justify her self in this tender point, that she walks in procession the next night with her Bride-grooms linnen Trouzers drawn over her head, ^{haveing} all the marks of Virginity upon them. And this Procession is lighted along the Streets with a great number of Flambeaux, that the whole Towne may witness that she had done her Husband Justice.[9]

[460] There are no more than 3 familys now remaining in Italy, which plainly are decended from the old Romans. The Colonna, Ursini, & Savelli Familys, from the last of which the English Savils claim their original, as the Lumlys do from the Lomelinis of Genoa, which is one of the best Familys there.

[461] When the Sun shines the Peacock spreads its Train, not unlike ^a Proud man who Struts and Swells in Prospérity, at which time he first forgets himself and then his friends.

[462] A Man may be said to be curst into Prosperity considering the Train of mischeif it deludes most People into, and only fats them ^{up} for Slaughter & distraction.

[463] In our degenerate ^{age} People are ashamd of nothing but Innocence & being thought old.

[464] A good name, like Virginity in a Woman, when once dead, must expect no Resurrection.

[465] Twas said of one who had been brought low by a very fashionable Distemper, that he was wasted to ^a Cinder.

[466] It was the hard Fate of a grave Philosopher to fall in love with a Damsel, with whome he desird to have an affair; He determind to put it to Her, but instead of makeing love in the language of other Mortals, when he got the girle alone, come my Dear said he, let you & I go this moment and make our Selves immortal; & since we must dye ourselves let us get a child that may represent us, & he another and so into all generations. This is the only way left for Man to live for ever in this world, & that way let us resolve to take

[467] [/78] A Poor Woman was indicted of Treason, for offering to take Charles the 9th of France by the privy Parts.

[468] There are many instances of Men who have 3 testicles, & some have only one, & others again have none that ever appear out of their Belly, and yet all these have begot Children. An Instance of those who have had 3, was Agathocles King of Sicily; & an Instance of those whose Testacles have not

---

9. Coded marks follow for half a line.

descended out of their Belly, was Monsieur Argentan, which hinderd not their Wives at least from haveing children.

[469] The Clitoris in a woman is in many things like a mans Penis, it has a nut & prepuse like that, & swells very much in the act & desire of copulation; however it is not perforated, but is the Supream seat of pleasure in the exercises of love.

[470] Tis said the Privitys of man grow less and dwindle away by excessive abstinence, of which St Martin is reported to be a remarquable Instance, who observd such strict Rules of abstinence, & exercisd such Austeritys upon himself, that when the women came to lay him out after he was dead, they coud hardly find out any Penis at all, at most not larger than a moderate Clitoris. So that the Fair are not much out of the way, when they choose a Lover by his stomach.

[471] In the formation of a male child, if there be any Superfluity of the generative matter, it is thrown in to the Penis, to make that larger than the common proportion; and if the same matter happen to fall short, the poor Penis must suffer for it by being less than the ordinary standard. But in the case of a Female child, this defect or abundance go's all into their **Feet**, & the Parts to which they bear the greatest proportion.

[472] [/79] Tis a standing observation, that men on whome nature has bestowd the largest Privitys, have the least understanding. The longer a Penis is, the surer work tis like to make in the business of Generation, because the Seed is injected with more certainty into the womb by reaching nearer to it. Except the length be monstrous, & then tis more likely to lessen the number of the liveing, rather than increase it.

[473] In Plato's commonwealth it was ordaind, that in case 2 Persons had thoughts of marriage, they shoud See one another stark naked before they were betrothed, reaconing it much better for the Peace of Familys, that defects in the person shoud be discoverd before wedlock than afterwards. Tis said the Muscovites are wise enough to follow this prudent method, and are not content to see one anothers Bodys naked: but desire also to unmask their very Souls too, by seeing each other very drunk, before the Engagement has gone too far; that so they may secure their Retreat, if any discoverys happen to be made to the disadvantage of either.

[474] T'is reported that Cornelia Mother of the Gracchi, was so narrow that she conceivd without looseing her maidenhead, and there was work for the Surgeon before any thing coud be done by the midwife.

[475] Some women in child-bed have so bad a time of it, that both overtures burst into one, and then Nature is so kind in the healing of the Breach, that the Entrance into Joy is much narrower then it was before.

[476] To rub the Penis with oyl of Lavender is of great use to procure Erection: but the drink usd in Provence calld Sambajeu, is much better for that purpose; which is compounded of Wine, yolk of Eggs, Saffran, Sugar, & mace, which may be boild together, or else drunk raw with glorious Success.

[477] A Strong decoction of Human scull & vitriol is a powerfull stopper of bloud in the case of any wound or amputation.

[478] A Decoction of what the French call grande consoude, is the best wash a lady of large naturall Parts can use to make them less. Steel medicines are also good for this purpose

[479] [/80] The best Receipt to make a very strait Maid penetrable, is, a Decoction made of Sheeps-feet, Hartshorn-shaveings, Beaf-marrow, marsh mallow Roots, Lineseed, & Flea-bané, to be taken inwardly & applyd outwardly for some time.

[480] The Romans of old erected a Statue in honour of Virginity. This Statue was calld Bucca Veritatis, & stood erect upon a Pedistal with its mouth open. If any Virgin was Suspected of haveing lost her Maidenhead she might claim the priviledge of justifying her Innocence by puting her finger into the Statues mouth, & if she drew it out whole, she was a woman of honour: but if she had been poluted her Finger was in danger of being bit off. By an Edict publisht by Tiberius no Virgin cou'd be executed for any crime til the Hangman had first deflowerd her, which was a cruel complement paid to Virginity.

[481] In some parts of Affrica the Privitys of Girles are sewd up from their Infancy, makeing the Stitches wide enough for the passage of their Water & their Terms. In this safe condition they continue til they come to be marryed & then the stitches are all rip't out again.

[482] Some women have been got with Child without looseing their maidenhead, when neither the Hymen nor nymphæ have been in the least torn or injurd, so that their pregnancy has appeard Miraculous.

[483] Some women have had milk in their Breasts who had never had amorous Commerce with man: nay there are instances too of Men who have had milk & given Suck without the help of a Miracle. Nay Travellors tell us tis no uncommon thing in the Eastern part of Affrick for the men to have milk & help Suckle the children.

[484] Some naturallists are of opinion, that any young woman of a healthy

sanguine complection, woud have the milk come into their breasts, without haveing had any commerce with a man, if they will let a child suck them every day for a few days successively, for then their Terms will be derivd that [w]ay and changed into milk.

[485] [/81] The Spartans had so much Regard for Marriag[e] that they enacted a Law by which they condemnd all old Bachelors above the age of 24 to be whipt publickly by the women upon a certain Festival, and the Women were sure to lay it on very heartily, for shewing so great a disregard to their charming Sex.

[486] Where there are twins of different sex tis observd that the Female Seldome lives because the Male takes from it too much the natural nourishment & starves it in its Mothers Belly.

[487] The good Women generally cut the Naval string of a boy as long as they can, & that of a Girle as Short, imagining that the Privitys of the Male will be the longer for it, & those of the Female the straiter.

[488] The Emperor Tiberius lovd lewdness more than Women, & his mind was more tainted wth uncleaness than his body. For this reason he caus'd all the various Postures that he found in the naughty book of Eliphatis (the most illustrious Harlot of his Reign) to be painted round his Bedchamber, & woud often be servd at Table by naked women: but all these moveing Prospects coud not stir his feoble constitution.

[489] The Lesbian Sappho was not more famous for her tender Muse, than she was for the unnatural Tast of loveing women better than men, which was a Species of Lewdness very much practiced amongst the Roman Ladys, and not altogether unknown to the Females of this Island.

[490] Twas said of King Charles the 2^d that he coud see things if he woud: but King James woud have seen them if he coud, the first had Talents without Inclination, but the last Inclination without Talents.

[491] In Malabar all nobility decends from the Mother as the surer side, for the Mother may prove her delivery of a child: but the Father can never prove his begetting it.

[492] Barren women are commonly more lascivious than fruitfull ones, because the Heat of the womb, which is often the cause of Sterility, & at the same time the fomenter of wantoness

[493] [/82] Popilia being askt by a very curious Person of her own Sex, why Brutes woud never admit the male after they had once conceivd? answerd with the true Spirit of a woman, because they are Brutes, and know no better.

[494] The Reason why a Cuckold is infamous in most Countrys, is because it is

supposd to happen either by his own ill-treatment of the Wife, or at least by his own folly in Suffering her to have liberty & opportunity to abuse Him. Accordingly twas the Custome formerly in France, in case the Wife was taken in adultery, for the Magistrate to set the poor Husband upon an Ass with His Face towards the Brutes Tail, and make the naughty wife lead him thro' the Streets, and proclaim with a loud voice, **Behold I can lead these 2 asses wherever I please**.

[495]   Semiramis was very strongly inclind to the passion of Love: but at the same time so great a Prude that she constantly took care to order every Man, with whome she had an affair, to be instantly bury'd alive that he might not either thro' vanity or levity, discover her Secret. Tis pity she had not respited their punishment til they had boasted of her Favors, and then I think they woud have had their Reward. But she took it for granted all men were Traytors to the Fair & therefore woud not wait for their Treason, but orderd their punishment before hand to make sure work of it

[496]   Josephus tells us a very Strange Story that Berenice sued out a Divorce from Seleucus, because he caressed her too often. T'is much to be suspected that she rather had an aversion to her Husband than his frequent Performances.

[497]   Man, considering how frail, how dependent, & depravd a creature he is, never makes so ill a figure, as when he is vain of his Perfections, & gives himself airs of Sufficiency. Nay rather than suffer him Self to be inconsiderable, he is vain of his follys, & had rather glory in his Shame, than not distinguish him Self at all. Amongst the rest of our [/83] Vanitys, there is none more ridiculous than when we make ostentation of our Exploits with the women. Whereas supposeing every word we said of our might in that particul[ar] were true, theres hardly a Brute in the Creation but is able to perform oftener with his Female than we can do. Nay a poor sparrow or even a diminutive Fly coud they Speak as well as they coud in Æsops time, might call the ablest of our Boasters a Fumbler. The Emperor Proculus pretended that he had laid with an Hundred Sarmatian Women, which he had taken in the wars, in less than a Fort'night. Mighty Feats for an Emperour to glory in, when a Ram will tup that number of Ewes in one night & impregnate them all! Crusius tells us a Story that a strong Dog of a Servant in his neighbourhood, got ten wenches with child in one night. This indeed was doing business, and no man upon Record ever did more, except Hercules himself, who is famed for having begot 50 boys in one night upon the Bodys of 50 Athenian Damsels, and if this was

true, it was the greatest of all his Atcheivements. The Spaniards are famous for doing handsome things with the Women as appears by the complaint of a Catalonian Lady exhibited against her Husband. She fell down at the Kings feet & implord his Protection. The good King askt her what might be her Grievanc[e] Lord Sire said she, I am a dead Woman unless your Majesty protect me from a hard hearted Husband. What dos he do to you Madam replyd the King? Alas Sire said she, he dos more to me than any Husband in all Spain dos to His Wife, He is impertinent at least ten times every [n]ight. By St Iago answerd the King if this be true he deserve[s] to dye, for he will make every other Woman in my Dominions despise her Husband. However he mitigated his punishment & made him give Security for his good behaviour, and strictly injoind him not to assault the complainant more than 6 times a night for the future.

[498] When the ancients painted Venus, they generally shewd Mercury in some part of the Picture, which carryd this notable instruction, [t]hat we shoud always let Reason have some Share in our Love, to direct [a]nd keep it with in bounds, least what is intended by Providence for our ha[. . .] [/84] be abused by our folly to our destruction. And therefore Solon who was [a] wise man, & studyd the preservation of his Athenians, made a law, that no man shoud on pain of castration caress his Wife or any other woman more than 3 times in a month. This Edict raisd a terrible Mutiny amongst the Women, which made it necessary for that grave Lawgiver to indulge them with one time more, and confine them to once a week. Indeed the Jews are more liberal to the lovely Sex, and allow the men to gratify their Spouses as often as they can but twice a week they must do it by the Law and in case the Husband fell short in this necessary duty, His wife might have right done her by the magistrate. The ancient Philosophers were much in disgrace with the fair Sex, for recommending moderation in the pleasures of Love: but none so much as Aeas who was marryd 6 years and yet solaced his Wife no more than **thrice** the whole time. Yet this was pure continence in him, & not the least incapacity, for he Struck out a child every **Flourish** he made. Messalina, who obliged 25 men in 20 hours, and Cleopatra, who in one night stood the attacque of 105 young Fellows, woud have made sad Disciples to that Philosopher. The first of these illustrious Ladys when she had passt thro' the whole number askt if there were no more, for tho she was tired she was not satisfyd, assata Sum Sed non satiata.

[499] In matters of Love the only sure way to conquer, is to run away according to Cato.

[500]

In Spite of all the Vertue we can boast
The Woman that deliberates is lost.

nor is this the case with the women only, but the men find it as true as they in every Instance of Temptation.

[501] Some who have found themselves of too amorous a complection, and by an im[. . .]e either of Vertue or discretion, have not thought fit to use the Remedy which nature has provided, have endeavourd to humble their constitution another way. They have wore for Example a Leaden Girdle upon their Loins, and Strewd their Beds with white Roses with much Success. They have also eat sower Lemons, and abundance of Lettuce to cool their concupiscence. Others have applyd a Plaister of White Lillys to the Small of their backs, and taken them inwardly to dry up their Seed, and Stiffle their disorderly Inclinations. A Decoction of Hemlock moder-ately taken will have the [s]ame Effect and so will an ointment made of the Leaves of the Pric[. . .] of Peru, if the [. . .]ty Parts are anointed frequently wi[th i]t

[502] [/85]¹⁰ [. . .] most envyed of Women. For [. . .] am in [. . .] you not happy, it were impossible I shoud be so, even tho' I were in possession of your dear enchanting Person. Such are my notions of Love, and such is my love for you, that there is nothing so difficult to do, or so dreadfull to suffer, that I woud not encounter cheerfully, to approve my Self &c.

[503] 12. To Charmante October 23. 1722.

Certainly the Breast of a man in love, is like the troubled sea, that n[eve]r rests; it heaves & swells like that, tosst & disturbd by sighs instead of storms. When the Wretches heart beats high, & is big with hopes of happiness, how it resembles the Waves that roll aloft, & seem to raise their sawcy Pride to Heaven! But when they fall again, & humbly retire into the Bosome of the deep, they represent the Lovers fears that sink His Spirits into Dispair. O that the good naturd Charmante woud please to figure to Herself the restlessness of such an unhappy man, and pity me. What heavenly scenes has hope sometimes opend to my Eyes, when your dear smiles seemd to promise all that was delightfull in this world! and then alas by a Turn as sudden and unaccountable as those that happen in the air, my Heaven was ove[r]cast by your Frowns, and a dreadfull gloom has Shut in all the pleasing Prospect. Ah let that gloom clear up again I

---

10. Some intervening pages are missing. The top of this page is torn and partly illegible.

conjure you, Madam and speak peace to a troubled Soul. Heaven knows I love my Dear Charmante not only beyond Expression, but beyond all Retreat. What hopes can there be of getting the better of a Passion, which even absence inflames? for tho' my Eyes behold her not, my most discerning Fancy surveys all her tempting Charms. Then tis impossible that good Sence can ever cure me; because tis that tells me you are lovely as an angel. Tho I shoud run about to places of Diversion, I shoud only find out, how infinitely better pleasd I shoud be in your delightfull company. What tho' I shoud conver[se] with other Ladys, they will only convince me how much yʳ Excellences out shine theirs. Nothing then can be done to make me love you less, it is not in nature, it is impossible. It is now [/86] alas too late, [. . .] Disease is too far gone, and even Matrimony the last Remedy in such cases can never cure it, because the more I know of the enchanting Charmante, the more I must love Her. Thus madam I am fated by invincible necessity to be intirely & unalterably yours. I intreat you therefore if you have any Pity, any compassion, smile upon my Inclinations and bless me with your favour. May you be as happy as Peace & health, content and love can make you, which is the never-ceasing wish of &c.

[504] 13. To Charmante Octobʳ 26. 1722.

My Imagination is so delighted with a Dream I had this morning at break of day, that I cant contain my self from telling it—you without any other Preface, but only that I wish sincerely it may ᵃˡˡ prove true. I went to sleep as I constantly do with my Dearest Charmante in my thoughts, & dreamt I saw her in a shady Grove sitting on a mossy Bank in a pensive posture, with her head reclind upon her hand. At my approach she started up with some marks of surprize, and discomposure. Her Face seemd lovely as a cherubim, her Stature just, her shape proportionable & unconstraind, and all her behaviour perfectly gracefull & engageing. Her dress was neat, and tight & well fashiond, which added no ᵒⁿᵉ beauty to her Person, but conceald a thousand. I addresst this Divine Female with wonder, counting over every visible perfection, but when I heard her speak, and observd the good nature which sat smileing upon every Features, I was so struck with the charms of her Mind, that I forgot those of her Body. I was astonisht, I was inflamd, and all my Soul was melted into the sincerest affection. For some time she ˢᵉᵉᵐᵈ ᵗᵒ listen to my tender Tale with patience, and I hoped with Pity, til on a sudden ᵗʰᵉ ʷⁱⁿᵈ ᶜʰᵃⁿᵍᵈ, she grew surprizeingly reservd, & seemd uneasy at my presence. Grievd to the Soul I ᵐᵒᵈᵉˢᵗˡʸ retird with all the anguish of a slighted Lover, hopeing my

absence might deliver the cruel charmer from a Wretch that was disagreable to her, & my self from an excess of passion that threatend to take
away my sences, as well as my Quiet. But alas! instead of being abated
[/87] by keeping away, the distemper increast, the Impression wore deeper
every d[ay] and seemd to be the last thing that woud dye of me. I[. . .]
belong to a Rover who can meet with never a Woman more perfect than
his old mistress; for me that is utterly impossible. My Heart was more
than constant for I lovd her better than before. For this uncommon vertue I
fancy I was rewarded in the following happy manner. At some distance I
seemd to hear a flourish of Trumpets Hautbois & kettledrums, which
drawing my Eys towards it, I perceivd a fine Procession advancing The
first Person that appeard was a grave Gentleman with a countenance very
composed, holding in his hand a lighted Flambeau made of Virgin wax.
Next to him rode Venus in her golden car, drawn by 2 Innocent Turtles
which bill'd and coo'd as they passt along. The Goddess lookt all the while
over her shoulder and smiled upon Charmante, who followd next the car,
reaching out to her the Cestus full of all the Enchantments of the Sex. No
sooner did the heavenly Charmante appear, but my Heart flutterd with
joy, and all my Spirits seemd to be in an unspeakable Hurry. She was
cloathd in a loose Robe of Spotless white with her Sable Tresses flowing in
Ringlets upon her shoulders. Thus unadornd she seemd to rival the
Goddess so much that the wanto[n] cupids left their mother to frisk and
play about her. Two of these ran [to] me took me by the hand, and lead me
to this charming woman, who told me with a blush & a smile that she
chose me from all mankind to lead her in that Procession. I receivd her hand
with a Transport no Language can express, and marcht along happyer far
than any Roman Hero at his own Triumph. On the Right of my dear Angel
walkt a comely Dame with a calm and steady countenance in a mantle of
the deepest Azu[re] holding a golden sphære in her Right hand, & with
her left leading a Dog that fixt his Eys wishfully upon her, and waggd his
Tail, and upon my left marcht a beautifull unaffected Virgin without any
ayres or ornament in the world and all she had on was only a lawn shift thro'
which one might discern every comely proportion. Next to us followd a
matron with a serene and peaceable Countenance, have[ing] an everlast-
ing smile upon her face, and pointing up to heaven. After Her came a
plump Damsel but very cheerfull and good humourd, pou[r]ing out of a
cournucope the finest fruit and gayest flowers in the greatest plenty &
perfection. And then followd in the Rear a jolly fresh coulourd Female
with a beautifull little Girle in her arms, and on each side a charming Boy

one of which was grave & wore a mitre on his head, and the other was more [/88] lively and carryd a Truncheon in his hand. We marcht in this order to the Temple of Honor, where a dignifyd Priest joind our hands and discending Angels sang in celestial notes, amen. The Joys that followd need the tongue of those very angels to tell you, for I can find no words that can reach 'em. Adieu my Dear Charmante may you be as happy all your life long as I was dureing the few moments of this delightfull dream, and may you be made so by &c.

[505] 14. To Charmante October 30 1722

[. . .] as in a face that is furiously deformd the more moderate blemishes of moles & Freckles are not observd so

While my Dearest Charmante continues unkind, all other misfortunes loose their sting. Indeed those that befall her charming self affect me after a—lively manner, & reach the very Quick of my Soul. A most feeling Instance of this concern is, what I now suffer for your Indisposition. Just this moment I have the grief to hear you are laid up with a cold & swelld face, which I'm affraid you have caught by the excess of care you take of your self. I am most sincerely and most sensibly sorry for it, and the impracticableness of comeing to see you just at this time, makes me almost distracted. However I beg the most charming of Womankind to believe, that my Heart, my soul, my tenderest wishes are with Her, & I protest solemnly I woud ease all her Pains at the Price of bearing them double my self. May you eternally frown upon me if this be not — true, & that's a curse I woud not pull down upon my head to enjoy any other Blessing. Neither can the Lovely Charmante doubt the certainty of what I say, if she believes I love Her. That Passion takes a disinterested delight in makeing its dear Object happy, and while tis conscious of that, all its pains are converted into pleasure, and tis meer luxury to a Lover to suffer for his mistresses service. That Luxury I shoud relish beyond all other, and if I coud make the Darling of my Soule easy by transplanting all her Greifs upon my self, I shoud not only count them things indifferent like a Stoick, but shoud even, revel in them like an Epicurean. If this be false Madam there is nothing true & I must henceforth pronounce that Life itself is a delusion, our sences all deceave us, and even Faiths a Lye. So sure as your Eys behold a Heaven [/89] above, & so sure as mine behold a Heaven below, when I see the excellent Charmante, so certainly I love you most unfeighisly & everlastingly. If after this you can stil be Infidel enough to disbelieve me, I must work a miracle to convince you, by shewing, that a man is constant, & that a Passion that is violent can be lasting. Adieu my

Dearest Charmante may you always be blesst with health & the full enjoyment of what you love; and may you have some sympathy for him who
plights you his eternal Faith and is with the most intire and never dying
affection &c.

[506] 15. To Charmante November 1. [1]722.

I might as easily go about to describe the Beauty of coulours to one
that was born blind, as to convey to the insensible Charmante, who never
lovd, a just notion of the Pain I feel whenever I am forced to leave Her.
The nearest Likeness I can draw of it, is, the horrid Regret a Wretch
almost famish't woud have, to be hurryed away from a Table, coverd with
all the Daintys that Luxury coud invent, or Expence coud furnish. For
Gods sake imagin, how his mouth woud water, and how he woud devour
with his Eyes, what he was forbid to touch with his Teeth. Just like that
Wretch I am greivd whenever I am separated from the lovely Female with
whome my soul, and every one of my sences are charmd. In her absence I
pine, I languish like a lonely Turtle, lamenting in plaintive notes that his
inconstant mate is parted from Him. In that situation the Picture I draw in
my own mind of your engageing Qualitys, makes my loss appear in all its
weight of affliction. For to speak the truth, I can never think of my Dear
Charmante with out forming the lovelyest Ideas of Female perfection.
From thence follow naturally those 2 certain conclusions, how much she
deserves to be happy herself, and how tranportingly so, she woud make
the man on whome she bestows her Heart. To me that were a Blessing in
good earnest, [/90] that woud hardly leave any room to lament the loss of
Paradise, because her charms and her Innocence woud make one fancy
ones self there. For my Part I can have no notion that any mortal Felicity
can reach higher than the joy of obtaining your affections, except it be the
pleasure of makeing you happy, and of meriting much more than our
modern nobility do theirs, the title of &c.

[507] 16. To Charmante Novr 9. 1722.

I beg the generous Charmante will please to forgive me if I presume to
write once more, & that she wont look upon that to be a transgression of
her orders, which is only a promise of obedience. Tho' I must confess her
last orders were very short & sudden, yet I will prove the intire Regard I
have for Her, by exactly observing them. I will endeavour to convince
Her, that the slightest Hint of her Pleasure shall be a Law to me, tho' never
so disagreable to my self. But Dear Madam what coud provoke you to
deliver your commands last night in that odd Place? I dont remember I
was asking an Alms of you, that you shoud deny me, like a common

Begger, in the street. You know very well, you have lately had more opportunitys than one of signifying your mind to me at your own house. That certainly had been a more proper Place, unless you intended by the surprize of the onset, to cut off all possibility of Reply. Surely you coud not apprehend, I shoud in the bitterness of my Soul have reproacht you with any Instances of your former conduct, in case you had attackt me in a fair Feild of Battle. You had been safe from such ungenerous treatment from me, madam, because I think it very absurd, to upbraid a Lady with lesser Favours, when I am desireing the greatest. God knows were I capable of finding any fault with you, it shoud be, that your behavior, instead of being too kind, had not been kind enough. But Madam you are safer from any Reproaches from me, than from your [/91] self, and let your treatment of me ever so cruel & ungenerous, stil my carriage to you shall be unblamable. Dureing my whole address to you, I have behavd with truth & honour, and shall always love you too well to do, or say any thing to your disadvantage. I coud not injure you madam for the whole world, nor for what is more valuable than 20 worlds, your dear self, and that's as high as honour can go. However if after all, you shoud determine to make me unhappy, I will submit to my hard Fate, without reproaching any thing but my stars, & in return of your unkind usage, shall earnestly pray, that every thing that is good, every thing that is prosperous may befal you and if ever you marry any other man, (oh dreadfull thought) may he set as just a value upon your fine Qualitys, & charming Person, & take as much pleasure in makeing you happy, as I shoud do, and more I'm sure will be impossible. May sprightly Health & gaiety of mind, may full Content, & all the Joys resulting from vertue & honour, attend you to the end of your days. Provided my Dearest Charmante is thus compleatly bles't, it matters not what becomes of &c

Her unfortunate humble servant

[508] These Passionate Billets were writ to a Lady who had more charms than honour, more wit than discretion. In the begining, she gave the writer of them the plainest marks of her favour. He did not only hint his Passion to Her, but also confirmd it by many a close hugg & tender squeeze, which she sufferd with the patience of a Martyr. Nay that she might have no doubt of his Intentions, he put the Question to Her in the plainest terms, which she seemd to agree to, not only by a modest Silence, but by permitting the same familiaritys for more than a month afterwards. She saw him every day, receivd his letters, and fed his Flame by the gentlest behaviour in the world, til at last on a sudden with out any Provocation on his part,

she grew Resty and in a moment turnd all her Smiles into Frowns, & all his Hopes into utter dispair. Whe[/92]ther this suprizeing change proceeded from any private scandal—she had receivd about him, or from pure Inconstancy of temper, I cant be sure. The first is not unlikely, because he had a Rival that had no hopes of Succeeding openly, & therefore it might be necessary to work underground, and blow him up by a mine. This Suspicion is a little confirmd by that Rival's marrying her afterwards, who was then so poor, that t'is likely that good naturd Woman might wed him out of Charity, especially since he was at the same time so unwholesome, that he stood in much greater need of a Nurse than a Wife. Tis true he did beget a child upon her Body, but he had not vigour enough to give it life. She did not choose him for his beauty and length of chin, tho possibly she might for those pure morals, wch recommended him to His Grace of W——n for a companion. But If after all she did not marry him for his Vertue neither, then it must certainly have been for the worst quality any Husband can have, for his wit. That I own he has his share of, yet so overcharg'd & encumberd wth words, that he do's more Violence to the Ear than a Ring of bells, for he's altogether as noisy, without haveing so many changes. But if he had never so much wit, a wife may be sure the Edge of it will be turnd mostly against her Self. Wit is a dangerous Quality both for the Owner, and every one that has the misfortune to belong to Him. He that is curs't with wit, has commonly too much Fire to think, too much Quickness to have any Discretion. If it be petulant it draws its owner into Quarrels, & very often the breaking an unseasonable Joke, ends in breaking of Bones. But supposeing the very best, that Wit be so very inoffensive and entertaining, as to make People fond of those that have it. This draws 'em into a train of Idleness & Intemperance, & makes 'em utterly neglect their affairs & their Familys. Besides it exposes them to very great expence, and seldome fails to end in the ruin both of their Health, and their Fortune. In one word, Wit rarely makes a man either happier or better, & much seldomer makes him Rich than immortal. Wit in a man, like beauty in a woman, may please & divert other People, but never dos its owner any good. But then wit is the worst domestick Quality in the world, It insults the Wife, it beggers the children, it starves the servants, and Spreads want & Poverty over the whole Family. Heaven defend Charmante from the dreadfull Effects of it!

[509] [/93] Most Creatures have there Sympathys and Antipathys, and man himself with all his boasted Reason is by no means exempt from them. The great Leviathan is not born without his Fears, for he dreads the

Sword Fish, which often wounds his fat sides. The Elephant too so terrible in war, will tremble at the sight of a little mouse, that is apt to creep into his Ears. The lordly Lyon too, which terrifys all other creatures is mortally affraid of a Cock, whose crowing makes him tremble like a Quartan ague. Nay the Devil himself, whose horns & cloven feet are such a terrour to mankind, is put into a cold sweat with musty Relicks and Holy water. No wonder then that man the Bully of this lower World, is dismayed at a cat, or a Toad, or a Slice of cheshire cheese; nor is it wonderfull that a Woman, who fears neither Devil nor Husband, is scard out of her sences at the sight of an harmless Spider, or a nimble Frogg, which have much more reason to be affraid of Her.

[510] The Elk is a sociable creature, and sets a fair example of generous Friendship to unfreindly man. For when any one of the Herd is wounded, the rest stand over & defend him til they are all kill'd upon the Spot.

[511] The Rain deer is the humblest of all Qadrupeds, & in Lapland will draw a Sledge over the Snow 100 miles a day. they use each Deer to one Journey only, which he performs without guideing, tho the Inhabitants pretend to direct them by a whisper

[512] Red-Deer are the only Brutes that Shed Tears, & then only in the article of death, or at times of extreem danger the Stags shed their Horns yearly, but the poor Cuckold never sheds his, but carrys them with infamy to his grave, while possibly the Kind spouse that planted them, survives him in good repute, has a Pension from the court, & is visited by all the Prudes of Quality about the Towne.

[513] The Wolf is tamed by the Indians, and used like a dog but a Fox like a Shrew, can never be made tame either by kind or by Cross usage. He sheds his coat every Summer: but Stinks as much in his new cloaths as in his old.

[514] T'is said meliciously of womens Tongues, that they are like Race Horses which run the faster the less weight they have to carry. Or like the Philosophical Wheel that has the greatest velocity in vacuo, because it meets with no Resistance.

[515] [/94] The Bones which support a humane Body are no less than 300, every one of which is of admirable use to our mortal frame all these are coverd with a thin Membrane extreemly sensible and are nourisht by the marrow they contain. The Joints are made to move about, by the insertion of the Head of one into the pan or socket of the other, and to prevent the 2 bones rubbing upon one another, they are lined with a Cartilage or Gristle wch is a Substance very tough & slippery. and to hinder them from

starting out of their place, they are knit together by a very strong liga-
ment. When these ligaments are stretcht by any spraine, they contract
again by the immediate application of cold Remedys.

[516]   The Muscles that cover our Bones are no less than 405, which are exactly
fitted to the Several motions of the body, and are divided from each other
by a thin membrane. These muscles are all movd by a Tendon, & that
tendon is twitcht by the animal Spirits, and those Spirits put in motion by
the Will after a manner wholly incomprehensible, tho tis perform'd
within our selves an hundred times in a day.

[517]   As the Heart is the orignal of the arterys, which from the Aorta Magna are
brancht into every part of the Body, so the Liver is the original of the
Veins, whose Ramification begins at the Vena Cava. But the nerves spring
all from the Brain and the Spinal Marrow, which is the same substance
with the brain, so that in truth a mans Brains reach quite down to his
Rump. These nerves altho' impervious to our Sight, are yet the chanels
thro' which the animal Spirits are conveyd to all Parts, and are the cause
of every Sence and Motion. The Vital Spirits flow with the artereal Blood
thro' the arterys, & give life & heat to the whole Body. But the natural
Spirits are conveyd thro' the Veins, & are employd in nourishing every
particular member. What these several Spirits are, & how they are produced is difficult to know, only we are sure they are only the fine parts of
matter, because they are common to all living creatures, and utterly
distinct from the Reasonable Soul, which is peculiar to man, & makes
him the Image of his Maker. All the acquaintance we have with this
Divine part of us, depends upon some of its Qualitys & effects. We [/95]
discern it to be the Power by which we think, reason, decide, and will any
thing, & particularly the faculty by which we arrive at the Knowledge of
the Supream Being. These are all Qualifications, of which the most Sensible Brute is not capable; tho' they have some Instincts ingrafted in their
Natures, which supply the place of Some of them. Of Instincts there seem
to be 2 sorts, which all animals seem to have planted in them, of which
the first is that of Self Preservation by which they all endeavour to preserve, support, and defend their own Being. The other is that of propa-
gating their Species, protecting their young, and training them up, til they
are in condition to provide for themselves. In all these cases Instinct
serves them instead of Reason, and sometimes so much resembles it, that
t'is mistaken by small Philosophers for Reason.

[518]   Our nourishment is conveyd thro' our whole Body in this manner. While
we are chewing our Meat, a firmentative liquor issues from the Glands of

the mouth, and not only moistens the food to make it slip easyer down the Gullet, but also disposes it the better to digest in the Stomach. By digestion there, tis reduced into a kind of Pap calld chyle, which being dischargd thro' the lower orifice of the Stomach into the Laetes, or Small guts the first separation is made. The grosser parts are thrown off into the great Gutts, thro' which by the peristaltick motion they are squeesd into the Rectum to be dischargd by Stool. and in healthy people they need about 48 hours to perform this Journey. But the Nutritive parts of the Chyle are suckt up by the mesaraick Veins, and by them transmitted thro' the Vena Porta into the Liver, where the Blood is separated from its 3 Recrements, that are carryd off by 3 Several channels. The first is the Serous, or watry part, which runs off thro the Emulgent Veins into the Kidneys, and from thence thro' the Ureters into the Bladder. The 2ᵈ being the more turbid part is attracted by the Spleen, and by that straind into the great Gut, as into a common shoar. But the adust particles are draind into the Gall bladder, & from thence are also voided into the Intestinum Crassum where by their stimulateing quality they help to provoke our Stools. When the Blood is thus cleansed from its [/96] Impuritys, and has receivd its purple coulour, it flows into the Vena Cava, & from thence is distributed by the help of the smaller veins into every part of the Body. While the bloud is makeing its circulation round the Body, which it performs in each part sucks in as much of the Dew of it as is Sufficient to nourish, & keep it in good Repair. This some call the 3ᵈ concoction, & the Excrements that are separated find a Passage thro' the skin by Sweat, or Insensible perspiration, which last is much the most plentifull evacuation, being in weight at least 2 thirds of what we eat & drink if we are in health. But if the Pores are shut up by the impression of the cold air, what ought to be dischargd this way, must seek a passage thro the Glands of the mouth, or the nose, or else will cause a cough or an Inflamaton, and possibly end in a Feaver or a consumption.

[519] The method of our being hungry is this, whatever part about us wants nourishment, twinges the fibrous Veins, these twinge the larger Veins, these again Sollicite the Liver, and that the mesaraick Veins, these importune the Stomack, and that shrivels it self up haveing nothing to bestow, which action of the Stomack gives us that sensation calld Hunger. and when it wants moisture, it Drains the Glands of the mouth & throat, and makes us suffer Thirst.

[520] Doctors differ very much concerning the Quantity of Blood that men of moderate Size have in their Whole Bodys. Some have been so niggardly as

to allow it no more than 20 Pounds or pints, but others are much more bountifull, & Dr Keil particularly gives it no less than 100. But the middle betwixt these 2 Extreems seems nearest the truth, and the Just Quantity is most probably between 6 & 7 Gallons, or about 50 Pints, includeing the other Juices of the Body wch are inconsiderable. By analyzeing the Blood, there has been discoverd a fixt Alcalious salt, and a Sulphur, but no Acid. But whether the heat of it proceeds from its rapid motion, or from an Ebullition occasiond by the mixture of Aerogenious Juices, is far from being determin'd. And stil the Learned are more at a loss to find out how it comes by its purple coulour, which seems to belong only to the Globules, or Earthy particles, which float in the Serum, and makes the whole appear of a florid Red while t'is warm, [/97] and blended together. The Blood moves with great velocity, being forced by the Systole & Diastole of the Heart into the Arteries, & returning to it again by the Veins. But there's an amazeing difference of opinion amongst the learned concerning the force of the Heart. Borellus says the force of the Heart in a healthy strong man, is equal to a weight of 35000 pounds, while Dr Keil computes it only equall to 5 pounds, which vast difference of sentiment shews how uncertain these things are, & how arrogant it is to decide them peremptorily & dogmatically.

[521] Travellors, who are Seldome Slaves to the Truth, tell us very gravely, that in the East Indies there's a sort of serpent call'd a Boa, which measures 120 feet in length & ^is big in proportion, So that he often swallows a Buck horns and all for his Dinner, & it don't sit heavy upon his stomach

[522] The Same grave authors assure us likewise, that in Egypt there is a large Fowl, calld an Ibis, that when he finds himself out of order will give himself a Glyster with his Beak, and that tis to the example of this Bird we owe that usefull operation.

[523] The Chinese letters are said to be real characters, which Several nations read ^each in their own Language. Just like the numeral Figures, Physical Weights, & the Marks for the Planets & signs of the Zodiack, which are the same to most nations of Europe, & constantly read in the Tongue of the country. Just like these are the Chinese letters, as Travellors tell us, which might serve for a universal Language, like that which Bishop Wilkins ^recommends under the name of a Real character.

[524] Always dine with as much Temperance in this World, as if you expected to sup in the next, said Leonidas.

[525] In Europe t'is computed that about 1020 fixt stars are visible to the naked Eye, tho' many more are Seen by the help of Telescopes. The nearest of

these is at so vast a distance from the Earth, that a cannon Ball shot from thence on Adams birth day woud hardly have reacht us at this time.

[526] [/98] The Revd Mr Wollaston in his book calld Natural Religion delineated, proves that all vice is either Speaking or acting contrary to some known Truth, or a denying, or behaveing as if we deny'd, things to be what they are, by which we give our maker the lye, and, as much as in us lyes, overturn & pervert the decrees of his Providence. Thus if I neglect to worship God, I treat him as if he were not the author & preserver of my Being, & of all the Beings in the universe. If I kill, beat, defraud or abuse my Fellow creature, I plainly deny by these actions that he has a right to his own life, Limbs, & Estate which I use as if they were not his, & as if I had a right to do with them as I pleasd, wch certainly I have not. If I am so hard hearted as not to pity his misfortunes, or forbear to Supply his wants, when I can do it without great inconvenience to my Self, I treat him as a Person that is not indigent or in affliction, which is directly against Truth. If I live riotously and gorge my Self with too much eating & drinking, I treat my Body as a machine not capable of suffering by these Excesses, and act against the great Truth that every creature ought to preserve its being as long as it can. If I am incontinent, and lye with every Woman I meet, I use those women as if they belongd to me when they really do not, and suffer my Self to be governd by appetite like a Brute, & not by Reason like a man, and is in effect Saying that I am a Brute, and not a Reasonable creature, which I shoud pronounce a Lye if any body else affirmd it. Besides by lying with any woman that I have not a Right to by marriage, I do an injury to another, to please my Self, which is acting against a fundamental Truth. Neither doth her consent alter the case, because I am not to do any thing mischeivous to a Woman, tho she when blinded by passion, or corrupted by mony or deluded by deceitfull Promises, shoud yeild to it. In all these instances her consent is not free, because she is inveigled and over-reacht, which is as much a Violence offerd to the mind, as a Rape is a force upon the Body. In the same manner he condemns all other vices by being violations of Some plain Truth, and consequently against all the Rules of Reason, and our own and other People's happiness. and that we may not plead Ignorance, what things are true & what not, the author of nature has endued us with Reason, which if duly attended to, will be our Sufficient Direction. Upon [/99] this Foundation all Natural Religion is built, according to our author, and the light by which any Person of common understanding may clearly discern the distinction betwixt moral Good & Evil. The same

author supposes the Residence of the Soul to be in the Brain, cloath'd with a Vehicle of the most refind matter, which Serves as the Band of Connection or union between the Soule & the Body. With this Vehicle of pure matter he imagins the Soule to fly away, at the Death or dissolution of the Body, to the Region allotted for departed Spirits. And when the soul comes to be disentangled from the grosser matter of the body, its activity will exert it self in a Surprizeing manner, all its Sensations, whether of pain or pleasure, will ᵇᵉ vastly quicker, than we find them at present, and its ideas will be more clear & extensive. Then we Shan't know things by the ˢˡᵒʷ assistance of the Sences, and by the tedious deductions of Reason but by Intuition, that is an instantaneous apprehension of every thing we have an inclination & capacity to know. Our author proves the certainty of a future State, from the Justice & goodness of the Supream Being, who woud no[t] suffer good men to be miserable, & ill men to prosper & be happy in this world, (not so much as in one Single Instance,) except He intended to make amends for all ⁱⁿ another State, and reward every reasonable Creature there for what he has done in the flesh whether it be good, or whether it be evil makeing just allowances for every ones Sufferings, and haveing due Regard to their Talents and opportunitys here below. He proves that the Deity knows every thing to come, even what will be done by free agents, as well as what is passt, because there is no Succession of time with the Eternal God, who Surveys all times & all Events at one view. Besides God sees every thing in its causes, wᶜʰ are all chaind together, and destind by his Providence to produce their certain effects. He discerns all the Seeds of action, as they lye in the hearts of free agents, knows all their passions, all their tendencies, and how far they are like to steer & direct them by Reason. Some sagacious men make a shrewd guess at many things that will happen hereafter, & Spirits much better than men: & what angels & men can do imperfectly God is able to do in the utmost perfection.

[527]   [/100] Paper was invented so long ago as in the time of Alexander the Great, about 480 years before the Birth of our Saviour. The use of the Needle, or Mariners Compass, was found out so lately as the year 1300. Printing was first discovered, (in Europe at least,) in the year 1412 ᵇʸ ᵃ ᴰᵘᵗᶜʰ ˢᵒᵘˡᵈⁱᵉʳ: tho' tis pretended it was known in China many ages before. About the Same ᵗⁱᵐᵉ a German Monk making some Experiments in Chymistry, stumbled upon the way of makeing Gunpowder, which Invention tho' it may seem a little pernicious, has however savd abundance of Blood. For by the help of this noisy composition ᴺᵃᵗⁱᵒⁿˢ come to a much quicker

decision of their Quarrels than they usd to do, and one Side gives way in a very few hours, whereas heretofore when other arms were in fashion, they woud renew a Battle ᵃᵍᵃⁱⁿ the next morning, and perhaps be hewing & hacking one another for Several days together. By this slow way method of destruction vast numbers of men usd to be killd on both Sides, and whole armys cut to pieces, whereas now tis a very bloody battle in which 10,000 are slain.

[528] We shoud to nick the proper Season of doing every thing, which is a considerable part of humane Prudence. Sʳ Francis Bacon instances in a very adroit Solicitor of his time, who never woud ask a favour of any Man til after he had dined, that so the appetites of his Freind might be quiet & ⁱⁿ good Humour.

[529] Mʳ Dryden usd to say, that good naturd people have a milkiness of Blood, without any mixture of Sharp humours.

[530] A Man of great Generosity caus'd this Epitaph to be engraved upon his Tombe, What I spent, I losst, what I leave behind, my Relations possess. Only what I gave away, I carry along with me to the other World.

[531] When a man keeps a woman, tho' he cant properly be said to be marryed, yet he may be said to live in the Suburbs of Matrimony.

[532] [/101] The Italians have a Proverb very big with good Sence to this Effect, the Man who lives by hope, will be in great danger of dying by Hunger.

[533] Tho' it be in every Fathers power to leave his son a Title or an Estate, yet he may if he please leave him a better thing, The Honour of being descended from a vertuous man, by which the Blessing of Heaven will be intaild upon the Family.

[534] Hesiods Paradox πλέον ἥμισυ πάντθ half is more than the whole, proves true in many Instances, particularly in politick Arithmetick. The Dutch burn one half of their Spices finding the remaining moity fetch more mony than the whole woud have done, and so it proves in every thing besides that overstocks the Market.

[535] An excellent water for the Eyes when troubled with any sharp humour. Of Eye-bright, White rose water, Plantain water and prepard Powder of Tutty, of Each one Penny worth. With this Water, gently wash the Eys every night & morning, & often if the case is very bad.

[536] Some Profligate Men undergo more Watchings & fatique in following a vicious Amour ⁱⁿ ʷⁱⁿᵗᵉʳ Qᵘᵃʳᵗᵉʳˢ than they do in following an Enimy for a whole Campaign together ⁱⁿ ᵗʰᵉ Sᵘᵐᵐᵉʳ and I have heard one of 'em so ingenuous as to confess, that he believd he coud conquer his corrupt Inclinations, with half the Pains he was at in gratifying them.

[537] There is a humourous Fragment of Apollodorus the Comique Poet, which Says, there's no barring up a house so fast, but a Cat & a whore-master will find the way into it.

[538] Eating Blood was forbid for 2 Reasons, 1 because the Soule of all Brutes consists in the fine parts of the blood, & we are only permitted to devour their Bodys. 2 because in sin-offerings the burning of the flesh was to expiate the polutions of our Bodys, and the sprinkleing of the Blood was to attone for the Sins and Impuritys of the Soule. The Eating therefore of blood woud have been to rob God of that sacrifise, & our Selves of the necessary benefit of it. Besides as the Soul or Essence of the Brute is in the Blood, the eating of it might in some measure graft it in our Selves.

[539] [/102] The Jews are Split into 2 Sects that are utterly irreconcileable, the 1st consists of the Posterity of Juda Benjamin & Levi, which after the destruction of Jerusalem by Titus were disperst all over Europe: & the 2d is the Posterity of the other ten Tribes, which were long before transplanted into Assyria and other parts of Asia, which are calld Karites. because they only read the Books of Moses & the Prophets, while the others are cheifly directed by the Traditions of their Rabbi contain in the Talmud.

[540] The Copti were baptizd both with water & Fire, for they were not only plunged overhead & ears in Some running water: but were cauterizd with the figure of the Cross upon their Breasts. & so did not only carry about them the inward Power, but also the outward marks of Christianity.

[541] The Mahometans are divided into 2 Sects, which hate one another heartily. Some Follow Ali believeing Him to be most genuin Interpreter of the Alchoran. The greatest part of the Persians are of this Sect: but the Turks prefer Ebubecar Omar & Omar to Ali, and embrace their Interpretation of Mahomets meaning. These oppose each other with a most furious Zeal, wch has been the occasion of most bloody wars betwixt those 2 nations.

[542] The Balsom-Tree is always wounded with Glass bone or Ivory to Let the Balsome distil from it, for if it is cut with any Iron Instrument that noble shrub will wither & dye in a very short time.

[543] Our English word Harlot is deriv'd from Arlotta the Skinners Daughter who was concubine to Robert Duke of Normandy & mother to our William the Conqueror.

[544] A Snail is thought to have no Eyes; but gropes out its way with its horns

[545] One who spoke very properly, said of an Englishman, that he was as drunk as a Spunge.

[546] A Bat is the only bird that has hair & teeth, & tis on account of that Singularity, being very bashfull. that it dos not appear in the day time

amongst the rest of the featherd kind, but sneaks abroad in the dusk when the others are retird to roost.

[547] [/103] A Wag said of my Ld Clarendon's & Mr Eachard's History, that they were like a Pudding very ill made, where the Plumbs run all to one side, so their commendations lean'd altogether to one party.

[548] The finest Gentleman in the world is an English Man that speaks, and a French man that thinks, says St Evremont

[549] It was said in complement of Julius Cæsar, that he thought nothing [at al] done, so long as any thing remaind undone

nil actum reputans si quid superesset agendum

[550] T'is a man's birth-right to Speak his mind: but often his Prudence to hold his tongue.

[551] A contempt for Defamation discredits it, and defeats its authors of the malicious pleasure of makeing us uneasy.

[552] Uneasiness at an ill-natured Story, puts it into the Power of every paltry Lyer to make us miserable.

[553] Men of business are accustomed to a style of dispatch, that makes them write below the Dignity of History

[554] When you find anger begin to disorder your mind Suffer it not to break out into any bitter words, or boistrous actions, til you have said over this pacifying Prayer, Forgive us O God our Trespasses, as we forgive them that trespass against us.

[555] By the French Kings Declaration it appears, that the Debt of that crown was in the year 1725 near 1800, millions of Livers which is almost 100 milions Sterling. The Interest hereof at 5$ cent is 90 milions of Livers, exactly one half of that monarchs Revenue. From the other moiety if you deduct the vast charge of collecting, which amounts to 60 milions at last, he has then no more than 30 milions remaining. Out of this He is to maintain 100,000 Men, all his civil list, & his most Expensive Pleasures, besides repairing the great Roads of the Kingdome, which is performd at His majestys charge. By this state it appears, that France is in a very wretched condition, and that either the great monarch or his unhappy creditors must be undone very soon.

[556] Tis certain the late Dauphine of France had his fortune told him long before Spain was bequeathd to the Duke of Anjou, that he shoud be the father of a King but never live to be a King himself. This Horoscope was in print long before his death.

[557] [/104] Old King Louis sent his Grandsons the Dukes of Burgundy and Berry, to accompany their Brother the King of Spain to the Frontiers. By

the way the arch Monsr de Berry askt the Duke of Burgundy why the King sent them so far with their Brother? Without doubt said the ^grave Duke that we might be better acquainted with the country. No no replyd the little Wagg It is, by shewing us all to the Spaniards, to convince them he has sent them the best of the three. And in truth the Duke of Anjou was the best natured of the whole Set, and did nothing else during the Journey but reconcile the eternal Quarrels of his Brothers.

[558] Bish^p Burnet going to a neighbour in the Country upon a visit, His coach ^happened ^to stick in a Hole so fast, that his 2 Horses coud not drag it out. All the Servants he had with Him lent a hand, but to no manner of Purpose. At last the coach man with a dispairing countenance told the B^p ^plainly, that while His Lord^p was by, it was impossible to make the Horses Stir an Inch but here we must stick. How so said the Bishop? Why said he because your Lord^p wont give his leave to Swear. Nay Richard replyd the good Prelate, if Swearing be necessary to get us out the mire, pray fetch us out as soon as you can. Upon this permission Richard Swore so many strong oaths that the Horses were put upon their mettle, and tuggd the coach out in an Instant.

[559] Bish^p Tr . . . had so much of the Rake in his constitution that neither holy orders nor consecration coud keep him within bounds. He woud swear like any officer of the Guards & now & then too woud covet his neighbours Wife. Amongs the rest of his Intrigues he had tempted the Spouse of a poor Poet to infidelity who happend unhappily to Suprize them in the flagrant Act. The Husband civilly begd his Lord^ps pardon & retird, into the Street, where he with great Solemnity gave his Blessing to every one he met. At last an old acquaintance inquireing how he came to be so free of his Benedictions? Why replyd the Poet, very humourously, Since my Ld Bish^p is takeing the trouble to do my business for me in the House, it is but just I Shoud be doing his in the Street.

[560] To shew that every thing was bought & sold in France in the days of old Louis, Madame de Montauban gave Madame de Harcourt 1000 crowns for her Turn of going with the King to Marli for 3 days. That monarch usd to take about a Dozin ^choice People with him, 6 men & 6 women as many & woud fill the Pavilions at that delightfull Place, calld the 12 Signs of the Zodiack.

[561] [/105] A mercenary young Fellow marryd an antique Lady with the expectation of a great deal of mony: but finding little, he treated the old Gentlewoman very unworthily. She Stomach't the ill usage, & resolvd to make her Tyrant smart for it. She had enterd deep into the occult Sci-

ences, and understood all sorts of Enchantment, so that She was compleatly qualifyd for the female Passion of Revenge, & had resentment
strong enough to put it in execution. After she had practiced about a
week upon the young Gentleman, he fell away so fast that he thought
himself in a galloping Consumption. This was the more Surprizeing,
because his appetite was keen as that [. . .] & his Digestion regular. He slept
very sound the whole night, but instead of being refresht by it, he found
himself so sore and tired that he coud hardly tur[n] in his bed. He consulted the Top Physicians, & tryd all sorts of Remedys to no purpose; so
that in less than a month he gave himself quite over. At last the maid
seeing her master in that wofull plight, told him, that the night before
hearing a noise in his bed-chamber, she got up & peept thro' the Kea hole,
& saw her mistress wave a White wand over him, & then mutter some
strange words, by which she turnd him into a Horse. Then she saddled
him, & put a glittering kirb into his mouth, and vaulting nimbly upon his
back, began to whip him unmercifully upon this the poor Horse kickt &
curvetted a little about the room, & at last flew away out of the Window.
The[. . .] at 4 in the morning She brought her nagg home just as foaming
hot, as if she had been ten miles & back again to fetch a midwife. After this
she unbewithct Him again, & restord him to his humane figure, & no
wonder if by such hard Rideing he came to be so sore & so fatigued as he
found himself every morning. Upon this information the sick man
caused his Wife to be instantly apprehended for a witch, and confessing
the fact at her tryall, and her Judge & Jury haveing a great deal of faith, she
was condemnd to be burnt, and the Sick man very soon recoverd.

[562] A young Girle was sent to a Nunnery for Education, but likeing neither
the sobriety nor confinement of that life, Slipt out at the Gate one evening
& made her escape: but not knowing where to go she got into a great
basket which she found in the market in which she intended to take up her
lodging that night. At [/106] 2 in the morning she was wakt with the high
words which 3 men seemd to have together, & being curious to see what
was the matter, she raisd her head so high out of the Basket that one of the
men perceivd the Pinners of a Female. Well said he we wont fall out about
the matter for here is one shall end the dispute. Haveing said this, he
luggd the poor girle out of her nest & made her go along with them away
they went to a neighbouring church, forced open the door, & then movd
away a great Stone that gave entrance into a Vault where an ancient
Gentlewoman had been interd the day before, who had orderd some of
her Jewells to be buryd with her. The 3 Rogues being more fearful of the

dead than the liveing had debated very warmly who shoud go down into the vault & rifle the corpse, but haveing brought the Girle along with them, they forced her upon this frightfull service. She beggd hard to be excusd: but D— Her, they said, she must obey, or they woud cut her throat that instant. However they furnisht her with Instruments to open the Coffin, and forct her down without loss of time. After a great deal of fear & fumbleing she brought them up a Ring, & a Pearl Necklace. This is not all you little Bitch, said the Ruffians, you must tear the Earrings from her Ears, or we'll put you to death. Upon these menaces down went the Girl the 2ᵈ time: but being longer than ordinary, they closd up the mouth of the vault, & left the poor creature to perish in that dismal place with fear & hunger. No case can be conceivd more dreadfull than what Miss was in for 24 hours, all the while lamenting her hard fate, & giveing her self over. But it happend the next night another Gang of Rogues came upon the Same pious Errand, & haveing opend the vault descended with a dark lanthorn: but perceiveing something stir, believd to be sure it coud be nothing but a Spirit, and therefore leting fall their lanthorn, they fled as fast as fear coud carry them. This happy accident gave the poor Girl an opportunity of retireing from those Regions of death, and reconciled her to all the Inconveniences of a Cloister.

[563] When some injudicious People get a word, or grow fond of any expression, they come in time to use it mechanically upon every occasion. The Lord F . . . h being a welbred Person, whenever he spoke of himself, he was extreemly apt to say he had the honour to do such a thing. According to this style he let the House of Commons once understand, he had the honour to live near one of the gates at Westminster; & acquanting the King how his Varlet of a coachman overturnd him in the street, he let his Majesty know, that he had the honour to be pure and dirty.

[564] [/107] Now & then a man makes his court to some great [. . .] by expressions that woud seem a little shocking to others. The great monarch of France complaind once to Monsʳ Cavois Mareschal des logis, that some of his officers had very straight lodgings. Tis impossible Sire Said the Mareschal, it can be otherwise, when your Majestys Court is so numerous. Why replyd the King, Fontainbleau usd to Serve my Father & my Grandfather very commodiously. Your Majᵗʸ Says very true, said the other but they were poor Kings indeed. The King Swallowd this implicit flattery with very good humour, tho it was at the expence of his immediate [mini]sters & Monsʳ Cavois grew into favour upon it.

[565] A certain Remedy for a bloody Flux or any other flux is as follows, Take

the yolks of new laid Eggs and beat them up very well together with double-refined Sugar. This put into a glass of Nants Brandy & mixing them well together drink 'em off, and if the case be very obstinate repeat this dose 3 day together, & youll not fail of a cure. Anothe[r] Remedy in these cases is take a vomit of Hypoᶜacanna, & if the cure dont follow immediately put about 3 grains of the same Hypocoacanna into conserve of Roses or in a glass of Canary & drink it off the 3 Succeeding nights takeing cheifly for your food fat mutton broth.

[566] In the case of continual vomiting the best Remedy is a grain of Opium repeated some days together which will comfort the stomach & bring it to its natural Tone.

[567] Monsʳ Hermenonville was a formal old fellow whose constant complement was that he humbly kisst your hands. His mouth was so accustomd to this way of expressing his courtesy, that he often came out with it very unseasonably. Particularly He told Monsʳ the Duke of Orleans one day that he humbly kisst his Highness'es hand. Upon which the Duke of Roquelaure instantly fetch't a bason of water, of which Monsʳ inquireing the Reason, It ⁱˢ replyd he, that your Highness may wash your hands after Monsʳ Hermenonville has taken the liberty to kiss them.

[568] My Lord Vicᵗ Gage introduceing a Gentleman to my Lady Strafford told her, that He had the pleasure of introdceing Mʳ D—— to Her Ladᵖ who was no means so great a fool as he lookt to be. My Lord tells you very true Madam said He, but I am sorry to let you know, that his Lordp̱ Appearance dos by no means bely his understanding.

[569] [/108] Monsʳ de Chamillart had the fortune to raise himself so high in the Kings favour as to be placed at the Head both of the War and the Finances and he owd this great advancement to his Skill at Billards. It seems the King was formerly very fond of this Game and so addroit at it that nobody coud play with Him without odds. and complaining one day to Monsʳ d'Armagnac the real master of the Horse, that nobody was able to play with him, Sire, said He, if your [. . .] away with [. . .] Lawyer, I know one that can play in perfection. Bring [. . .] as soon as you will, replyd the King, upon which he brought Monsʳ Chamillart the next day, who play'd himself so [. . .] favour that [h]e became one of the first men in the Kingdome, tho he had otherwise no very remarquable merit.

[570] The French have a very Significant Proverb which says, that in a Country where the Inhabitants are Blind, a [o]ne-eyed man woud be a great Prince.

[571] When Clovis King of France was converted to Christianity, Heaven shewd

its approbation by a miracle. For a Banner descended from the Sky, which the French call oriflame, with 9 flower de lis, which the Kings of France have born ever since for their arms. His Predecessors gave 3 Toads before that, to which Nostradmus alludes in one of his Predictions. Besides this oriflame, there ^also^ came down the sacred Ampoule or Vial, containing a never failing Spring of oil, with which all the Kings of France have been ever since anointed. This like the widdow's Cruse is Self Supplyd, if you'll believe the Priests, and is kept at Reims, whose A. Bishop always assists at the Coronation of the French Monarchs. Sed credat Juddus Apella.

[572] It was said of Sr Wm Young that he coud Speak much better than he coud think, and consequently woud have made a better Parrot than a man.

[573] Medina the Jew let a House to a French Refugié for a term of years. Monsr insisted upon haveing a clause in the lease that in case the French King shoud revoke the Edict of Nants and call home the Hugenots he might relinquish his lease

Commentary

As we have discussed in the Prologue, a commonplace book is a record of notions gleaned by an individual from reading and conversation. William Byrd's commonplace book, unlike most others, neither sorts entries under topical headings nor registers the sources of the entries. His practice has presented an editorial challenge not encountered by scholars working with such orderly manuscripts as Thomas Jefferson's commonplace books. Therefore, we have developed an approach to annotation necessarily different from most precedents we have seen. We thus provide several kinds of information: (1) the immediate source of the entry, whenever possible, and analysis of the evidence of transcription or translation; (2) the identification of possible sources, especially those to which we know Byrd had access; (3) the identification of historical personages named or discussed in an entry; (4) discussion of the general historical context of entries; (5) discussion of the relation of material in the entries to issues relating to Byrd's private and public life.

Whenever possible, we have tracked down Byrd's immediate sources. We were able to compare the manuscript with a number of books Byrd owned (thanks to the availability of Kevin Hayes's work with the catalog of Byrd's library) and other texts with which Byrd was likely familiar. We have identified a number of early modern sources with reasonable certainty—specifically Joseph Addison, Gilbert Burnet, Nicolas Venette, William Wollaston, and the Awnsham and John Churchill volumes of travel narratives. Classical authors, including Cicero, Lucian, and Plutarch, also make frequent appearances. In some cases, we have made judgments concerning what edition Byrd used, as in the case of Venette (see discussion in Chapter 9). Another such case is Byrd's use of the *Spectator*. Although he owned a copy of the 1723–1724 Jacob Tonson edition (Hayes 870), it could not have been the source of the commonplace book references, because the commonplace book includes sequential extracts from *Spectators* not included in that edition.

At the same time, it has not always been possible to establish whether Byrd's classical entries spring from the ultimate source or from any of a number of classical or early modern references. Plutarch is a case in point: Byrd certainly owned and had access to the works of this moralist, historian, and compiler of ancient wisdom, yet we have no internal evidence whether his commonplace book entries draw from the original source or from any of a vast number of intervening texts. Early modern readers did not always draw on the earliest texts; thus, in many cases when an ancient philosopher is named, Byrd might well have been referring to reinterpreters of Greek tradition such as the Roman writers Cicero and Seneca, to the third-century Greek historian of philosophy Diogenes Laertius, the sixteenth-century Dutch compiler of aphorisms Ioannes

Stobaeus, the seventeenth-century English historian of philosophy Thomas Stanley, or authors of early modern conduct books and moral essays such as Richard Allestree, Addison, Richard Brathwaite, Theophilus Dorrington, Richard Steele, and so forth. We have thought it valuable to note the early sources of the material as well as later instances that might have caught Byrd's eye. Whenever we have strong evidence that Byrd consulted a specific source, we will say so; otherwise, the references should be construed as registering possible sources and analogues.

We have also attempted to provide historical background interesting and useful to both general readers and specialists. Our approach here should be for the most part self-evident. In the case of certain entries, when we consider the topic of particular importance to Byrd, our annotations provide more detail and discussion. Thus, we have provided extended discussion of certain entries relating to topics such as aging, human sexuality, moral philosophy, physic, and public life.

Many entries must have come from conversation and table talk, and as such they defy any attempt to discover sources. Few of the manuscript's humorous anecdotes, jokes, scandalous tales, and gossip seem to appear in print before the commonplace book period. We have provided some background when it seems appropriate; otherwise, we have assumed that the material was "in the air."

Finally, it will be evident that we have not undertaken comprehensive annotation. Much remains to be discovered; opportunities to extend the research we have initiated here abound. We welcome future developments.

§5. The procedure of variolation (inoculation from pustules of mild cases) for smallpox first became widely known in England upon the return of Lady Mary Wortley Montagu from Turkey in 1718. During the serious outbreak of smallpox in London in 1721, Lady Mary had her four-year-old daughter variolated. In "A Plain Account of the Innoculating of the Small Pox by a Turkey Merchant," published in the *Flying-Post* in 1722, she criticized the English treatment of the disease, comparing it unfavorably with the successful system practiced in Constantinople. A trial of variolation on a group of Newgate prisoners was conducted by physicians under the guidance of Royal Society president Sir Hans Sloane. In 1723, the Princess of Wales had her daughters inoculated, along with the earl of Bathurst's children. The success of the project was prevented by the death of a footman, either from the smallpox virus from his own variolation or from contact with the inoculated children. The resulting controversy and hysteria ended the variolation campaign.

Byrd might have based this entry on Lady Mary's "Plain Account," but there is also a distinct possibility that he learned of the Turkish procedure of variolation several years earlier. According to Derrick Baxby: "Accounts of variolation were sent to the Royal Society in 1714 by Timoni of Athens and in 1716 by Pylari, a Venetian. They described how in Turkey a mild form of the disease could be produced by inserting the virus into the skin. The first English people known to be variolated, the sons of the secretary of the Ambassador to Turkey, arrived back in England in 1716" (*Jenner's Smallpox Vaccine: The Riddle of the Vaccinia Virus and Its Origin* [London, 1981], 22). These letters appear in Royal Society, *Philosophical Transactions,* nos. 339, 347. Byrd owned a full run of these volumes (Hayes 197, 199–203), which he consulted in his research for his tract on the plague.

During the commonplace book period many authors discussed inoculation; for instance, Charles Maitland's *Account of Inoculating the Small Pox* (London, 1722) explains: "The Method I here propose, is no other than that very plain one of raising the *Small Pox* by *Inoculation.* A Method, new indeed, and utterly unknown here, till of late, tho' universally practis'd with Success all over *Turky* these threescore Years past; and in other Parts of the *East,* an hundred, or, for ought we know, some hundreds of Years before" (2). Dr. Maitland attended the Wortley Montagu family at Constantinople, where he observed the practice, as did "the Ambassador's ingenious Lady," who was so convinced of its safety that she submitted her own six-year-old son to it (7). In 1722, Walter Harris published *A Description of Inoculating the Small Pox;* in *St. James's Journal,* XVI (August 1722), the reviewer points out Harris's tract is based on Timoni's letter. Aubry de La Mottraye, in *Travels through Europe, Asia, and into Part of Africa* . . . (London, 1723), describes the success of inoculation in Turkey and London (II, 396) and includes "Dr. Timone's Historical Dissertation upon the Inoculating of the Small Pox, Such as He Gave It to Me at Constantinople in 1712" (app. 9, separate pagination, II, 13–16). For further discussion, see Baxby, *Jenner's Smallpox Vaccine;* Genevieve Miller, *The Adoption of Inoculation of Smallpox in England and France* (Philadelphia, 1957).

This topic had special meaning for Byrd, for his first wife, Lucy, died in 1716 of smallpox soon after she arrived in London to join him. Fear of the disease kept Byrd from sending his son (William Byrd III) to England for schooling. Several of Byrd's fellow Virginians did lose sons to smallpox.

In any case, we see here evidence of Byrd's continued interest in medicine. His work on epidemic disease, his membership in the Royal Society, and his correspondence with Sloane all suggest that he was familiar with these early reports.

§6. Byrd's diet included goat's milk. Generally, he followed the regime recommended by George Cheyne's *Essay of Health and Long Life,* 3d ed. (London, 1724), a copy of which was in his library (Hayes 669); on Byrd's diet, see Ulrich Troubetzkoy, "Enough to Keep a Byrd Alive," *Virginia Cavalcade,* XI, no. 2 (Autumn 1961), 36–41. See also §315.

§7. Alexander, king of Macedonia, was known for his pursuit of military greatness, for the instability of his temper, and for the oddity of some of his whims (such as the deification of his horse Bucephalus and of his friend Hephaestion). Although in fact Hephaestion was not named a god, but a hero (Arrian 7.6; Plutarch *Lives,* "Alexander" 72.2; Quintus Curtius 10.4.3 in the Freinshem supplement), Diodorus Siculus (17.115.6) and Justin (12.12.11) report inaccurately that he was deified, and most early modern accounts accept the deification. A *freak* is "a sudden causeless change or turn of the mind; a capricious humour, notion, whim, or vagary" (*OED*); the way Alexander's followers catered to his whimsies served as an exemplum of the excesses of flattery and the absurdities of deferential courtiers. This story serves the same exemplary function.

The source for Byrd's entry is the *Slander* (17–19) of Lucian, the Greek satirist, who reports the seriousness of failing to worship Hephaestion among Alexander's followers. Flatterers competed with more and more outrageous flattery. Alexander was pleased to think himself "not only the son of a god but also able to make gods." Some of Alexander's friends, however, fell out of favor for not honoring Hephaestion sufficiently, especially Agathocles of Samos, one of Alexander's captains, who was charged with weeping as he passed Hephaestion's tomb. Perdiccas rescued him, "swearing by all the gods and by Hephaestion to boot that while he was hunting the god had appeared to him in the flesh and had bidden him to tell Alexander to spare Agathocles, saying that he had not wept from want of faith or because he thought Hephaestion dead, but only because he had been put in mind of their old-time friendship" (*Works,* I).

There were several editions of Lucian in Byrd's library, including the Dryden translation of 1710–1711 (Hayes 966), or Byrd could have found this passage in Freinshem's supplement to Quintus Curtius. Byrd reported in his diaries intensive sessions of reading Lucian in Greek; for instance, during the first two weeks of October 1710, he read more than thirty leaves of him in Greek and French.

§10. The Roman general and consul Cornelius Scipio Africanus defeated Hannibal's Carthaginians and persuaded the Roman senate to support his campaign against Carthage, which he conquered in 202 B.C.E. The source of this anecdote is Valerius Maximus, *Acts and Sayings of the Romans*, who reports that Scipio prevented the senators from retreating from the Carthaginian attack by drawing his sword in the Forum and threatening "death to every man that would not take an Oath never to forsake his Countrey" (240).

§12. Sir George Savile, marquess of Halifax (1633–1695), was an English statesman and man of letters. As an author he is best known as a master of the prose character and for his *Advice to a Daughter*. In his own time his reputation as a politician with shifting loyalties surpassed his literary fame, though this reputation was certainly connected with his authorship of "A Character of a Trimmer." He was an active Royalist before the Restoration, then an opponent of Charles II's policies, an ardent anti-Papist during the Popish Plot frenzy, an opponent of James II's policies, an opponent of William of Orange's intervention, a supporter of the Glorious Revolution, a member of the opposition, and at last (perhaps) a Jacobite. Bishop Gilbert Burnet said that Halifax "went backwards and forwards, and changed sides so often, that, in the conclusion, no side would trust him" (*History,* 103).

The source of this anecdote is possibly Burnet's *History,* which we are confident Byrd read (see notes to §22, 23, 45, 302, 396, 406), though there was not a copy in his library at its dispersal. Burnet comments: "He let his wit run much on matters of religion, which got him the reputation of a confirmed atheist; but he denied the charge, though he could not, as he said, digest iron as an ostrich, or to take into his belief things that would burst him" (103). Thus, in the light of his reputation for political changeability, the altered saying may be construed as advice to those entering political life—it may be needful to "swallow" new developments. Byrd knew Halifax as a member of the Royal Society; how close their acquaintance might have been is not known, but a portrait of Halifax was among the paintings Byrd hung in his library at Westover.

The entry also introduces a classical parallel with Milo of Croton, who, according to legend, carried a full-grown ox around the stadium at Olympia, which he was able to do because he started carrying it when it was a calf. This story most often appears in support of acquiring virtuous habits through resolution and practice; see Quintilian (*Institutio oratoria* 1.9.5); Lucian *Charon; or, The Inspectors* 8 (*Works,* II); Erasmus, *Adages,* 1.2.51 ("Taurum tollet qui vitulum sustelerit").

§13. Fort St. George (now Madras) was founded by the British East India Company in 1639. Byrd might have drawn on discussion of the East India trade in Charles Lockyer's *Account of the Trade in India . . .* (London, 1711), a copy of which was in his library (Hayes 111).

§14. Byrd's source was the *Octogenarians* (24–25) (of Lucian?) (*Works*, I). Other sources vary: Valerius Maximus, *Acts and Sayings of the Romans* (470) has Philemon (not Polemon) die from laughter at the ass eating figs, and Anacreon the poet die choking on a raisin; cf. Pliny *Natural History* 7.7.94; and Addison, *Guardian*, no. 67 (May 28, 1713). Diogenes Laertius (*Lives* 7.185) tells the same story of Chrysippus. Montaigne mentions these deaths in his list of curious deaths (*Essays*, "That To Think as a Philosopher Is to Learn to Die," 108).

§15. The cry of the soldier's wife, "dow[n] with the Rump," refers to the so-called Rump Parliament, the remnant of the Long Parliament, dissolved by General George Monck upon the Restoration in 1660.

§17. Source unidentified. There may an obscure jest within the anecdote, rooted in English traditions of mocking Scotland. John Ray's *Collection of English Proverbs* (Cambridge, 1678) defines a "Scotch *warming-pan*" as a "wench," adding a jocular story about Scottish country customs: "The story is well known of the Gentleman travelling in Scotland, who desiring to have his bed warmed, the servant-maid doffs her clothes, and l[a]ys her self down in it a while. In Scotland they have neither bellowes, warming-pans, nor houses of office" (83–84).

§21. Source unidentified. Sir William Davenant (1608–1668) was an English poet and dramatist; a copy of his *Works* was in Byrd's library (Hayes 915).

§22. John Bazilovitz (Ivan the Terrible, 1530–1584), czar of Russia, was a tyrant of legendary proportions. Adam Olearius (Hayes 187, 194) noted that historians unanimously condemned him as the most violent of all tyrants—"the reign of *John Basilouits*, whose Scepter was of Iron, and his Government more cruel and violent than that of any Prince mentioned in History" (*The Voyages and Travells of the Ambassadors . . .* , trans. John Davies, 2d ed. [London, 1669], I, 72). He was often called into service to represent the arbitrary cruelty characteristic of absolute rulers. Interestingly, J[odocus] C[rull], *Antient and Present State of Muscovy . . .* (London, 1698) (Hayes 36), uses this image of oppression analogically to condemn the seventeenth-century policy of passive obedience (widely considered inimical to the English love of liberty): "The wiser sort among them were perhaps sensible, that those who are good Slaves, make the worst Freemen in the World; not only their natural Inclination, but also their Education, having infused into them the Principles of *Passive Obedience,* in so transcendent a Degree, as not to have the true Sense of that Liberty we enjoy in these Parts" (170). In *The Present State of Russia . . .* (London, 1671) (Hayes 114), Samuel Collins discusses the czar's tyranny and mentions his exaction of fleas: "He once sent to *Vologda* for a *Colpack* of Fleas, and because they could not bring him full measure, he fined them" (48). The proverbial reputation of Muscovite tyranny may be seen in Burnet's criticism of General Drummond, who "had too much of the air and temper of Russia," expecting power and bribery as part of his position (*History,* 96).

§23. Percy Kirke (1646–1691), colonel of the Fourth Regiment of Foot, returned from northern Africa at the time of Monmouth's rebellion. In 1680, the army was charged with suppressing forces sympathetic to Monmouth in the western counties, where the ferocity of his regiment's actions earned them the ironic name "Kirke's Lambs." Burnet observes, "Kirk, who had commanded long at Tangiers, was by the neighbourhood of the Moors become so savage, that some days after the battle he ordered several prisoners at Taunton to be hanged up; and being then at an entertainment, as every new health was drunk he had a fresh man turned off; and observing how they shaked their legs in the agonies of death, he called it dancing, and ordered music to play to them" (*History,* 234).

Kirke and George Jeffreys (who hanged more than six hundred at the Bloody Assizes) became examples among Whig writers of the grave danger of tyranny in the absolutist Stuart monarchy. The actions of Kirke and Jeffreys, they argued, had been ordered by the king, who in this (and elsewhere) showed himself not unwilling to suspend the constitutional rights of freeborn Englishmen.

See also §97, 408; for Jeffreys, see §382.

§24. This entry comes from Bishop Gilbert Burnet, *Some Letters Containing an Account of What Seemed Most Remarkable in Switzerland, Italy, Etc.* (Amsterdam, 1686). Burnet, who states in his *History* that this work had been "written on purpose to expose Popery and tyranny" (263n), compares Protestant Switzerland and Papist Italy, pointing out the natural alliance of Roman Catholicism and tyranny. Geneva's charitable policy concerning grain benefits the commonwealth, but Rome's policy only enriches the pope, whom he characterizes as having "particular Stiffness of Temper, with a great Slowness of Understanding, and an insatiable Desire of heaping up Wealth" (*Letters,* 7–8, 184). Burnet claims he heard the assertion that papal oppression is worse than Turkish oppression from a Roman Catholic priest (186). Byrd had a copy of Burnet's *Letters* in his library (Hayes 290) as well as Antoine Varillas's *Reflexions on Dr. Gilbert Burnet's Travels* (1688) (Hayes 277).

§25. The opening lines of this entry resemble Plutarch's discussion of the term *virtus* in his *Lives,* "Caius Marcus Coriolanus" (1.4): "It is perfectly true, however, that in those days Rome held in highest honour that phase of virtue which concerns itself with warlike and military achievements, and evidence of this may be found in the only Latin word for virtue, which signifies really *manly valour;* they made valour, a specific form of virtue, stand for virtue in general." The meditation on female honor that follows comes either from an as yet unidentified source, from conversation, or from Byrd's own thoughts on the matter.

§26. This entry is essentially a précis of key parts of Addison's "Dialogue III: A Parallel between the Ancient and Modern Medals" (*The Works of the Right Honourable Joseph Addison, Esq* [London, 1721], I, 526–539). Addison opens with a discussion of the popular view of collecting antique coins and medals— many consider it (as Byrd notes) trifling, useless knowledge. The dialogue then introduces arguments establishing the real utility of the study of medals as a historical science. The first sentences of Byrd's entry establish the background; the sentences that follow draw directly on Addison, with a generalized conclusion. A comparison of the texts suggests that Byrd compiled his entry from notes taken while reading Addison's "Dialogue." He arranges the elements he has extracted from Addison's text as if he too were interested in justifying the study of medals, which probably held an actual interest for him—in his library there were a number of books on emblems, medals, and related curiosities. He records in his diary (July 29, 1718) a visit to the public library in London, where he "saw abundance of rarities, particularly some rare manuscripts and medals" (*LD*, 154).

Addison comments: "One may understand all the learned part of this science, without knowing whether there were Coins of iron or lead among the old *Roma[n]s,* and if a man is well acquainted with the Device of a Medal, I do not see what necessity there is of being able to tell whether the Medal it self be of copper or *Corinthian* brass. There is however so great a difference between the antique and modern Medals, that I have seen an Antiquary lick an old coin among other trials, to disti[n]guish the age of it by its Taste. I remember when I laught at him for it, he told me with a great deal of vehemence, there was as much difference between the relish of ancient and modern brass, as between an apple and a turnep. It is pity, says *Eugenius,* but they found out the Smell too of an ancient Medal. They would then be able to judge of it by all the senses. The Touch, I have heard, gives almost as good evidence as the Sight, and the Ringing of a Medal is, I know, a very common experiment" (*Works,* I, 527). While Addison reports the amazing intricacies of the virtuoso's knowledge, he manages both to recount the "curious" facts urbanely and to be facetious in the matter of smelling medals. Byrd here alters Addison's text, retaining the primary ironic posture by calling the virtuosi "nice" (that is, committed to overly scrupulous distinctions), but omitting (or missing) the olfactory joke.

Byrd's comments on the utility of medals in illustrating history, providing poetry and painting with ancient imagery, and furnishing the likenesses of historical figures, the outlines of architecture and machinery, and impressions of daily life—all are condensed from Addison's treatise.

Addison also discussed medals in the *Guardian*, no. 96 (July 1, 1713). Here he touches on other matters, without providing any clear parallels with either the "Dialogue" or Byrd's transcription; however, one passage closely resembles the opening of the commonplace book entry: "The ancient *Romans* took the only effectual Method to disperse and preserve their Medals, by making them their current Mony." Because the *Guardian* essay was reproduced in the 1721 edition of Addison's *Works*, we believe Byrd consulted the version of the "Dialogue" printed there, incorporating this element from a related essay into his commonplace book entry.

The work to which Addison refers (that draws history from the evidence of medals) is [Obadiah Walker], *The Greek and Roman History Illustrated by Coins and Medals* . . . (London, 1692). Walker defines "*Corinthian* Brass" as the metal made "accidentally at the burning of *Corinth* by *L. Mummius,* where all the Statues of Gold, Silver and Brass running together, made a very beautiful and much-prized Composition, or of such as was made in imitation of it" (18). The unidentified *History of Coins and Medals* in Byrd's library (Hayes 2451) was probably this book.

§27. Byrd's attack on the dishonesty of Jesuit discourse is typical of the English mistrust of the Society of Jesus. Protestants in the seventeenth and eighteenth centuries were certain that Jesuits hatched plots against the Protestant church and commonwealth and that the Jesuits' primary weapon was a unique form of persuasion involving plausible lies, equivocation, and prevarication. Thus *jesuitical* came to be a common term for dissembling. In *A Journey to the Land of Eden*, Byrd wittily participates in this long-established tradition: "It was impossible for us to strike the tents till the afternoon and then we took our departure and made an easy march of four miles to another branch of Hyco River, which we called Jesuit's Creek because it misled us" (*Works*, 402).

Lucilio (or Giulio-Cesare) Vanini was born in Naples in 1585, studied law, and became a Jesuit priest. He traveled widely in France, Italy, and England and was known for two controversial books. Byrd may be referring to his first book, *Amphitheatrum aeternae providentiae divino-magicum* (1615), which ostensibly attacked atheism, apparently in an attempt to clear himself of suspicions of being anti-Christian. His second book, *De admirandis naturae reginae deaeque mortalium arcanis* (1616), may come nearer to expressing his real views. In 1619 he was executed in France for atheism.

§29. Plutarch *Lives*, "Alexander" 8.3; cf. Erasmus, *Apophthegmes*, "Alexander," no. 41; Stanley, *History*, I, 355; *Guardian*, no. 111 (July 18, 1713).

§30. Plutarch *Moralia* ("Sayings of Kings and Commanders") 189d. Byrd's entry seems close to Jacques Amyot's preface in Sir Thomas North's translation of Plutarch, *The Lives of the Noble Grecians and Romans* ... (Cambridge, 1676): "And therefore *Demetrius Phalerius* (a man renowned as well for his skill in the good Government of a Common-weal, as for his excellent Knowledge otherwise) counselled *Ptolomy*, first King of *Egypt* after the death of *Alexander* the Great, that he should often and diligently read the Books that treated of the Government of Kingdoms, because (said he) thou shalt find many things there, which thy servants and familiar friends dare not tell thee" (sig. [A4]r).

This story belongs to the tradition of comparing life in the courts unfavorably with a simple life, primarily because of the dangers of flattery. Byrd was aware of the tradition and consciously participated in it. In an early letter to Governor Francis Nicholson (Apr. 12, 1699), Byrd assures him that his wishes that the governor will remain in Virgina for many years are sincere, "without any thing of the courtier" (*Correspondence*, I, 207).

§34. Byrd includes several entries on the topic of clamorous women (§75, 107, 223) and used similar expressions in his own work; for instance, in the *History of the Dividing Line*: "About four miles beyond the river Irvin we forded Matrimony Creek, called so by an unfortunate married man because it was exceedingly noisy and impetuous. However, though the stream was clamorous, yet like those women who make themselves plainest heard, it was likewise perfectly clear and unsullied." "Not far from where we went over is a rock much higher than the rest that strikes the eye with an agreeable horror, and near it a very talkative echo that like a fluent helpmeet will return her goodman seven words for one and after all be sure to have the last" (*Works*, 256, 317).

§36. Byrd (or his unidentified source) names those who study the animal kingdom "fellow creatures" of the mule, participating in the tradition satirizing virtuosos. The notion that a mule is proof against intoxication apparently has its origin among the ancients. See Diogenes Laertius "Aristippus": "To one who boasted that he could drink a good deal without getting drunk, his rejoinder was, 'And so can a mule'" (*Lives* 2.73). The saying suggests that excessive drink makes men stupid; with a mule, the change would be harder to discern.

§39. Thales of Miletus, the first of the Seven Sages. The source of this saying has not been identified. It parallels Seneca's comment in *De beneficia* 4.20.3: "He is ungrateful who in the act of repaying gratitude has an eye on a second gift—who hopes while he repays" (*Moral Essays*, trans. John W. Basore, 3 vols., LCL [1928–1935], II).

§41. Epaminondas commanded the Boeotians at the battle of Leuctra. According to Diodorus Siculus (15.54–57), more than four thousand Spartans were killed, but the Boeotians lost only three hundred; Xenophon estimates the Boeotian losses at closer to one thousand. This anecdote appears in Plutarch's *Moralia* ("Sayings of Kings and Commanders"): "He used to say that of all the fair and goodly fortune that had fallen to his lot the thing that gave him the greatest gratification was that his victory over the Spartans at Leuctra came while his father and mother were still living" (193a). Cf. *Moralia* 786d ("Whether an Old Man Should Engage in Public Affairs"), 1098b ("That Epicurus Actually Makes a Pleasant Life Impossible"), and Plutarch *Lives*, "Caius Marcius Coriolanus" 4.3. Byrd could also have found this story in Montaigne's *Essays*, "Of the Most Eminent Men."

§43. Plutarch *Moralia* 198e ("Sayings of Romans"): "He said that he preferred to receive no thanks when he had done a favour rather than to suffer no punishment when he had done a wrong, and that he always granted pardon to all who erred, with the single exception of himself." Cf. Plutarch *Lives*, "Marcus Cato" 8.9; see also §139.

§45. Source unidentified. John, Lord Somers (1651–1716), served as solicitor-general, attorney general, lord keeper, and lord chancellor. He was admired for his learning, patience, and equitable nature. Burnet praised him for his learning, patience, and equity, finding him the model of a just magistrate (*History*, 379). Jonathan Swift dedicated *A Tale of a Tub* to Somers, praising him for generosity and learning (in Herbert Davis, ed., The Prose Works of Jonathan Swift, I [Oxford, 1957], 13–16), and Addison praises his eloquence (*Freeholder*, no. 39 [May 4, 1716]). Somers's translation, *Several Orations of Demosthenes* (London, 1702), was in Byrd's library (Hayes 860).

§46. Horace *Epistles* 1.2.58–63: "He who curbs not his anger will wish that undone which vexation and wrath prompted, as he made haste with violence to gratify his unsated hatred. Anger is short-lived madness. Rule your pasion, for unless it obeys, it gives commands. Check it with bridle—check it, I pray you, with chains" (*Satires, Epistles, and Ars Poetica*, trans. H. Rushton Fairclough, LCL [1929]). The first half of the saying recorded in this entry is proverbial; Plutarch attributes it to Cato in *Moralia* ("Sayings of Romans"): "He had an idea that the man who has lost his temper differs from him who has lost his mind only in duration of time" (199a); cf. *Moralia* 503e ("Concerning Talkativeness"); Seneca *De ira* 1.1.2 (*Moral Essays*).

§49. This passage resembles part of a letter Byrd wrote to John Custis; see §91.

§52. Hippocrates (469–399) was considered the father of medical science, though many of the works circulated under his name were not authentically his. Byrd might have found the material for this entry in any of a number of early modern medical texts. However, it refers to a specific medical aphorism and is therefore almost certainly drawn from *The Aphorisms of Hippocrates*, two copies of which were in Byrd's library (Hayes 672, 783) as well as his *Opera* (Hayes 637):

Aphorism I, 2:

In Loosenesses and Vomitings that happen spontaneously, if such things be purged as ought to be purged, they are profitable and easily endured; otherwise it falls out contrary. So likewise an Evacuation of Vessels (if done as it should be) is beneficial and easily suffered; otherwise contrary Effects ensue. Wherefore Respect must be had to the Region, Time, Age, and Diseases, in which it is agreeable or not.

Explanation

The Guts are, as it were, the Common-shore of the Body, into which are thrown not only the *Foeces* of our own Food from the Stomach, but likewise the excrementitious Parts of the neighbouring *Viscera*, as the Liver, Mesentery, *&c.* and of the Blood it self. Now if either the Blood should be vitiated, or the *Viscera* be overcharged and disordered with Crudities, then such offensive Particles are gradually by the benign and constant natural Motions, congested, separated, and so extruded into the Guts, where by their saline *Spicula*, they stimulate the Membranes of the Intestines to a violent Contraction, and sometimes to such a Degree, as to draw the Stomach it self into a Consent, wherewith all the Contents are thrown forth upward and downwards, and in this manner the Body is reliev'd from noxious Humours. This natural Stimulation is imitated by artificial Purging and Vomiting Medicines, thereby to assist Nature, if of herself too weak, and not forward enough, and so do that by Art, which she was not able to do without. But if they are not rightly administer'd, they rather cause than mitigate Pains and Disease. (C. J. Sprengell, M.D., ed., *The Aphorisms of Hippocrates, and the Sentences of Celsus* ... [London, 1708], 3)

§53. Plutarch *Moralia* ("Sayings of Kings and Commanders"): "To those who found fault with him for accomplishing most things through deception (a procedure which they asserted was unworthy of Heracles) he used to say in reply that where the lion's skin does not reach it must be pieced out with the skin of the fox" (190e). In the *Lives,* Plutarch offers a harsher view: Lysander "seemed to be unscrupulous and subtle, a man who tricked out most of what he did in war with the varied hues of deceit, extolling justice if it was at the same time profitable, but if not, adopting the advantageous as the honourable course, and not considering truth as inherently better than falsehood, but bounding his estimate of either by the needs of the hour. Those who demanded that the descendants of Heracles should not wage war by deceit he held up to ridicule, saying that 'where the lion's skin will not reach, it must be patched out with the fox's' " ("Lysander" 7.3–4). Cf. *Moralia* 229b ("Sayings of Spartans," no. 2); Montaigne, *Essays,* "Should the Commanders Go Forth to Parley."

§54. Diogenes Laertius *Lives* 1.87: "He would rather decide a dispute between two of his enemies than between two of his friends; for in the latter case he would be certain to make one of his friends his enemy, but in the former case he would make one of his enemies his friend" ("Bias"). Cf. Stanley, *History,* I, 41; see also §142.

§56. Diodorus Siculus thus describes the ancient monuments of Diospolis, known to the Greeks as the Egyptian Thebes: "In this hall there are many wooden statues representing parties in litigation, whose eyes are fixed upon the judges who decide their cases; and these, in turn, are shown in relief on one of the walls, to the number of thirty, and without any hands, and in their midst the chief justice, with a figure of Truth hanging from his neck and holding his eyes closed, and at his side a great number of books. And these figures show by their attitude that the judges shall receive no gift and that the chief justice shall have his eyes upon the truth alone" (1.48). Cf. Peter de La Primaudaye, *The French Academie . . .* (London, 1618), 162.

§57. See also §140.

§59. See Cicero *De officiis* 1.19.63: "This, then, is a fine saying of Plato's: 'Not only must all knowledge that is divorced from justice be called cunning rather than wisdom' " (trans. Walter Miller, LCL [1968]).

§60. Diogenes Laertius "Heraclitus": "Again he would say . . . 'The people must fight for the law as for city-walls' " (*Lives* 9.2).

§61. Stanley, "Arcesilaus": "He said, Where there are many Medicines, and many Physicians, there are most Diseases; and where there are many Laws, there is most iniquity" (*History,* I, 220).

§64. The death of a young man, according to Cicero (*De senectute* 19.71), is like a flame suddenly extinguished, while the death of an old man is like a fire going out of its own accord. "So, with the young, death comes as a result of force, while with the old it is the result of ripeness. To me, indeed, the thought of this 'ripeness' for death is so pleasant, that the nearer I approach death the more I feel like one who is in sight of land at last and is about to anchor in his home port after a long voyage" (*De senectute, De amicitia, De divinatione*, trans. William Armistead Falconer, LCL [1971]).

§65. Plutarch "Letter to Apollonius": "It is said that Pindar himself enjoined upon the deputies of the Boeotians who were sent to consult the god that they should inquire, 'What is the best thing for mankind?' and the prophetic priestess made answer, that he himself could not be ignorant of it ... but if he desired to learn it by experience, it should be made manifest to him within a short time. As a result of this inquiry Pindar inferred that he should expect death, and after a short time his end came" (*Moralia* 109a–b).

§66. Stanley: "To one that asked him, how a Man might be Rich, he answered, by being Poor in Desire" (*History*, II, 482).

§68. Plutarch "Whether an Old Man Should Engage in Public Affairs": "Dionysius the Elder, when someone asked him if he was at leisure, replied: 'May that never happen to me!' " (*Moralia* 792c). Note that Plutarch is here discussing the continuation of the active life well into old age. Cf. *Moralia* 176a ("Sayings of Kings and Commanders"); see also §153.

§69. Stanley lists this as one of the apothegms of Theophrastus: "The Envious are more unhappy than others in this respect, that they are troubled not only at their misfortunes, but also at the good fortunes of others" (*History*, II, 395). See also §72.

§71. Diogenes Laertius "Antisthenes": "As iron is eaten away by rust, so, said he, the envious are consumed by their own passion" (*Lives* 6.5). Cf. Stanley, "Antisthenes," *History*, II, 405.

§72. Diogenes Laertius "Bion": "To a slanderer who showed a grave face his words were, 'I don't know whether you have met with ill luck, or your neighbour with good' " (*Lives* 4.51). Cf. Bacon, *Apophthegmes*, no. 237; Stanley, "Bion," *History*, I, 142.

§79. Source unidentified. The course of physic adopted by these men reflects medical practices of the day, which sought to counteract the heat of a venereal disorder with "Alterative Drinks." According to Richard Wiseman (*Several Chirurgical Treatises*, 2d ed. [London, 1686]), a cooling diet and anodyne draughts should be taken to counteract the "heat and acrimony of the humours" disturbed and fired by the disease (557). Byrd's copy of this book (Hayes 632) is now in the Historic Library of the Pennsylvania Hospital. On the cultural history of venereal disease and its treatment in the eighteenth century, see Linda E. Merians, *The Secret Malady: Venereal Disease in Eighteenth-Century Britain and France* (Lexington, Ky., 1996).

§80. This story appears to be a favorite among travelers describing Russia. Byrd might have drawn it from one of several books about Muscovy, such as [Adam Olearius], *The Voyages and Travells of the Ambassadors . . .* (London, 1669) (Hayes 187, 194). Describing the architecture of Moscow, Olearius describes the wooden structures most common throughout Muscovy: "Those who have their houses burnt, have this comfort withall, that they may buy houses ready built, at a market for that purpose, without the white-Wall, at a very easy rate, and have them taken down, transported, and in a short time set up in the same place where the former stood" (I, 43). Jodocus Crull provides a similar account in *The Antient and Present State of Muscovy . . .* (London, 1698) (Hayes 36): "As for their Houses, they are almost as soon repaired as lost, there being a certain Market without the white Wall of this City, where at a very easie rate (Wood being so over-plenty in this Country) they buy a House of what bigness they please, ready built, which, in a little time is taken down, and transported to the Place, where the other House stood before" (8). Byrd's use of the phrase "in a very little time" suggests he was consulting Crull.

§81. Plutarch "Isis and Osiris": "The crocodile, certainly, has acquired honour which is not devoid of a plausible reason, but he is declared to be a living representation of God, since he is the only creature without a tongue; for the Divine Word has no need of a voice" (*Moralia* 381b); cf. Herodotus (*History* 1.68). Erasmus explains the proverb: "Crocodile tears, is used of those who pretend to be deeply affected by the distress of anyone for whose destruction they are themselves responsible or for whom they are planning some great disaster" (*Adages*, "Crocodili lachrymae," 2.4.60). The notion that women use tears as a stratagem for manipulating men is ubiquitous, and the connection between women's tears and crocodile tears is also proverbial. See, for instance, the misogynistic verses in [William Ramsey], *Conjugium Conjurgium; or, Some Serious Considerations on Marriage . . .* (London, 1675), 16:

> Oh Heavenly Powers! Why did you bring to light
> That thing called WOMAN, Natures oversight?
> A Wayward, a Froward, a constant evil,
> A seeming Saint, sole Factor to the Devil:
> That *She-born Tyrant* full of Misery,
> A guilded wethercock of Vanity:
> That being Damn'd, she first began to fall,

> From bad to worse, from worse to worst of all.
> So is she wretched, nay she's far more vile,
> Than the deceitful weeping Crocadile.

§82. Eastern travel narratives usually featured detailed descriptions of the Seraglio, the palace of the grand signior (or sultan) in Constantinople. The legend of accumulated treasure was particularly fascinating to Western travelers (see, for instance, Joseph Pitton de Tournefort, *A Voyage into the Levant . . .* [London, 1718], II, 6). The lands of the Grand Mogul, or emperor of Delhi, included most of Hindustan. Both monarchs were thought to be fabulously wealthy. As such, they served Western commentators as examples of the corruption of absolute tyrannical power.

§90. Stanley, "Aristotle": "Being demanded how a man should come to be rich; he answer'd, *by being poor in desire*" (*History*, II, 359).

§91. On April 10, 1723, John Custis, Byrd's brother-in-law, wrote to Byrd in London, reproaching him for writing so seldom: "I will impute your long silence to love; and am allmost confirmed in a report I have heard, i.e.; that your thoughts are wholly taken up with matrimony; or something like it. It is said that you have a keene appetite to a young wider morsell of about 16 years old; if so, I do not wonder any thing else can enter your thoughts; all that I shall pretend to say on that head, is that your vigorous ability may answer the sallies of your inclinations &c" (*Correspondence*, I, 342).

The Charmante episode had recently concluded; Byrd comments in his letter to Custis on July 29, 1723 (*Correspondence*, I, 346) that "love has no more such violent operation" upon him as to keep him from thinking of his friends and that "my reason begins at last to get the better of my inclination"—but he insists that it is *not* age that has delivered him. Byrd then criticizes the way age is reckoned in years instead of in vigor, a passage clearly copied (with only a few minor adjustments) from this part of his commonplace book.

§94. Plutarch tells that after the death of his sons, Aemilius Paulus said he had "no fears or misgivings about his country, since Fortune had thrust upon his house the retribution due for all their good fortune, and he had received this in behalf of all" (*Moralia* ["Sayings of Romans"] 198d). Cf. Plutarch *Lives*, "Aemilus Paulus" 35.1–36.6; Seneca *Ad Marciam de consolatione* 13; Valerius Maximus 5.10.2; Velleius Paterculus 1.10.3–6; Montaigne, *Essays*, "The Hour of Parley Is a Dangerous Time."

§95. Plutarch *Moralia* ("Ancient Customs of the Spartans") 238e–f; Plutarch *Lives*, "Lycurgus" 27.3–4.

§96. This topic was frequently the subject of sermons in Byrd's time; the entry might have been based on such a sermon, or on a similar passage in [Richard Allestree], *The Whole Duty of Man* . . . (London, 1673), which Byrd (like nearly every literate Englishman and Virginian) had in his library (Hayes, 145, A25): "But besides this of the weekly *Lords* day, there are other times, which the Church hath set apart for the *remembrance* of some *special mercies of God,* such as the *Birth* and *Resurrection of Christ,* the *Descent* of the *Holy Ghost,* and the like; and these dayes we are to keep in that manner which the Church hath ordered, to wit, in the *solemn worship* of *God,* and in particular *thanksgiving* for that special blessing we then remember. And surely whoever is truly thankful for those rich mercies, cannot think it too much to set apart some few dayes in a year for that purpose. But then we are to look that our Feasts be truly spiritual, by imploying the day thus holily, and not make it an occasion of intemperance and disorder, as too many, who consider nothing in *Christmas* and other good times, but the good cheers and jollity of them. For that is doing despight in stead of honour to Christ; who came to bring all *purity* and soberness into the world; and therefore must not have that coming of his remembred in any other manner" (49–50).

Another source possibility is Erasmus, *Adages* ("Ignavis semper feriae sunt"): "Today the common run of Christians misuse the holy days, devised in old days for pious purposes, in drinking, wenching, gambling, quarreling and fighting; and at no season are more crimes committed than at those when crimes are most clearly out of place. Never do we so clearly imitate the pagans as on the days when we have a special duty to behave like Christians; and . . . a practice designed for the advancement of religion now tends to put religion itself in peril" (2.6.2).

§97. See commentary on §23.

§98. This information is a usual feature in European travel literature concerning Barbary, the Islamic region of northern Africa (now Morocco, Tunisia, and Algeria). See, for instance, [John Windus], *A Journey to Mequinez* . . . (London, 1725): "Adultery is punished with Death; and if a Christian or Jew is found to have to do with a Moorish Woman, they must either turn to the Mahometan Religion or be burnt" (37). Cf. Joseph Pitton de Tournefort, *A Voyage into the Levant* (London, 1718), II, 73. For Western attitudes toward Barbary, see Ann Thompson, *Barbary and Enlightenment: European Attitudes towards the Mahgreb in the Eighteenth Century* (Leiden, 1987). See also §100, 459.

§100. Another commonly cited "fact" in accounts of travels to Barbary; see

[Windus], *Journey to Mequinez:* "The fattest and biggest are most admired, for which Reason they cram themselves against Marriage, with a Food called *Zummith;* it is a Compound of Flower, Honey and Spices, made into little Loaves for that Purpose" (37). See also §98, 459.

§101. Possibly Charles Mordaunt, third earl of Peterborough (1658–1735), admiral, diplomat, wit, and patron of men of learning.

§105. See §341.

§106. Xenophon recounts Socrates' use of the net metaphor (catching helpless men) to explain the appeal of the courtesan Theodoté's beauty (*Memorabilia* 3.11.10). Cicero notes that Plato in the *Timaeus* (69d) calls pleasure " 'the bait of sin'—evidently because men are caught therewith like fish" (*De senectute* 13.44 [*De senectute, De amicitia, De divinatione,* trans. William Armistead Falconer, LCL (1971)]). The metaphor is extended to matrimony in Stanley: "To others that asked his opinion concerning marriage, he said, *As Fishes in a net would fain get out, and those without would get in, take heed young Men it not be so with you*" (*History,* I, 77).

The verses Byrd records here as Chaucer's are not now considered genuine. The earliest attribution we have discovered is [William Ramsey], *Conjugium Conjurgium; or, Some Serious Considerations on Marriage . . .* (London, 1675), 49:

If *Women,* then, in general, be so bad, *Philogynus, what an hazard is it then to Marry?* And if so, I admonish thee again, keep thy self as thou art ('Tis best to be free, and at liberty.) For as honest *Chauser* well observes:

> Marriage is like a Re[v]el Rout,
> He that is out would fain get in,
> And he that's in would fain get out.

And, therefore, with the *Philosopher,* make answer to thy Friends that importune thee to Marry, *Adhuc intempestivum,* 'Tis yet unseasonable, (and so let it always be.)

Other possible sources are the preface (sig. [A5]r) to [Edward "Ned" Ward], *Nuptial Dialogues and Debates . . .* (London, 1710), or the "letters" on marriage, in [Charles Gildon], *The Post-Man Robb'd of His Mail . . .* (London, 1719), 20. Any of these books could have been among those Byrd consulted during his course of reading works attacking women and marriage.

§108, 109, 110. The sequence replicates a passage from Erasmus, *Apophthegmes:* "With the Musicians also he found faulte, for that about their harpes and other musicall instrumentes, thei would bestowe great labour and diligence to sette the strynges in right tune, and had maners gerrying quite and clene out of all good accord and frame. He reproued also the professours of the Mathematicall sciencies, for that thei wer alwayes gazyng and staryng vpon the soonne, the moone, and the sterres, and yet could not see what thynges laye before their feete. At the oratours also he had a saiyng, for that thei wer buisie enough to speake thynges standyng with right and iustice, but to putte the same in execucion, and to dooe thereafter, thei wer veraye slacke" ("Diogenes," nos. 17–19). Cf. Stanley, *History*, II, 411; see also §166, 167, 217.

§111. Stobaeus, *Sententiae*, LXV ("Laus nuptiarum"), 412. Diogenes Laertius *Lives* attributes this saying to Bion (4.48), and elsewhere to Antisthenes (6.3); see also §340. This is the first of three topically linked entries, found in the early modern collection of ancient wisdom, *Ioannis Stobaei Sententiae, ex Thesauris Graecorum Delectae*. The fact that §112 and 113 follow each other immediately in Stobaeus may be considered a strong indication that Stobaeus is Byrd's source (though there is, of course, the possibility that Byrd consulted an unknown source that itself drew upon and recapitulated the order of the sayings in Stobaeus).

§112. Stobaeus, *Sententiae*, LXVIII ("De uxoris petitione, et amplius de nuptiis"), attributes the saying to Pericles. Plutarch attributes it to another Athenian statesman, Themistocles, in *Moralia* ("Sayings of Kings and Commanders") 185e. Cf. Plutarch *Lives*, "Themistocles" 18.4; Cicero *De officiis* 2.20.71; [Abel] Boyer, *The Wise and Ingenious Companion* . . . (London, 1700), 35; Addison, *Spectator*, no. 311 (Feb. 26, 1712). Themistocles, as Plutarch points out, gained his glory through his own merit; his father belonged to a less than influential Athenian family, and his mother was of foreign birth. About the time Byrd was writing entries in his commonplace book, he had reason to be concerned about the the proper role of fathers in the marriage of daughters. In 1717–1718, he had himself been courting Mary Smith (see Byrd's letters to "Sabina," *ASD*, 298–359) and had experienced her family's disapproval of his suit. Writing to her father John Smith in an attempt to win his favor and suggesting Smith consult Lord Perceval, Edward Southwell, or any of his many other friends who could testify to his good character, Byrd uses a phrase not unlike the commonplace book entries on finding a good match for a daughter: "I own Sir you may marry your daughter to a better estate, and to higher quality: but there is nothing necessary to make her happy, which may not be compasst by my fortune" (*Correspondence*, I, 313). But Sabina's family married her in 1719 to the propertied "booby" Sir Edward Des Bouverie.

Ironically, five years after these events, Byrd found the position reversed when his daughter Evelyn was courted by a baronet (as yet unidentified) of whom Byrd strongly disapproved. See his stern letter to "Amasia," *ASD*, 381–383; *Correspondence*, I, 343–345.

§113. Stobaeus, *Sententiae*, LXVIII ("De uxoris petitione, et amplius de nuptiis"), 428.

§116. Addison recommends a good conscience as proof against detraction: "The way to silence Calumny, says *Bias,* is to be always exercised in such Things as are Praise-worthy." According to Addison, Plato also shared this position: "Being told that he had many enemies who spoke ill of him, 'Tis no matter, said he, I'll live so none shall believe 'em" (*Guardian,* no. 135 [Aug. 15, 1713]). Addison's source is unclear; neither aphorism appears in this form in Diogenes Laertius.

§117. That speech reveals far more than the literal content of a statement is a common observation. See Erasmus, *Adages* ("Stultus stulta loquitur"): "There is a verse . . . current in Greek: 'Man's character is known from what he says.' In [Diogenes] Laertius, the philosopher Democritus called speech 'the mirror of life,' a sort of reflection of it, as it were. Nothing could be said more truly. For no mirror reflects the bodily appearance better or more definitely than speech reflects the image of the heart. Men are discerned by their words just as brazen vessels are by their resonance" (1.1.98). Other writers similarly tell of Socrates addressing a young man, "Speak that I may see you"; see Cesare Ripa, *Iconologia . . .* (Rome, 1593); Richard Brathwait, *The English Gentleman . . .*, 2d ed. (London, 1633), 77; Addison, *Spectator,* no. 86 (June 8, 1711).

§120. The source of this exemplary tale is Plutarch's *Lives*, "Phocion." Just as Phocion was held forth as an example of heroic service to the common good, so his wife served as an example of modesty. See, for example, the account in [Theophilus Dorrington], *The Excellent Woman Described by Her True Characters and Their Opposites . . .* (London, 1695): "Let them only observe the Modesty of the Wife of *Phocion,* who was often praised in full Theater, with the general Applause of the Spectators, and the universal Approbation of all the World. When one of her Friends shewed her, her Rings, Necklaces, and Jewels, she made answer, These were not the things that she cared to adorn her self with; that all the Luster of precious Stones and Pearls could not come near the Vertues of *Phocion:* That she had more Glory in being his Wife than she could have from being proudly drest. This Lady who was an Enemy to Luxury, was a Lady of no mean Spirit, nor of a small Fortune: Her Husband was chosen for twenty Years together General of the *Athenian Armies,* and she the mean while went about the Streets of *Athens* with but one Servant: She was as modest in her Habit and Train, as the greatest part of our Age to endeavour to be sumptuous and extravagant" (II, 279–280).

Reversing the precedent of this classical example, Britain demonstrated gratitude to its great general, the duke of Marlborough, with copious rewards. On his death in 1722, the duke left his widow, Sarah Churchill, a jointure of fifteen thousand pounds per annum; she was also allowed a budget of fifty thousand pounds for completing the palace at Blenheim. The duchess quarreled and litigated bitterly and tirelessly with numerous parties on many issues, largely concerning her property. Both the size of the estate and her litigiousness were well known during the commonplace book period, and Byrd owned a number of books about the controversies over her maintenance and her relations with the court, including *An Account of the Conduct of the Dowager Duchess of Marlborough* (Hayes 1887), and James Ralph's answer, *The Other Side of the Question; or, An Attempt to Rescue the Characters of the Two Royal Sisters Q. Mary and Q. Anne, out of the Hands of the D——s D—— of ——* (Hayes 1888). Byrd's commonplace book entry ironically attributes the title "poor woman" to one of the richest (and least satisfied) of women.

§121. The sexual appetites of Charles II were legendary. John Wilmot, earl of Rochester (1647–1680), the king's favorite, was also a well-known libertine, satirist, and bawdy poet—hardly the "bashful" earl, though Burnet maintains Rochester was naturally modest until the court corrupted him. See Rochester's "Satyr on Charles II" (David M. Vieth, ed., *The Complete Poems of John Wilmot, Earl of Rochester* [New Haven, Conn., 1968], 60–61) for his frank estimation of the sexual prowess of the "merry monarch." For discussion of the sexual representation of Charles in Restoration political writing, see Paul Hammond, "The King's Two Bodies: Representations of Charles II," in Jeremy Black and Jeremy Gregory, eds., *Culture, Politics, and Society in Britain, 1660–1800* (Manchester, 1991), 13–48.

§124. Plutarch *Moralia* ("Sayings of Kings and Commanders"): "When Alexander the king sent him twenty thousand pounds as a present, he asked those who brought the money why it was that, when there were so many Athenians, Alexander offered this to him only. They replied that their king considered him only to be upright and honourable. 'Then,' said he, 'let him suffer me both to seem and to be such'" (188c); cf. Plutarch *Lives,* "Phocion" 18.1–3; Erasmus, *Apophthegmes,* "Phocion," no. 2; Bacon, *Apophthegmes,* no. 205.

§125. Epaminondas, the Theban general and statesman, was one of the principal classical types of nobility and incorruptibility. This story appears in Plutarch's *Moralia* ("Sayings of Kings and Commanders"): "When the king of the Persians sent twenty-five thousand pounds to him, he assailed Diomedon bitterly because he had made such a long voyage to corrupt Epameinondas; and he bade him say to the king that if the king should hold views conducive to the good of the Thebans, he should have Epameinondas as his friend for nothing; but if the reverse, than as his enemy" (193c). Cf. Cornelius Nepos, *The Lives of Illustrious Men*, 2d ed. (London, 1685); [Abel] Boyer, *The Wise and Ingenious Companion . . .* (London, 1700), 15.

§126. This verse, attributed to Jonathan Swift and called "A Certificate of Marriage" in Charles Henry Wilson's edition, *Swiftiana* (London, 1804), was "said to have been composed by Swift for a man and pregnant woman whom he united beneath an oak on the London-Chester road near Lichfield" (Harold Williams, ed., *The Poems of Jonathan Swift*, 2d ed., III [Oxford, 1958], 1146):

> Under an oak, in stormy weather,
> I join'd this rogue and whore together;
> And none but he who rules the thunder
> Can put this whore and rogue asunder.

Byrd does not identify Swift in his entry, and there is no certainty that Swift was named by all those who retold the anecdote and verse. Still, at the time this anecdote was probably circulating in London and was collected by Byrd, Swift's reputation would have justified the appellation "merry Priest." The twenty-fifth article of the Church of England specifies that there are only two sacraments, baptism and the Eucharist, unlike Roman Catholic doctrine. The term used in this entry—"holy Ordinance"—is accurate, though whether Swift joked on marriage for the purpose of demonstrating his doctrinal position is not possible to determine. (The editors would like to thank A. C. Elias, Jr., and James Woolley for directing our attention to the Swift attribution, and to Father H. James Considine, John O'Neill, and Françoise Deconinck-Brossard for guidance concerning Anglican doctrine.)

§127. The orator Gorgias, Socrates' contemporary, was a rhetorician, teacher, and author of some merit, though he is best remembered as a sophistical disputant in Plato's dialogue bearing his name. Quintilian states that he lived to the age of 109 years (*Institutio oratoria* 3.1.9) and that he continued answering questions into "extreme old age" (12.11.21). According to Valerius Maximus, *Acts and Sayings of the Romans* (415), Gorgias lived to be 107. In *De senectute* 5.13, Cicero introduces him as an example of unburdensome old age.

§129. Sir David Colyear, earl of Portmore (d. 1730). In 1712 he was made Knight of the Thistle, an order worn on a green ribbon ("ruban").

§130. William North (1678–1734), sixth Baron North and second Baron Gray, lost his right hand at Blenheim in 1704 serving under Marlborough.

§132. Cleanthes (331–232) was a Stoic philosopher, writer, and student of Zeno.

§133. Socrates' lack of interest in material prosperity was proverbial; Diogenes Laertius relates: "He prided himself on his plain living. . . . He used to say that . . . he was nearest the gods in that he had the fewest wants" (*Lives* 2.24–27). Cf. Xenophon *Memorabilia*, esp. 1.2.1, 1.6.1–10; Plato *Apology* 30b; Stanley, "Socrates," *History*, I, 75; Addison, *Spectator*, no. 574 (July 30, 1714): "*Content is natural Wealth*, says *Socrates*." Byrd owned several editions of works by Xenophon, including at least one edition in Greek and Latin (Hayes 1604). He also owned the 1578 Stephanus edition of Plato (Hayes 1730) as well as an English version of André Dacier's French translation (Hayes 972). See also §48, 329.

§135 Plutarch *Moralia* ("Sayings of Spartans"): "When someone said to him, 'You have agreed,' and kept repeating the same thing, Agesilaus said, 'Yes, of course, if it is right; but if not, then I said so, but I did not agree.' And when the other added, 'But surely kings ought to carry out "whatsoe'er they confirm by the royal assent,"' Agesilaus said, 'No more than those who approach kings ought to ask for what is right and say what is right, trying to hit upon the right occasion and a request fitting for kings to grant' " (208d).

§139. See §43.

§140. See §57.

§142. See §54.

§143. Source unidentified. The entry resembles many examples of the early modern reinvention of the ancient philosophers in a newer image. This saying attributed to a somewhat Christianized Plato resembles Dacier's view of Plato's *Laws:* "In fine, he shows, that *sooner or later God renders to every Man according to his Works*. The Righteous, who have been expos'd to Troubles in this Life, are recompensed in the other; and the Wicked who have always enjoy'd the Pleasures of the World, are punished in Hell. This is necessarily inferr'd from the Justice of God: 'Tis impossible to avoid this Judgment, which the Gods have fix'd" (*The Works of Plato Abridg'd . . .* [London, 1749], 87). Byrd owned an edition of this book (Hayes 972). See also §144, 178.

§144. Diogenes Laertius "Plato," *Lives* 3.25, claims that Plato was the first to write of divine providence; cf. Stanley, *History*, I, 164.

§148. A commonplace of classical moral wisdom, frequently cited as a corrective to the pretensions associated with "good" lineage. Charles Gildon's iteration of the principle is characteristic:

> *Qui Genus jactat suum, aliena laudat.* And
> *Et Genus & Proavos, & quae non fecimus ipsi,*
> *Vix eas nostra voco* —— And
> *Nobilitas sola est atque unica Virtus.*

Virtue is the only Nobility, and he who boasts an old Family, boasts of another's Merit, not his own. *Ovid,* who was himself of the *Equestrian* Order, makes the wise *Ulysses* speak the second Quotation." ([Gildon], *The Post-Man Robb'd of His Mail* . . . [London, 1719], 196–197)

§149. Diogenes Laertius relates the Scythian Anacharsis's response to impertinent reproof: "When some Athenian reproached him with being a Scythian, he replied, 'Well, granted that my country is a disgrace to me, you are a disgrace to your country' " (1.104). Cf. Stanley, *History,* I, 56.

§152. Antigonus was one of Alexander's chief generals and successors, the grandfather of Antigonus Gonatus. Early modern writers drew on Plutarch to counter the notion that nobility of birth and virtue are the same thing; Plutarch *Moralia* ("Sayings of Kings and Commanders"): "When a young man, son of a brave father, but not himself having any reputation for being a good soldier, suggested the propriety of receiving his father's emoluments, Antigonus said, 'My boy, I give pay and presents for the excellence of a man, not for the excellence of his father' " (183d). Cf. *Moralia* 534c ("On Compliancy"); see also Montaigne, *Essays,* "On Certain Verses of Virgil."

§153. "Denis" is a name often given to Dionysius the Elder, tyrant of Syracuse (430–377); see §68.

§155. Diogenes Laertius "Anaxagoras": "And at last he went into retirement and engaged in physical investigation without troubling himself about public affairs. When some one inquired, 'Have you no concern in your native land?' 'Gently,' he replied, 'I am greatly concerned with my fatherland,' and pointed to the sky" (*Lives* 2.7).

§156. Lucius Cornelius Sulla (or Sylla) was dictator of Rome in the second century B.C.E. This story appears in Plutarch's *Moralia* ("Precepts of Statecraft"): "For when Sulla, after the capture of Praenestê, was going to slaughter all the rest of the citizens but was letting that one man go on account of his guest-friendship, he declared that he would not be indebted for his life to the slayer of his fatherland, and then mingled with his fellow-citizens and was cut down with them" (816a). Cf. Plutarch *Lives,* "Sulla" 32.1.

§158. Byrd's entry refers to the problem of moral contagion. During the London years Byrd often sought out bad company, though he boasted in "Inamorato L'Oiseaux" that he was unaffected. His claim is not substantiated by the facts of his life at the time, according to his diary's account of alternating bouts of illicit activity and guilt. Byrd might have sought guidance at this time from classical moral philosophers, who were unanimous in their advice *against* the position Byrd adopted. Xenophon warns, "The society of honest men is a training in virtue, but the society of the bad is virtue's undoing" (*Memorabilia* 1.2.20). Similarly, Seneca, in *De ira* (3.8.1–2) explains: "We adopt our habits from those with whom we associate, and as certain diseases of the body spread to others from contact, so the mind transmits its faults to those nearby" (*Moral Essays,* trans. John W. Basore, LCL [1928], I). Erasmus touches on this subject in several places; Byrd might have read these words in the *Adages*: "Faults pass from man to man more easily than good qualities. . . . Association with wicked men is very dangerous, because faults of the body and still more faults of the mind pass like an infection. . . . A man's moral corruption rubs off on those who live in his company" (1.10.73, "Si juxta claudum habites, subclaudicare disces").

The topic also appears in early modern handbooks of manners in public life, as in this warning in [Jacques de Caillières], *The Courtier's Calling: Shewing the Ways of Making a Fortune . . .* (London, 1675): "Alas, how dangerous is it for a Gentleman to mistake himself in the choice of his ordinary Conversations? and with what circumspection ought he to avoid Debauch'd and Sottish Company! This is a point of that importance, that from it depends the whole course of his manners, and of his Life. The frequenting with wicked men, brings us acquainted with Vice, and makes us behold it without any emotion; by degrees we begin to act it with some pleasure; time breeds in us a habit, and the habit will at last be converted into a necessity" (217–218). A copy of this book was in Byrd's library (Hayes 900). Cf. Montaigne, *Essays,* "Of the Art of Conversation"; see also §263.

§159. "To those who said to him, 'You are an old man; take a rest,' 'What?' he replied, 'if I were running in the stadium, ought I to slacken my pace when approaching the goal? ought I not rather to put on speed?'" (Diogenes Laertius "Diogenes," *Lives* 6.34).

§160. A version of the saying appears in [Abel] Boyer, *The Wise and Ingenious Companion . . .* (London, 1700): "*Simonides* being asked which was most to be desired, either Riches or Wisdom: *I am,* answered he, *very much in doubt about it; for I see a great many Wisemen make their Court to the Rich*" (73).

§162. Thales, according to Stanley, originally commented that enduring political tyranny was less difficult than a life without self-knowledge and self-control: "Being demanded what was difficult, he answered, To know ones self; what easie, to be ruled by another" (*History,* I, 11–12). This differs from Diogenes

Laertius, who has Thales saying only that giving advice to others is easy (*Lives* 1.36). See also §336.

§163. Plutarch *Moralia* ("Sayings of Kings and Commanders"): "When [Agesilaus] was dying he gave orders that his friends have no 'plaster or paint' used, for this was the way he spoke of statues and portraits. 'For,' said he, 'if I have done any noble deed, that is my memorial; but if none, then not all the statues in the world avail'" (191d). Cf. *Moralia* 210e, 215a ("Sayings of the Spartans"); Diodorus Siculus 15.93.

§164. During the ten years Demetrius held chief power in Athens, the assembly decreed 360 bronze statues of him. Diogenes Laertius blames his fall from power on "all-devouring envy." Ancient and early modern writers alike included Demetrius in the company of public benefactors like Demosthenes and Phocion who suffered at the hands of an ungrateful populace: "When he heard that the Athenians had destroyed his statues, 'That they may do,' said he, 'but the merits which caused them to be erected they cannot destroy'" (*Lives* 5.76–77, 82).

§166. See §109, 110, 217.

§167. For the comments of Diogenes on orators, see §109, 110. The verses critical of Charles are from Rochester's "Impromptu on Charles II," first published in the 1707 edition of his verse (David M. Vieth, ed., *The Complete Poems of John Wilmot, Earl of Rochester* [New Haven, Conn., 1968], 134):

> God bless our good and gracious King,
>> Whose promise none relies on;
> Who never said a foolish thing,
>> Nor ever did a wise one.

Byrd owned a copy of "Rochester's Poems" (Hayes 1013). See also §110.

§168. We have not identified the "Duke Hamilton" of this anecdote. Curiously, James Douglas, fourth duke of Hamilton (1658–1712), did not inherit his father's honors and estate in Scotland on his death in 1694, because the title and property passed to his mother. However (in distinction to the story told here), she resigned her honors to her son only four years later, by permission of the king.

§169. Probably Cleomenes, king of the Spartans, son of Anaxandrides. Stanley records a similar saying attributed to Socrates: "Hunters take Hares with Hounds, many take Fools with their own praises" (*History,* I, 77).

§171. After his first failed attempts at oratory, Demosthenes was advised by Satyrus the actor, who demonstrated what could be done with the proper delivery. Demosthenes had already mastered the content of speaking but needed to consider form; thus Plutarch, in the *Lives*, concludes, "Persuaded, now, how much of ornament and grace action leads to oratory, he considered it of little or no use for a man to practise declaiming if he neglected the delivery and disposition of his words" ("Demosthenes" 7.2). Cf. Quintilian on Demosthenes' emphasis on the *manner* of presenting a speech (*Institutio oratoria* 11.3.5–6); and Valerius Maximus, *Acts and Sayings of the Romans*, 406.

§172. According to Plutarch, Demosthenes shaved one side of his head during his early period of intensive study in oratory, during which he secreted himself away in an underground study: "And into this he would descend every day without exception in order to form his action and cultivate his voice, and he would often remain there even for two or three months together, shaving one side of his head in order that shame might keep him from going abroad even though he greatly wished to do so" (*Lives*, "Demosthenes" 7.3). Plutarch, however, makes no mention of Phryne, the Greek courtesan legendary for her beauty.

§173. The notion of "washing an Ethiopian white" is proverbial, denoting an impossible attempt to change inherent natural qualities. Erasmus applies the saying to attempts to disguise vice with facile words (*Adages*, 1.4.50: "Aethiopem lavas; Aethiopem dealbas"), attempts whose eventual failure is inevitable. In Byrd's version the proverb is literalized by the incestuous miscegenation of the "wicked West Indian." Byrd's ironic reference to the "honourable" descent of his issue, in conjoining the whitening process with a tone of opprobrium, may indicate familiarity with the moral censure implicit in the Erasmian passage.

Nonetheless, Byrd refers to miscegenation elsewhere without any note of opprobrium, as in his discussion about intermarriage with the Indians: "Nor would the shade of the skin have been any reproach at this day, for if a Moor may be washt white in three generations, surely an Indian might have been blancht in two" (*History of the Dividing Line*, in *Works*, 160–161). His interest in matters of race and pigmentation may also be seen in the paper he read before the Royal Society in 1697, "An Account of a Negro-Boy That Is Dappel'd in Several Places of His Body with White Spots," Royal Society, *Philosophical Transactions*, XIX (1695–1697), 781–782 (and see above, Chapter 7). Kathleen M. Brown explains this anecdote in terms of a belief in the transgressive power of white slaveowners to sidestep the power of nature, overcoming "white male anxieties about sexual and racial potence" through "sexual virility and willingness to violate incest taboos." Brown concludes this signifies the racial dominance of the slaveowners accomplished by "effacing any trace of African parentage in their descendants" (*Good Wives, Nasty Wenches, and Anxious Patriarchs: Gender, Race, and Power in Colonial Virginia* [Chapel Hill, N.C., 1996], 333). However, as the history of miscegenation in colonial Virginia indicates, such effacement does not in fact occur. A child with any admixture of African blood continues to be classified as African, thus confirming the futility of the attempt to erase racial ancestry, implicit in the aphorism itself.

§174. The notion of besting an enemy by outdoing him in virtue is a common theme with ancient moralists. See, for example, Plutarch *Moralia* ("How to Profit by One's Enemies"), where Diogenes names the best defense "proving yourself good and honourable" (88b).

§175. It should not be surprising to see Byrd recording such an opinion about the significance of a tolerance for bawdy talk in a woman. Traditional preceptual writers consider the refusal to participate in such talk a necessary part of feminine modesty. In Byrd's time, it was expected that a proper woman's modesty would be deeply offended by lascivious discourse. Such scruples had practical value; female tolerance of bawdy talk was a sign of "lightness" (openness to sexual advances). Many writers warn against the danger of even appearing immodest. Richard Allestree recommends this defense: "The best way therefore to countermine those Stratagems of men, is for women to be suspiciously vigilant even of the first approches. He that means to defend a Fort, must not abandon the Outworks, and she that will secure her Chastity, must never let it come to too close a siege, but repass the very first and most remote insinuations of a temter. Therefore when we speak of modesty in our present notion of it, we are not to oppose it only to the grosser act of Incontinentcy, but to all those misbehaviors, which either discover or may create an inclination to it; of which sort is all lightness of carriage, wanton glances, obscene discourse; things that shew a woman so weary of her honor, that the next comer may reasonably expect a surrender, and consequently be invited to the Assault" (*The Ladies' Calling* . . . [Oxford, 1673], I, 16). Female purity is endangered by every step away from absolute probity, because men tend to view such developments as encouragement. Halifax therefore cautions his daughter never to countenance any "*Forwardness*": "*Mankind*, from the double temptation of *Vanity* and *Desire*, is apt to turn every thing a *Woman* doth to the *hopeful side*; and there are few who dare make an impudent Application, till they discern something which they are willing to take for an *Encouragement*" (*Advice to a Daughter*, in *Miscellanies by the Right Noble Lord, the Late Lord Marquess of Halifax* . . . [London, 1700], 98).

Byrd here aligns himself with those men against whom such authors warn their female readers. It is not necessary for women to participate actively in lewd discourse, for even to tolerate it is construed as a form of encouragement (or a tacit acknowledgment of lasciviousness). Byrd's last words go further, suggesting that in most cases female modesty is no more than a tactical position, assumed for pride and politics (that is, out of self-interest and calculation, not out of moral conviction).

§177. Saint John Chrysostom, the fourth-century patriarch, theologian, and bishop of Constantinople. This saying is collected by Stobaeus in *Loci communes sententiarum,* XV ("De malis et improbis viris"), 27: "Qui saepe peccant nec puniuntur, metuere & vereri debent: augentur enim illis supplicia per supplicii tarditatem & divinam lenitatem" ("Those who sin often and are not punished ought to be filled with fear and dread; for their penalties are increased by the delay in their punishment and the slowness of divine justice").

§184. Source not identified. This entry and several of the next entries (and several other clusters later in the manuscript) refer to points of Anglican doctrine and might have been notes from sermons Byrd read or heard. This entry addressed the doctrine that compassion is the essential moral ingredient of human character; people incapable of feeling for the joys and sorrows of others are no better than beasts devoid of reason and virtue. See, for instance, Richard Allestree's definition of compassion in *The Ladies' Calling* ... (Oxford, 1673): "I need not say much to raise an estimate of this Vertu, since 'tis so essential to our Nature, so interwoven in the composition of Humanity, that we find in Scripture phrase, compassion is generally seated in the most inward sensible part of our frame, the bowels.... So that a cruel and ruthless person unmans himself, and is by the common vote of mankind to be listed among brutes; nay, not among the better, but only the more hateful, noxious sort of them" (I, 48).

§186. That Jesus was known to express all human emotions (save laughter) was an early modern commonplace. A similar constancy of expression (indicating mastery of the passions) was attributed to a number of philosophers and great men, including Pericles, Socrates, Cato, and others. Phocion was an exemplar of heroic virtue, unselfish devotion to the well-being of his people, and philosophical self-control. Byrd's reference to Phocion is based on Plutarch *Moralia* 187f ("Sayings of Kings and Commanders"), or Plutarch *Lives,* "Phocion" 4.2.

The duke of Alba, ambassador from the duke of Anjou, represented the court of France at the 1709 peace conferences.

§187. This story is found in Diogenes Laertius *Lives* 4.43 ("Archelaus"). Cf. Stanley, "Arcesilaus," *History,* I, 220; Bacon, *Apophthegmes,* no. 280; Montaigne, *Essays,* "Of Cruelty." Byrd records the same story again in §290.

§192. The Church of England, in laying claim to primitive Christianity uncorrupted by the rulings of popes and councils and in arguing that Anglican doctrine could be comprehended by reason, often characterized Roman Catholicism as superstitious and labeled several of its beliefs (notably transubstantiation) as contradictory.

§194. Plato *Laws* 808b: "Overmuch sleep, indeed, is naturally as unsuitable to us in body and mind as it is incongruous with business of all these kinds. In fact, a man asleep is of no more account than a corpse" (*The Collected Dialogues,* trans. Edith Hamilton and Huntington Cairns, [Princeton, N.J., 1961]). Cf. *Republic* 537b; Diogenes Laertius *Lives* ("Plato") 3.40; Plutarch *Moralia* 8d ("The Education of Children"); Montaigne, *Essays,* "Of Experience"; and Stanley, "Plato," *History,* I, 272.

§198. Alexander rejected Parmenion's recommendation of a night attack as dishonorable; Quintus Curtius maintains that he rejected the plan on strategic grounds, rendering the moral question moot. Alexander says: "The craft which you recommend to me is that of petty robbers and thieves; for their sole desire is to deceive. I will not suffer my glory always to be impaired by the absence of Darius, or by confined places, or by deceit by night. I am determined to attack openly by daylight; I prefer to regret my fortune rather than be ashamed of my victory. Besides, this consideration too is added; I am well aware that the barbarians keep watch by night and stand under arms, so that it is not really possible to deceive them" (4.13.3–10). Arrian speculates that Alexander might have used the claim of honor "since others were listening," to disguise an essentially strategic decision about the difficulty of maintaining control of nocturnal battles (*Anabasis Alexandri* 3.10.1–4, trans. P. A. Brunt, LCL [1976–1982]); cf. Plutarch *Lives,* "Alexander" 31.5.

§199. King Philip of Macedon thus advised his son Alexander, according to Plutarch: "And so Philip once said to his son, who, as the wine went round, plucked the strings charmingly and skillfully, 'Art not ashamed to pluck the strings so well?' It is enough, surely, if a king have leisure to hear others pluck the strings, and he pays great deference to the Muses if he be but a spectator of such contests. Labour with one's hands on lowly tasks gives witness, in the toil thus expended on useless things, to one's own indifference to higher things" (*Lives,* "Pericles" 1.5–2.1). Older translations such as Sir Thomas North's present the advice more pointedly: "He that personally shall bestow his time, exercising any mean Science: bringeth his pains he hath taken in matters unprofitable, a witness against himself, to prove that he hath been negligent to learn things honest and profitable" (*The Lives of the Noble Grecians and Romans* . . . [Cambridge, 1676], 132). See also Montaigne, *Essays*, "Reflection concerning Cicero."

§200. The story appears in the *Encheiridion* of Epictetus: "If one come and tell thee, Such a man slaundered you thus or thus: never stand to apologize for thy selfe: but answere him againe onely thus: he knoweth not mine other faults, for if he did, he would never have reckoned only those you tell me of" (*Epictetus Manuall, Cebes Table, Theophrastus Characters*, trans. Jo. Healey [London, 1616], 68–69).

§202. This entry warns of the power of love to distort a man's ability to perceive the true character of a woman. In many cases, the angelic appearance of women conceals a devilish nature, a fact that a man whose judgment is not impaired by passion might discern, thus saving him from torment. Some years later Byrd employed some of the same phrases about female deceptiveness in a letter to Mrs. Jane Pratt Taylor on Mar. 20, 1736/7: "Another thing is, the ladys study all the arts of dress and disguise more than the men. They have the secret of setting off their charms with more advantage, and covering their irregularitys. They know how to place their perfections in the fairest light, and cast all their blemishes in shade, so that the poor men who know no better, take them to be cherubims, and gems without flaw. But when upon a better acquaintance we come to discover, that the fair creature has some failings and we begin to judge a little by sence and not altogether by fancy, our vast expectations are disappointed, upon which the appetite will naturally pall, and after we have misst of Paradise in one place, we are apt to look for it in another. It is therefore wrong for any damsell to endeavour to make the men in love with her, that she intends to marry. Lovers are all idolators and fondly fancy a kind of divinity in their mistresses. But after a [. . .] the angel will certainly disappear, and the very wo[. . .] the inconstancy of our sex is owing to the disappointments it meets with from yours, who are too solicitous to hide their blemishes before they throw themselves into a mans arms and too little afterwards. These are abominable truths, but there's no such thing as perfection in this poor world, the sun itself has its spots, no wonder then that the next bright thing to that shoud have her failings" (*Correspondence*, II, 505). In this later discussion, the misogyny of Byrd's earlier view is qualified by the acknowledgment that both sexes are party to deception.

§203. Byrd here may be alluding to Theseus's anatomy of love in Shakespeare's *Midsummer Night's Dream*: "The lunatic, the lover, and the poet are of imagination all compact" (5.1.7–8).

§205. Xenophon *Memorabilia* 1.3.11–13. Xenophon does not stipulate that kissing a beautiful *woman* is dangerous—it is the sight of a beautiful *face* that can have the same numbing or fatal effect as the scorpion's venom.

§206. Source of the saying attributed to Demosthenes unidentified. Several extant anecdotes establish Socrates' unwillingness to stoop to rude disputes or brawls, either with belligerent strangers (Xenophon *Memorabilia* 3.13.1; Diogenes Laertius *Lives* 2.21) or his wife, Xanthippe (Xenophon *Symposium* 2.10; Diogenes Laertius *Lives* 2.36–37). Cf. Stanley, *History,* I, 91–92; see also §243.

§212. This observation, common to many discussions on friendship, is well articulated by Cicero in *De amicitia* 7.29.

§213. On mutual accord, active goodwill, and faith in friendship, see Cicero *De amicitia* 6–7 and *De officiis* 1.17.55–57.

§214. Diogenes Laertius attributes an ironic version of this teaching to Demetrius of Phalerum: "In prosperity friends do not leave you unless desired, whereas in adversity they stay away of their own accord" (*Lives* 5.83).

§215. The ultimate source is *Magna moralia* 2.11, attributed to Aristotle, where a friend is defined as a second self and it is said that the souls of friends are one. The saying is ubiquitous. Cf. Diogenes Laertius *Lives* 5.20; Erasmus, *Adages,* 1.1.2 ("Amicitia aequalitas; Amicus alter ipse"); Stanley, "Aristotle," *History,* II, 359; R[oger] L'Estrange, *Seneca's Morals by Way of Abstract . . . ,* 6th ed. (London, 1696), 545–546.

§216. This extract comes from Dominick Fernandez Navarette, *An Account of the Empire of China:* "There is one thing very remarkable in the Province of *Kuei Chu,* that is a Bridg of one only Stone, and is twenty Fathom in length, and three in breadth. F. *Michael Trigaucius* a Jesuit, and my Companion in Persecution, had noted this down as a Rarity; he told me of it, and I thought it worth writing. The manner of carrying that Stone, and placing it on to pieces of Wall, very high and broad, built on both sides of the River, was no small Subject of discourse. Of all the Men in the World, the *Chineses* only are the fittest to conquer such difficultys. They have excellent Contrivances, and a ready Wit for all worldly Affairs" (Churchill, *Voyages,* I, 32; Byrd owned a copy [Hayes 79]). A fathom is a measure of six feet. Byrd translates Navarette's figures accurately into feet: "120 feet long, and 18 feet broad." For other entries based on the travel writings collected by Churchill, see §238, 419, 423, 425, 426.

§217. Diogenes Laertius *Lives* 6.39; cf. Stanley, *History,* II, 412. See also §109, 166.

§218. Byrd might have encountered this anecdote in any of a number of places. It appears in Plutarch's *Moralia* 179d ("Sayings of Kings and Commanders"),

331b ("On the Fortune or the Virtue of Alexander"); Plutarch *Lives,* "Alex-ander" 4.5. Cf. Erasmus, *Apophthegmes,* "Alexander," no. 2; Bacon's *Ap-ophthegmes,* no. 171; [Abel] Boyer, *The Wise and Ingenious Companion . . .* (London, 1700), 77. Or Byrd might have encountered the story in the *Specta-tor,* no. 157 (Aug. 30, 1711): "My common-place Book directs me on this Occasion to mention the Dawning of Greatness in Alexander, who being asked in his Youth to contend for a Prize in the Olympick Games, answered he would if he had Kings to run against him."

§219. Plutarch *Moralia* 179d ("Sayings of Kings and Commanders"); Plutarch *Lives,* "Alexander" 5.2.

§220. Gaius Julius Caesar (ca. 100–44), the first Roman emperor of that name— his successors took his name as an honorific worthy of an emperor—was a popular exemplar of bold, great-spirited ambition. This anecdote is found in Plutarch *Moralia* 206b ("Sayings of Romans"). Cf. Plutarch *Lives,* "Caesar" 11.2; Suetonius "The Deified Julius" 23, *Lives of the Caesars;* Bacon, *Ad-vancement of Learning,* 2.32.36; [Abel] Boyer, *The Wise and Ingenious Com-panion . . .* (London, 1700), 27.

§222. A different version of this tale appears in Addisons's *Guardian* essay on good conscience as proof against detraction: *"Diogenes* was still more severe on one who spoke ill of him: No Body will believe you when you speak ill of me, any more than they would believe me should I speak well of you" (no. 135 [Aug. 15, 1713]). Byrd believes Diogenes is referring to Plato; this difference may indicate another source, or (perhaps) a conflation caused by hasty refer-ence or reliance on memory, since in Addison's essay two related stories concerning Plato immediately follow the tale of Diogenes.

§223. Plutarch *Moralia* 174c ("Sayings of Kings and Commanders"); Cf. *Specta-tor,* no. 427 (July 10, 1712).

§224. It was Anaxarchus, not Anaxagoras, whose discourse on the plurality of worlds reduced Alexander to tears. Diogenes Laertius records that Anax-archus traveled to India with Alexander (*Lives* 9.58). On Alexander's tears, see Plutarch *Moralia* 466d ("On Tranquillity of Mind"); Valerius Maximus thought Alexander's tears revealed immoderate desire for honor, for he "thought his Honour too much confin'd that had not all which suffices for the Habitation of the Gods" (*Acts and Sayings of the Romans,* 419–420).

§225. Plutarch *Moralia* ("Sayings of the Spartans"): "Damis, with reference to the instructions sent from Alexander that they should pass a formal vote deifying him, said, 'We concede to Alexander that, if he so wishes, he may be called a god'" (219e).

§226. Croesus was the last king of Lydia (ca. 560–546); his immense wealth is still proverbial. Herodotus *History* 1.29–33 tells the story of Solon's visit to Croesus, who attempted to impress the lawgiver with the spectacle of his treasure and was surprised when Solon declined to number him among the most happy of men, explaining that happiness springs, not from gold, silver, or power, but from honesty, duty, and virtue. According to Diogenes Laertius, Solon told Croesus that the natural colors of cocks and pheasants and peacock were more beautiful than his riches (*Lives* 1. 51). Cf. Plutarch *Lives*, "Solon" 28.1–7; Lucian *Charon; or, The Inspectors* 10–11, in *Works*; Stanley, "Solon," *History*, I, 29.

§228. Stanley notes that this saying is attributed to both Zeno and Socrates (*History*, II, 424). In the *History of the Dividing Line*, Byrd modifies this proverb in one of his regular ironic swipes at Virginia's southern neighbors: "And, considering how Fortune delights in bringing great things out of small, who knows but Carolina may, one time or other, come to be the seat of some other great empire?" (*Works*, 186).

§229. It is not clear to whom the manuscript refers here; the handwriting appears to indicate "Pitho[. . .]rius," but no such name appears in Greek or Roman history.

§230. Permutations of this saying abound, beginning with Diogenes the Cynic: "Being asked what creature's bite is the worst, he said, 'Of those that are wild a sycophant's; of those that are tame a flatterer's'" (Diogenes Laertius *Lives* 6.51). The basilisk is a supremely poisonous mythical serpent; it kills humans if they look at its eyes, destroys bushes with its touch as it passes, and sets fire to grass and rocks with its breath (Pliny *Natural History* 7.77–78). Plutarch attributes a different version to Thales, who denounced the tyrant and the flatterer, in *Moralia* 147b ("Dinner of the Seven Wise Men") (cf. Stanley, "Thales," *History*, I, 3), and to Bias in *Moralia* 61c ("How to Tell a Flatterer from a Friend"). Cf. Erasmus, *Parabolae*, trans. R. A. B. Mynors, *Collected Works of Erasmus*, XXIII (Toronto, 1978), 250; [Abel] Boyer, *The Wise and Ingenious Companion . . .* (London, 1700), 31; Addison, *Whig-Examiner*, no. 5 (Oct. 12, 1710).

§233. On the duty of a friend to rebuke on fit occasions and the dangers of complaisance and flattery, see Cicero *De amicitia* 34.88–89. See also Plutarch *Moralia* ("How to Tell a Flatterer from a Friend") 48e–49b.

§234. The danger of flatterers is a common theme among the ancient moralists. See, for instance, Plutarch's warnings in *Moralia* ("The Education of Children"): "There is no class of persons more pernicious than flatterers, nor any that more surely and quickly gives youth a nasty tumble. They utterly ruin both fathers and sons, bringing to sorrow the old age of those and the youth of these, and dangling pleasure as an irresistible lure to get their advice taken" (13a). See also Cicero *De amicitia* 25.91–94.

§235. In "How to Tell a Flatterer from a Friend" (*Moralia* 48e–49b), Plutarch attributes to Plato a similar warning about the dangerous flattery of self-love (*Laws* 731d–e).

§236. Alexander Pope, the English poet, had many literary enemies. His authorship of this epigram has not been substantiated, nor has a written or published source been found; thus it is probable that this entry came from conversation. If Pope was indeed the author, C——y might have been Walter Cary (1685–1757), later clerk of the Privy Council. Pope told Joseph Spence in 1738 that Cary had contributed something—"scarce anything"—to the *Spectator* or the *Guardian*, but, because he flattered adroitly, Steele "mentioned him purely to do him a service" (Joseph Spence, *Observations, Anecdotes, and Characters of Books and Men, Collected from Conversation*, ed. James M. Osborn [Oxford, 1966], no. 497, I, 212). Thus, the epigram, pointed at a wit who does not write, fits Cary.

However, if this witty attack originated with Pope, it is surprising that Spence did not record it in conjunction with Pope's comment on Cary or anywhere else in the large section devoted to Pope (Spence's favorite part of the collection). Moreover, this identification becomes problematic when we consider that Spence *does* include much later in the *Observations* a remarkably similar epigram (no. 1053, I, 403), credited to Spence himself, and dated as late as 1756:

> Argyle has wit they say; for what?
> For writing? No; for writing not.

This time the target is Archibald Campbell, third duke of Argyll (1682–1761), the younger brother and heir of Byrd's friend and patron John Campbell, the second duke (1678–1743).

§238. Byrd here begins with a transcription from Dominick Fernandez Navarette, *An Account of the Empire of China:* "The Elephants Trunk they affirm to be a mighty dainty, and a bit for a King, the same they say of a Bear's Paw" (Churchill, *Voyages*, I, 65). The list of the three most wealthy monarchs is an interpolation, perhaps from elsewhere in the collection of voyages, which often treat of the wealth of eastern potentates. The beaver tail is also added, perhaps from Byrd's own familiarity with indigenous delicacies of North America.

§239. Diogenes Laertius "Bias": "When an impious man asked him to define piety, he was silent; and when the other inquired the reason, 'I am silent,' he

replied, 'because you are asking questions about what does not concern you'"
(*Lives* 1.86).

§241. Matthew Barker, *Flores Intellectuales; or, Select Notions, Sentences, and Observations* . . . (London, 1691): "The Wine mixt with Myrrh, offer'd to Christ upon the Cross, was usually given to stupifie the Sense, and to mitigate the Pain, as some say, but Christ refused it, he was supported under his Pain by other means, and was willing to suffer to the utmost for our sakes" (66). Byrd owned a copy of this book (Hayes 2271).

§243. See §206.

§244. For some historians, this incident demonstrates Alexander's magnanimity. Arrian praises him for his "compassion for the women" (*Anabasis Alexandri* 2.12.8), and Athenaeus introduces the story of Alexander's restraint in not forcing himself upon the captive women, usually considered fair game in war (*Deipnosophistae* 12.603c). Plutarch also praises Alexander's magnanimity, noting that he told the women Darius was still alive, gave them permission to bury their dead, and maintained them in their usual dignity. His emphasis on Alexander's self-control is similar:

> But the most honourable and most princely favour which these noble and chaste women received from him in their captivity was that they neither heard, nor suspected, nor awaited anything that could disgrace them, but lived, as though guarded in sacred and inviolable virgins' chambers instead of in an enemy's camp, apart from the speech and sight of men. And yet it is said that the wife of Dareius was far the most comely of all royal women, just as Dareius himself also was handsomest and tallest of men, and their daughters resembled their parents.
>
> But Alexander, as it would seem, considering the mastery of himself a more kingly thing than the conquest of his enemies, neither laid hands upon these women, nor did he know any other before marriage, except Barsiné. . . . But as for the other captive women, seeing that they were surpassingly stately and beautiful, he merely said jestingly that Persian women were torments to the eyes. And displaying in rivalry with their fair looks the beauty of his own sobriety and self-control, he passed them by as though they were lifeless images for display. (*Lives*, "Alexander" 21.3–5)

Cf. Aulus Gellius *Attic Nights* 7.8.1–2.

§246. Plutarch *Moralia* 177e ("Sayings of Kings and Commanders"); cf. Bacon, *Apophthegmes*, no. 103. Plutarch also attributes a similar saying to Pyrrhus, in *Lives*, "Pyrrhus" 8.5.

§248. Plutarch *Moralia* ("Sayings of Spartan Woman") 241c–d.

§249. Cf. D[aniel] T[uvill], *Essaies Politicke and Morall* (London, 1608): "There are few, that can say, & say truly, as that *Graecian* of former times did, who beeing told that his breath did smell, answered, that it was by reason of the many secrets, which had a long time layne rotting, and putrifying within him" (fol. 80r).

§256. The notion that the best governors are themselves aware of their own subjection to the law is ubiquitous. Plutarch states that Agesilaus "had been educated to obey before he came to command. For this reason he was much more in harmony with his subjects than any of the kings; to the commanding and kingly traits which were his by nature there had been added by his public training those of popularity and kindness" (*Lives*, "Agesilaus" 1.2–3).

§259. Diogenes Laertius reports that Aristippus remarked that "it was better for the money to perish on account of Aristippus than for Aristippus to perish on account of the money" (*Lives* 2.77).

§260. Plutarch *Moralia* ("Sayings of Spartans"): "A Spartan, being asked why he wore his beard so very long, said, 'So that I may see my grey hairs and do nothing unworthy of them'" (232e).

§261. Plutarch *Moralia* ("Whether an Old Man Should Engage in Public Affairs"): "Cato, for example, used to say that we ought not voluntarily to add to the many evils of its own which belong to old age the disgrace that comes from baseness" (784a). Cf. Plutarch *Moralia* 199a ("Sayings of Romans"), 829f ("On Borrowing"), and *Lives*, "Marcus Cato" 9.6–7. Similar advice attributed to Cato appears in Cicero *De senectute* 18.65.

§263. See §158.

§265. The Cynic philosopher Diogenes considered dependency worse than need: "When some one was extolling the good fortune of Callisthenes and saying what splendour he shared in the suite of Alexander, 'Not so,' said Diogenes, 'but rather ill fortune; for he breakfasts and dines when Alexander thinks fit'" (Diogenes Laertius *Lives* 6.45). Cf. Stanley, *History*, II, 413.

§267. See §301.

§269. The topos of the transience of life is common among classical writers, especially those concerned with the need to be prepared for sudden changes in fortune or for death. Xenophon in his *Memorabilia* (1.1.8) observed that knowledge of the future is reserved for the gods: "You may plant a field well; but you know not who shall gather the fruits: you may build a house well; but you know not who shall dwell in it" (*Memorabilia, Oeconomicus, Sumposium, Apology*, trans. E. C. Marchant and O. J. Todd, LCL [1979]). Another possible source for this entry is Lucian's *Charon; or, The Inspectors* 17, in which Hermes wonders at the surprise of mortals at their own death, for "they never expected to be torn away from their gear. For example, that man who is busily building himself a house and driving the workmen on; what would not he do if he knew that although the house will be finished, as soon as he gets the roof on, he himself will depart and leave his heir the enjoyment of it without even dining in it, poor fellow?" (*Works*, II). On the other hand, Cicero, in *De senectute*, praises the nobility of those aged farmers who continue to work, planting trees for posterity (8.24).

§274. Stobaeus, *Sententiae*, XXI, 176 ("De cognoscendo seipsum"): "Socrates roganti cur nihil scriptum ederet: Respondit, Quia video chartam multo preciosorem, quàm scribenda forent" ("Socrates, asked why he set nothing down in writing, answered, Because I see so much precious paper ruined by scribbling").

§277. This entry alludes to the topos of man's confusion about what is truly valuable. Xenophon attributes the principle of praying only for what God sees fit to give to Socrates (*Memorabilia* 1.3.2); cf. Valerius Maximus, *Acts and Sayings of the Romans*, 310. Montaigne draws on the same source in his *Essays*, "Apology for Raimond Sebond," reminding his readers that Midas wished for the power of turning whatever he touched to gold, which turned out to be an "intolerable benefaction."

§278. Alexander reproves his flatterers with verses from Homer; Plutarch *Moralia* 180e ("Sayings of Kings and Commanders"), 341b ("On the Fortune of Alexander"); *Lives*, "Alexander" 28.2. Cf. Dio Chrysostom *Orations* 44; Seneca *Moral Epistles*, no. 59, "On Pleasure and Joy" 12–13; Erasmus, *Apophthegmes*, "Alexander," no. 16. Diogenes Laertius tells the story as if another speaker thus counseled Alexander (*Lives*, "Anaxarchus," 9.60). See also Montaigne, *Essays*, "Of the Inequality between Us."

§279. Aulus Gellius reports "that Olympias, the wife of Philip, wrote a very witty reply to her son Alexander. For he had addressed his mother as follows: 'King Alexander, son of Jupiter Hammon, greets his mother Olympias.' Olympias replied to this effect: 'Pray, my son,' said she, 'be silent, and do not slander me or accuse me before Juno; undoubtedly she will take cruel vengeance on me, if you admit in your letters that I am her husband's paramour.' This courteous reply of a wise and prudent woman to her arrogant son seemed to warn him in a mild and polite fashion to give up the foolish ideas which he had formed from his great victories, from the flattery of his courtiers, and from his incredible success—that he was the son of Jupiter" (*The Attic Nights* 13.4, trans. John C. Rolfe, LCL [1927]).

This is the source for early modern versions of the story, usually exemplifying modesty; see Thom[as] Heywood, Γυναικειον; or, Nine Books of Various History concerninge Women . . . (London, 1624), 144, and General History of Women (London, 1657), 174). Cf. The Accomplish'd Lady; or, Deserving Gentlewoman . . . (London, [1684]), 121–122; [Abel] Boyer, The Wise and Ingenious Companion . . . (London, 1700), 81.

§280. "All the days of the afflicted are evil, but a cheerful heart hath a continual feast." Prov. 15:15.

§281. Travelers "bait" during a journey; that is, they "stop at an inn . . . to rest and refresh themselves" or "make a brief stay or sojourn" (OED). The source of the comment about recreation attributed to Plutarch has not been identified.

§283. "Plato once saw some one playing at dice and rebuked him. And, upon his protesting that he played for a trifle only, 'But the habit,' rejoined Plato, 'is not a trifle' " (Diogenes Laertius Lives 3.38). See also Montaigne, Essays, "Of Custom and the Inadvisability of Changing an Established Law."

§287. See §311.

§288. This ironic saying, suggesting that the general public rarely knows what is good for it, is attributed to different figures, most frequently to Phocion. Plutarch Moralia 188a ("Sayings of Kings and Commanders"); Bacon, Apophthegmes, no. 30; Addison, Spectator, no. 188 (Oct. 5, 1711). See also §247, 289.

§289. Like §288, this saying disparages the judgment of the multitude. "Applauded by rascals," Antisthenes remarked, "I am horribly afraid I have done something wrong." Diogenes Laertius Lives 6.5, 8.

§290. See §187.

§291. Saint Basil (329–379), bishop, theologian, classicist, and patriarch of the Byzantine Church, instituted rules for monastic life.

§292. Plutarch Moralia 241a–e ("Sayings of Spartan Women," nos. 3, 10, 12).

§293. Anacharsis is one of the ancient philosophers often introduced by classical and early modern writers to exemplify self-mastery, especially in regard to the government of the tongue. The common source is Plutarch Moralia ("Concerning Talkativeness"): "Now of the other affections and maladies some are dangerous, some detestable, some ridiculous; but garrulousness has all these qualities at once; for babblers are derided for telling what everyone knows, they are hated for bearing bad news, they run into danger since they cannot refrain from revealing secrets. So it is that Anacharsis, when he had been entertained and feasted at Solon's house and lay down to sleep, was seen to have his left hand placed upon his private parts, but his right hand upon his mouth; for he believed, quite rightly, that the tongue needs the stronger restraint. It would not be easy, for example, to enumerate as many men who have been ruined by incontinent lust as is the number of cities and empires which a secret revealed has brought to destruction" (504e–505a).

The image of the philosopher's defensive posture took on emblematic significance for some early modern writers. Nicolas Venette, for example, explains:

On pourroit peut-être me dire icy que, bien que dans la matiere que je traite je menage avec dessein les expressions du langage, qui semblent être d'elles-mesmes trop libres, je garde une certaine bienseance & un certain menagement dans les paroles, dont je me sers pour exprimer ma pensée, & qu'enfin je ressemble au sage Tartare *Anacarsis,* qui n'estoit jamais representé par les Peintres qu'avec la main droite sur la bouche, & la gauche sur ces parties amoureuses, pour nous apprendre qu'il ne faloit parler de ces parties & de leur action qu'avec modestie & retenuë. (Preface, *Tableau,* sig. [*10v–r])

It could perhaps be said of me here, that even though the subject at hand concerns expressions of language concerning conjugal relations, and that these expressions seem too unrestrained in themselves, nevertheless I maintain a certain decorum and tact in the words I use to express my thought, and that in short I resemble the Tartar sage Anacharsis, whom the painters always depict with his right hand over his mouth and his left over his private parts, in order that we may learn that these parts and their action should be spoken of only with modesty and restraint.

Byrd had two copies of Venette in his library (Hayes 1405, 1469).

§296. See §291.

§298. The *Physiognomonics* once attributed to Aristotle proposes that "mental character is not independent of and unaffected by bodily processes, but is conditioned by the state of the body. . . . And contrariwise the body is evidently influenced by the affections of the soul—by the emotions of love and fear, and by states of pleasure and pain" (805a) (trans. T. Loveday and E. S. Forster, in Jonathan Barnes, ed., *The Complete Works of Aristotle,* I [Princeton, N.J., 1984], 1237). The other classical source is Cicero *Tusculan Disputations* 4.37. Cf. Montaigne, *Essays,* "Of Physiognomy."

§300. Socrates explains the significance of the Delphic Oracle's statement that he was the wisest of men in Plato's *Apology* 20d–23b. The story recurs frequently throughout antiquity and early modern times. See also Diogenes Laertius *Lives* 2.37.

§301. This point of view appears to be a Christianized view of a classical notion, in the light of the parable of talents, which Anglican divines interpreted as teaching that both abilities and material goods are held by individuals in trust (ownership remaining with God) and must be improved. The saying attributed to Bion might have been drawn from his comments about the way misers misunderstand ownership of property, recorded by Diogenes Laertius: "Misers, he said, took care of property as if it belonged to them, but derived no more benefit from it than if it belonged to others" (*Lives* 4.50). See also §267.

§304. Plutarch *Moralia* ("Sayings of the Spartans"): "A beggar asked alms of a Spartan, who said, 'If I should give to you, you will be the more a beggar; and for this unseemly conduct of yours he who first gave to you is responsible, for he thus made you lazy'" (235e). The *OED* defines a *handsel* as a "gift or present (expressive of good wishes) at the beginning of a new year, or on entering upon any new condition, situation, or circumstances, the donning of new clothes, etc."

§305. Diogenes Laertius *Lives* 6.56; cf. Stanley, *History*, II, 414; Bacon, *Apophthegmes*, no. 94; [Abel] Boyer, *The Wise and Ingenious Companion . . .* (London, 1700), 195.

§307. A modernization of an anecdote from Diogenes Laertius: "He asked a spendthrift for a mina. The man inquired why it was that he asked others for an obol but him for a mina. 'Because,' said Diogenes, 'I expect to receive from others again, but whether I shall ever get anything from you again lies on the knees of the gods'" (*Lives* 6.67).

§311. See §287.

§312. See §29.

§314. Ligarius had sided with Pompey against Caesar, as had Cicero himself, which makes the success of his defense all the more remarkable. Plutarch relates the story in his *Lives:* "It is said also that when Quintus Ligarius was under prosecution because he had been one of the enemies of Caesar, and Cicero was his advocate, Caesar said to his friends: 'What is to prevent our hearing a speech from Cicero after all this while, since Ligarius has long been adjudged a villain and an enemy?' But when Cicero had begun to speak and was moving his hearers beyond measure, and his speech, as it proceeded, showed varying pathos and amazing grace, Caesar's face often changed colour and it was manifest that all the emotions of his soul were stirred; and at last, when the orator touched upon the struggles at Pharsalus, he was so greatly affected that his body shook and he dropped from his hand some of his documents. At any rate he acquitted Ligarius under compulsion." "Cicero" 39.5–6.

Cicero's defense of Ligarius became an example for early modern writers of the power of reason (or oratory) to persuade men to alter determined courses of action. See, for instance, D[aniel] T[uvill], *Essaies Politicke and Morall* (London, 1608), fol. 26r–v, who relates that Caesar initially jested about hearing Cicero since the defendant was already irrevocably condemned.

It is quite possible that Byrd here draws on Thomas Baker's discussion of Cicero's powers of persuasion in [Baker], *Reflections upon Learning, Wherein Is Shewn the Insufficiency Thereof . . .* , 2d ed. (London, 1700), 39–40 (also based on Plutarch): "It must be confest this is a remarkable instance; here was the Greatest Orator and the Greatest Judge (for *Caesar* is allowed by *Cicero* to be one of the most Eloquent Persons of his time) *Caesar* comes into the place of Judicature, breathing revenge against *Ligarius,* and with an obstinate resolution to condemn him, but with difficulty is prevail'd with to hear *Cicero* in his Defense, which he gives way to, rather as a thing of meer form, than with any thoughts of yielding to his perswasion: However, no sooner is he heard, but he moves and affects, and when he comes to touch upon *Pharsalia,* the Conqueror has no more Soul left, he takes fire and is transported beyond himself, he shakes and trembles, and drops the Paper that he held in his hand, and in spite of all his resolutions, absolves the Criminal, whom he was determin'd to condemn." Byrd's own copy of this book is now in the library of the Virginia Historical Society (Hayes 1092). See also §391.

§315. Byrd read widely in medical books, and his personal health regimen was probably developed from a myriad of sources. A comparison of Byrd's notes with one source, George Cheyne's *Essay of Health and Long Life,* 3d ed. (London, 1725), may serve to indicate the way Byrd drew selectively from his readings for commonplace book entries.

Item 1: Cheyne (90–91) discusses the salubrious effects of exercise, especially in preventing the thickening of bodily fluids, but he does not appear to distinguish between sweating and perspiration, as Byrd's entry does; Cheyne also warns against exercise to the point of weariness (108).

Item 4: Cheyne recommends watering wine: "The rich, strong, and heavy Wines ought never to be tasted without a sufficient Dilution of Water; at least they should be used, like Brandy or Spirits, for a Cordial (i.e. *At most to take but three small Glasses of such.*) *Ad summum tria pocula sume.* Whatsoever is more cometh of *Sin,* and must be diluted with the Waters of *Repentance*" (50–51).

Item 5: Cheyne (86) recommends against going to sleep before digestion of the great meal of the day is over.

Item 6: Cheyne recommends cold bathing (102–103) and observes that the "free open *Air* is a kind of a *cold Bath*" (84). Cold baths were often part of the healthful regimen prescribed by medical writers. Byrd himself made such a prescription in a letter to "Irene": "How transported shou'd I be if Irene shou'd get a robust constitution by my advice of plungeing into cold water! For then I shou'd not only have the pleasure of seeing her in perfect health, but likewise have the comfortable conscience of haveing been the instrument of so great a blessing to the world. The cold Bath will infallibly make you as much proof agst catching Cold, as Grace is against Temptation. Twill prevent the attacks both of ague and feaver, and make you as chearful as a mocking-Bird. Twill cure the Head-ach more effectually, than Infidelity dos Love, and give you a ruddiness of complection that will make it dangerous to see you" (*ASD*, 222).

Another possible influence (though both may draw on common sources) is Addison's essay on the health-giving effects of temperance, *Spectator*, no. 195 (Oct. 12, 1711). He discusses several items on Byrd's list, including: (1) the benefits of exercise to the point of perspiration; (4) limiting oneself to eating one thing at a time: "Nature delights in the most plain and simple Diet. Every Animal, but Man, keeps to one Dish." "Make your whole Repast out of one Dish." Addison recommends the work of Luigi Cornaro, who writes of the importance of frugality and temperance in achieving a healthy, vigorous old age; see *Sure and Certain Methods of Attaining a Long and Healthful Life*, 3d ed. (London, 1722), esp. 3, 6. Addison's puff is reproduced facing the title page. Though Cornaro's book does not appear in the catalog of Byrd's library, it is probable that Byrd knew it. See also §6.

§316. Aristotle's definition is found in Diogenes Laertius: "He was asked to define hope, and he replied, 'It is a waking dream'" (*Lives* 5.18); cf. Stanley, "Aristotle," *History*, II, 359. Abel Boyer attributes the saying to Plato in *The Wise and Ingenious Companion* . . . (London, 1700), 33.

§317. Stobaeus, *Sententiae*, CIX ("De spe"), 581; Stanley, "Socrates," *History*: "A Woman cannot conceive without a Man, nor a good hope produce any benefit without labour" (I, 74).

§324. Diogenes Laertius *Lives*, "Diogenes": "Seeing a notice on the house of a profligate, 'To be sold,' he said, 'I knew well that after such surfeiting you would throw up the owner'" (6.47). Cf. Stanley, "Diogenes," *History*, II, 413.

§325. The topos of the ultimate greatness of self-knowledge and self-mastery may be found everywhere in classical antiquity and in the writings of those self-consciously influenced by the ancients. It is enforced here by contrasting two radically different notions of greatness: in comparison with philosophical self-mastery, the military achievements of Alexander and Caesar appear little more than barbarous violence. Although the source of this entry has not been established, the presence in the commonplace book of entries representing both categories of greatness is intriguing.

Byrd might have been influenced by something he encountered in his sermon reading; Isaac Barrow, for instance, describes the strengths of the pious man in a sermon "The Profitableness of Godliness": "He conquereth and commandeth himself, which is the bravest victory, and noblest empire: he quelleth fleshly lusts, subdueth inordinate passions, and repelleth strong temptations. He, *by his faith, overcometh the world* with a conquest far more glorious than ever any *Alexander* or *Caesar* could do. He, in fine, doth perform the most worthy exploits, and deserveth the most honourable triumphs that man can do" (*The Works of the Learned Isaac Barrow, D.D.* . . . [London, 1686–1687], I, 20).

The most common view of Alexander was positive; he was the primary exemplar of daring, courage, magnanimity, and ambition. Nonetheless, there exists among classical writers an opposing tradition. Quintus Curtius records the frank and fearless words of a Scythian to Alexander, who called the conqueror no better than a thief (7.8.19–26). Lucan calls Alexander "a man who was born to teach this bad lesson to the world" (*The Civil War [Pharsalia]* 10.20–35, trans. J. D. Duff, LCL [1962]). Seneca considers it an unworthy thing to praise "the robberies of a Philip, or of an Alexander, or of others who were no less famous for the destruction of the human race than a flood that inundated every plain or a conflagration that burned up the majority of living creatures" (*Naturales quaestiones* 3.Pref.5, trans. Thomas H. Corcoran, LCL [1971]). Later in the same work he calls wars of conquest such as those waged by Caesar and Alexander "madness" (5.18.4–10), and in *De clementia* he censures Alexander's cruelty and blood-lust as ill befitting a man (*Moral Essays* 1.25.1–2). In "On the Supreme Good" Seneca rates self-conquest far above military achievements (*Moral Epistles* 71.37); see also *De beneficiis* 1.13.3, 4.31.2, in *Moral Essays;* "On Reforming Hardened Sinners," *Moral Epistles* 113.29–31. Valerius Maximus, *Acts and Sayings of the Romans*, 444, notes that Alexander's anger and inability to control his passions kept him out of heaven. Julian's *Oration to Sallust* questions whether Alexander is best understood as the model of ambition for greatness or of excessive valor leading to sinful pride (*The Works of the Emperor Julian* 8.251b, trans. Wilmer Cave Wright, LCL [1913–1923]).

Erasmus, discussing in the *Adages* the choice of greatness and folly kings have made, introduces Alexander, *not* as a dauntless conqueror, but as a man driven by foolish whims (1.3.1: "Aut regem aut fatuum nasci oportere"); he blasts the education of princes, who are allowed to imbibe zeal for "pernicious" heros such as Caesar, Xerxes, or Alexander. Cf. *Adages*, 2.5.1 ("Spartam nactus es, hanc orna"). Cf. Augustine *De civitate dei* 4.4. A number of early modern writers also questioned the positive view of Alexander. Byrd is likely to have read a number of such texts during the commonplace book period. Montaigne considers the virtue of Alexander inferior to that of Socrates, who knew how to subjugate his own passions (*Essays*, "Of Repentance"). Again, Montaigne considers Epaminondas greater than Alexander or Caesar because he possessed heroic virtue in a well-ordered soul ("Of the Most Eminent Men").

John Dunton, in the *Athenian Mercury*, I, no. 5 (Apr. 7, 1691), answers the question whether Alexander or Caesar was the greater man: "We may do well to consider them as *Men* or *Generals*. The *greatest Conquest* is that over our *selves*, as to Ambition, Revenge, or Love. For Ambition they might be pretty even, but *Caesar* at least *conceal'd* the *weakness* of his *Mind* better than the other; he never *cry'd* because he could not *conquer* other *Worlds;* nor desire to be a *God* in this. For *Revenge Alexander* on the least *pique* wou'd kill his *best Friends; Caesar* very often forgave his *worst Enemies*. As for *Love*, the *Grecian* by his carriage towards *Darius's Wives and Daughters* is indeed worthy of Eternal *Honour,* and seems to me to deserve greater *Trophys* than for his *Conquering the World*." Byrd owned a copy of the collection *The Athenian Oracle* (Hayes 1099). It is interesting to note that this brief answer emphasizes several points made by the commonplace book entries on Alexander the Great: his tears at his inability to conquer other worlds (§224), his immoderate claim to godhead (§225, 278), and his restrained treatment of Darius's women (§244).

There is a strong tradition in English letters comparing the conquest of nations unfavorably with self-knowledge and self-control. In *Paradise Lost* (11.688–699), Milton's archangel Michael censures antique notions of greatness:

> Such were these Giants, men of high renown;
> For in those days Might only shall be admir'd,
> And Valor and Heroic Virtue call'd:
> To overcome in Battle, and subdue
> Nations, and bring home spoils with infinite
> Man-slaughter, shall be held the highest pitch
> Of human Glory, and for Glory done
> Of triumph, to be styl'd great Conquerors,

Patrons of Mankind, Gods, and Sons of Gods,
Destroyers rightlier call'd and Plagues of men.
Thus Fame shall be achiev'd, renown on Earth,
And what most merits fame in silence hid.

Pope, in the *Essay on Man* (4.217–236), declares that the conquerors Alexander of Macedon and Charles II of Sweden fall short of Socrates, who was truly great. When in John Gay's ballad opera *Polly* (1729), Morano, captain of a band of thieves and ruffians, dismisses virtue, conscience, honesty, shame, and honor, setting in their place ambition and rapine, he answers his judge's shocked protestations by saying: *"Alexander* the great was more successful. That's all." Addison in the *Guardian,* no. 122 (July 31, 1713), calls Alexander "a Man of great Virtues and of great Faults," and in the *Freeholder,* no. 51 (June 15, 1716), condemns Alexander's inflammation "by false notions of glory" when he cruelly imitated Achilles' triumph over Hector by dragging a defeated governor behind his own chariot. Sir William Temple, in the essay "Of Heroick Virtue" published (among other places) in Swift's edition *The Works of Sir William Temple, Bart. . . .* (London, 1720), considers Alexander, like Caesar, a mixed character, and is unable to determine "whether his Virtues or his Faults were greatest" (I, 194). Sir R[oger] L'Estrange, *Seneca's Morals by Way of Abstract . . .* (London, 1696), 423, discusses the way vices give rise to other vices, as when luxury produces avarice, and avarice the abuse of power; in the same way the excessive ambition of Alexander and Caesar gave rise to wanton bloodletting: "Cruelties . . . in *Princes . . .* are a War against Mankind."

The presence in the commonplace book of this criticism indicates Byrd's familiarity with this historical-literary tradition (he owned copies of nearly every book cited here). In fact, he incorporated it into his own writing. In the *History of the Dividing Line,* Byrd tempers the usual censure of the cruelty of Indians to their captives by showing it is in no way unique to them; indeed, it is no worse than the "inhuman" treatment of captives by Homer's Achilles and by Alexander "with all his famed generosity" (*Works,* 259). Finally, the commonplace book contains more than a few entries representing the uncritical tradition, which sees Alexander as a model of ambition and valor. The fact that Byrd also included this entry strongly criticizing Alexander's thirst for greatness may be related to his own need to reconcile himself to a less ambitious political position.

§326. Diogenes Laertius *Lives,* "Diogenes": "To the question what wine he found pleasant to drink, he replied, 'That for which other people pay' " (6.54); cf. Stanley, "Diogenes," *History*, II, 414. The comment about parasitism is added.

§328. Byrd here discusses the charge that some women tamper with their physiological constitution to attain an attractive appearance. A regular program of clysters (enemas) and issues (incisions or artificial ulcerations made to induce discharge of blood) would produce a visual effect of paleness and fragility. Byrd may here be drawing on William Law, *A Serious Call to a Devout and Holy Life* (1728; London, 1906). In his character of a woman obsessively concerned with maintaining the delicacy of her daughters' appearance, which must never appear too vigorous, Law relates: "She stints them in their meals, and is very scrupulous of what they eat and drink, and tells them how many fine shapes she has seen spoiled in her time. . . . Whenever they begin to look too sanguine and healthful, she calls in the assistance of a doctor; and if physic or issues will keep the complexion from including to coarse or ruddy, she thinks them well employed" (251).

One of the most frequent uses of the word "physic" is to indicate a purge; thus, the wording of Byrd's entry (substituting his own favorite synonym "clyster") parallels Law closely. It is also possible, of course, that Byrd was actually referring to one of Law's sources among contemporary medical texts.

§329. The moderation of Socrates was proverbial. Diogenes Laertius praises his independence and dignity of character: "Often when he looked at the multitude of wares exposed for sale, he would say to himself, 'How many things I can do without!' " (*Lives* 2.25). "He prided himself on his plain living. . . . He used to say . . . that he was nearest to the gods in that he had the fewest wants" (2.27). See also §48, 133.

§330. This entry could refer (like the previous one) to Socrates' patience; in this case the trial is his marriage to Xanthippe, whose difficulty is legendary. According to Diogenes Laertius, Socrates learned to master his passions by enduring this domestic discord: "He said he lived with a shrew, as horsemen are fond of spirited horses, 'but just as, when they have mastered these, they can easily cope with the rest, so I in the society of Xanthippe shall learn to adapt myself to the rest of the world' " (*Lives* 2.37). Without mastering his passions, Socrates explains, he might have been led to do foolish things, such as brawling in public.

§332. Pythagoras taught that the soul comprised three parts: intelligence, reason, and passion. Reason (the only immortal part) resides in the brain, and the passions in the heart. If the passions govern, the proper order is inverted. See Diogenes Laertius *Lives*, "Pythagoras," 8.30–31. Stanley, *History*, records several related sayings: "Temperance is the strength of the Soul; for it is the light of the Soul clear from Passion. To serve Passions is more grievous than to serve Tyrants. It is impossible he can be free, who serves passions, and is governed by them" (II, 542).

§335. This maxim, not uncommonly used by later writers in a Christianized form, first appears in Xenophon's account of the teachings of Socrates: "To me at least it seemed that by these sayings he kept his friends from impiety, injustice, and baseness, and that not only when they were seen by men, but even in solitude; since they ever felt that no deed of theirs could ever escape the gods" (*Memorabilia* 1.4.19, in *Memorabilia, Oeconomicus, Symposium, Apology*, trans. E. C. Marchant and O. J. Todd, LCL [1979]).

§336. Early modern English political writers sometimes pointed to Switzerland and the Low Countries—the "Seven Provinces" are the United Provinces of the Netherlands, allied by the Treaty of Utrecht in 1579—as examples of constitutional government, free from tyranny and maintained by civic virtue.

§339. Although many early accounts have Socrates claiming he learns patience from his wife Xanthippe's fury, later writers extrapolate misogyny from the fact that he was married to the archetypal scold. Perhaps this explains the transference of the saying attributed to Diogenes the Cynic by Diogenes Laertius: "Seeing some women hanged from an olive-tree, he said, 'Would that every tree bore similar fruit'" (*Lives* 6.52).

§340. This anecdote is one of the interchangeable stories of antiquity; Stanley, for instance, attributed it to Aristippus (*History*, I, 137), to Bias (I, 41, citing Aulus Gellius), and to Bion (I, 142). See also §111.

§341. See §105.

§342. On the Egyptian limitation of female mobility by prohibiting footwear, see Plutarch *Moralia* ("Advice to Bride and Groom"): "The women of Egypt, by inherited custom, were not allowed to wear shoes, so that they should stay at home all day; and most women, if you take from them gold-embroidered shoes, bracelets, anklets, purple, and pearls, stay indoors" (142c). The comment by Hyperides, the Greek orator and pupil of Plato and Isocrates, may spring from his reputation for maintaining three mistresses simultaneously, one of whom was reputedly the most expensive woman in all Greece.

§343. Byrd's entry resembles Steele's comment in the *Tatler*, no. 147 (Mar. 18, 1709/10): "I shall leave this tale to the consideration of such good housewives who are never well dressed but when thay are abroad, and think it necessary to appear more agreeable to all men living than to their husbands; as also to those prudent ladies, who, to avoid the appearance of being over-fond, entertain their husbands with indifference, aversion, sullen silence, or exasperating language."

§344. Plutarch, *Lives,* "Aemilius Paulus": "A Roman once divorced his wife, and when his friends admonished him, saying: 'Is she not discreet? is she not beautiful? is she not fruitful?' he held out his shoe (the Romans call it 'calceus'), saying: 'Is this not handsome? is it not new? but no one of you can tell me where it pinches my foot?' For, as a matter of fact, it is great and notorious faults that separate many wives from their husbands; but the slight and frequent frictions arising from some unpleasantness or incongruity of characters, unnoticed as they may be by everybody else, also produce incurable alienations in those whose lives are linked together" (5.1–2). See also *Moralia* 141a ("Advice to Bride and Groom"); [Abel] Boyer, *The Wise and Ingenious Companion* . . . (London, 1700), 33.

§345. The phrase "Critical Minute" is proverbial; it indicates an opportunity, of very short duration, in which one may be able to take decisive action to effect a major change in one's circumstances. For instance, John, Baron Somers, in *The True Secret History of the Lives and Reigns of All the Kings and Queens of England* . . . (London, 1722), writes of the "Critical minute" of Queen Elizabeth's affection for Essex, when he had requested and she had granted a token of her favor that could protect him from his enemies (319). Again, in [Eustache Du Refuge], *The Art of Complaisance* . . . (London, 1677), a popular courtesy book, the author advises that patience is necessary to spot such opportunities: "There is in the Court, as there is said to be in Love, one Critical minute, and a Prince having sometimes need of so many kind of Persons, that he who is thought the most unprofitable may once meet with such a fortunate occasion, which may render him serviceable and agreeable" (25).

Halifax counsels his daughter, in the case of difficulty with a parsimonious husband, to watch for the occasional times (as when he has been drinking wine) when he might be inclined to a better humor, and not to let one of "these *critical moments* . . . slip without making your advantage of it" (*Works of George Savile, Marquis of Halifax,* ed. Mark N. Brown [Oxford, 1989], 56).

§346. Another typical eighteenth-century mixture of classical and Christian teachings. Byrd might have started this entry with a transcription or a memory of the beginning of Addison's *Spectator,* no. 93 (June 16, 1711): "We all of us complain of the Shortness of Time, saith *Seneca,* and yet we have much more than we know what to do with."

§350. Diogenes Laertius records this saying of Solon: "Learn to obey before you command" (*Lives* 1.60). Cf. Stanley: "Being demanded how a City might be best ordered, he answer'd if the Citizens obey'd the Magistrates, the Magistrates the Laws" (*History,* I, 26).

§354. "Buy truth, and sell it not; also wisdom, and instruction, and understanding." Prov. 23:23.

§356. A fairly typical eighteenth-century homiletic warning about the dangers of allowing the pursuit of material goals to corrupt conscience; cf. Matt. 16:26.

§358. Diogenes Laertius attributes this saying to Aristippus, not Antisthenes: "When Dionysius inquired what was the reason that philosophers go to rich men's houses, while rich men no longer visit philosophers, his reply was that 'the one know what they need while the other do not' " (*Lives* 2.69). Bacon, however, credits Diogenes with the saying, in *Apophthegmes,* no. 161; this was probably the source for Steele's version of the story in the *Guardian,* no. 94 (June 29, 1713), which in turn might possibly have been Byrd's source: "It was a fine Answer of *Diogenes,* who being ask'd in Mockery, why Philosophers were the Followers of Rich Men, and not rich Men of Philosophers, replied, Because the one knew what they had need of, and the other did not."

§360. This saying is attributed to Bion, rather than Solon, by Diogenes Laertius *Lives,* "Bion," 4.51; Cf. Stanley, "Bion," *History,* I, 142.

§365. The sharpness (and obscenity) of this criticism depends upon the double meaning of *looseness,* which can indicate both "moral laxity" and laxity "of the bowels," or diarrhea (*OED*).

§366. Homer describes the mighty Otus and Ephialtes, whose mother, Iphimedeia, declared them the sons of Poseidon and not of her husband Aloeus: "men whom the earth, the giver of grain, reared as the tallest, and far the comeliest, after the famous Orion. For at nine years they were nine cubits in breadth and in height nine fathoms." They threatened Olympus with war but were stopped by Zeus, who slew them before they had time to mature fully (*Odyssey* 11.305–320, trans. A. T. Murray, LCL [1984]). Homer elsewhere mentions that they did manage to bind the war god Ares in a brazen jar for a number of years (*Iliad* 5.385).

   According to traditional measures, a fathom is equivalent to 6 feet, and a cubit to 18 inches (*OED*). The arithmetic of this calculation is accurate. The young giants were 9 fathoms (54 feet) tall and 9 cubits (13 feet, 6 inches) at the waist, exactly four times longer than their breadth.

§367. A *Cadi* is "a civil judge . . . of a town or village" in countries governed by Islamic law (*OED*).

§368. The "old Song of *Chevy Chase*" was a well-known English ballad, which Addison discussed in some detail as an example of the poetic value of traditional anonymous verse; see *Spectator*, no. 70 (May 21, 1711), no. 74 (May 25, 1711). Byrd here refers specifically to this stanza:

> To drive the Deer with Hound and Horn
> Earl *Piercy* took his Way;
> The Child may rue that was unborn
> The Hunting of that Day.

It is interesting to note that the ballad (by way of the *Spectator*) was learned and recited in eighteenth-century Virginia; see Douglass Adair, ed., "Autobiography of the Reverend Devereux Jarratt, 1732–1763," *WMQ*, 3d Ser., IX (1952), 346–393.

§369. Byrd employed the proverb in his *History of the Dividing Line*: "By this means they shot a brace of fat bears, which came very seasonably, because we had made clean Work in the morning and were in danger of dining with St. Anthony, or His Grace Duke Humphry" (*Works*, 273). "Dining with Duke Humphry" is a proverbial expression for going hungry.

§370. Francis Atterbury (1662–1732), bishop of Rochester, was a Tory politician, man of letters, friend of Pope and Swift, and a Jacobite. He was tried and condemned for treason in 1722 and exiled to France. The source of this anecdote has not been found, nor has the identity of Lord L——e been established. Philip, duke of Wharton (1698–1731), opposed the bill against Atterbury in debate in the House of Lords on May 15, 1723. To the remark on the secrecy implicit in the exchange of sealed letters, Wharton replies that the use of the "Great Seal" is more significant. This is the royal seal used "for the authentication of documents of the highest importance issued in the name of the sovereign" (*OED*)—in this case used not by the ruling monarch, but falsely appropriated by the Pretender.

§371. James Butler (1610–1688), first duke of Ormonde and lord lieutenant of Ireland, had the favor of Charles II and owned lands in both England and Ireland. Around 1663 he angered Lady Castlemaine by opposing the king's grant to her of Phoenix Park near Dublin. Barbara Villiers Palmer (1641–1709), countess of Castlemaine, later Baroness Nonsuch, countess of Southampton, and duchess of Cleveland (1670), was mistress to Charles II, and mother of six of his children, from about 1660 to 1674, when Charles took another mistress. She was reputed to be very beautiful, imperious, and manipulative.

§372. The question of the independence of the Irish Parliament had been a controversial matter since the Restoration. There were several books on the history of this matter among Byrd's legal library, including John Molyneux,

The Case of Ireland's Being Bound by Acts of Parliament in England (Dublin, 1698); and [John Cary], *An Answer to Mr. Molyneux His Case of Ireland's Being Bound by Acts of Parliament in England* . . . (London, 1698). During the commonplace book period, another development took place, the Declaratory Act of 1720, which finally eliminated the independence of the Irish legislature and judiciary. The consequences of this change continued to be a major concern for the Anglo-Irish community, with several of whom Byrd was on friendly terms. The earl who declared his disapproval of the Irish Lords' concurrence with the act was probably Arthur Annesley, earl of Anglesey. He was educated in England and took his seat in the English house in 1710 and in the Irish house in 1711.

§377. Byrd here refers to a passage in Herodotus, which tells of an unnamed daughter of Cheops, the pyramid-building Egyptian king: "And so evil a man was Cheops that for lack of money he made his own daughter to sit in a chamber and exact payment (how much, I know not; for they did not tell me this). She, they say, doing her father's bidding, was minded to leave some memorial of her own, and demanded of everyone who sought intercourse with her that he should give one stone to set in her work; and of these stones was built the pyramid that stands midmost of the three, over against the great pyramid; each side of it measures one hundred and fifty feet" (*Herodotus* [*History*] 2.126, trans. A. D. Godley, LCL [1920–1922]).

This story is often conflated with another tale of a pyramid built by the lovers of another indefatigable woman, the courtesan Rhodope, or Rhodopis; this version may be found in Strabo, Pliny (*Natural History* 36.82), Diodorus Siculus, and Herodotus (2.134–135), who debunks it.

In his treatise *Pyramidographia; or, A Description of the Pyramids in Aegypt*, originally published in 1646 and reprinted in Churchill (Hayes 79), John Greaves traces the story: "The same *Herodotus* also writes, That *some of the* Grecians *make the third Pyramid the work of* Rhodopis *a Curtizan: an Errour in Opinion of those who seem not to know who this* Rhodopis *might be of which they speak; for neither could she have undertaken such a Pyramid, on which so many thousand Talents were to be spent; neither lived she in this Man's time, but in the time of King* Amasis. Now this *Amasis*, as he elsewhere shews, lived long after these Pyramids were in being. The same Story is recited by *Strabo*, and *Pliny*, both of them omitting the Names of the Founders of the former two. *Strabo* gives her a double Name; *The third Pyramid is the Sepulchre of a Curtizan, made by her Lovers, whom* Sappho *the Poetress calls* Doricha, *Mistress to her brother* Charaxus; *others name her* Rhodope. But whether we name her *Doricha*, or *Rhodope*, the Relation is altogether improbable, if we consider either her Condition or the infinite vastness of the Expense. For *Diodorus,* though he rightly acknowledges this Pyramid to be much less than either of the former two, yet in respect of the exquisite Workmanship, and richness of the Materials, he judges it not inferiour to either of them. A Structure certainly too great and sumptuous to have been the design and undertaking of a Curtizan, which could hardly have been performed by a rich and potent Monarch. And yet *Diodorus* hath almost the same Relation, only a little altered in the Circumstances: *Some say, that this is the Sepulchre of the Strumpet* Rhodope, *of whom, some of the* Nomarchae (or Prefects of the Provinces) *being enamoured, by a common Expence to win her Favour, they built this Monument"* (*Voyages,* II, 691–692).

See also Erasmus, *Parabolae,* trans. R. A. B. Mynors, *Collested Works of Erasmus,* XXIII (Toronto, 1978), 224; Thom[as] Heywood, Γυναικειον; *or, Nine Bookes of Various History concerninge Women* . . . (London, 1624), 306–307. In both forms the legend serves many writers as an example of sexual excess, even after early modern scholars cast doubt on the story's truth. In none of these sources have we encountered the ironic tone of Byrd's entry.

§378. *Toledo* is a short, familiar term for a sword such as those made in the Spanish city (*OED*).

§380. To *daggle* means "to clog with wet mud; to wet and soil a garment, etc., by trailing it through mud or wet grass" (*OED*). John Ray defines the term in *A Collection of English Words Not Generally Used* . . . , 2d ed. (London, 1691): "DAG; Dew upon the Grass. Hence daggle tail is spoken of a Woman that hath dabbled her Coats with Dew, Wet, or Dirt" (95). *Trapes* is "an opprobrious name for a woman or girl slovenly in person or habits" (*OED*).

§382. This anecdote depicting the brusque wit of Chancellor Jeffreys is one of several commonplace book entries dealing with major political figures of the late seventeenth century. In the ensuing years, including Byrd's commonplace book period, these stories took on powerful political associations. Sir George Jeffreys (1648–1689)—named chief justice of the King's Bench in 1683 and lord chancellor in 1685—became an important symbol for Whig historians of the abuses of the Stuart monarchy. Jeffreys was best known for his harsh treatment of supporters of Monmouth in 1680, where at the Bloody Assizes he condemned an unprecedented number of Englishmen to death. Thus he stood for the tyranny implicit in Stuart absolutism.

§383. Tanner's bark is "the crushed bark of the oak or of other trees, an infusion of which is used in converting hides into leather" (*OED*). Because the spent bark was widely used as mulch in gardening, Byrd probably encountered this tip in one of the many books on gardening in his collection.

§385. Runnet, or rennet, is the "curdled milk found in the stomach of an un-weaned calf or other animal, used for curdling milk in making cheese," or by extension other preparations having a similar effect (*OED*).

§387. Triton was a Greek and Roman sea god; in England the term was figura-tively applied "to a seaman, waterman, or person connected in some way with the sea" (*OED*).

§388. Book 22 of Homer's *Odyssey* (302–305), which tells of the slaughter of Alcinous and the other suitors by Odysseus with his great bow, uses a heroic simile comparing the flight of the panic-stricken wooers to the flight of small birds from birds of prey—"and men rejoice at the chase" (trans. A. T. Murray, LCL [1919]). Nets are not mentioned.

Hammersmith, a town west of London, was, at the time, a primarily rural area with a few large estates.

§390, 391. The comparison of the two great orators of Greece and Rome, Demos-thenes and Cicero, has a long history. See, for instance, Quintilian *Institutio oratoria* 10.1.105–112, 12.1.14–22, 12.10.12; Plutarch *Lives*, "Comparison of De-mosthenes and Cicero."

§391. See §314.

§393. Henry Roper, Lord Teynham (1676–1723), shot himself while at his house in Haymarket on May 16, 1723. The coroner's verdict was lunacy.

§394. Byrd's discussion of the relative merits of Homer and Virgil follows the well-established lines of the classical party in the battle between the ancients and the moderns. In its major points it strongly resembles the (rather con-ventional) comparison of poets in Sir William Temple's essay "Of Poetry": "*Homer* was, without Dispute, the most Universal *Genius* that has been known in the World, and *Virgil* the most accomplish'd. To the first must be allowed the most fertile Invention, the richest Vein, the most general Knowl-edge, and the most lively Expression: To the last, the noblest Ideas, the justest Intuition, the wisest Conduct, and the choicest Elocution. To speak in the Painter's Terms, we find in the Works of *Homer,* the most Spirit, Force, and Life; in those of *Virgil,* the best Design, the truest Proportions, and the greatest Grace. . . . *Homer* had more Fire and Rapture, *Virgil* more Light and Softness; or at least the Poetical Fire was more raging in one but clearer in the other, which makes the first more amazing, and better allay'd to make up excellent work" (*The Works of Sir William Temple, Bart.* . . . [London, 1720], I, 237). For other parallels, see *Spectator*, no. 273 (Jan. 12, 1712); Henry Felton, *A Dissertation on Reading the Classics and Forming a Just Style* . . . (London, 1715), 20–28. Felton praises the coolness of Virgil's judgment, which he sug-gests produces a finer poem than Homer's unregulated though fiery genius.

For the ancients/moderns debate in England, see Joseph M. Levine, *The Battle of the Books: History and Literature in the Augustan Age* (Ithaca, N.Y., 1991).

§396. Although this entry initially appears to be little more than a highly complimentary eulogy to a gifted physician, in fact it deals with a highly politicized sequence of events in British history. Dr. John Radcliffe (1650–1714), a High Church Tory, was educated at Oxford and came to London in 1684. In 1686 he became chief physician to Princess Anne and served as physician to the royal family, saving the life of the infant duke of Gloucester in 1691. He became well known for his diagnostic ability, paying special attention to key physical symptoms of illnesses—a practice that may not seem unusual to modern readers but that was by no means universally practiced among physicians of Radcliffe's day. However, he fell out of favor in 1694 when, with characteristic directness, he refused one evening to attend Princess Anne, saying that her condition was nothing more than vapors and could wait until morning. He lost his position as royal physician, though he was consulted privately on several occasions. Political points were scored by his Whig adversaries. Bishop Burnet complained unfairly that the doctor's treatment of Queen Mary in her last days brought about her death: "I will not enter into another's province, nor speak of matters so much out of the way of my own profession; but the physicians' part was universally condemned, and her death was imputed to the negligence, or unskilfulness of Dr. Radcliffe. He was called for, and it appeared but too evidently that his opinion was chiefly considered, and was most depended on. Other physicians were afterwards called, but not till it was too late" (Burnet, *History,* 359).

In fact, the queen herself delayed treatment, and Radcliffe was called at the last, when he judged that it was too late for human skill. Burnet reversed the order of events, attributing the sad event to Radcliffe's character as "an impious and vicious man who hated the Queen much, but virtue and religion more. He was a professed Jacobite, and by many thought a very bad physician, but others cried him up to the highest degree imagineable" (Campbell Richard Hone, *The Life of Dr. John Radcliffe, 1652–1714* ... [London, 1950], 57).

Radcliffe brought Whig mockery upon himself for his courtship at nearly sixty of one of his patients—a young, rich, beautiful heiress—going to the length of outfitting himself with a fancy coach and a fashionable new wardrobe. Steele satirized Radcliffe's folly in his portrait of *Aesculapius* in the *Tatler,* nos. 44, 47 (July 21, 28, 1709). In 1714 Radcliffe was seriously ill himself when he was called to attend Queen Anne, who was upon her deathbed, and he refused. She died only two hours after the message was sent to him; the court was riddled with intrigue, some hoping for a return of the Stuart line (James Stuart, the Old Pretender), and others preparing to send for the Protestant heir, the elector of Hanover (George I). In this context, the medical care of Queen Anne became a party issue. Radcliffe himself was accused of causing the queen's death for political motives, received assassination threats, and was summoned to Parliament to face censure. Tory accounts of her death generally deny the antiphysician rumors, as in [Thomas Salmon], *The Life of Her Late Majesty Queen Anne . . .* (London, 1721): "Various Reports have been spread concerning her Majesty's Death, but whatever might be the immediate Occasion of it, nothing is more evident, than that her Constitution was very much impair'd by many severe Strokes of Fortune, from which her high Station was so far from exempting her, that some of them are found to be almost the inseparable Attendants of Crown'd Heads" (II, 608).

Radcliffe died on November 1, 1714, only four months after Queen Anne's death. The main authority for Radcliffe's life is [William Pittis], *Some Memoirs of the Life of John Radcliffe, M.D. . . .* , 2d ed. (London, 1715), first published shortly after the doctor died. However, Pittis is *not* Byrd's source; neither the anecdotes here recorded nor the patients Fountain and Abney appear in his biography. Moreover, there are clear contradictions of testimony. Byrd's entry mentions that one of Radcliffe's diagnostic methods was examining a patient's urine. Pittis records Radcliffe's contempt for those *"Quacks* and *Intermedlers"* in medicine known as "Piss-pot *Prophets,* and *Urinal-Casters,"* who professed the ability to diagnose illness from the appearance of urine samples. He tells a humorous story of Radcliffe's reply to the wife of a bootmaker who brought him a bottle of her husband's urine for diagnosis. Emptying the bottle and refilling it with his own urine, the doctor returned it to her, declaring, "Take this with you Home to your Husband, and if he will undertake to fit me with a Pair of Boots by the sight of my Water, I'll make no Question of prescribing for his Distempre, by a View of his" (11–12). Nich[olas] Culpeper, in *The English Physitian Enlarged . . .* (London, 1656), 398, also mocks the practice with the story of a quack whose shrewd guesses and leading questions allowed him to convince a woman that he had successfully diagnosed her husband's injuries—falling down some thirty stairs—by examining a sample of his urine. Still, within reasonable limits, diagnosis of illness by examining urine was a respected practice; see George Cheyne, *An Essay of Health and Long Life,* 3d ed. (London, 1725), 121–125.

Although the original source for Byrd's entry has not been found, it is worth noting that the commonplace book account of Radcliffe's life passes over all damaging episodes in silence, including the absurdities of his courtship and the disfavor with the royal family. Indeed, this account not only omits any reference to charges of neglect but includes an opposite anecdote testifying to the efficacy of Radcliffe's diagnostic talents in a case (parallel to that of the queen) where he encountered no difficulty restoring a patient to health despite an overnight delay in attending him.

Byrd continued to be interested in Dr. Radcliffe; he is mentioned in three extant letters. Byrd names Radcliffe (as a proverbially good physician) in a letter to Sir Hans Sloane (May 31, 1737, *Correspondence,* II, 512). Several days later, in a letter to John Perceval, earl of Egmont (July 2, 1737, *Correspondence,* II, 520), Byrd suggests he might "improve the late [Dr. Rad]cliffes scheme" by providing a collection of Virginia flora for traveling physicians to study; he repeats the proposal in a letter (on the medicinal properties of ginseng) to Peter Collinson (July 5, 1737, *Correspondence,* II, 524). For further discussion of Radcliffe, see Hone, *Life of Radcliffe;* Pittis, *Some Memoirs;* William Macmichael, *The Gold-Headed Cane* (New York, 1932).

Dr. Radcliffe's patients: Sir Andrew Fountaine (1676–1753), educated at Christ Church, Oxford, was a virtuoso known for his collections of classical coins, pictures, china, and miscellaneous antiquities. He traveled widely in Europe, was intimate with Swift (another patient of Dr. Radcliffe), and corresponded with Leibniz. He was seriously ill in 1710; Swift visited him and foretold his recovery, though the doctors had given him up. Later he kept a portrait of Dr. Radcliffe at his home in Narford. Sir Thomas Abney (1640–1722) was descended from an ancient family of gentry in Derbyshire. He was a fishmonger in London and rose to the status of alderman in 1692, sheriff in 1693–1694, lord mayor of London in 1700–1701, and member of Parliament for the City of London in 1701–1702.

§398. Homer *Iliad* 1.50–53: pestilence is figured as arrows from Apollo's bow: "The mules he assailed first and the swift dogs, but thereafter on the men themselves he let fly his stinging arrows, and smote; and ever did the pyres of the dead burn thick" (trans. A. T. Murray, LCL [1924]).

§399. When Pisistratus became tyrant of Athens, he drove Solon into exile. His facile ability to represent his regime as beneficial to Athens is expressed in his letter to Solon included in Diogenes Laertius *Lives,* "Solon," 1.53–54.

Plutarch, in *Lives,* tells of Lycurgus's discovery of Homer's epics in Asia: "There too, as it would appear, he made his first acquaintance with the poems of Homer, which were preserved among the posterity of Creophylus; and when he saw that the political and disciplinary lessons contained in them were worthy of no less serious attention than the incentives to pleasure and license which they supplied, he eagerly copied and compiled them in order to take them home with him. For these epics already had a certain faint reputation among the Greeks, and a few were in possession of certain portions of them, as the poems were carried here and there by chance; but Lycurgus was the very first to make them really known" ("Lycurgus" 4.4).

§400. This entry refers to elements in the background of the Battle of the Books, in which Swift participated. In 1690 William Temple's *Essays on Ancient and Modern Learning* appeared and was attacked by William Wotton's *Reflections upon Ancient and Modern Learning* (1694). Charles Boyle (later the earl of Orrery, and Byrd's friend) published *Dr. Bentley's Dissertations on the Epistles of Phalaris* in 1698, with a preface attacking Richard Bentley, who retaliated with *A Dissertation upon the Epistles of Phalaris,* published as an appendix to a second edition of Wotton's *Reflections* (1698). Boyle had been educated at Christ Church, and the "Christ Church wits" (principally Francis Atterbury, later dean of Westminster) drafted a humorous response on his behalf, *Dr. Bentley's Dissertation and the Fables of Aesop, Examin'd by the Honourable Charles Boyle, Esq.* (1698). Swift was editing the works of Temple, who had been his mentor, and made Wotton the target of satire in *A Tale of a Tub* and *Battle of the Books* (1697, first published in 1704). Christ Church's reputation was legendary; more than a century later, Thomas Babington Macaulay wrote in his copy of *Dr. Bentley's Dissertation:* "The Christ Church men were drunk with the vanity which has always characterized their college" (cited in Jonathan Swift, *A Tale of a Tub, with Other Early Works, 1696–1707,* in Herbert Davis, ed., The Prose Works of Jonathan Swift, I, [Oxford, 1957], xvii).

Byrd owned a complete collection of the major works of the Battle of the Books. In his library there were copies of many of Temple's works, including editions of his letters (Hayes 71, 1110, 1111) and the Swift edition of Temple's *Miscellanies* (Hayes 55, 1112), Boyle's edition of the *Epistolae Phalaris* (Hayes 1814), Wotton's *Reflections* (Hayes 251, 1093), Boyle's *Dr. Bentley's Dissertations . . . Examin'd* (Hayes 829), Bentley's *Dissertations upon the Epistles of Phalaris, with an Answer to the Objections of the Hon. C[harles] Boyle* (Hayes 821), a 1705 English translation *The Epistles of Phalaris* including Temple's "character" of the epistles (Hayes 842), and Swift's *Tale of a Tub* (Hayes 962).

The source of this anecdote (and of §401) has not been identified. In the light of Byrd's friendship with Charles Boyle, Lord Orrery, the presence in the commonplace book of a story relating the vanity of this particular college is interesting.

§401. Thomas Stratford (1703–1729) was canon of Christ Church College, Oxford. On the associations of this college, see §400.

§402. François Michel Le Tellier, marquis de Louvois (1641–1691), was war minister under Louis XIV. He improved discipline and organization in the army, but was known for his harshness when carrying out policies; his cruel and arbitrary punishment of the "prating Frenchman"—according to English writers of Byrd's time—was typical French tyranny. Byrd owned a copy of Gatien de Courtilz, *Testament politique du marquis de Louvois, premier minis-tre d'etat, sous le regne de Louis XIV. roy de France, ou, l'on voit ce qui s'est passé de plus remarquable en France jusqu'a sa mort* (Cologne, 1695, 1696, 1697) (Hayes 1477), and he mentions Louvois in a letter dated Aug. 8, 1738 (*Corre-spondence,* II, 526–527).

§403. According to eighteenth-century medical science, the internal organs of the body (especially the stomach) gave off exhalations which could injure the health. A person with the "vapours" suffered "a morbid condition supposed to be caused by the presence of such vaporous exhalations; depression of spirits, hypochondria, hysteria, or other nervous disorder" (*OED*).

§405. "How is possible, says Madam B—— for a Woman to keep her Cabinet unpicked, when every Raskal has got a Key to't? Ay but Madam, the Raskal's Key signifies not a Farthing, unless the Owner of the Cabinet at least goes halves with him" (*Laconics; or, New Maxims of State and Conversation . . .* [London, 1701], 82).

§406. George Buchanan (1506–1582) was a noted Scottish poet (his Latin verse appeared in many editions throughout the seventeenth and eighteenth cen-turies), historian, and scholar; see also §456.

§408. Colonel Percy Kirke served in Tangiers with his regiment (later known as Kirke's Lambs) in 1681; he sent an embassy to the emperor of Morocco at Meknes (Mequinez). In 1682, he was named governor of Tangiers and was elevated to the rank of general in 1685. This anecdote comes from the section in Burnet's *History of His Own Time* dealing with the attempts of James II to draw over English Protestants to the Roman Church: "And what was as smart a reply as any, when Kirk was asked to change his religion, he told them he was unhappily pre-engaged, for that if ever he changed he had promised the King of Morocco to turn Mahometan" (Burnet, *History,* 249). See also §23, 97.

§410. The story of defamation in Pyrrhus's army appears in Plutarch *Moralia,* "Sayings of Kings and Commanders" : "Hearing that some young men had made many defamatory remarks about him while in their cups, he ordered that they should all be brought before him the next day. When they were brought, he asked the first whether they had said these things about him. And the young man replied, 'Yes, Your Majesty; and we should have said more than that if we had had more wine' " (184d). Cf. Plutarch *Lives,* "Pyrrhus" 8.5; [Abel] Boyer, *The Wise and Ingenious Companion . . .* (London, 1700), 172.

§412. Charles V, Holy Roman emperor, 1519–1556.

§416. See §430.

§417. The impudent apothecary's apprentice in this jest is named for an imple-
ment probably found in such shops: a *squirt* is "a small tubular instrument by
which water may be squirted; a form of syringe" (*OED*).

§418. This Talmudic story appears in a discussion of the wisdom of not ques-
tioning the workings of Providence, in the *Spectator,* no. 237 (Dec. 1, 1711).
Byrd's version follows Addison's very closely: "I shall relieve my Readers from
this abstracted Thought, by relating here a *Jewish* Tradition concerning
Moses, which seems to be a kind of Parable, illustrating what I have last
mentioned. That great Prophet, it is said, was called up by a Voice from
Heaven to the Top of a Mountain; where, in a Conference with the Supreme
Being, he was permitted to propose to him some Questions concerning his
Administration of the Universe. In the midst of this Divine Colloquy he was
commanded to look down on the Plain below. At the Foot of the Mountain
there issued out a clear Spring of Water, at which a Soldier alighted from his
Horse to Drink. He was no sooner gone than a little Boy came to the same
Place, and finding a Purse of Gold which the Soldier had dropped, took it up
and went away with it. Immediately after this came an Infirm old Man, weary
with Age and Travelling, and having quenched his Thirst, sat down to rest
himself by the side of the Spring. The Soldier missing his Purse returns to
search for it, and demands it of the old Man, who affirms he had not seen it,
and appeals to Heaven in witness of his Innocence. The Soldier, not believing
his Protestations, kills him. *Moses* fell on his face with Horror and Amaze-
ment, when the Divine Voice thus prevented his Expostulation; 'Be not surprised, *Moses,* nor ask why the Judge of the whole Earth has suffer'd this thing
to come to pass: the Child is the Occasion that the Blood of the old Man is
spilt; but know, that the old Man whom thou sawest, was the Murderer of
that Child's Father.' "

Donald Bond, the editor of the *Spectator,* traces the story to Henry More's
Divine Dialogues and notes that the *Spectator* piece appears again in the
British Mercury, Jan. 28, 1712, and that the theme is developed in the *British
Mercury,* Feb. 1, 4, 1712.

§419. This is the first of a series of entries drawn from the fourth volume of the
collection of voyages published by Awnsham and John Churchill. Two earlier
extracts (§216, 238) came from the first volume. Byrd's two entries on Hottentots (§419, 425) are taken from William ten Rhijne's *Account of the Cape of
Good Hope and the Hottentotes, the Natives of That Country,* in Churchill,
Voyages, IV, 829–845.

On the English representation of the Cape Khoekoe people known as Hottentots, see Linda E. Merians, "What They Are, Who We Are: Representations of the 'Hottentot' in Eighteenth-Century Britain," *Eighteenth-Century Life*, XVII, no. 3 (November 1993), 14–39. Merians demonstrates the pervasive construction of the Hottentot as a lower level on the chain of being, the most bestial of human kind: "The collective British voice seemed to proclaim that 'we' are different and better than 'they' are; yet some level of fear, be it unconscious or conscious, told them that while 'they' can never be like 'us,' we can become like 'them' " (15). Many of the travel books cited as the sources of the English notion of the Hottentots were in Byrd's library (specifically, Awnsham Churchill and John Churchill's *Collection of Voyages and Travels*, including accounts by Ten Rhijne and Maxwell (Hayes 79); Captain Edward Cooke, *A Voyage to the South Sea, and Round the World* (Hayes 125); William Dampier, *A New Voyage Round the World* (Hayes 58); William Funnell, *A Voyage Round the World* (Hayes 243); William Hacke, ed., *A Collection of Original Voyages* (Hayes 59); *Collection of Voyages* (Hayes 2033); Peter Kolb, *The Present State of the Cape of Good Hope; or, A Particular Account of the Several Nations of the Hottentots* (Hayes 128); John Maxwell, *Account of the Cape of Good Hope*, in Royal Society, *Philosophical Transactions* (1706–1707) (Hayes 197); and the English translation *A New Voyage to the East Indies by François Leguat and His Companions* (Hayes 120). The notion of the degraded Hottentot enters the proverbial English vocabulary, and thus Byrd must have encountered many examples in any number of writers (including Addison).

Byrd frequently refers to the low condition of the Hottentots in exactly the way Merians outlines. For instance, in his *History of the Dividing Line*, in yet another of his ironic jabs at Virginia's southern neighbor, Byrd mocks the benighted North Carolinians by likening them to the Hottentots as examples of the lowest imaginable condition of human life: "'Tis natural for helpless man to adore his Maker in some form or other, and were there any exception to this rule, I should suspect it to be among the Hottentots of the Cape of Good Hope and of North Carolina" (*Works*, 193). Byrd mentions Hottentots again on several occasions: as a figure of speech for novelty (200); as a figure of speech for a liking for certain foods—"Certainly no Tartar ever loved horseflesh or Hottentot guts and garbage better than woodsmen do bear" (277)—in the context of a discussion of ginseng (291–292); declaring that people learned the principles of sailing from observing the flying squirrel, "as the Hottentots learnt the physical use of most of their plants from the baboons" (307). The entries on Hottentots in the commonplace book actually predate the earliest references to Hottentots in the Byrd correspondence

(John Perceval, Viscount Perceval, to Byrd, Dec. 28, 1730, *Correspondence,* I, 440).

This entry is drawn selectively from an extended passage in which Ten Rhijne describes the extremely lascivious nature of the Hottentots. "Their innate Barbarity, their idle and solitary Life, join'd with the want of Knowledge and true Virtue, makes them prone to all manner of Vices, as Levity, Inconstancy, Lust, Deceits, Perfidiousness, and most shameful Debaucheries. . . . Their inordinate way of living and Lust, makes them grow old before their time" (Churchill, *Voyages,* IV, 837–838). Byrd's entry is constructed from material taken from nearby: "In Copulation they choose to perform it from behind, the Woman lying upon one side, something higher than the Men, scarce differing in this point from the Bruits" (IV, 838). "They cut out one of the Testicles to all their Male Children, immediately after they are born, to make them run with the more swiftness" (IV, 842). "As these barbarous Pagans live without Laws, so they only follow their Instinct without controul. Their manner of sitting is just like the posture of a Child in the Womb, bending their Heads betwixt both Knees, which they embrace with their Arms" (IV, 838).

The fact that the order of the elements as they appear in Byrd's entry breaks Ten Rhijne's sequence invites speculation about the way Byrd took notes.

§420. Richard Allestree, in *The Whole Duty of Man . . .* (London, 1673), observes that encouragement is the most effective stimulant to moral education: "To the great duty of Educating of Children there is required as means, first, Encouragement; secondly, Correction[.] Encouragement is first to be tried, we should endeavour to make children in love with duty, by offering them rewards and invitations, and whatever they do well, take notice of it, and encourage them to go on" (286).

A similar observation occurs frequently among educational writers; Byrd may be referring here to John Locke's *Some Thoughts concerning Education,* a book he owned (Hayes 837) and that he might have consulted in reference to the education of his own children: "I have seen little Girls exercise whole Hours together, and take abundance of pains to be expert at *Dibstones,* as they call it: Whilst I have been looking on, I have thought, it wanted only some good Contrivance, to make them employ all that Industry about something that might be more useful to them; and methinks 'tis only the fault and negligence of elder People, that it is not so. Children are much less apt to be idle, than Men; and Men are to be blamed, if some part of that busie Humour be not turned to useful Things; which might be made usually as delightful to them, as those they are employed in, if Men would be but half so forward to lead the way, as these little Apes would be to follow" (*Some Thoughts,* ed. John W. Yolton and Jean S. Yolton [Oxford, 1989], 210–211).

§421. Philip's paternal counsel is found in Plutarch's *Moralia* 178f ("Sayings of Kings and Commanders"): "He bade Alexander give heed to Aristotle, and study philosophy, 'so that,' as he said, 'you may not do a great many things of the sort that I am sorry to have done.'"

§422. This entry consists of an extract from the account of Indostan by Dr. John Francis Gemelli Careri, in *A Voyage Round the World.* The Indostanis capture elephants by using a sexually active female: "They carry a Female into the Woods just at the time when she is in her Lust; at her Cries the wild Male comes, and couples with her contrary to other Beasts, Belly to Belly, in the narrow Place where she was left. When the Male would be gone, he finds the way stopp'd up, and the Hunters at a distance, throw over him great and small Ropes; so that his Trunk and Legs being secur'd they can come near without Danger. However they lead him away between two tame Elephants, and beat him if he makes a noise. Afterwards he grows tame among the rest of his kind; and then he that has them in charge, teaches him to Salute Friends with his Trunk, to Threaten, or Strike whom he pleases, and to kill a Man Condemn'd to that sort of Death, with an Iron fix'd at the end of a Pole, and then the Manager sits upon his Neck. It is of it self a very tractable Creature, when it is not Enrag'd or in Lust; for then he that Rules it is in Danger. They quiet him with Artificial Fire-works, or directing him into a River, where, tho' so large, he swims extraordinary well. The She Elephants carry their young 12 Months; they live 100 years; and carry about 3200 Pounds weight *Spanish*" (Churchill, *Voyages,* IV, 254–255). See also Aristotle *Historia animalium* 571b on the elephant's furious copulation.

§423. This story comes from Careri's historical account of the Tartar conquest of China in *A Voyage Round the World:* "In the mean while *Li,* leaving a sufficient Garrison in *Peking,* prepar'd to give Battle to the General *Usanquey,* who had the Supreme Command of the *Chinese* Army, consisting of 60000 Men; and was employ'd in the Province of *Leaotung,* against the *Tartars.* He advanced to attack the City, where finding *Usan-quey,* who defended it bravely, he caus'd his Father to be brought before the Wall, threatning to put him to a most cruel Death, if he did not Surrender the City. *Usan-quey,* being on the Wall in that Condition, knelt down and begg'd his Father's Pardon, telling him, *he ow'd a greater Duty to his King and Country than to him, and that it was better to die, than to live Subject to Robbers.* The Father commended his Son's generous Resolution, and willingly bowing his Neck was put to Death" (Churchill, *Voyages,* IV, 387).

§425. As with §419, Byrd's other Hottentot entry, this is taken from William ten Rhijne's *Account of the Cape of Good Hope and the Hottentotes, the Natives of That Country:* "If we are oblig'd to the Brutes for the discovery of several wholesome Remedies; as to the *Dogs* for *Emetics,* to the *Egyptian* Bird *Ibis* for *Clysters,* for *Phlebotomy* to the Sea-horse, for the use of *Ditany* or *Garden Ginger* to the *Goats,* of the *Swallow-wort* to the Swallows, of *Fennel* to the *Snake,* of the *narrow small row leav'd Plantin* to the *Toads,* of the *Rue* to the *Weesel,* of the *Origanum* to the *Stork,* of the *Ground-Ivy* to the *wild Boar,* and of the use of the *Artichoak* to the *Stag,* what wonder is it, if these Hottentotes, tho' never so brutish, have their own way of curing Distempers? I don't say all Distempers. . . . *Suction* and *Unction* are two chief, if not the only Remedies used among the *Hottentotes;* their main dread being from the Poison of Arrows or venomous Beasts: If they are wounded by them, they beat the afflicted part with a small stick, till it be deprived of all sense; then they scarifie and suck it till the Blood follows" (Churchill, *Voyages,* IV, 843). The passage from which Byrd extracted the snakebite remedy introduces the popular notion that medical treatments were discovered through observation of animal behavior; see also §522.

§426. This story comes from Dr. John Francis Gemelli Careri's account of the superstitions of the Indostanis in *A Voyage Round the World,* where it appears with the marginal caption, "A foolish Opinion of theirs": "They are so Silly, or Ignorant as to conceit a Woman may Conceive by strength of Imagination; and that tho' they are many thousand Miles distant, and that for several Years, yet their Wives imagining they Lie with them, may become with Child, and therefore when they hear of their being brought to Bed, they make great Rejoycing. To this purpose, *F. Galli,* Prefect of the *Theatins* of *Goa,* told me a pleasant Story. *D. Francis de Tavora,* Earl of *Alvor,* arriving from *Portugal,* to be Vice-Roy of *India;* News was brought that his Wife, whom he left big with Child, was deliver'd of a Son. Among the rest a *Pagan* Merchant went to Congratule him, and thinking to make the Vice-Roy a great Complement said, *I wish your Excellency Joy, and hope you will have News every Year of the Birth of a Son.* This would have put him in a Passion, had not some told him that the Idolaters held that preposterous Opinion. The Women are Happy, that can take their Liberty, and make their silly Husbands believe they Conceiv'd by thinking on them" (Churchill, *Voyages,* IV, 260).

§429. *Varlet* is a term of abuse for "a person of a low, mean, or knavish disposition; a knave, rogue, or rascal" (*OED*).

§430. See §416.

§435. Cerberus was the three-headed dog guarding the gates of the infernal regions in classical mythology. The word sometimes appears allusively in early modern English writing as a humorous title for a porter.

§439. This entry is the first of a number of translations from Nicolas Venette's *De la génération de l'homme, ou tableau de l'amour conjugal,* two copies of which were in Byrd's library (Hayes 1405, 1469), both in French, probably different editions. Byrd's copies have not been found, so it is difficult to determine with certainty which edition he was consulting when he wrote in the commonplace book. A comparison of the Venette entries with the English translations clearly indicates they were not sources. And because a small part of the Venette material found in the commonplace book does not appear in earlier editions, it appears likely that Byrd used a later French edition, quite likely the one we cite. See also the discussion above, Chapter 9 n. 14.

This entry comes from Venette's discussion of female sexual appetite:

L'experience nous apprend, qu'une femme grosse est plus amoureuse au commencement de sa grossesse qu'auparavant. Beaucoup plus de sang & d'esprits occupent ses parties naturelles, & si on la baise en ce temps-là, c'est de l'eau que l'on jette sur le feu d'une forge, qui, plus il est arrosé, plus il est ardent.

Les François ne sont pas si retenus à caresser les femmes grosses que quelques autres Nations. Il y a mesme de Médecins qui font d'avis qu'on les doit baiser avec plus d'ardeur, pour obeïr aux loix de la Nature, qui les rend alors plus amoureuses. Mais à dire le vray, si nous suivons le sentiment d'*Hippocrate,* elles sont de plus vehementes couches, quand elles ne sont point caressées pendant leur grossesse, & nous voyons souvent arriver des accidens funestes aux femmes qui se divertissent avec un homme, quand elles sont grosses, car si elles ne font pas de fausses couches, au moins deviennent-elles grosses une seconde fois.

Les femmes de Bresil sont bien plus retenuës que nos Françoises, puis que des qu'elles se sentent grosses, elles se separent de la compagnie de leurs maris. Elles n'apprehendent pas que les fortes secousses de l'amour ébranlent un enfant qui est fort delicat dans ses premier mois, & que les regles, qui sont souvent provoquées par la chaleur, que les baisers réïterez excitent dans les parties d'une femme, l'éttouffent & le suffoquent. Il ne peut mesme s'en garantir sur la fin de sa prison, lorsqu'il est plus robuste. Les liens qui le tiennent faisi se relâchent par sa pesanteur, aux moindres efforts amoureux de la mere: & il est ainsi contraint de perdre la vie en naissant, avant le temps, luy qui ne l'a presques encore recüe. (*Tableau,* 116–118)

Venette, like most of his contemporaries, believed that sexual intercourse during pregnancy was dangerous because a second impregnation (or superfetation) was possible at any time. Byrd, however, apparently did not share this concern; his diaries record intercourse with his first wife, Lucy, during her pregnancy (*SD*, 272, 345); see also Lockridge, *Patriarchal Rage*, 35.

§441. This entry comprises Venette's most sensational example of the suppression of sexual passion: "Je ne saurois passer icy sous silence le réméde horrible, dont se servit *Faustine* fille de l'Empereur *Antoine* le débonnaire, pour calmer l'amour déreglé qu'elle portoit à un *Gladiateur*. L'Empereur qui l'aymoit tendrement se persuadoit qu'elle avoit esté enchantée, & il croyoit qu'il estoit impossible sans charmes qu'une femme abandonnast un mary qui avoit de si belles qualitez comme avoit *Antoine* le Philosophe pour aymer un *Gladiateur*. C'est ce qui l'obligea à envoyer consulter les Caldéens qui luy firent réponse que *Faustine* devoit boire du sang de celuy qu'elle aymoit, & coucher ensuite avec son mary pour haïr horriblement ce prémier homme. En effet le succez répondit à la promesse: & *Antonius Commodus* nasquit de ces embrassemens qui dans le temps se délecta au meurtre, comme le meurtre avoit esté la cause de sa vie" (*Tableau,* 209–210). The commentary in the last sentence appears to be Byrd's own reaction to the story.

§442. Byrd's discussion of sexual positions follows Venette:

La plus commune des postures est celle qui est la plus licite & la plus voluptueuse; on se parle bouche à bouche, on se baise & on se caresse, quand on s'embrasse par devant.

Si un homme est trop pésant, & que la femme soit extrémement delicate, il me semble qu'on n'agiroit pas contre les loix de la Nature, si l'on se caressoit de costé à l'imitation des renards. On éviteroit par cette posture tous les accidens ausquels une femme delicate peut estre exposée dans la posture la plus commune, & il n'arriveroit jamais par là de suffocations ny de fausses couches.

Je mettrois icy la posture de caresser une femme par derriere parmy celles qui sont contre les loix de la Nature, si un Philosophe & deux Medecins ne me disoient le contraire. En effet, toutes les bestes, si nous en exceptons quelques-unes, se joignent de la sorte; & pour engendrer, la Nature ne leur a point appris d'autre moyen que celuy-là. La matrice des femelles est alors plus en estat de recevoir la semence du masle, elle la retient & la fomente plus commodément, si bien que ne s'écoulant pas si aisément de leurs parties naturelles que dans une autre posture, l'experience leur a fait voir que l'on rendoit ainsi des femmes fécondes qu'estoient steriles auparavant.

Il est certain que l'Anatomie nous montre que la matrice est beaucoup mieux située pour la conception, lors qu'une femme est sur ses mains & sur ses pieds que quand elle est sur dos. Le fond de cette partie est alors plus bas que son orifice, & il n'y a qu'à y jetter de la semence, elle y coule d'elle-mesme, & par sa propre pesanteur elle tombe où elle doit être conservée pour la génération. Cette posture est la plus naturelle & la moins voluptueuse. . . .

Mais encore, puisque la loy commande à un mari de rendre le devoir à sa femme, quand elle témoigne l'aimer ardemment, elle oblige aussi la femme de rendre ce mesme devoir à son mary quand il ne peut dompter sa passion. Si par hazard il veut éteindre sa concupiscence sur la fin de la grossesse de sa femme, ne pourroit-on pas alors luy permettre de la caresser par derriere plûtost que d'étouffer l'enfant qui est sur le point de naistre, on que d'aller luy-mesme chercher ailleurs à faire un crime? Dans cette posture il n'y aura point de crainte pour une fausse couche, l'épine du dos souffre plutost que le ventre les secousses que l'amour inspire aux hommes dans cette rencontre. (*Tableau,* 237–239)

§443. The source of this anecdote has not been identified. On the superiority of the sexual position here described for conception, see Montaigne, *Essays,* "Apology for Raimond Sebond."

§445. This jest resembles a humorous tale told by John Taylor, *Wit and Mirth . . .* (London, 1635), no. 50: "A Cardinall kept a knavish foole for his recreation, to whom he said, Sirrah foole, suppose that all the world were dead but thou and I, and that one of us should be turned to a Horse, and the other of us to an Asse, say which of these two wouldest thou choose to bee? The foole answered, Sir, you are my master, and for that respect it is fit that your worship should chuse first, and I will bee contented to take that which you leave. Why then said the Cardinall, I would be a horse: no said the foole, let me intreat your worship to be an Asse, for I would be an Asse to chuse of al things: why, quoth the Cardinall: marry, said the foole, because that I have knowne many Asses come to be Justices, but I never knew any horse come to the like preferment." A slightly modernized version appears in [Richard Head], *The Complaisant Companion . . .* (London, 1674), 4.

§447. Taylor, *Wit and Mirth,* no. 48: "A Gentlewoman cheapned a close stools in Pauls Church-yard, and the shopkeeper did aske her too much money for it, as shee thought. Why mistris, said hee, I pray you consider what a good locke and key it hath: Shee replyed, that shee had small use for either lock or key, for she purposed to put nothing into it, but what shee cared not who stole out." Cf. [Head], *The Complaisant Companion,* 22.

§449. Taylor, *Wit and Mirth,* no. 80: "Divers Gentlemen being merry together, at last one of their acquaintance came to them (whose name was Sampson)

Aha, said one of them, now we may bee severely merry, no serjeant or Bailiffe dare touch us, if a thousand Philistins come, there is Sampson, who is able to brain them all: to whom Sampson replyde, Sir I may boldly venture against so many as you speake of, provided, that you will lend me one of your Jaw-bones." Cf. [Head], *The Complaisant Companion*, 23.

§456. See §406.

§458. The *hadj*, or *hajj* (or sometimes *hagge*), is the pilgrimage to Mecca expected of devout Muslims (*OED*).

§459. On the fattening of prospective brides in Barbary, see §100.

§465. The "very fashionable Distemper" is the pox (syphilis). The jest depends upon current medical theories, which considered syphilis a disease of heat, which, if not stopped, literally consumed the body, beginning with the nose.

§467. From Venette's discussion of the penis: "En effet, dans ces derniers siecles aussi-bien que dans les premiers, on a eu beaucoup de vénération pour cette partie-là, parce qu'elle est le pere du genre humain, & l'origine des parties qui nous composent. Villandré, ainsi que remarque l'Histoire de France, commit un crime de Léze Majesté pour avoir touché de la main les parties naturelles de Charles IX." *Tableau*, 3.

Note that Byrd erroneously translates this passage as if a woman had touched the king's penis; he probably accidentally conflated this line with the next, which refers to the punishment accorded by Old Testament law for a woman who injures a man's penis.

§468. From Venette, *Tableau*, 6–8:

Chaque homme a ordinairement deux testicules; si l'un est incommodé, fletry ou blessé, l'autre peut servir à la génération, & il s'en trouve qui n'en ont naturallement qu'un, comme autrefois les Sylles & les Cottes; mais la Nature renferme dans cette seule partie toute la vertu qui devoit estre dans les deux.

Ceux qui en ont trois ou quatre, sont bien plus communs que ceux qui n'en ont qu'un: & nos Histoires de Medecine remarquent qu'il n'y a guere de Royaumes, qui ne fournissent des familles où il n'y ait des hommes à trois testicules, mais ceux-cy n'ont pas l'avantage des premiers, puisqu'au lieu d'estre fertiles par la multitude de leurs parties, ils en deviennent impuissants, la vertue prolifique estant divisée en trop de parties pour avoir de la force. *Agathocles* Roy de Sicil & Mr. *Pint*... de cette ville, connurent bien que le plus grand nombre de testicules n'estoit pas le meilleur pour la génération, bien qu'il le fust pour l'ardeur & pour le plaisir: & qu'il vailloit beaucoup mieux n'en avoir qu'un ou deux que d'ens avoir d'avantage.

§469. This entry appears to have originated with Venette: "On voit au haut des nymphes une partie plus ou moins longue que la moitié du doigt, que les Anatomistes appellent Clitoris, & que je pourrois nommer la fougue & la rage de l'amour. C'est-là que la Nature a mis le trône de ses plaisirs & de ses voluptez, comme elle a fait dans le gland de l'homme. C'est là qu'elle a placé ses chatoüillemens excessifs, & qu'elle a établi le lieu de la lasciveté des femmes. Car dans l'action de l'amour, le Clitoris se remplit d'esprits, & se roidit ensuite comme la Verge d'un homme: aussi en a-t-il les parties toutes semblables. On peut voir ses tuyaux, ses nerfs & ses muscles, il ne luy manque ny gland ny prepuce, & s'il estoit trouüé par le bout, on diroit qu'il est tout semblable au nombre viril. C'est de cette partie qu'abusent souvent les femmes lascives." *Tableau*, 20.

   Nicholas Culpeper's *Directory for Midwives* . . . ([London, 1671]), I, 22, II, 3, describes the clitoris in similar terms: "The *Clitoris* is a sinewy and hard Body . . . in form it represents the yard of a man, and suffers erection and falling as that doth, this is that which causeth lust in a woman, and gives delight in Copulation, for without this a woman neither desires copulation, or hath pleasure in it, or conceives by it." "The part at the top is hard and nervous, and swells like a Yard in Venery, with much spirit." Cf. *Aristotle's Master-Piece* . . . (London, 1698), 77, 85–86.

§470. From Venette: "La mortification de la chair & la chasteté sont souvent de puissantes causes pour diminuer nos parties naturelles. L'example de *St. Martin* nous le fait bien voir, lui qui pendant la vie avoit tellement maceré son corps par des austerités inouïes, & qui s'estoit tellement roidi contre les libertés de son siécle, qu'aprés sa mort, si nous en croyons *Sulpice,* sa verge estoit si petite, que l'on ne l'auroit point trouvée, si l'on n'eust seu le lieu qu'elle devoit occuper." *Tableau*, 34.

§471. From Venette:

Les verges trop longues ou trop grosses ne sont les plus propres, ny pour la copulation ny pour la génération. Elles incommodent les femmes & ne produisent rien, si bien que pour la commodité de l'action, il faut que la partie de l'homme soit mediocre, & que celle de la femme y soit proportionée, afin de s'unir l'une à l'autre, & de se toucher agréablement de toutes parts.

   Il n'y a point d'autre cause de ce vice naturel que l'abondance de la matiere dans les premieres semaines de la conception, si bien que l'Intelligence, qui a soin de la formation de cette partie aussi bien que des autres, ne sachant que faire de tant de matiere qui reste aprés les principales parties formées, elle l'employe à faire une grosse & longue verge. (*Tableau*, 34–35)

The detail about abundance of material going to the feet of the female is not found in Venette.

§472. From Venette:

> S'il est vray ce que les Physionomistes nous disent que les hommes qui ont de grands nez ont aussi de grandes verges, & qu'ils sont plus robustes & plus courageux que les autres, nous ne devons pas nous étonner de ce qu'*Heliogabale,* que la Nature avoit favorisé de grandes parties genitales, comme l'ecrit *Lampridius,* choisissoit des soldats qui avoient de grands nez, afin d'estre plus en estat avec moins de troupes de faire quelque grande expedition de guerre, ou de resister plus fortement aux efforts de ses ennemis; mais il ne s'appercevoit pas en mesme temps, que ces gens aux grandes verges estoient les plus étourdis & les plus stupides des hommes. . . .
>
> On doute si la semence est prolifique qui passe par une longue verge. *Galien* aprés *Aristote* a agité cette question. Ils disent tous deux que les esprits, qui resident abondamment dans la semence, se dissipant par la longeuer du chemin, la semence n'est plus ensuite capable de production. Mais plusieurs Medecins, & entre autres le savant *Hucher,* sont d'un tout autre sentiment. Car la semence se portant directement dans le fonds de la matrice sans estre alterée de l'air, ny par aucune autre cause étrangere, elle a toutes les dispositions necessaires pour la génération, & les histoires que ce dernier Médecin nous rapporte sur ce sujet, nous font bien voir que la verité est toute pour luy. . . . Je ne parle point icy de la grosseur prodigieuse de la Verge de quelques hommes: on sait qu'ils ne sont pas destinez pour le mariage, & l'on auroit eu grand tort si l'on avoit voulu rémarier l'homme, dont parle *Fabrice de Hilden,* qui l'avoit aussi grosse qu'un enfant nouvellement né. (*Tableau,* 35–37)

§473. From Venette: "Si nous suivons en France ce que *Platon* nous a laissé par écrit pour une Republique bien reglée, nous ne verrions point tant de desordres dans les mariages que nous en observons quelquefois. On se marie à l'aveugle, sans avoir auparavant consideré si l'on est capable de génération. Si avant que de se marier on s'examinoit tout nud, selon les loix de ce Philosophe, ou qu'il y eust des personnes établies pour cela, je suis assuré qu'il y auroit quelques mariages plus tranquiles qu'ils ne le sont; & que jamais *Hammeberge* n'eust esté repudié par *Theodoric,* si ces loix eussent esté alors établis." *Tableau,* 41–42.

Venette erroneously credits Plato with this suggestion, for in the *Republic* he only proposes that women and men should exercise together in the nude (457a), and in *Laws* (771e–772a) recommends mutual viewing before marriage. Venette conflates Plato's position with the more blunt recommendations of Thomas More in *Utopia,* an error Venette might have drawn from Montaigne, *Essays,* "On Certain Verses of Virgil."

In June 1729, Byrd again discussed premarital viewing in a humorous letter on marriage to Mrs. Anne Taylor Otway: "And that both sexes may hereafter come together fairly and squarely, without concealing their personal defects, I wou'd have it also enacted that the partys shoud view each other stark naked thro' an iron grate for the space of half an hour, the woman if she please to have a mask upon her face all the while to save her modesty. This will hinder their being surprised after marriage with any deformitys and disproportions, which they did by no means expect. Likewise to prevent their imposeing on each other with any counterfeit good humour, it shou'd be further enacted, that they see one another drunk 3 several times, to discover the true temper and disposition of their souls. By acting thus fairly and above-bord, many unhappy matches will be avoided, to the great peace of familys, and to the propagateing a strong and vigorous posterity." *Correspondence,* I, 401; other material from this commonplace book (§485) appears in the same letter.

An account of the Muscovite practice of premarital viewing appears in [Samuel Collins], *The Present State of Russia . . .* (London, 1671), a copy of which was probably in Byrd's library (Hayes 114). Most betrothals there are undertaken by family members or brokers: "And the Yo[u]ng-man seldom sees his Wife till they come into the brides Chamber; if she be ugly she pays for it soundly, it may be the first time he sees her. To prevent future mistakes, the Bride-grooms Friends, *viz.* five or six Women see the Bride stark naked, and observe whether she has any defect in her Body" (36–37). This account differs from Byrd's in that the viewing is done by proxy (and sober). Still, Collins, imperfectly recollected, might have been subsumed into Byrd's comments on the utopian practice.

§474. From Venette's discussion of the maladies and irregularities of the female natural parts: "Souvent les caroncules jointes, qu'on nomme *Hymen,* sont percées pour donner passage aux humeurs qui sortent de la matrice, & qui y entrent aussi quelquefois; & il ne faut s'étonner s'il y a eu des femmes qui ont conceu ne pouvant mesme souffrir d'homme; comme il arrive à *Cornelia* mere des *Gracques;* & comme il arrive encore tous les jours à plusieurs femmes de l'Amerique Meridionale, qui conçoivent sans estres ouverte, mais aussi qui meurent souvent en mettant un homme au monde." *Tableau,* 68.

Cornelia, Roman matron, mother of the Gracchi (Tiberius and Gaius, reformers of the Roman government), was often celebrated as a type of patriotic motherhood.

§475. From Venette: "L'accouchement est quelquefois accompagné d'accidens si facheux, que les femmes se fendent d'une maniere étonnante, & j'en ay vû une dont les deux trous n'en faisoient qu'un. Ces parties se déchiverent d'un telle façon, & la Nature en les repoussant y envoye tant le matiere qu'il s'y engendre plus de chair qu'auparavant, si bien qu'aprés cela l'ouverture en est presque tout bouchée, & quand ces femmes sont un jour en estat d'estre embrassées par leurs maris, elles sont fort surprises de n'être pas ouvertes comme auparavant." *Tableau,* 42–43.

§476. From Venette's discussion of the remedies popularly prescribed for male impotence: "On a beau frotter ces parties malades d'huile de vers de terre, d'huile de lavande ou de *palma Christi,* parmy lesquelles on aura meslé un peu de poudre du nerf d'un taureau ou d'un cerf, tout cela reproduit rien, & ne sert qu'a embrasser davantage le malade." *Tableau,* 546.

Venette warns against placing much trust in such purported remedies; however, Byrd appears to pay attention only to Venette's reports of traditional methods of stimulating an erection, adding his own recommendation and blithely ignoring the pessimistic context. Byrd's diaries reveal only occasional problems with impotence; see the entry for Oct. 8, 1718: "Then I walked the street and picked up a woman and carried her to the tavern and gave her a broiled chicken for supper but she could provoke me to do nothing because my roger would not stand with all she could do." *LD,* 182.

§477. The source of this entry has not been identified. Vitriol (sulfate of iron; *not* oil of vitriol, which is sulfuric acid) is a common ingredient in styptic preparations, along with alum, sugar, extenders (lint), and binding agents (egg whites). Such recipes may be found in any of the many books of physic in Byrd's library.

§478. From Venette's discussion of large female sexual parts: "Les femmes des regions chaudes previennent le defaut que nous avons marqué en se lavant les parties naturelles avec l'eau de myrthe distillé, qu'elles aromatisent avec un peu d'essence de girofle, ou avec quelque goutte d'esprit de vin ambré, ou avec des concoctions astringentes. Mais la concoction de grande consoude est encore meilleure que tout cela, si nous en croyons la femme, dont parle *Sennert,* qui s'estant mise dans un bain, que sa servante avoit preparé pour soy-mesme, fut fort fatiguée la nuit suivante par son mary, parce qu'elle se trouva presque tout fermée. Cette experience n'est pas seule; *Benivenius* nous fait une semblable histoire sur ce sujet, & nous en produirions quelques autres, si l'on pouvoir douter de cette verité." *Tableau,* 64.

The materia medica may be of interest: *girofle* is clove; *grande consoude* is comfrey; and *myrthe* is sweet cicely. The astringent bath treatment was widely used; Nicholas Culpeper's *Directory for Midwives* . . . (London, 1671), II, 99, mentions "a Wench that was married, and to appear a Virgin, she used a Bath of Comfry roots." According to Joannis Cruso, whose book *Medicamentorum Εὐποριστῶν Thesaurus* . . . (London, 1701) was in Byrd's library (Hayes 757), *sympitum* (comfrey) is a specific applied externally for "Vulvam Adstringunt," providing "pro deliciis noviter nuptorum" (138). The term "Steel medicines" does not appear in Venette. Byrd here probably refers to other astringents such as "Salts of steel," usually iron chloride, or to another medicament containing iron (*OED*).

§479. From Venette: "La fille d'un chauderonnier que je vis il y a deux ans, n'auroit pas gardé toutes ces mesures avec son mari, si je n'avois donné ordre d'élargir ses parties naturelles par des décoctions de pieds de mouton, de corne de cerfs, de moële de boeuf, de racines de guimauves, de semence de lin, d'herbe aux puces bouïllie dans l'eau." *Tableau*, 66–67.

§480. From Venette:

Les Romains autrefois lui firent bâtir un temple & éléver un statuë, qu'ils appelloient *Bucca Veritatis*. Cette statuë décidoit de la Virginité ou de l'infamie des filles. Témoin la fille du Roy de *Volaterre*, qui aprés luy avoir mis le doigt dans la bouche n'en fut point morduë, & ainsi se justitia de l'injure qu'un vielle femme avoit faite à sa pudicité. Il n'en arriva pas de mesme, à ce qu'on dit, à l'égard d'une autre qui estant accusée du mesme crime, eut le doigt emporté par la bouche de la statuë.

On fait encore quelle vénération ont eu ces mesmes peuples pour les *Vierges Vestales*, & le fameux Edit que l'Empereur *Tibere* fit publier. La fille de *Sejan*, qui n'avoit pas encore atteint l'âge de puberté, fut deflorée par le bourreau, avant que d'estre étranglée pour ne faire pas deshonneur à la Virginité. (*Tableau*, 76–77)

Bucca Veritatis translates as "the mouth of truth." Here (as elsewhere) the emperor Tiberius serves as a type of tyrannical and perverted cruelty; cf. Pierre de Bourdeille, seigneur de Brantôme, *The Lives of the Gallant Ladies*, trans. Alec Brown (London, 1961), 346. On the other hand, Sejanus appears not infrequently in later literature as a type of heroic military integrity. Addison draws on Suetonius to offer a comic version of the story in the *Guardian*, no. 114 (July 22, 1713).

§481. From Venette: "Le meilleur expédient pour conserver la pudicité de filles, selon la distinction qu'en font les Médicins, & pour en estre bien assuré, ce seroit de coudre leurs parties naturelles, dés quelles sont nées, ainsi que *Pierre*

Bembo dit qu'on fait aux vierges Africaines" (*Tableau*, 80–81). Venette wryly adds that, since this practice is not customary in France, it must suffice to rely instead upon female education and wisdom to preserve modesty.

§482. From Venette: "Il n'y a donc rien, je le diray encore une fois, de si difficile à connoître que la Virginité, puisque mesme une femme grosse, si nous en croyons *Severin Pinay,* peut en avoir toutes les marques. A moins qu'une fille n'ait esté trouvée entre les bras d'un homme, & qu'on ne l'examine au mesme instant, il n'y a guere de moyen de connoître sa defloration." *Tableau*, 86–87.

"Ce qui a donné lieu aux Théologiens, aux Jurisconsultes, & à quelques Medecins de croire qu'une femme pouvoit engendrer sans l'application des parties naturelles d'un homme, ce sont sans doute les Histoires qu'*Averroês, Amatus Lusitanus,* & *Delrio* nous ont laissées par écrit." *Tableau*, 608–609.

§483, 484. From Venette's account of the signs of virginity:

L'on croit que le sang qui s'épanche la prémiere nuit des nôces, & que le lait qu'on trouve dans les mamelles d'une fille sont des marques manifestes de la perte de sa Virginité. . . . Le lait ne peut couleur du sein d'une fille qu'elle n'ait auparavant conceu dans ses entrailles, & l'on ne doit pas appeller vierge, celle qui donne à têter à un enfant.

Mais l'on me permettra de dire que le sang & le lait ne sont pas toûjours des marques d'une fille prostituée. . . .

Si le sang des regles cesse de couleur à une fille, ce sang rémontant aux mamelles se change en lait, selon le sentiment d'*Hippocrate,* & la petite fille dont *Alexandre Benoist* nous fait l'histoire, qui fut sterile toute sa vie, donna des marques de sa prostitution dépuis son enfance, si le lait est un signe assuré d'une mauvais conduite. Mais ce qui est encore de plus remarquable sur ce sujet, c'est que le Syrien du mesme *Benoist,* & le Soldat *Benzo* de *Cardan* avoient tous deux du lait, bien qu'ils fussent des hommes robustes.

Dans l'Orient d'Afrique du côte de Mozambique & au pays des Caffres, si nous en croions les Historiens, plusiers hommes nourissent leurs enfants du lait de leurs mammelles. (*Tableau,* 83–84)

The notion of male lactation is also recorded by Aristotle *Historia animalium* 1.12.10.

§485. From Venette: "Car les Spartiates d'un costé instituerent une feste, où ceux qui n'estoient pas mariez, estoient foüettez par des femmes, comme indignes de servir la Republique, & de contribuer à son honneur & à son progrés" (*Tableau*, 104). Venette does not specify the age of 24; however, several pages later he does divide the life of man into ages: youth, from birth to 25; "la fleur de l'âge de l'homme," from 25 to 35 or 40 (*Tableau*, 104–106).

Byrd seems to have incorporated part of this entry (and part of §473) into a letter to Mrs. Anne Taylor Otway in June 1729. The beginning of the letter is missing, but the fragmentary first remaining sentence probably refers to the Spartan regime here described: "... live unmarryd to the age of five and twenty, he shall be whipt every Munday morning as long as he continues single, by at least 2 of the oldest virgins in the neighbourhood." *Correspondence*, I, 401.

§487. On the currency of this practice, see Nicholas Culpeper's *Directory for Midwives* ... [London, 1671], I, 133–134: "Midwives ... leave a longer part of the Navel-string of a male than they do of a female, and their supposed reason is this, because in males they would have the instruments of generation long, that so they may not be Cowards in the Schools of *Venus*. But in females they cut it shortyer, and that they think forsooth, makes them modest, and their Privities narrower."

§488. From Venette's chapter on the best ways for married couples to engage in lovemaking: "Toutes les postures que la Courtisane *Cyréne* inventa autrefois jusqu'au nombre de douze pour se caresser, que *Pheilenis* & *Astyanasse* publierent, qu'*Elephanits* composa en vers *Leonins,* & que l'Empereur *Tibere* fit ensuite peindre autour de sa sale, nous font bien voir que les femmes savent mieux que nous toutes les soupplesses de l'amour, & qu'elles s'abandonnent plus aux voluptés amoureuses; en effet leur passion est plus violente & leur plaisir dure plus long temps; c'est comme un feu qui s'entretient dans du bois verd par la foiblesse & la legereté de leur jugement." *Tableau,* 235.

Tiberius's fascination with the illustration of sexual positions also appears elsewhere in Venette (155). Venette's source is Suetonius "Tiberius" 43, *The Lives of the Caesars.* Eliphantis was a Greek poet who wrote amatory verse; she was reputedly also the author of a book of sexual positions. See Pierre de Bourdeille, seigneur de Brantôme, *The Lives of the Gallant Ladies,* trans. Alec Brown (London, 1961), 27.

§489. Venette introduces Sappho as an example of female sexual furor: "Cette fureur amoureuse vient souvent à tel point qu'elle la force à solliciter un homme de l'embrasser tendrement, & à se prostituer mesme au premier venu. ... Au reste, toutes les femmes amoureuses ne sont pas semblables, l'on en voit d'agiles, d'inconstantes, de babillardes, de hardies ou d'inquiétes. D'autres paroissent mornes, solitaires, timides ou languissantes. ... On en a vû d'autres qui craignant les suites facheuses de l'amour se divertissoient avec des filles, comme si elles eussent esté des hommes, c'est ce que le Poëte *Martial* reproche aigrement à *Bassa.* On fait encore que *Megille* meritoit le mesme réproche: & que *Sappho Lesbienne* avoit chez elle quantité de servantes pour un pareil divertissement." *Tableau,* 155–156.

Sappho, the Greek lyric poet, was later known as much for her intimate relations with the young girls in her order devoted to Aphrodite and the Muses as for her verse. She became the prototype of the Lesbian woman.

§490. A saying generally attributed to George Villiers, second duke of Buckingham.

§491, §492. From Venette: "On dit qu'une femme stérile est plus amoureuse qu'une femme féconde; & l'on ne manque point de raisons là dessus, car si on considere l'envie déreglée qu'a la premiere de se perpétuer par la génération, & la cause la plus ordinaire de sa stérilité, qui est l'ardeur de ses entrailles, on avoüera qu'elle doit estre plus lascive que l'autre: témoin les femmes de Malabar qui ne sont pas les plus fecondes du monde à cause de la chaleur du pays, & qui à cause de cela ont la permission de prendre autant de maris qu'il leur plaist; parce que les enfants selon leur loy ne sont nobles que de leur côte. C'est asseurement un piperie pour le libertinage où les Orientaux sont plongés." *Tableau*, 156–157.

It is instructive to consult Nicholas Culpeper's *Directory for Midwives . . .* ([London, 1671]), II, 21–22, for further light on the seventeenth-century understanding of the relation of sexual appetite to the heat of the womb: "They who have hot wombs, desire Copulation sooner and more vehemently, and are much delighted therewith. . . . The hot and dry have great Lust and Frenzy if they want it: but they are quickly tired, because there are few Spirits. . . . Heat of the Womb is necessary for Conception; but if it be too much, it nourisheth not the Seed of the man, but disperseth its heat, and hinders the Conception."

§493. Writing on the amorous temperament of women, Venette introduces this story into his discussion of sex during pregnancy: "Mais une femme qui devient grosse, & qui devroit avoir assouvi sa passion, ne laisse pas encore d'aymer éperdûment. J'en prends à témoin *Popilia*, qui, estant un jour interogée, sur la passion déreglée d'une femme grosse par rapport aux autres animaux, respondit fort spirituellement, qu'elle ne s'estonnoit pas de ce que les femelles des bestes fuyoient alors la compagnie des masles, parce qu'en effet elles estoient des bestes" (*Tableau*, 157). The story is recorded in the *Saturnalia* of Macrobius (2.5). Cf. Thom[as] Heywood, Γυναικειον; *or, Nine Books of Various History concerninge Women* (London, 1624), 127, and *The Generall History of Women* (London, 1657), 174. See also Culpeper's *Directory for Midwives*, I, 108, on the desire for copulation during pregnancy.

§494. The source for this entry has not been found. Curiously, according to Joseph Pitton de Tournefort, *A Voyage into the Levant . . .* (London, 1718), II, 73, the Turks accord a similar punishment, not to the cuckold, but to the adulterous man, who (if not killed by the offended husband) may be compelled to marry his lover, and to ride through the streets seated backwards upon an ass.

§495. Discussing excessive female sexual appetite—*fureur amoureuse*—Venette introduces Semiramis among the examples of insatiable women: "J'en appelle à témoin la Reine *Semiramis,* qui aprés avoir pleuré la mort de son mary, se prostitutua à beaucoup de personnes, & qui, pour cacher ses desordres amoreux, fit bâtir quantité de mausolées pour enterrer tout vivants ceux avec qui elle avoit pris des plaisirs illicites, afin que son impudicité fust cachée aux yeux des hommes" (*Tableau,* 156). Queen Semiramis was the widow of King Ninus. After his death, she ruled for many years, led the Assyrians in battle, and built the city of Babylon. Historians differ about her character; according to some she was the daughter of the goddess Derceto, was nursed by doves, and was transformed to a dove at her death. Conversely, she was held in ill repute, becoming one of the major negative exempla of dissolute women. See, for instance, Thomas Heywood's *Generall History of Women* (London, 1657), 231: "In her latter years [Semiramis] grew to that debauch'd effeminacy and sordid lust, that she did not only admit but allure and compell into her goatish embraces, many of her souldiers, without respect of their degrees or places, so they were well featured, able and lusty of performance, whom when they had wasted their bodies upon her, she caused to be most cruelly murthered."

§496. Discussing excessive female sexual appetite, Venette introduces Berenice as a counterexample: "Toutes les femmes estoient d'un autre temperament que *Berenice,* qui, au rapport de *Josephe,* se sépera de son mary pour en estre trop carressée. En effet, une personne amoureuse l'est en toute forte d'estat, elle a beau estre fille ou femme mariée ou veuve, vuide ou pleine, stérile ou feconde, tout cela n'empêche pas qu'elle ne soit plus lascive qu'un homme" (*Tableau,* 164–165). Venette's source is unclear; the story does not appear to be preserved in modern editions of Josephus.

§497. From Venette's chapter, "Combien de fois pendant une nuit l'on peut caresser amoureusement sa femme":

La vanité est un passion naturelle à l'homme. Il s'y laisse aller quand il y pense le moins; & nous pouvons dire sans exageration, qu'elle est un des plus grands maux auxquels il est sujet. En effet l'homme n'est qu'un songe d'ombre si nous en voulons croire un Poëte Grec, & à se bien considerer, il n'est que foiblesse & que misere. Il ne paroist jamais plus ridicule & plus foible que dans la vanité, & c'est sans doute ce qui obligea *Democrite* à se mocquer de luy.

Mais il n'y a point d'occasion où la vanité se fasse voir davantage que dans les matieres de l'amour, quand pour nous faire admirer, nous nous attribuons des exploits que n'avons jamais faits. C'est ainsi que l'Empereur *Proculus* nous en impose, lors qu'écrivant à son amy *Metianus,* il nous veut persuader qu'ayant pris en guerre cent filles *Sarmates,* il les avoit toutes baisées en moins de quinze jours; & le Poëte, qui est le maître de la galanterie, se vante aussi de l'avoir fait neuf fois pendant une nuit.

J'avoüe que nous sommes vaillains en parlant de l'amour; mais nous sommes souvent bien lâches, quand il faut exécuter ses ordres. Ce n'est pas assez que de badiner avec une femme, il faut encore quelque chose de réel par où il paroisse qu'on est homme, & qu'on peut produire son semblable.

Je say qu'il y en a qui sont d'un temperament si lascif, qu'ils pourroient baiser plusieurs femmes plusiers nuits de suites; ils se sentent presque toûjours en estat d'en satisfaire quelqu'une; mais enfin ils s'affoiblissent, & ils s'énervent d'une telle façon, que leur semence n'est pas féconde, & que leurs parties naturelles réfusent mesmes de leur obeïr. . . .

Il faut tenir pour fabuleux ce que *Crucius* nous rapporte d'un serviteur, qui engrossa dix servantes pendant une nuit, & ce que *Clement Alexandrin* nous dit d'*Hercules,* qui ayant couché pendant 12. ou 14. heures avec 50. filles *Atheniennes,* leur fit à chacune un garçon qu'on appella ensuite les *Thespiades.* . . .

Il faut donc croire que les plus grands efforts que l'on puisse faire auprés d'une femme pendant une nuit, ne sauroient aller qu'à quatre ou à cinq embrassemens. Tous ces grands excez d'amour que l'on nous raconte sont autant de fables que l'on nous debite, & si nous en voulions croire les hommes sur ce qu'ils nous disent là-dessus sans consulter la raison, nous nous laisserions aller aussi bien qu'eux à l'imposture & à la foiblesse d'ame.

Un Roy d'Aragon rendit autrefois un Arrest autentique sur cette matiere. Une femme mariée à un *Catelan* fut obligée de se jetter un jour au pied du Roy, pour implorer son secours sur les frequentes caresses de son mary, qui, selon son rapport, luy osteroit bientost la vie, si l'on ny mettoit ordre. Le Roy fit venir le mary pour en savoir la vérité. Le *Catelan* avoüa sincérement que chaque nuit il la baisoit dix fois. Sur quoy le Roy luy deffendit sur peine de la vie de [ne] la baiser plus de six fois, de peur qu'il ne l'accablast par les excez de des embrassemens. (*Tableau,* 186–188, 193–194)

Democritus was known as the "laughing philosopher" for his legendary ridicule of human pretensions. Heracles, the most popular and revered of the Greek heroes, was enormously brave and strong. The story told by Clement of Alexandria of the hero's sexual relations with all fifty daughters of Thespius comes originally from Apollodorus; cf. Athenaeus *Deipnosophistae* 13.556; Diodorus Siculus 4.29.

Venette himself was probably drawing upon Montaigne's *Essays,* "On Certain Verses of Virgil," where three stories in §497 (the Roman emperor deflowering ten Sarmatian virgins, the tale of Messalina, the hyperactive Catalan husband) and Solon's ruling about sexual frequency (in §498) all appear (1158–1159). The tale of the Catalan husband also appears in Pierre de Bourdeille, seigneur de Brantôme, *The Lives of the Gallant Ladies,* trans. Alec Brown (London, 1961), 236–237.

See also §437 for another reference to the ram's prowess.

§498. From Venette:

Les Anciens avoient accoûtumé de mettre *Mercure* prés de *Venus,* quand ils faisoient le portrait de cette Déesse, pour nous apprendre que la raison, dont ils pensoient que *Mercure* estoit le Dieu, devoit toûjours ménager nos voluptez. En effet, nous les goûtons avec plus de tranquilité, lorsque l'usage n'en est pas si frequent. Souvent nous nous d'égoûtons des alimens que nous avons en abondance, & quelquefois nous sommes bien aises de quitter la table des Grands pour celle d'un pauvre homme.

Si la modération est loüable en quelque chose, c'est sans doute dans l'amour. *Solon* qui fut estimé de l'Oracle l'un des plus sages de la Gréce, prévoyoit bien les malheurs qui devoient arriver aux hommes par l'usage indiscret de l'amour, lors qu'il ordonna à ses Citoyens qu'il ne falloit baiser sa femme que trois fois le mois.

Les caresses trop fréquentes des femmes nous épuisent entierément, au lieu que, si elles sont moderées, nostre santé s'en conserve, & nostre corps en devient beaucoup plus libre qu'auparavant: si bien que je ne conseillerois à une jeune homme ny de fuir *Venus* avec horreur, ny de se laisser aller à ses charmes avec trop de molesse & de complaisance. Je ferois ici le souhait qu'*Euripide* faisoit autrefois en parlant à *Venus.*

> Venus, en beauté si parfaite,
> Inspire de grace à mon coeur
> Ta plus belle & plus vive ardeur,
> Et rends dans mes amours mon ame satisfaite:
> Mais tiens si bien la bride à mes ardens désirs,
> Que sans en ressentir ny doleur ny foiblesse,
> Jusques dans l'extrême viellesse,
> Je prenne part à tes plaisirs.

Je ne saurois loüer le Philosophe *Aéας* qui ne baisa sa femme que trois fois pendant son mariage, bien qu'il lui fist un garçon chaque fois. Pour *Xeno-crate*, qui parut plûtost une pierre qu'un homme auprés de la Courtisane *Phyrné*, on doit croire que ce fut en effet de la continence, qu'il devoit à l'étude de la Philosophie, plûtost que le défaut du mouvement de ses parties naturelles.

Le temperament, l'âge, le climat, la saison, & la façon de vivre réglent toutes les caresses que nous faisons aux femmes. Un homme de 25. ans qui est d'une complexion chaude, rempli de sang & d'esprits, qui habite les plaines fertiles de Barbarie, qui est l'un des plus aisez de ces contrées-là, baisera plûtost cinq fois une femme pendant une nuit du mois *d'Avril*, qu'un un autre de 40. ans, qui est d'un temperament froid, & demeure dans les mon-tagnes stériles de Suede, & qui avec cela a de la peine à vivre, n'en connoîtra une autre deux fois pendant une du mois de *Ianvier*.

Les femmes n'ont pas leurs voluptés bornées comme nous les avons, autre-ment les Nobles de *Lithuanie* ne permettroient pas aux leurs, comme ils font, d'avoir des aides dans leur mariage. En effet, les femmes ne se sentent pas épuisées, quand mesme elles souffriroient long-temps de suite les attaques amoureuses d'une multitude d'hommes. Témoin l'impudique *Messaline* & l'infame *Cleopatre*. La premiére, ayant pris le nom de *Lysisca*, fameuse Cour-tisane de Rome, surpassa de 25. coups en moins de 24. heures, dans un lieu public la Courtisane, qu'l'on estimoit la plus brave en amour, & aprés cela, elle avoüa qu'elle n'estoit pas encore tout à fait assouvie. L'autre si nous en voulons croire la lettre de *Marc-Antoine*, l'un de ses Amans, souffrit pendant une nuit les efforts amoureux de cent six hommes sans témoigner d'en estre fatiguée. (*Tableau*, 195–197)

At the beginning of this passage, Venette refers to Plutarch's *Moralia* ("Ad-vice to Bride and Groom"): "Indeed, the ancients gave Hermes a place at the side of Aphrodite, in the conviction that the pleasure in marriage stands espe-cially in need of reason" (138c–d). But Venette appears to have misunder-stood Solon's strictures about the frequency of sexual congress, which were specifically prescriptive, not generally restrictive. According to Plutarch's *Lives*, a man who marries an heiress must "approach her thrice a month without fail" ("Solon" 20.3); cf. Stanley, *History*, I, 21. [Thomas Salmon], *A Critical Essay concerning Marriage* . . . (London, 1724), stipulates that heiresses "had this further Privilege above other Wives, that their Husbands were oblig'd to lye with them three Times in a Month" (219).

We have not identified the moderate but fertile philosopher Aeas. Messalina, wife of Roman emperor Claudius, was notorious for her decadent sexual exploits. See Pliny *Natural History* 10.83.172; and Juvenal *Satires* 6. 130, which is the ultimate source of the Latin tag, "[L]assata Sum Sed non satiata" ("I was worn out but not satiated"). The story resurfaces frequently in accounts of insatiable female sexuality; see, for instance, *A Discourse of Women, Shewing Their Imperfections Alphabetically* . . . (London, 1662), 16; Jacques Olivier, *Alphabet de l'imperfection et malice des femmes* (Rouen, 1683), 22; and Brantôme, *Lives of Gallant Ladies*, 18–19.

The history of Cleopatra, queen of Egypt, is colored by the fact that her enemies, the Romans, wrote it. She was the lover first of Julius Caesar and later of Marc Antony; the legend of her voracious sexual appetite grew in later years, when writers felt the need for shocking examples of female depravity.

§499. Addressing the complaint that old age brings a diminution of sensual pleasure, Cato (in Cicero *De senectute* 14.47) quotes Sophocles' reply to one who asked whether he still indulged in the delights of love. " 'Heaven forbid!' he said. 'Indeed I have fled from them as from a harsh and cruel master' " (*De senectute, De amicitia, De divinatione,* trans. William Armistead Falconer, LCL [1971]). There may also be a parallel with the Catonian aphorism about the wisdom in withdrawing from an encounter with an overpowering adversary: "When you're outmatched, to meet the case, retreat: / Oft-times the vanquished will the victor beat" (*Dicta Catonis* 2.10, in J. Wight Duff and Arnold M. Duff, trans., *Minor Latin Poets*, LCL [1961]).

§500. The last two lines of act 4, scene 1, of Joseph Addison's tragedy *Cato* (London, 1713). The editors would like to thank Lisa Berglund of Connecticut College for this identification.

§501. From Venette's discussion of remedies used to subdue male sexual appetite by limiting the production of semen. Byrd's treatment of this passage is characteristically selective:

En quelque lieu que vive homme lascif, il est toûjours embarassé de son temperament amoureux. La vertu ne peut rien où l'amour agit naturelle-ment: & la Religion mesme a trop peu de pouvoir sur son ame pour rétenir ses prémiers mouvemens, & pour vaincre sa complexion qui luy fournit à toute heure des objets amoureux, dont son imagination est échauffée.

Dans le chagrin ou il en est, il cherche par tout des rémédes qui puissent dompter sa passion. Celuy que la Nature luy présente pour éteindre son feu luy plairoit plus que tous les autres, s'il estoit permis; mais il a de certaines considerations pour ne le pas prendre. Cependant tous les autres rémédes, dont on peut user par dedans ou par dehors, sont tous en quelque façon inutiles ou dangereux pour luy. Leur fraîcheur éteint presque nostre chaleur naturelle, leur astriction épaissit trop nos esprits; & l'un & l'autre détruisent presque nostre memoire & sont tort à nostre jugement. . . . En effet, si l'on s'opiniastre à détruire nostre humeur amoureuse, on détruit en mesme temps nostre temperament, & par là on nous cause des maladies, dont souvent nous ne guérissons jamais.

Cependant, si nostre passion est si forte qu'elle nous apporte quelques incommodités facheuses, & que mesmes elle nous en fasse apprehender d'autres qui ne le sont pas moins, nous pouvons alors nous servir des rémédes que les Medecins nous proposent sur ce sujet, mais avec une telle moderation, que nous ne fassions rien dont nous ayons lieu ensuite de nous repentir.

L'expérience nous apprend que l'air froid, les alimens qui font peu de sang & d'esprits, le jeûne, l'eau en boisson, l'application à l'etude, le travail, & les veilles sont des rémédes propres à combattre un amour déreglé. De plus, éviter la compagnie de la compagnie de la personne que l'on ayme eperdûment, & se lier d'amitié avec une autre, fuir la nudité dans les portraits & dans les statuës, ne lire jamais de livres qui nous excitent à l'amour, & ne regarder point d'animaux qui se caressent, sont encore de puissans moyens pour corriger cette passion: car le grand secret pour vaincre icy, & pour remporter la victoire, c'est de ne combattre point ou de ne combattre qu'en fuyant.

Mais tous ces rémédes sont peu de chose pour un homme qui aime passionément; & qui d'ailleurs est d'un telle complexion qu'il aymeroit, quand il ne voudroit pas aymer. Il faut quelque autre réméde qui fasse plus d'impression sur luy mesme, & qui lui arrache par force, pour parler ainsi; l'amour déreglé dont son imagination est blessée.

Je ne m'arresteray point icy à décrire tous les rémédes que nos Médecins employent à combattre cette passion. Je proposeray seulement ceux qui ont le plus de force à la détruire ou plûtost à la diminuer. Mais avant que de les proposer, il ne semble que l'on doit savoir, que tous les temperamens ne sont pas égaux, & qu'il y a des rémédes qui diminuent le sang, les esprits & la sémence, en émoussant la pointe dans les uns, qui cependant en d'autres en produissent abondamment.

Ce que j'avance seroit difficile à croire si l'experience, par laquelle nous savons presque tout ce que nous savons, ne nous en instruisoit. La laituë & la chicorée, par exemple, s'opposent presque dans tous les hommes à la génération de la sémence; mais je say certainement, que dans quelques-uns, principalement s'ils en mangent le soir, elles en engendrent une telle abondance qu'ils se polluent la nuit en dormant. . . .

Je ne diray rien icy des ceintures rafraîchissantes, des lames de plomb que l'on s'applique sur les reins, des roses blanches dont on parséme son lit, de la mandragore, des groseilles rouges, du citron aigre, & de tous les autres ré- médes qui s'opposent à la génération de la sémence, en nous rafraîchissant, & en nous dessechant beaucoup. Je diray seulement quelque chose de ceux, qui ont le plus de force à éteindre nostre feu & à détruire nostre sémence.

Le lis d'estang blanc, que quelques-uns appellent *Volet*, & que nos Apothi- caires nomment *Nenupar*, aussi-bien que les Arabes, a une qualité si par- ticuliere pour combattre nos desirs amoreux, qu'au rapport de *Pline*, son usage pendant douze jours consécutifs empeche la génération de la sémence; & si nous en usons pendant 40. nous ne sentirons plus les éguillons de l'amour. Sa sécheresse jointe à la froideur de cette plante est si active, qu'elle desseche & rafraîchit toutes nos parties sans que d'ailleurs nous en ressen- tions aucune incommodité. C'est par ces qualitez, si nous en croyons *Galien*, qu'elle entretient nostre voix & nourrit nostre corps, & que s'opposant à la génération de la sémence, elle empêche la dissipation des esprits, qui se pourroit faire par les mouvemens de l'amour. . . .

Bien que nous n'ayons pas la *Ciguë* des Atheniens qui est d'un verd obscur & d'une puanteur insupportable, cependant la nostre ne laisse pas de nous incommoder par sa froideur quand nous la mangeons. (*Tableau*, 199–205)

The calming power of lettuce is traditional; Nich[olas] Culpeper's *English Physitian Enlarged . . .* (London, 1656) explains that the plant is ruled by the moon, cools the heat and dryness caused by Mars, and "abateth Bodily Lust, represseth Venerious Dreams, being outwardly applied to the Cods with a little Camphire" (141–142).

It is particularly interesting that Byrd's translation skips Venette's serious account of methods of avoiding the *occasions* of increasing desire, espe- cially rational, moral self-control, and focuses instead on specific medicinal applications.

Venette refers cryptically to masturbation as a method of releasing the pressure of a surplus of seed, but Byrd skips this as well. Note that, according to Venette and contemporary physiologists, women cannot pollute them- selves, since they do not discharge the female seed during orgasm (*Tableau*, 462).

§502. This entry is a fragment of letter 11 of a series of letters Byrd wrote to "Charmante," and five more follow, together with a severe commentary on the courtship (§508). The complete series of extant Charmante letters is published in *Correspondence*, I, 332–341. Byrd numbered the letters in the manuscript 12–16; the missing letters were almost certainly once included here in the commonplace book. The Huntington Library owns fragments of three other letters. The Charmante pages are distinguished from the rest of the manuscript by a penned-in vertical marginal line; between each two letters is a horizontal line extending from the inner margin to the right-hand side of the page. The handwriting in this section of the commonplace book varies only slightly from that employed in the rest of the manuscript, but enough to suggest that it might have been written at a different time, as noted in the Prologue.

Byrd might have chosen the name he assigned to his beloved in emulation of Sir Richard Steele, who features in one of his papers, the *Lover,* no. 31 (May 6, 1714), a letter from a young man suddenly stricken with love for a beautiful young woman he calls *"Ma Charmante"* (*The Lover and the Reader . . .* [London, 1715], 215). There was a copy in Byrd's library (Hayes 866).

§504. The dream recounted in this letter includes much of the traditional elements of the Triumph of Venus, as recounted by Roman poets. The "Cestus full of all the Enchantments of the Sex" is the girdle of Venus, which represents all the powers of the goddess of love.

§510. In the *History of the Dividing Line* Byrd relates the same information: "They commonly herd together, and the Indians say if one of the drove happen by some wound to be disabled from making his escape, the rest will forsake their fears to defend their friend, which they will do with great obstinacy till they are killed upon the spot" (*Works,* 269).

§513. In the *History of the Dividing Line,* Byrd mentions the Indians' domestication of the wolf: "This beast is not so untamable as the panther, but the Indians know how to gentle their whelps and use them about their cabins instead of dogs" (*Works,* 240).

§518. Source not identified. Byrd's comments about digestion may be understood by referring to Clopton Havers, "A Short Discourse concerning Concoction," in Edmond Halley, *Miscellanea Curiosa: Containing a Collection of Some of the Principal Phaenomena in Nature . . .* (London, 1708), a book Byrd owned (Hayes 1091), now in the library of the College of Physicians in Philadelphia. Saliva not only moistens food for easy passage, "but seems to be the Ferment, by the Benefit of which the Food is dissolved and digested" (I, 163). Foods are thus broken down "until they are at last so far attenuated as to mix more equally with the Fluid, and with them to make one Pulp or Chylous Mass" (I, 170).

§520. Source not identified. The Scottish physician James Keill (1673–1719) was an important proponent of experimental science in medicine and author of *The Anatomy of the Humane Body Abridged . . .* (London, 1698), which Byrd had in his library (Hayes 752). Keill, *Essays on Several Parts of the Animal Oeconomy* (London, 1717), 87, corrects Giovanni Alfonso Borelli's estimate of the quantity of blood and the motive power of the heart in *De motu animalium* (Rome, 1680–1681).

§522. Like many of Byrd's references to animals in the manuscript, the story of the ibis is a legendary commonplace of ancient natural history. Byrd might have encountered this in Pliny, Aelian, or any of a multitude of later narratives, including medical texts or travel books (see note to §425). Pliny tells how the ibis "makes use of the curve of its beak to purge itself through the part by which it is most conducive to health for the heavy residue of food-stuffs to be excreted. Nor is the ibis alone, but many animals have made discoveries destined to be useful for man as well" (*Natural History* 8.41.97, trans. H. Rackham et al., LCL [1940–1962]). Aelian *On the Characteristics of Animals* 2.35 also comments on animal discoveries: "The Egyptians assert that a knowledge of clysters and intestinal purges is derived from no discovery of man's, but they commonly affirm that it was the Ibis that taught them this remedy. And how it instructed those who were the first to see it, some other shall tell" (trans. A. F. Scholfield, LCL [1958–1959]).

Byrd refers to this tradition in the *History of the Dividing Line:* "And this long-necked fowl will give itself a clyster with its beak whenever it finds itself too costive or feverish" (*Works,* 305). As with many other scientists of his day, Byrd's real interest in empirical observation of wildlife in their natural habitat did not preclude consultation of ancient authorities. He was also aware of the controversy over the achievements of the New Science, for he owned [Thomas Baker], *Reflections upon Learning, Wherein Is Shewn the Insufficiency Thereof...*, 2d ed. (London, 1700) (Hayes 1092). Baker was one of those who questioned the newness of some of the "inventions" of seventeenth-century science; interestingly, the autocathartic bird appears in Baker's argument illustrating the ancient origin of several procedures of physic: "If any Credit may be given to *Pliny* we shall have no reason to boast of the Invention of Physic, two great Operations in that Art, having been owing to two inconsiderable Creatures. Bleeding amd purging have been taught us by the *Hippopotamus* and *Ibis,* the former of which being over-charg'd with Blood, breaths a Vein by rowling himself among the sharp Reeds of the *Nile;* and the latter sucking in the Salt Water, administers a Cathartic, by turning her Bill upon her Fundament" (172).

§523. John Wilkins (1614–1672), bishop of Chester, was one of the founders of the Royal Society and its secretary. In his *Essay towards a Real Character, and a Philosophical Language* (London, 1668), he proposed the development of a universal language, based on a more direct correspondence between things themselves and the signs used to describe them. Byrd owned a copy of several of Wilkins's works, including this one (Hayes 93).

Byrd might have been referring again (see §522) to Baker's *Reflections upon Learning*. Baker discusses Bishop Wilkins's project for a real character and concludes it is impracticable: because people cannot agree about the nature of things themselves, a real character based on things themselves is chimerical (17–18).

§524. Leonidas, king of Sparta, died at Thermopylae with three hundred companions holding a mountain pass against the entire Persian army (Herodotus 7.204–238). He came to be regarded as the embodiment and type of military valor, determination, love of glory, and fearlessness (expressed in laconic, understated comments) while facing certain death. The original version of this laconic saying of Leonidas suggested such fearlessness, rather than temperance. Plutarch *Moralia* ("Sayings of Spartans"): "He bade his soldiers eat their breakfast as if they were to eat their dinner in the other world" (225d). Cf. *Moralia* ("Greek and Roman Parallel Stories") 305c–e.

§526. Byrd here discusses [William Wollaston], *The Religion of Nature Delineated . . .* (London, 1724.) Wollaston sets out to demonstrate what part of religion may be apprehended through reason, "that light which *nature* affords" (211). David A. Pailin, in "The Confused and Confusing Story of Natural Religion," defines the term "natural religion" as referring to "religious beliefs and practices that are based on understanding that all people allegedly can discover for themselves and can warrant by rational reflection" (*Religion*, XXIV [1994], 99). Wollaston considers natural religion the conclusion of rational reflection; his purpose is, not to claim that reason alone is sufficient without the help of revelation, but to demonstrate that the foundations of Christian belief are reasonable (Pailin, 201). Wollaston's concentration on the rational later earned him a reputation for deism, in large part because the term "natural religion" was adopted by those who indeed sought a wholly rationalistic system of belief. Nonetheless, *The Religion of Nature Delineated* was consistent with contemporary Anglican doctrine and was warmly received in its day. Wollaston explains that he considers natural religion complementary to revelation, an attitude central to Anglican thought in the early eighteenth century. Consider, for instance, the full title of Samuel Clarke's Boyle Lectures for 1705, *A Discourse concerning the Unchangeable Obligations of Natural Religion, and the Truth and Certainty of the Christian Revelation: Being Eight Sermons Preach'd at the Cathedral-church of St. Paul, in the Year 1705, at the Lecture Founded by the Honourable Robert Boyle, Esq* (London, 1706), an author Byrd was familiar with (Hayes, 1197, 1198). Among the other books dealing with natural religion in Byrd's library were William Derham's *Astro-theology* and *Physico-theology* (Hayes 2298, 1095); John Locke, *The Reasonableness of Christianity* (Hayes 2453); Alexander Ross, *Pansebeia: A View of All Religions in the World* (Hayes 2436); and several books by John Wilkins: *Of the Principles and Duties of Natural Religion* (Hayes 1240), *A Discourse concerning the Gift of Prayer* (Hayes 1174), and sermons (Hayes 1173, 1238). Significantly, Byrd owned none of the major books of deist authors. On the difference between contemporary reception—hardly anybody questioned Wollaston's orthodoxy—and modern critics and historians of religion, see Chester Chapin, "Was William Wollaston (1660–1724) a Deist?" *ANQ: A Quarterly Journal of Short Articles, Notes, and Reviews,* VII (1994), 72–76.

Byrd's continuing interest in natural religion may also be seen in the *History of the Dividing Line,* where he relates the religious tenets of the Indian scout Bearskin. Byrd outlines the correspondence between the beliefs Bearskin attained without benefit of revelation and the eighteenth-century (Anglican) understanding of that part of the truths of Christianity accessible through reason alone. Byrd reports: "It contained, however, the three great articles of natural religion: the belief of a god, the moral distinction betwixt good and evil, and the expectation of rewards and punishments in another world" (*Works,* 248).

Byrd's précis of Wollaston clearly indicates a careful reading. He skips the detailed logical demonstrations and most of the complex metaphysics, going directly to the material that defines the personal, experiential part of religion: what virtue and vice really are, what the soul consists of, what its role is in understanding, what changes will occur after death; and finally he discusses the future state of rewards and punishments, including references to God's knowledge of secret motives. Byrd's synopsis of Wollaston follows the original text fairly closely, with certain elements introduced, evidently to relate the text to his own circumstances. In the notes that follow we will compare Byrd's synopsis with the original text.

Wollaston's opening section, "Of Moral Good and Evil," defines morality as a matter of conduct congruent with truth as it can be found in created nature. In acting morally, man conforms to God's will, as "reveald in the books of nature"; failure to do so contradicts "axioms and truths eternal" (14). Wollaston defines both sins of commission and sins of omission (16) as nothing more than denial of recognizable, eternal truths established by God.

In his version, Byrd's colloquial phrase indicating such denials of truth—to "give our maker the lye"—emphasizes the enormity of denying God through refusing his truth.

Byrd notes that neglecting worship is the same as treating God as if he were not in truth the "author & preserver" of his being. This is a simplified version of Wollaston's explanation of the duty of worship: "If I should not say my prayers at such a certain *hour,* or in such a certain *place* and *manner,* this would not imply a denial of the existence of God, His providence, or my dependence upon Him: nay, there may be reasons perhaps against *that particular* time, place, manner. But if I should *never* pray to Him, or worship Him at all, such a *total* omission would be equivalent to this assertion, *There is no God, who governs the world, to be adored:* which, if there is such a being, must be contrary to the truth" (18).

Following Locke, Wollaston discusses the moral laws that govern society in terms of property rights, explaining violations of these laws as contradictions of known truths. Byrd adapts this point: "If I kill, beat, defraud, or abuse my Fellow creature, I plainly deny by these actions that he has a right to his own Life, Limbs, & Estate which I use as if they were not his, & ᵃˢ if I had a right to do with them as I pleasd, wᶜʰ I certainly have not." Here Byrd follows the original argument in a general sense, but the specific conduct and phrasing are Byrd's own.

In the sentences dealing with the duty of charity and moderation in eating and drinking, Byrd adapts Wollaston's general argument, but the specifics (the vices named and the phrasing) are Byrd's own. This personalized adaptation becomes more pronounced in the part of the synopsis dealing with sexual continence. Wollaston states that the adulterer "does what no man in his wits could think *reasonable* . . . : briefly, he impudently treats a woman as *his own woman* (or *wife*), who is *not his* but *another*'s, contrary to *justice, truth,* and *fact*" (142). Byrd adds to Wollaston's explanation the term "incontinent" and the note of absurdly general promiscuity ("If I . . . lye with every Woman I meet").

The heart of Wollaston's argument is that vicious conduct denies truth. In failing to live by the truth through rationality (the one characteristic that separates man from beast), "a *man* cancels his *reason,* and as it were strives to metamorphize himself into a *brute.* And yet this he does, who pursues only sensual objects, and leaves himself to the impulses of appetite and passion" (170). Byrd encapsulates this teaching in his words, "and suffer my Self to be governd by appetite like a Brute, & not by Reason like a man," adding that he would vigorously deny such a charge if anyone else should affirm it.

Wollaston continues his discussion of the social evils of sexual immorality by calling attention to the harm done to the husband of a corrupted wife: "In the case of case *of adultery,* when any one insnares, and corrupts the wife of another. . . . The adulterer denies the *property* a husband has in his wife by compact, the most express and sacred that can possibly be made: he does that, which tends to subvert the peace of families, confounds relations, and is altogether inconsistent with the *order* and *tranquillity* of the world, and therefore with the laws of human nature: he does what no man in his wits could think *reasonable,* or even *tolerable,* were he the person wronged: briefly, he impudently treats a woman as *his own woman* (or *wife*), who is *not his* but *another's,* contrary to *justice, truth* and *fact*" (141–142). The concept of adultery as a violation of the husband's property rights is conventional eighteenth-century thinking; see [Richard Allestree], *The Whole Duty of Man* . . . (London, 1673), on "the especial and peculiar right that every man hath in his Wife" (217). Byrd's succinct version of this argument acknowledges, "By lying with any woman that I have not a Right to by marriage, I do an injury to another, to please my Self, which is acting against a fundamental Truth."

In the next part of his synopsis, Byrd considers whether a woman's consent to seduction alters the charge that adultery deprives another man of his rights. He concludes that no consent declared in blind passion or inveigled through deceit can be considered valid. The discussion of seduction as suborning a woman's will appears to be Byrd's own interpolation, though it might have been suggested by Wollaston's terms (that the male adulterer ensnares and corrupts the woman).

A similar principle governs all other moral issues. Wollaston explains: "But if the *formal ratio* of moral good and evil be made to consist in a conformity of mens acts to the *truth of the case* or the contrary, as I have here explained it, the *distinction* seems to be settled in a manner undeniable, intelligible, practicable. For as what is meant by a *true proposition* and *matter of fact* is perfectly understood by every body; so will it be easie for any one, so far as he knows any such propositions and facts, to compare not only *words,* but also *actions* with them. A very little skill and attention will serve to interpret even these, and discover whether they *speak truth,* or not" (25). Wollaston couples rational virtue with consideration of the happiness of others: "The way to happiness and the practice of truth incur the one into the other" (40). "No man can have a right to begin to interrupt the happiness of another" (131). Byrd's concise rendition of Wollaston's argument covers all the main points: "He condemns all other vices by being violations of Some plain Truth, and consequently against all the Rules of Reason, and our own and other People's happiness."

When Byrd writes, "We may not plead Ignorance, what things are true & what not, the author of nature has endued us with Reason, which if duly attended to, will be our Sufficient Direction," he is following Wollaston's contention that all human beings are governed by natural law, which is readily accessible by reason. As well as the heading, "There is such a thing as right reason: or, Truth may be discovered by reasoning," Wollaston adds another: "To be governed by reason is the general law imposed by the Author of nature upon them, whose uppermost faculty is reason: as the dictates of it in particular cases are the particular laws, to which they are subject" (48, 51).

Byrd next summarizes Wollaston's position on the location and nature of the human soul. Wollaston proposes "that the human *soul* is a *cogitative* substance, clothed in a *material* vehicle, or rather united to it, and as it were *inseparably* mixt . . . with it: that these act in *conjunction*, that, which affects the one, affecting the other: that the *soul* is detaind in the *body* (the head or brain) by some *sympathy* or *attraction* between this material vehicle and it, till the habitation is spoild, and this mutual tendency interrupted . . . by some hurt, or disease, or by the decays and ruins of old age, or the like, happening to the body: and that in the *interim* by means of this vehicle motions and impressions are communicated to and fro" (192–193).

Byrd's account of the departure of the soul at death is a close paraphrase of Wollaston: "And so, in general, that, which now can know many things by the impressions made at the end of the nerves, or by the intervention of our present organs, and in this *situation* and *inclosure* can know them no other way, may for all that, when it comes to be *loosed* out of that prison, know them *immediately*, or by some *other medium*. That, which is now forced to make shift with *words* and *signs* of things in its reasonings, may, when it shall be set at liberty and can come at them, reason upon the intuition of *things themselves*, or use a language more *spiritual* or *ideal*" (196).

The account of the future state of rewards and punishments also faithfully records Wollaston's argument. Wollaston introduces many examples of human suffering, injustice, and misery (200–203), arguing against the notion that God would allow this if there were no future state of rewards and punishments in which such things will be rectified: "And then, how can we acquit the *justice* and *reasonableness* of that Being, upon whom these poor creatures depend, and who leaves them such great losers by their existence, if there be no *future state*, where the proper amends may be made? So that the argument is brought to this undeniable issue: if the *soul* of man is not *immortal,* either there is *no God,* upon whom we depend; or he is an *unreasonable Being;* or there never has been *any man,* whose sufferings in this world have exceeded his injoyments, without his being the cause of it himself. But surely *no one* of these three things can be said" (203).

Byrd concludes his notes on Wollaston's book by noting his proof of divine foreknowledge, and God's power to discern the secrets of men's hearts. In his discussion of providence, Wollaston declares:

It seems to me not *impossible,* that God should know *what is to come:* on the contrary, it is highly reasonable to think, that He does and must know things *future.* Whatever happens in the world, which does not come immediately from Him, must either be the effect of *mechanical* causes, or of the motions of living beings and *free* agents. . . . Now as to the former, it cannot be *impossible* for Him, upon whom the being and nature of every thing depends, and who therefore must *intimately* know all their powers, and what effects they will have, to see through the whole *train* of causes and effects, and whatever will come to pass in *that way:* nay, it is *impossible,* that He should *not* do it. . . . Now He, who knows what *is* in man's power, what not; knows the make of their bodies, and all the *mechanism* and propensions of them; knows the *nature* and *extent* of their understandings, and what will determin them this or that way; knows all the process of natural (or second) causes, and consequently how these may work upon them; He, I say, who knows all this, may know *what* men will do, if He can but know this one thing more, *viz.* whether they *will use* their rational faculties or *not.* And since even we our selves, mean and defective as we are, can *in some measure* conceive, how so much as this may be done, and seem to want but one step to finish the account, can we with any shew of reason deny to a *Perfect* being this one article more, or think that He cannot do that too; especially if we call to mind, that this very power of *using* our own faculties is held of Him?

Observe what a sagacity there is in some *men,* not only in respect of physical causes and effects, but also of the future actings of mankind; and how very easie it is many times, if the persons concernd, their characters, and circumstances are given, to foresee what they will do: as also to foretell many general events, tho the intermediate transactions upon which they depend are not known. Consider how much more remarkable this penetration is in *some* men, than in *others:* consider further, that if there be any *minds* more perfect than the human . . . they must have it in a still more eminent degree, *proportionable* to the excellence of their natures: in the last place, do but allow (as you must) this power of discerning to be in God *proportionable* to His nature, as in lower beings it is proportionable to *theirs*, and then it becomes *infinite*; and then again, the *future* actions of free agents are at once all unlocked, and exposed to His view. For that knowledge is not infinite, which is limited to things *past* or *present* or which come to pass *necessarily*. (99–101)

Here too, as throughout, Byrd carefully records the essence of Wollaston's ideas, sometimes translating them into his own terms and sometimes preserving the language of the original.

§528. Byrd here transcribes a part of the second paragraph of the *Spectator*, no. 177 (Sept. 22, 1711), before extracting an important idea from the first (for which see the next entry). In this essay, Addison discusses the moral effects of Good Nature, a disposition of mind he had earlier defined as combining "Compassion, Benevolence and Humanity" (*Spectator*, no. 169 [Sept. 13, 1711]). Addison describes that part of Good Nature produced by the physiological and psychological (or constitutional) makeup of human beings as a "Supply of Spirits, or a more kindly Circulation of the Blood." This notion— perhaps attractive to Byrd because the physiological metaphor matches his own interests—is illustrated with a reference to Bacon: "Sir *Francis Bacon* mentions a cunning Sollicitor, who would never ask a Favour of a great Man before Dinner; but took care to prefer his Petition at a time when the Party petitioned had his Mind free from Care, and his Appetites in good Humour."

§529. Here Byrd transcribes the *earlier* part of Addison's discussion of the two kinds of Good Nature, *Spectator*, no. 177 (Sept. 22, 1711): "In one of my last Week's Papers I treated of Good-nature, as it is the effect of Constitution; I shall now speak of it as it is a Moral Virtue. The first may make a Man easie in himself, and agreeable to others, but implies no Merit in him that is possessed of it. A Man is no more to be praised upon this Account, than because he has a regular Pulse or a good Digestion. This Good-nature however in the Constitution, which Mr. *Dryden* somewhere calls a *Milkiness of Blood*, is an admirable Ground-work for the other."

§530. In the same essay, *Spectator*, no. 177, Addison goes on to discuss the scriptural imperative for charity, especially in the New Testament, "where our Saviour tells us in a most pathetick manner that he shall hereafter regard the cloathing of the naked, the feeding of the hungry, and the visiting of the imprisoned, as Offices done to himself, and reward them accordingly. Pursuant to those Passages in Holy Scripture, I have some where met with the Epitaph of a charitable Man which has very much pleased me. I cannot recollect the Words, but the Sense of it is to this purpose: What I spent I lost. What I possessed is left to others. What I gave away remains with me."

§531. This phrase is also drawn from the *Spectator*, no. 176 (Sept. 21, 1711); this essay features a letter about the perils of marriage to a strong-willed woman, from one "Nathaniel Henroost," who calls himself henpecked and urges: "When you have considered Wedlock throughly, you ought to enter into the Suburbs of Matrimony, and give us an Account of the Thraldom of kind Keepers and irresolute Lovers; the Keepers who cannot quit their fair ones tho' they see their approaching Ruine; the Lovers who dare not marry, tho' they know they shall never be happy without the Mistresses whom they cannot purchase on other Terms."

§534. *Spectator*, no. 200 (Oct. 19, 1711): "That Paradox therefore in old *Hesiod* . . . [that] Half is more than the Whole, is very applicable to the present Case; since nothing is more true in political Artihmetick, than that the same People with half a Country is more valuable than with the whole."

§535. *Tutty* is zinc oxide, a medicinal substance gathered in flakes from the flues of brass foundries, or from mines (*OED*).

§536. *Spectator*, no. 203 (Oct. 23, 1711): Byrd's transcription is quite close to the original: "What makes this Generation of Vermin so very Prolifick, is the indefatigable Diligence with which they apply themselves to their Business. A Man does not undergo more watchings and fatigues in a Campaign, than in the Course of a vicious Amour. As it is said of some Men, that they make their Business their Pleasure, these Sons of Darkness may be said to make their Pleasure their Business. They might conquer their corrupt Inclinations with half the Pains they are at in gratifying them."

§537. This entry is a close transcription of a passage from an essay by Addison, *Spectator*, no. 203 (Oct. 23, 1711), on the prolific and indefatigable "loose Tribe" of profligate men who deceive women and father numerous illegitimate children: "Nor is the Invention of these Men less to be admired than their Industry and Vigilance. There is a Fragment of *Apollodorus* the Comick Poet (who was Contemporary with *Menander*) which is full of Humour as follows. *Thou may'st shut up thy Doors*, says he, *with Bars and Bolts: It will be impossible for the Blacksmith to make them so fast, but a Cat and a Whoremaster will find a way through them.* In a Word, there is no Head so full of Stratagems as that of a Libidinous Man." Addison follows this ironic tribute with a proposal that (though not included in this commonplace book transcription) might well have afforded Byrd, himself a founder of colonial settlements, with special amusement: "Were I to propose a Punishment for this infamous Race of Propagators, it should be to send them, after the second or third Offence, into our *American* Colonies, in order to People those Parts of her Majesty's Dominions where there is a want of of Inhabitants, and in the Phrase of *Diogenes* to *Plant Men*."

§542. Pliny writes of the balsam tree: "The branch is thicker than that of a myrtle; incision is made in it with a piece of glass or a stone, or with knives made of bone—it strongly dislikes having its vital parts wounded with steel, and dies off all at once, though it can stand having superfluous branches pruned with a steel knife" (*Natural History* 12.44.115, trans. H. Rackham et al., LCL [1940–1962]).

§543. This etymological myth has been popular since the sixteenth century. The word *harlot* actually derives from the masculine Old French word *herlot*, or "lad, young fellow, base fellow, knave, vagabond." The later sense of the word indicating an "unchaste woman" seems to have originated "only after the earlier senses and uses of the word had been forgotten" (*OED*).

§544. Pliny on snails: "They have no eyes, and consequently explore the way in front of them with their little horns" (*Natural History* 9.41.101, trans. H. Rackham et al., LCL [1940–1962]).

§547. Byrd here refers to two historiographers of the events of the preceding century, whose accounts were generally understood to follow party lines. The Tory historian was Edward Hyde, first earl of Clarendon, (1609–1674), adviser to Charles I and Charles II and participant in the Royalist cause. Clarendon's *True Historical Narrative of the Rebellion and Civil Wars in England* (known as *History of the Rebellion*), first published in 1702–1704, vindicated the constitutional Royalists and commemorated the great men of the king's party. His *History* was much influenced by Roman historiographers and was admired for its style and eloquence.

Laurence Echard (1670?–1730) was educated at Cambridge and served as chaplain to the bishop of Lincoln. He wrote many works on history and geography and translated some classic texts. His best-known work was his *History of England, from the First Entrance of Julius Caesar and the Romans to the End of the Reign of James the First*, which first appeared in 1707 and was later updated in 1718 and 1720.

The "wag" to whom Byrd refers might have been John Oldmixon, whose *Critical History of England, Ecclesiastical and Civil* features extensive comparative discussion of Clarendon and Echard. He also discusses the comparison in his *Essay on Criticism as It Regards Design, Thought, and Experience, in Prose and Verse* (London, 1728) using a similar analogy for evaluating the imbalance of Archdeacon Echard's *History*: "The Historians Reflections upon Events are entirely his own, and we shall see in the following Pages, how wise and how weighty they are: But as they bear all on one Side, like an ill ballasted Ship, it is much, if in the Course of a few Years, it does not overset the History" (20).

§548. Charles de Saint-Denis, seigneur de Saint-Évremond (1613–1703), was a soldier and political exile in England, known for his wit and good living. Byrd owned copies of his works in French and English (Hayes 963, 1478, 2445) and Charles Cotolendi's *Dissertation sur les oeuvres de Monsieur de Saint-Évremont* (Hayes 1479). Byrd mentions Saint-Évremond's death in a letter of Sept. 11, 1703 (*Correspondence*, I, 241).

§549. Lucan *Pharsalia* 2.657. Byrd might have found this Latin phrase in *Spectator*, no. 374 (May 9, 1712), where it serves as the essay's motto; the essay provides this commentary and translation: "The Man who distinguishes himself from the rest, stands in a Press of People; those before him intercept his Progress, and those behind him, if he does not urge on, will tread him down. *Caesar*, of whom it is said, *that he thought nothing done while there was any thing left for him to do*, went on in performing the greatest Exploits, without assuming to himself a Privilege of taking Rest upon the Foundation of the Merit of his former Actions." Cf. Montaigne, *Essays*, "Of Experience."

§554. Byrd here advises (himself) to resort to the Lord's Prayer to prevent anger from leading to rash acts.

§556. Louis de France (1661–1711) was grand dauphin and heir to the French throne, but, as the astrologer predicted, he died of smallpox. His son the duke of Anjou was declared king of Spain in 1700, Philip V. See §557.

§557. Charles II of Spain had no immediate heir. Louis XIV, realizing this, had prepared by having one of his grandsons, the duke of Anjou (second son of the grand dauphin), educated in Spain. Upon his death Charles II left Spain to the duke of Anjou, who thus became Philip V (1683–1746). The other two grandsons, the duke of Bourgogne (1682–1712) and the duke of Berri (1685–1714), both died before they had the chance to rule France, thus leaving the crown to Louis XIV's great-grandson.

§558. Gilbert Burnet (1643–1715), bishop of Salisbury, author of *History of His Own Time* (London, 1724) and *History of the Reformation* (1679–1714). Burnet was a Whig propagandist; this anecdote probably derives from an as-yet-unlocated Tory source.

§560. Louis XIV began building on his estate at Marly near Versailles in 1679. Marly, designed by Jules Mansart with gardens laid out by André Le Nôtre, consisted of a central chateau for the royal family and twelve pavilions for visitors; eleven of these could house two couples each, and the twelfth contained the bathrooms. The etiquette here was much more relaxed than at court, and invitations to visit were much sought after. The company was entertained by balls, concerts, gambling, and so forth.

§563. Lord F——h is the fictional Lord Froth. His habit of speech appears in the *Guardian*, no. 137 (Aug. 18, 1713): "He has indeed nothing but his Nobility to give Employment to his Thoughts. Rank and Precedency are the important Points which he is always discussing within himself. A Gentleman of this Turn begun a Speech in one of King *Charles*'s Parliaments: *Sir, I had the Honour to be born at a time*—upon which a rough honest Gentleman took him up short, *I would fain know what that Gentleman means, Is there any one in this House that has not had the Honour to be born as well as himself?* . . . But there are many who have had their Education among Women, Dependants or Flatterers, that lose all the Respect, which would otherwise be paid them, by being too assiduous in procuring it."

§565. A *flux* is "an abnormally copious flowing of blood, excrement, etc., from the bowels or other organs," often a term for dysentery (*OED*). The treatment recommended here was standard for Byrd's day, alternating diet to stabilize the digestive disturbance with purgatives or emetics (specifically ipecacuanha).

§567. Philippe I, duke of Orléans (1640–1701), the brother of Louis XIV, was known as Monsieur. Antoine Gaston Jean Baptiste, duke of Rouquelaure (1656–1738), was marshal of France (1724).

§569. Michel Chamillart (1652–1721) was controller general of finance (1699) and secretary of state (1700). The story of Chamillart's game is well known, according to William Hendricks, *History of Billiards* (Roxana, Ill., 1977), 8:

There were actually two tables, "the great billiard-table of eleven feet eight inches long and six feet wide" as well as a smaller eight foot table, "on which the king usually played." Rene d'Allemagne recalls Louis's Parliamentary Counselor Chamillard who parlayed his billiards skill and good manners into a ministry and became the target of a famous contemporary doggerel epitaph:

> Here lies the famous Chamillard
> Partner of his king
> Who was a hero at billiards
> And a zero in the ministry.

INDEX